WASHINGTON DC

SAMANTHA SAULT

CONTENTS

Although every effort was made to make sure the information in this book was accurate when going to press, research was impacted by the COVID-19 pandemic. Some things may have changed during this crisis and the recovery that followed. Be sure to confirm specific details when making your travel plans.

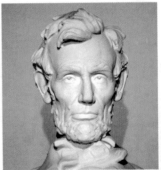

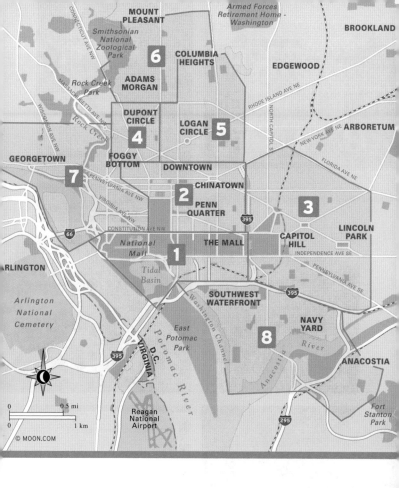

MAPS

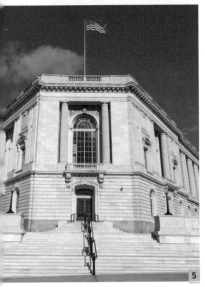

1 18th Street in Adams Morgan

2 Georgetown and Foggy Bottom

3 Women's March on Washington

4 Smithsonian Institution

5 Senate office building

6 Martin Luther King Jr. Memorial

DISCOVER
WASHINGTON DC

Oh, you're from Washington DC? It's changed so much. It's gotten so cool.

This common trope is pushed by residents, those who've come and gone and everyone whose kid interned on Capitol Hill, by media and Hollywood and glossy travel magazines and the Michelin Guide. Waxing poetic about the newest starred fusion restaurant where you can't get a reservation, or off-the-beaten-path gallery in a "redeveloped" neighborhood far from the tourist drags, is a sign you're a tastemaker, that you're in the know.

It misses the point—and it's not true.

To say new, slick, high-tech concert venues and galleries and museums have made Washington DC a cultural center brushes aside the capital's rich history as a center of black theater and jazz before Harlem and Motown, of performance halls and parks and churches that have witnessed world-changing events. And sure, there are more restaurants now, but Washington's always had a unique flavor, a blend of soul food and Ethiopian and sizzling Chesapeake Bay seafood served in the backrooms of classic steakhouses where history was made over martinis. And yes, celebrity chefs and slick shopping developments and scores of social media influencers have brought revenue and new visitors, but they'll never, ever be as influential as former residents like Frederick Douglass, Duke Ellington, Toni Morrison, Eleanor Roosevelt, Marvin Gaye, Langston Hughes, Katharine Graham, and José Andrés.

Never mind the intoxicating political intrigue, which has drawn so many to the capital, and enticed them to stay, not because they don't want to live anywhere else, but because they truly can't imagine a life without that pulse.

Yes, Washington's changed so much—it changes every four years. But it's always been cool, in its own way. And no matter which way the political winds blow, it always will be.

10 TOP
EXPERIENCES

1 **Stroll the National Mall:** Get up close and personal with monuments—and see if you can spot the tiniest monument on the National Mall (page 44).

2 **Walk the Halls of Power:** Ask your Member of Congress for a tour of the **U.S. Capitol Building** (page 106).

^
^
^

3 **Experience the Magnitude of the Washington Monument:** Visit the tallest structure in the city then ride the elevator to the top (page 48).

4 **See the Lincoln Memorial at Night:** After the crowds have dispersed, the interior monument light casts a dramatic glow on the Great Emancipator (page 49).

<<<

5 **Admire the Cherry Blossoms:** Spring in DC means an explosion of cherry blossoms. Brave the crowds at the Tidal Basin to rent a paddleboat during the **National Cherry Blossom Festival** (page 70).

>>>

6 **Take a Memorable Selfie:** Make your friends jealous with a photo outside the **White House** (page 76).

>>>

7 **Walk in the Footsteps of Frederick Douglass:** Visit the historic site of one of the country's most important abolitionists, where he lived during the end of his life (page 219).

8 **Visit the Smithsonian Institution Museums and Galleries:** Find the Star-Spangled Banner, the Hope Diamond, Chuck Berry's red Cadillac, and a real lunar module at the Smithsonian Institution's museums and galleries (page 50).

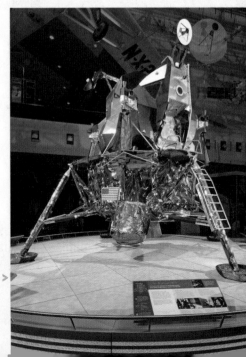

9 Pay Your Respects at Arlington National Cemetery: Visit the Tomb of the Unknown Solider and JFK's gravesite (page 236).

10 Become a Washington Insider: Partake in **happy hour** in a Capitol Hill pub or a posh cocktail bar—and keep your ears open for political gossip (page 89).

<<<

EXPLORE
WASHINGTON DC

THE BEST OF WASHINGTON DC

History, politics, power—and the world's best free museums. To experience the best of Washington DC in a few days, stay downtown in a hotel like Penn Quarter's Hotel Monaco, a short walk or just a few Metro stops away from the halls of power and the best restaurants and nightlife. You don't need a car; everything in this itinerary is accessible by Metro, a taxi or ride-share, or walking.

>DAY 1: DOWNTOWN, PENN QUARTER, AND CAPITOL HILL

Start your day at **Pete's Diner,** one block from the U.S. Capitol. You'll be joined by Hill staffers and perhaps a few lawmakers; former Speaker of the House John Boehner famously had eggs and coffee here almost every day.

>> **Public Transit:** To get from downtown/Penn Quarter to the U.S. Capitol, take the Metro Blue, Orange, or Silver Line from Metro Center to Capitol South.

Head west on Independence Avenue SE to the **U.S. Capitol.** You

U.S. Capitol

BEST VIEWS

U.S. CAPITOL DOME

It's not easy to get a tour of the Capitol building's dome, but it's worth the trouble. You'll have to plan in advance—and perhaps have a close connection in your member of Congress's office—to climb the winding staircase to see the amazing view from the exterior walkway (page 106).

FREDERICK DOUGLASS NATIONAL HISTORIC SITE

The abolitionist spent the last years of his life at his Anacostia mansion, perched on a 51-foot hill offering expansive views all the way to the U.S. Capitol (page 219).

POV

The posh rooftop bar and lounge at the W Hotel overlooks the White House—though you'll pay dearly for the only-in-Washington view, especially if you want a preferred table on the edge (page 87).

TOP OF THE GATE

The Watergate Hotel's huge rooftop bar has 360-degree views, including the Washington Monument, Pentagon, Georgetown, and Potomac River (page 198).

can explore the grounds and see the imposing dome from every angle; get a spectacular up-close selfie on the west side. No matter how many times you've seen photos—or passed by on your way to work—it's always awe-inspiring. If you'd like a tour, reserve one in advance via the **U.S. Capitol Visitor Center** or through your member of Congress; same-day passes are sometimes available at the information desk on the visitor center's lower level, but don't count on it.

The visitor center has public exhibits about the Capitol and Congress, as well as a gift shop.

Across from the visitor center entrance on 1st Street, get a glimpse of the **Library of Congress** and the **Supreme Court of the United States.** If you did not take a Capitol tour, you'll have time before lunch to pop inside the **United States Botanic Garden,** a hidden gem on the Capitol grounds full of thousands upon thousands of plant specimens from around the world.

For lunch, go to **Eastern Market** on 7th Street SE between C Street NE and North Carolina Avenue SE, 15 minutes from the Capitol by foot. The crab cake at **Market Lunch,** the casual counter inside the main market building, is one of the best in DC, but if you prefer finer dining, try **Acqua Al 2** across the street. On the weekend, people-watch and shop for local, DC-inspired artwork at the outdoor market; on weekdays, drop by **Bullfeathers** back at 1st Street and D Street for happy hour and political gossip.

>> **Public Transit:** To get from Eastern Market to downtown/ Penn Quarter, take the Metro Blue, Orange, or Silver Line from Eastern Market to Metro Center.

Celebrate your first night in the city with the seafood tower at **Old Ebbitt Grill.** Before you sit down, however, detour one block past the restaurant to see the **White House** and **Lafayette Square** during the golden hour. End with a nightcap at the historic **Round Robin Bar** at the **Willard InterContinental.**

>DAY 2:
NATIONAL MALL

If you have tickets to the Smithsonian's **National Museum of African American History and Culture,** grab coffee at **Compass Coffee** on 7th and F Streets NW, then beeline to the museum to be in line a few minutes before your entry time. You'll need the better part of a day to see everything, but it's worth it; start in the basement and work your way up, then have lunch at **Sweet Home Café** before the pop culture exhibits.

>> **Public Transit:** To get from downtown/Penn Quarter to the National Mall, simply walk south on 7th Street or 9th Street to Constitution Avenue. It's 10-20 minutes by foot to the major museums.

If you didn't get tickets, the Smithsonian's **National Museum of American History** and **National Air and Space Museum** are the other must-see museums. If you try to do both, don't miss the Star-Spangled Banner and first ladies' dresses at the former and, of course, the spaceships at the latter. **Mitsitam Native Foods Café** at the **National Museum of the American Indian** is a good option for lunch.

You can stay in the museums if you have foul weather, but otherwise, explore the memorials on the National Mall. Follow the **walking tour** on page 44 to hit the **Washington Monument, Martin Luther King Jr. Memorial, Franklin Delano Roosevelt Memorial, Thomas Jefferson Memorial,** and **Tidal Basin.**

BEST PEOPLE-WATCHING

LAFAYETTE SQUARE
The park on the north side of the White House is a popular gathering spot for tourists and protesters alike (page 77).

DUPONT CIRCLE
The park at the center of the traffic circle draws all kinds of people to read the paper, picnic, exercise, sunbathe, play chess on the permanent boards—and even get married (page 130).

THE PALM
This famous steakhouse is frankly better for the people-watching than the food, especially during the lunch hour, when the Washington VIPs whose faces are painted on the walls pack the tables (page 132).

MERIDIAN HILL PARK
This historic park is a prime spot for impromptu soccer games, engagement photo shoots, or just relaxing on a blanket. Since the 1970s, every Sunday afternoon around 3pm a drum circle has drawn musicians, dancers, and a crowd of spectators (page 183).

>> **Public Transit:** To get from the memorials on the southwest side of the Mall back to downtown/Penn Quarter, take the Metro Green or Yellow Line from L'Enfant Plaza to Gallery Pl-Chinatown.

Relax before a late dinner at **Jaleo,** the José Andrés Spanish restaurant that ignited the nation's tapas obsession. After, grab a taxi or ride-share to the **Lincoln Memorial,** which absolutely must be seen at night.

>DAY 3:
NATIONAL MALL, U STREET, AND SHAW

Start the day at the **National Gallery of Art.** If you didn't have breakfast, grab coffee and a pastry in the **Pavilion Café** in the **Sculpture Garden.** There's something for every art lover here: Choose the West Building for the French Impressionists and Da Vinci's only painting on view in the United States, or the East Building for modern art.

When you get hungry, head to CityCenterDC, where you can parse the works over leisurely brunch or lunch at **Centrolina** or **DBGB Kitchen & Bar,** or grab a healthy juice at **Fruitive.** Enjoy an afternoon of window shopping the luxury stores, or walk about 15 minutes south to the **National Archives Museum** to see the Declaration of Independence and U.S. Constitution in a new light.

>> **Public Transit:** To get from downtown/Penn Quarter to U Street/Shaw, take the Metro Green or Yellow Line from Gallery Place-Chinatown to U Street/African-Amer Civil War Memorial/Cardozo, or grab a taxi/ride-share.

Spend the evening in **U Street and Shaw,** DC's nightlife hub, bustling with trendy restaurants, cocktail and wine bars, and dance clubs. This is the neighborhood to try Ethiopian food—the Washington area has the largest Ethiopian population in the United States, and restaurants here include **Dukem Ethiopian Restaurant** and the more upscale **Chercher.** For the definitive DC nightlife experience, catch a show at the **9:30 Club,** followed by a late-night half-smoke (a spicy half-pork/half-beef sausage, served on a bun and smothered in chili) at the famous **Ben's Chili Bowl.**

With More Time

You could spend days—weeks—touring DC's museums and memorials, and if you're visiting for more than a few days, it's worth choosing one or two museums to explore at a more leisurely pace.

With more time, spend a morning in Dupont Circle. Take your coffee in the park at the center of the circle, a great spot to people-watch among locals, and meander to Kramerbooks, one of DC's essential bookstores, stocking top fiction and nonfiction, including the latest political tomes. The Phillips Collection, the country's first modern art museum, is worth a few hours.

Spend an afternoon in Georgetown, shopping top brands on the brick-lined streets or, in exceptionally beautiful weather, renting a boat on the Potomac River. Enjoy a predinner drink at one of the neighborhood's stylish hotels—The Lounge at Bourbon Steak at the Four Seasons has good cocktails and people-watching—before dinner at Fiola Mare, where you should ask for a table in the see-and-be-seen dining room for some of the best Italian seafood in the city.

Before you go, make time for a performance, because DC has a vibrant theater scene on par with the world capitals. Get tickets for anything at The John F. Kennedy Center for the Performing Arts before your Georgetown dinner, or better yet, see a thought-provoking new play at the Woolly Mammoth Theatre Company in Penn Quarter or Studio Theatre in Logan Circle.

THE CITY WITH KIDS

Washington DC is a wonderful city to visit with children, with a plethora of interactive museums and easy-to-use public transportation. And parents won't feel like they're missing out, because the top museums and attractions for kids are among the top museums and attractions in the city, period.

There are lots of family-friendly hotels, but two stand out. Steps from the Smithsonian's National Zoo and the Metro Red Line, the Omni Shoreham Hotel is a quiet hideaway with an outdoor pool and children's amenities; if you want to be closer to the National Mall, the Mandarin Oriental is a surprisingly kid-friendly choice, with a peaceful spa for tired parents.

>DAY 1

Whether you have dinosaur-loving toddlers or hard-to-please teens, the museums and memorials are sure to wow the entire family. Head to **Union Station** for breakfast at one of the many quick-serve restaurants, then pick up the **DC Ducks** tour out front to see the major sights, including the **Washington Monument, White House,** and **Thomas Jefferson Memorial** by land and water. The 90-minute tour will take you back to Union Station, from where you can walk to the **National Mall** by heading southeast on Louisiana Avenue past the **U.S. Capitol** and **Reflecting Pool,** or catch the DC Circulator.

Union Station

CAPITAL BY DESIGN

Architecture lovers should first fly into Dulles International Airport in Virginia. The main terminal, designed by Eero Saarinen, evokes flight. Here are just a few of the architectural highlights of the city:

UNION STATION

The city's major railroad station was designed by Daniel Burnham, architect of New York's Flatiron Building. Don't miss the restored Main Hall with soaring granite arches (page 110).

WASHINGTON NATIONAL CATHEDRAL

The imposing, neo-Gothic cathedral is an architectural delight, with 215 stained glass windows and 112 unique gargoyles (page 243).

HIRSHHORN MUSEUM

The circular contemporary art museum is a striking work of art itself, designed by Gordon Bunshaft (page 63).

NATIONAL GALLERY OF ART EAST BUILDING

Reopened in 2016 following an extensive renovation, the gallery's modern art wing was designed by I. M. Pei (page 63).

MARTIN LUTHER KING JR. MEMORIAL LIBRARY

Completed in 1972, DC's flagship library was Mies van der Rohe's last building (page 94).

>> **Public Transit:** The Metro Red Line goes directly to Union Station, where you can walk to the National Mall and Capitol Hill. The DC Circulator National Mall route goes from Union Station to the National Mall; take the bus in the direction of Lincoln Memorial.

The **National Museum of Natural History** is a good choice no matter your kids' interests, with dinosaurs, mummies, and sparkling gems, as is the **National Air and Space Museum,** with amazing aircraft and spacecraft. When hunger pangs strike, skip McDonald's at the latter; the Natural History Museum has a standard food court, with burgers, pizza, and barbecue, or if you're feeling adventurous, try **Mitsitam Native Foods Café** at the **National Museum of the American Indian.** Food trucks often cluster on Constitution Avenue around 15th Street and 17th Street. Round out the day in another museum, or head to the **Franklin Delano Roosevelt Memorial,** a kid favorite with larger-than-life statues and waterfalls.

>> **Public Transit:** To get from the National Mall to Capitol Hill, take the Metro Blue, Orange, or Silver Line from Smithsonian to Capitol South. If you're closer to the FDR Memorial, you can catch the DC Circulator National Mall route from the Lincoln Memorial toward Union Station four stops to Jefferson Drive and 12th Street, then transfer to Metro.

After a long day of sightseeing, have a casual dinner at **Good**

National Air and Space Museum

International Spy Museum

Stuff Eatery or **We, the Pizza** on Capitol Hill, serving inexpensive, tasty, kid-approved food with local, farm-raised ingredients (and adult beverages for you). You can walk by the **U.S. Capitol** illuminated in the evening before turning in.

>DAY 2

After breakfast at your hotel, head to **The White House.** You can get a good look, and teach your kids a lesson about the freedom of assembly, from **Lafayette Square,** where you may see (calm, peaceful) protesters on any given day. The **White House Visitor Center** is open to the public daily, though more suitable for older children.

>> **Public Transit:** The Metro stations closest to the White House are Farragut West and McPherson Square, serving the Blue, Orange, and Silver Lines; you can transfer from the Red Line at Metro Center or walk from Farragut North.

A few blocks away, you'll find several good lunch options, including the bustling **Old Ebbitt Grill,** which has an expansive menu that will satisfy even picky eaters, or **Astro Doughnuts and Fried Chicken,** a fast-casual spot for yummy fried treats. After lunch, visit the highly interactive **International Spy Museum,** which has lots of flashy, fun exhibits about free speech and major news events, or take older children to learn about the past at the **National Archives Museum** or the **United States Holocaust Memorial Museum**. If you're visiting during the holiday season, the magical production of A Christmas Carol at **Ford's Theatre** will appeal to children of all ages, and children at heart.

For dinner, the energetic **Jaleo** is a good restaurant to introduce the family to tapas, especially if you can get one of the glass-topped foosball tables; after all, pan con tomate (grilled bread with tomato), patatas bravas (fried potatoes), and croquetas de pollo (chicken croquettes) are Spanish riffs on kid palate pleasers, and parents can kick back with refreshing gin and tonics or a pitcher of

California sea lions. The zoo has a train and carousel, as well.

>> **Public Transit:** The Metro stations closest to the zoo are Woodley Park-Zoo/Adams Morgan and Cleveland Park, serving the Red Line. The main entrance is about the same distance from both stations, but it's an uphill walk from the former and a flat walk from the latter.

After relaxing at your hotel, get a taxi or ride-share to Cathedral Heights to see if you can find the Darth Vader gargoyle at the **Washington National Cathedral,** before enjoying D.O.C.-certified pizza at family favorite **2 Amys,** one of the city's best pizza joints.

Open City

sangria in the famous hot spot.

>DAY 3

Start your day in Upper Northwest at **Open City,** which serves breakfast all day, plus sandwiches, salads, pizza, and a full bar in a casual, family-filled diner. From there, it's a half-mile, 10-minute walk up Connecticut Avenue to the main entrance of **Smithsonian's National Zoo.** There's tons to explore: the great ape house, grand cats, and lots of indigenous American beasts, like bald eagles and chipper

>DAY 4

If time permits, the day trip to George Washington's home, **Mount Vernon,** is a fantastic family outing, no car required, where you can learn about Washington and how he lived. When visiting with children, don't miss the farm and the 4-D film about life during the American Revolution; the estate frequently hosts story hours and special holiday events.

The best route from DC is by boat; you can take the *Spirit of Washington river cruise* from the Southwest Waterfront directly to Mount Vernon from March to October. It's also reachable by car/taxi or public transportation (see the *Day Trips* chapter for details). Detour through **Old Town Alexandria** on the way back to DC for dinner on the waterfront.

PLAYING POLITICS

Whether you have a pet issue you want to discuss, or simply want to say hello, you, too, can play lobbyist for a day and visit your member of Congress. Afterward, see the city like the VIPs do.

> MORNING

If you want to say hello to your **senator** or **representative,** visit their website to get the office location and hours; some host weekly or monthly meet-and-greets for constituents, while others explicitly welcome you to drop by when you're in Washington. Regardless, **Senate** and **House office buildings** are open to the public, and anyone, including international visitors, is free to visit even without an appointment, though there's no guarantee the representative will be available.

If you have a specific issue or bill you want to discuss, contact the office to see if you can arrange a **15-minute meeting** with the member or relevant staffer. If you get a meeting, here are some tips from the pro lobbyists: First, make a clear "ask"—such as how you want them to vote on a bill. If possible, bring a one-page document or other materials with facts to make your case. You may get a vague answer, but follow up with a thank you note. And keep in mind House representatives will be easier to meet than, say, a senator or someone in a leadership position.

If you contact the office in

view of the White House from Lafayette Square

BEST FOR PATRIOTIC PRIDE

THE STAR-SPANGLED BANNER
See the original flag that inspired Francis Scott Key to pen the national anthem in the National Museum of American History (page 52).

NATIONAL AIR AND SPACE MUSEUM
See the results of America's race to the moon in this must-see museum (page 54).

THE WHITE HOUSE
No matter who's in charge, it's impossible not to feel a swell of patriotic pride when you pass by the White House. You'll have a great view from Lafayette Square (page 76).

NATIONAL 9/11 PENTAGON MEMORIAL
The site of the terrorist attack at the Pentagon on September 11, 2001, is a poignant memorial to the 184 souls killed (page 237).

NATIONAL ARCHIVES MUSEUM
Get an up-close look at several of the nation's founding documents, including the Declaration of Independence, U.S. Constitution, and Bill of Rights (page 52).

advance, they can arrange a U.S. Capitol tour led by an intern, as well as tours of the White House, Pentagon, and other major sights.

An alternate activity for wonks is seeing a committee hearing in action. Most are open to the public. (Check www.congress.gov for more information and the congressional schedule.)

> **AFTERNOON**

Make a reservation for lunch at The Palm in Dupont Circle, where lobbyists and reporters go to shake hands with other VIPs whose faces are painted on the walls. (Yes, the person at the next table over was probably on CNN earlier.)

Washington is all about who you know, and many lunch meetings turn into happy hour. And Washingtonians can drink, a lot, so don't attempt to keep up. Instead, put on your running shoes and go for a jog (or walk) around the National Mall and monuments, a favorite activity of DC's active VIPs before the schmoozing resumes in the evening.

> **EVENING**

Spend your evening in Georgetown, where DC's power set has historically lived and socialized. Start with a cocktail at one of the bars at The Watergate Hotel, followed by dinner at Cafe Milano, where you may very well see a cabinet secretary or senator enjoying pasta or branzino on any given night. Or, head downtown to Old Ebbitt Grill for a beer and White House gossip.

SUMMER IN THE CITY

Washingtonians will tell you to avoid DC during July and August, when the city is feeling the swampiest due to extreme heat and humidity, but don't let the weather deter you from visiting during congressional "recess." When locals go on vacation, enjoy DC's many air-conditioned museums, patios and rooftops, and waterfront views. The only requirement for your hotel? An outdoor pool. The Washington Plaza Hotel in Logan Circle and Liaison Capitol Hill have good ones.

>MORNING

After coffee by your hotel's pool—the Liaison Capitol Hill has resort-style cabanas and weekend yoga, too—beat the heat in one of the lesser-known (but still air-conditioned) museums. Tourists continue to pack the most popular museums even at the height of summer, but others are far enough off the beaten track to provide respite. Try the Asian art galleries **Freer Gallery of Art and Arthur M. Sackler Gallery** or the **National Museum of African Art,** the only museum dedicated exclusively to African art in the United States.

>AFTERNOON

Head to the water. Take the Metro Green Line from L'Enfant Plaza to Navy Yard-Ballpark; you'll have several options for patio dining with a view of the Anacostia River. On the weekend, **The Salt Line** serves classic brunch dishes until 3pm,

summer in Navy Yard

BEST FOR ROMANCE

Lincoln Memorial at night

LINCOLN MEMORIAL
Conclude your date night at the Lincoln Memorial—the 19-foot statue gives a powerful jolt to your heart when illuminated against the dark backdrop of the National Mall (page 49).

FIOLA MARE
Impress your date at this very fine Italian restaurant in Georgetown, which has a glamorous interior and crowd, plus excellent seafood (page 196).

TINY JEWEL BOX
If you're looking for a special gift, you can't go wrong with something in a red and gold box from the jewelry store where presidents and first ladies have shopped since 1930 (page 97).

THE JEFFERSON
The luxurious Dupont Circle hotel inspired by Thomas Jefferson's estate has gorgeous suites, a Michelin-starred restaurant, and private nooks near the bar for canoodling (page 267).

and a fun crowd gathers on the patio before the baseball games.

After, walk west along the river to **Ballpark Boathouse** to rent a kayak or canoe; paddle west toward the Potomac River for monument views.

>EVENING
If it's a game day, stick around to catch the **Washington Nationals** at **Nationals Park,** where concessions serve local foodie favorites like Ben's Chili Bowl half-smokes and DC Brau beers.

On Fridays, however, go back to the National Mall for **Jazz in the Garden** at the National Gallery of Art's **Sculpture Garden.** Washingtonians love to skip out of work early for the free outdoor jazz concert every Friday 5pm-8:30pm. You can bring a blanket and picnic or purchase hors d'oeuvres, sandwiches, and barbecue, plus beer, wine, and sangria from the **Pavilion Café.**

Another favorite summer activity: **outdoor movie screenings.** Throughout the summer, you'll find free, family-friendly film screenings in several neighborhoods, including Navy Yard; check www.dcoutdoorfilms.com for locations and schedules.

>LATE NIGHT
Head to Shaw for a plethora of rooftops, patios, and beer gardens; the Shaw-Howard U Metro station is just five or six stops on the Green Line from Navy Yard-Ballpark or Waterfront. **Dacha Beer Garden** is a laid-back spot for international craft beer, while the roof deck at **Nellie's Sports Bar** is one of the most fun gay bars in the city. Or, grab a seat on the patio at **Maxwell Park,** which has about 50 wines by the glass that rotate every month, plus innovative cocktails.

BEST BITES

Washington DC once was a city where steakhouses were the only options for a nice meal out—and where lunch was more about who you schmoozed with than the food. In recent years, however, it's emerged as a culinary capital with something for every palate and budget, from filets and Chesapeake Bay crab cakes in old-school dining rooms, to innovative fusion cuisine and extravagant tasting menus by celebrity and rising-star chefs, to authentic fare from Ethiopia, Afghanistan, and the Philippines, to American Southern and soul food traditions. And with new restaurants opening practically every week and recognition by Michelin Guides and *Bon Appétit*, it's clear people are now moving to DC to open restaurants, not just to regulate them.

So, what's good? Around the White House and U.S. Capitol, you'll find steakhouses, oyster bars, and other buzzy spots teeming with power players.

U Street and Shaw are home to the essential Washington flavors—half-smokes at Ben's Chili Bowl, soul food, Ethiopian—as well as hip eateries favored by 20- and 30-somethings with disposable income to drop on creative small plates and strong cocktails. And foodies looking for something new will have much to explore, from José Andrés' empire in Penn Quarter, to the international flavors in Adams Morgan and Columbia Heights, where you can taste how DC is a global melting pot.

MITSITAM NATIVE FOODS CAFÉ

The café at the National Museum of the American Indian serves native foods from throughout the Western Hemisphere (page 61).

OLD EBBITT GRILL

Since 1856, White House staffers, lobbyists, and visitors have downloaded the day over oysters and beers at **Old Ebbitt Grill** (page 81).

JALEO

José Andrés started his empire with **Jaleo** in Penn Quarter, and since then he's changed dining and disaster response around the world (page 85).

CHARLIE PALMER STEAK

You're likely to see U.S. Senators and Representatives enjoying steak and American wine at **Charlie Palmer Steak** (page 111).

Ben's Chili Bowl

HANK'S OYSTER BAR

It's hard to beat the half-price oysters from 10pm to midnight at **Hank's Oyster Bar** (page 133).

BAGELS ETC.

Enjoy the best bagels in DC at cash-only **Bagels Etc.** (page 135).

ANNIE'S PARAMOUNT

The historic **Annie's Paramount** has 24-hour dining on weekends (page 133).

BEN'S CHILI BOWL

Your trip to Washington isn't complete without a half-smoke and milkshake at **Ben's Chili Bowl** (page 153).

Blue Duck Tavern

DUKEM ETHIOPIAN RESTAURANT

Ask anyone who loves Ethiopian food where to go, and they'll tell you **Dukem Ethiopian Restaurant** (page 155).

BUSYBOYS AND POETS

Busboys and Poets has responsible, affordable American food and a history of activism (page 158).

A RAKE'S PROGRESS

Meals are events at hyperlocal, hyperseasonal showpiece restaurant, **A Rake's Progress** (page 174).

JOHNNY'S HALF SHELL

Enjoy excellent crab cakes at friendly neighborhood **Johnny's Half Shell** (page 175).

ELLĒ

Stop by **Ellē** for bakery goods during the day and creative dinners at night (page 175).

BLUE DUCK TAVERN

Blue Duck Tavern's local, seasonal cuisine is some of the best any time of day (page 193).

CAFE MILANO

Cafe Milano is the place to see and be seen, serving Italian fare to cabinet secretaries, ambassadors, and socialites (page 195).

FIOLA MARE AND MASSERIA AT UNION MARKET

Take your date to the sexy **Fiola Mare** (page 196) for superb seafood on the waterfront, or **Masseria at Union Market** (page 245) to experience the Michelin-starred menu in the starry courtyard.

PRIMROSE

Primrose raises the bar for French food in DC, with a whimsical atmosphere and excellent selection of calvados, too (page 244).

DC AFTER DARK

In Washington DC, presidential debates, snow days, and sensational congressional hearings or trials call for booze, and lots of it.

Washingtonians work hard but party harder. DC residents guzzle more alcohol per capita than residents of every state except New Hampshire. As a result, the city's nightlife centers around bars: cocktail bars, wine bars, beer gardens, posh hotel lounges, and of course, historic bars, where lobbyists, staffers, and reporters grease the wheels among the ghosts of presidents and policymakers past.

You'll find a few noteworthy dance clubs and late-night music venues, especially in trendy neighborhoods like U Street, Shaw, and the Atlas District, which are humming on weekend nights. But for the most part, DC is an early town, with the nightlife scene most vibrant around 5pm-8pm for happy hour, especially downtown, and relatively quiet on weekends. After all, Washingtonians need time to sleep off the hangover before the 10am hearing.

POV

The exclusive **POV** boasts expansive views of the White House and monuments (page 87).

ROUND ROBIN BAR

Senator Henry Clay mixed DC's first mint julep with Kentucky bourbon at **Round Robin Bar,**

POV at the W Washington D.C.

Round Robin Bar

which has served drinks to many U.S. presidents (page 87).

WILD DAYS

From happy hour until late, local artists and DJs mingle with buttoned-up lobbyists loosening their ties at **WILD DAYS** (page 90).

TUNE INN

Tune Inn serves cheap beer and fried food in a funky space to an incredibly diverse crowd on Capitol Hill (page 116).

MR. HENRY'S

This Capitol Hill institution is a welcoming pub serving reliable pub fare and happy hour specials. You'll enjoy great live music at **Mr. Henry's,** too (page 118).

JR'S BAR

Located on the parade route, the patio at **JR's Bar** is the place to celebrate during Capital Pride in June (page 137).

BLACK CAT

Dance the night away at **Black Cat** (page 161).

9:30 CLUB

Even *Rolling Stone* agrees the **9:30 Club** is an institution (page 161).

NELLIE'S SPORTS BAR

The all-you-can-eat drag brunch and expansive roof deck are just two of the draws of **Nellie's Sports Bar** (page 163).

JACK ROSE DINING SALOON

Jack Rose Dining Saloon has more than 2,500 bottles of whiskey and Scotch from around the world (page 178).

DAN'S CAFÉ

One of the best dive bars in the area, **Dan's Café** serves cheap beers and mix-your-own cocktails (page 180).

THE LOUNGE AT BOURBON STEAK

You never know who you'll meet at **The Lounge at Bourbon Steak,** located in the top choice hotel among celebrities and socialites (page 198).

THE ANTHEM

Curious about the best reason to visit the Wharf? It's probably to see a major headliner at **The Anthem** (page 224).

CULTURE CAPITAL

The first American city to have a black majority, Washington DC was a vibrant hub for African American arts and culture even before Harlem and Motown—and as the home of Duke Ellington, Marvin Gaye, and Chuck Brown, DC's most important contribution to American arts is the music. From the early 20th century until the 1960s, U Street and Shaw were known as "Black Broadway," with jazz clubs and iconic theaters like The Howard Theatre and The Lincoln Theatre, which remain the best spots to experience DC's jazz, soul, and go-go sounds.

Sphere No. 6 by Arnaldo Pomodoro at Hirshhorn Museum and Sculpture Garden

This history set the stage for DC's rich cultural scene today, with world-class performing arts, eye-popping historical homes and gardens, and of course, dozens of museums and galleries—many of which are free and open to the public almost every day of the year. You could spend weeks exploring the National Mall's museums, but you'll find hubs of niche history and art museums downtown and in Dupont Circle, as well.

DC likewise has a theater and performing arts scene on par with the world capitals, with theaters citywide showcasing Broadway-quality productions of classic and contemporary dramas and musicals as well as premieres of quirky new plays and fringe theater. And in Foggy Bottom, The John F. Kennedy Center for the Performing Arts is one of the country's premier venues, home to the National Symphony Orchestra as well as jazz, opera, and dance programs.

HIRSHHORN MUSEUM AND SCULPTURE GARDEN

The **Hirshhorn Museum and Sculpture Garden** boasts more than 12,000 modern and contemporary works, housed in a circular building designed by Gordon Bunshaft (page 63).

East Building of the National Gallery of Art

NATIONAL GALLERY OF ART

The **National Gallery of Art** has something for every fan of art— Da Vinci, Dutch masters, and

French impressionists in the West Building, and cool modern art in the East Building (page 63).

The John F. Kennedy Center for the Performing Arts

UNITED STATES HOLOCAUST MEMORIAL MUSEUM

The **United States Holocaust Memorial Museum** tells the story of the Holocaust in moving detail (page 65).

WOOLLY MAMMOTH THEATRE COMPANY

Any production by the **Woolly Mammoth Theatre Company** is sure to be groundbreaking—and maybe even shocking (page 92).

THE PHILLIPS COLLECTION

The Phillips Collection was founded in 1921 and is considered America's first modern art museum (page 137).

HOWARD THEATRE

The historic **Howard Theatre** regularly hosts go-go bands, a uniquely DC style of music (page 164).

THE JOHN F. KENNEDY CENTER FOR THE PERFORMING ARTS

The John F. Kennedy Center for the Performing Arts showcases world-class music, theater, opera, dance, and comedy for all tastes, with a free performance daily (page 201).

ARENA STAGE

Since 1950, Southwest's **Arena Stage** has been premiering award-winning plays and reviving classic American dramas and musicals (page 226).

HILLWOOD ESTATE, MUSEUM & GARDENS

The former estate of Marjorie Merriweather Post, **Hillwood Estate, Museum & Gardens** is the closest thing to Versailles in DC, thanks to the extravagant gardens and art collection (page 247).

NATIONAL CHERRY BLOSSOM FESTIVAL

Every spring at the **National Cherry Blossom Festival** you'll get the chance to see thousands of the pink and white flowering trees in bloom (page 70).

PLANNING YOUR TRIP

WHEN TO GO

Ask any local when you should visit DC, and they'll likely tell you **spring.** While these months are susceptible to unseasonably cold or hot weather and rain, you'll have plenty of mild, sunshine-filled days to explore the sights and join Washingtonians with "spring fever" on patios and rooftops. The cherry blossoms bloom in March or April, covering the National Mall and memorials in pink, and the **National Cherry Blossom Festival** is a bucket-list event with about three weeks of parades, parties, and special deals. There are two major downsides to visiting in the spring: high hotel prices and large crowds.

The **summer** months are hot, sticky, and jam-packed with tourists, though the **Smithsonian Folklife Festival, Capital Pride,** and, of course, **Independence Day,** are among the reasons to brave the humidity and expensive hotel rooms. The **fall** is crisp and lovely as the leaves begin to change colors and tourists disperse, and **winter** is even quieter, though often very cold.

The **holiday season** is a wonderful time to explore Washington, thanks to the **National Christmas**

cherry blossoms along the Tidal Basin

TOURIST TIPS

- **Stand to the Right:** On Metro escalators, stand to the right and walk to the left. You don't want to get in the path of a late, disgruntled staffer careening down one of the escalators.

- **Don't Hold the Doors:** Metro train doors are not like elevator doors—they won't slide open again if you stick your arm out when the door is closing. You'll hold up the train and possibly injure yourself.

- **Don't Mind the Sirens:** You may be walking downtown when police cars, motorcycles, and ambulances start barreling down the street, sirens blazing. Stay in place, and don't be alarmed—it's the presidential motorcade. Keep your eyes peeled and you might see the POTUS in "The Beast," an armored black limo with secure communication lines and its own air supply. (The jaded locals around you, however, will likely just roll their eyes and check their phones while waiting for the motorcade to pass.)

- **Prep for Security:** Government buildings and museums require you to pass through a metal detector before entering, while your belongings get X-ray screening. Many items are prohibited, ranging from scissors to food to luggage, so check the building's website if you're unsure whether you can bring something inside.

- **It's Probably Open:** Many sights managed by the U.S. Government or Smithsonian Institution are open daily year-round except Christmas Day; a few sights are closed on major holidays like Thanksgiving Day or New Year's Day, too. While it's probably open, it doesn't hurt to check before showing up at a museum or park on a federal holiday. Most outdoor memorials are accessible 24 hours daily, 365 days per year.

Tree and lighter crowds, and every four years, January gets busy the week of the **Presidential Inauguration.**

ENTRY REQUIREMENTS

All international visitors are required to have a **valid passport** to enter the United States. Canadian citizens traveling by air need a passport or NEXUS card, but those arriving by land may show an enhanced driver's license/identification card instead. Depending on your country of origin, a visa may be required, or you may be eligible for the Visa Waiver Program (VWP), allowing travel to the United States for business or leisure for 90 days or less without a visa. All visitors and their baggage may be subject to an interview or inspection by U.S. Customs and Border Protection; be prepared to provide details about the purpose of your visit, where you are staying, and when you plan to leave. For more information on entry requirements and restrictions, including prohibited items, visit www.cbp.gov.

TRANSPORTATION

The Washington metropolitan region is served by three airports: **Ronald Reagan Washington National Airport** in Arlington, Virginia; **Washington Dulles International Airport** in Dulles, Virginia; and **Baltimore/Washington International Thurgood Marshall Airport** in Maryland.

Amtrak serves **Union Station,** a convenient travel method between DC, Baltimore, Philadelphia, and New York.

It's not necessary or recommended to rent a car in DC. Public transportation options include Washington Metrorail and Metrobus, DC Circulator, and DC Streetcar service between Union Station and the H Street Corridor/Atlas District; all accept the Metro SmarTrip card, and the streetcar is currently free.

Ride-hailing services like Uber and Lyft are recommended and will take you throughout DC, Maryland, and Virginia.

RESERVATIONS

Washington DC is increasingly a reservations-recommended town. Reservations/tickets are required for **U.S. Capitol and White House tours** as well as the Smithsonian's **National Museum of African American History and Culture.**

Generally, if you have the option to reserve a ticket or tour in advance, you should if the sight is on your must-see list. On the other hand, with the exception of special exhibits, most museums are free and don't require tickets, and many tours, especially during nonbusy seasons, have walk-up availability. You can usually acquire tickets to theatrical or musical performances a day or two in advance, except for major, one-night-only concerts.

Reserve your hotel as far in advance as possible, especially if you're visiting during cherry blossom season, the first week of July, or inauguration weekend. You can almost always find available rooms, but prices get extremely high during prime tourist seasons or major conferences, and hotels offering good deals always sell out.

Museum of African American History and Culture

WHAT'S NEW?

If you haven't been to Washington DC in a while, you'll hardly recognize it.

- **Metro Silver Line:** Beginning service in 2014, the Metro Silver Line was the first new line to open in over two decades. When it's complete in 2021, it will connect Washington Dulles International Airport to the city center.

- **National Mall Additions:** A new memorial dedicated to the 34th president, Dwight D. Eisenhower, opened in May 2020, while the newest Smithsonian, the National Museum of African American History and Culture, remains the must-visit museum.

- **Museum Hopping:** Sadly, the Newseum closed in December 2019. However, the National Children's Museum moved from Maryland to DC in February 2020, while the International Spy Museum moved to a larger, cooler space.

- **District Wharf:** This mile-long complex on the Potomac River opened in October 2017 and changed the landscape with several new hotels, restaurants, and a concert venue.

- **Union Market:** The revitalized historic market continues to grow as new restaurants, entertainment venues, and local distilleries pop up.

- **Michelin Guide:** The French tastemaker now publishes a Washington DC guide annually, recognizing the city's culinary scene.

- **New Hotels:** Riggs Washington DC, Conrad Washington DC, and The LINE are among the many brand-new or fully restored hotels, boasting world-class amenities and destination dining and bars, while some hotels cater to specific political views.

Reservations are required for the most popular fine dining restaurants, especially those included in the Michelin Guide, which typically book up 2-3 weeks in advance, though it's possible to score a last-minute table if you're willing to dine early or late. Some exceptionally buzzy restaurants will have their own system for reservations and you'll want to call the first day possible; for example, **minibar by José Andrés** accepts reservations two calendar months at a time, starting at 10am on the first Monday of each month, while **Komi** accepts reservations exactly one month in advance by phone only. For most other restaurants, reservations are recommended a few days in advance, especially on weekends, though not always required. Check **OpenTable** or **Resy** for last-minute availability.

PASSES AND DISCOUNTS

One of the best things about a trip to Washington DC? The majority of the city's sights and museums—including the most exclusive ones, like the U.S. Capitol and White House, are free. Aside from the high cost of hotel accommodations, it's possible to have a relatively inexpensive vacation in DC thanks to dozens of free museums, memorials, and parks, plus excellent fast-casual restaurants and diners. The museums that charge admission fees usually offer discounts for seniors, students, military, and young children, and typically, these museums, like The Phillips Collection, are worth the price.

GUIDED TOURS

There are many options for guided tours of the major sights, including the **Old Town Trolley Tours,** open-air tours with live guides around DC and Arlington National Cemetery, and **DC Ducks,** 90-minute tours of the National Mall, Capitol Hill, and White House by land and water. Several traditional bus tours depart from Union Station, including double-decker buses, nighttime monuments tours, and day trips; look for (friendly, albeit pushy) uniformed operators at the southwest corner of the station. For something more active, choose a bike or Segway tour, including **Segs in the City,** from Pennsylvania Avenue, or **Bike and Roll** (202/842-2453, www.bikeandrolldc.com; prices vary), with departure points from the National Mall, Capitol Hill, and Old Town Alexandria; both offer guided and self-guided tours. **Smithsonian National Mall Tours** combine the Smithsonian Institution's knowledge with Segway/walking tour operators for educational experiences.

Like many things in DC, some of the best tours are free. The **National Park Service** offers a huge variety of free, ranger-led **walking tours** (www.nps.gov/nama/planyourvisit) around the National Mall and at major monuments and memorials, while guided tours of the U.S. Capitol, White House, and other key buildings are available for free if you plan in advance. In addition, the Smithsonian Institution museums and National Gallery of Art offer free, docent-led tours daily; check the museum's website for the schedule or inquire at the information desk, usually located just after the security screening.

CALENDAR OF EVENTS

JANUARY

Every four years, the city comes together for the **Presidential Inauguration.** Since the second inauguration of FDR in 1937, the swearing-in ceremony has taken place on January 20 after an election; if the date falls on a Sunday, the public ceremony occurs on Monday, January 21. Details on how to obtain tickets for festivities including the swearing-in ceremony, parade, and balls are usually available within a few weeks after the November election.

Dr. King had an enormous impact on Washington, which celebrates **Martin Luther King Jr. Day** (www.mlkholidaydc.org) with special events, including the Memorial Peace Walk and parade through Southeast DC.

Beat the January doldrums with the winter edition of the **Metropolitan Washington Restaurant Week** (www.ramw.org/restaurantweek), during which hundreds of local restaurants offer prix fixe menus for brunch ($22), lunch ($22), and dinner ($35) for one week in late January.

MARCH-APRIL

For 3-4 weeks in March and April, the **National Cherry Blossom Festival** (www.nationalcherryblossomfestival.org) celebrates the cherry trees, given to the United States by Japan in 1912. (The festival is timed to coincide with peak bloom, though it can be unpredictable if

White House Easter Egg Roll

winter is unusually long or unusually warm.) The festival includes tons of free events like a parade, kite festival, Japanese street festival, fireworks, special exhibits and museum events, and of course, the main event: the magnificent pink and white blossoms around the Tidal Basin and National Mall.

On Easter Monday, the **White House Easter Egg Roll** (www.whitehouse.gov/easter-egg-roll) welcomes more than 20,000 people to the South Lawn for children's egg-rolling races as well as celebrity performances, arts and crafts, and meet-and-greets with high-level officials. The free tickets are available approximately one month in advance by online lottery.

Every spring, the White House opens the gardens and grounds to the public for just two days in April for the **White House Spring Garden Tours** (www.whitehouse.

gov), allowing you to explore the Jacqueline Kennedy Garden, Rose Garden, White House Kitchen Garden, and South Lawn. The White House announces the date and ticket information approximately 3-4 weeks in advance, and free, timed tickets are distributed first come, first served the morning of the tours.

MAY

The Sunday before Memorial Day, the free **National Memorial Day Concert** (www.pbs.org/national-memorial-day-concert) takes place on the U.S. Capitol West Lawn, featuring celebrity performers, military heroes, the National Symphony Orchestra, and several U.S. military bands and choral groups. On Memorial Day, the **National Memorial Day Parade** runs along Constitution Avenue NW; check local news outlets for details.

JUNE

One of the largest pride festivals in the country, **Capital Pride** (www.capitalpride.org) is a colorful parade and street festival through Dupont Circle with more than 180 floats, entertainers, and participating groups. In recent years, the event has expanded to include a festival and concert, which has featured stars like Miley Cyrus, The Pointer Sisters, and the Gay Men's Chorus. The Dupont Circle neighborhood stays alive into the evening as parade-goers continue the celebration.

JULY-AUGUST

Independence Day in Washington DC is a bucket-list event. It begins with the **National Independence Day Parade** (www.july4thparade.com) on Constitution Avenue NW before crowds move to the U.S. Capitol West Lawn for **A Capitol Fourth** (www.pbs.org/a-capitol-fourth), the free, patriotic concert with celebrity guests who've included The Beach Boys and Trace Adkins. The concert ends with the iconic **fireworks at the Washington Monument,** which are best viewed from the National Mall but can be seen from rooftops and vistas across the city.

Starting late July, tennis fans make their way to the Rock Creek Park Tennis Center in Upper Northwest for **Citi Open** (www.citiopentennis.com; $15-100), one of the first open tennis tournaments in the United States. The outdoor event features professional men and women players from around the world.

The summer edition of the

fireworks at the Washington Monument

biannual **Metropolitan Washington Restaurant Week** (www.ramw.org/restaurantweek) provides a great opportunity to try the DC culinary scene with prix fixe menus for brunch ($22), lunch ($22), and dinner ($35) at hundreds of restaurants.

SEPTEMBER

In early September, the Library of Congress organizes the annual **National Book Festival** (www.loc.gov/bookfest), a free, one-day event at the Walter E. Washington Convention Center where more than 100 authors and illustrators across genres read and sign their books and participate in panel discussions.

OCTOBER

As the foliage changes colors, the White House opens the gardens and grounds to the public for the annual **White House Fall Garden Tours** (www.whitehouse.gov), allowing you to explore the Jacqueline Kennedy Garden, Rose Garden, White House Kitchen Garden, and South Lawn. The White House announces the date and ticket information approximately 3-4 weeks in advance, and free, timed tickets are distributed first come, first served the morning of the tours.

NOVEMBER

Veterans Day is a somber day in the capital as visitors pay respects at war memorials throughout DC and Virginia. The **wreath-laying ceremony at Arlington National Cemetery** (www.arlingtoncemetery.mil) on November 11 is open to the public.

DECEMBER

For nearly 100 years, the president of the United States and First Family have hosted the **National Christmas Tree Lighting** (www.thenationaltree.org) on the Ellipse, kicking off the holiday season in Washington DC with a festive performance featuring A-list celebrities. The free, coveted tickets are available by lottery beginning in October; check in late September for details. The tree is lit daily through January 1, along with 56 trees representing the states and territories.

Every Chanukah, politicians and Jewish community leaders light the **National Menorah** (www.nationalmenorah.org), the largest in the world at 30 feet tall. The ceremony features Jewish performers; free tickets are required and available online in advance.

National Mall

Map 1

The National Mall is America's lawn, where people gather for major events like Independence Day and presidential inaugurations, as well as festivals, concerts, and protests for every issue imaginable. In addition to being the location of the **national monuments and memorials,** it's a national park with more than 1,000 acres of **green space** and photo-op-worthy areas for picnics, jogging, biking, and boating. The National Mall is also home to many of the **Smithsonian Institution museums and galleries,** which are free and open to the public every day except Christmas Day.

TOP SIGHTS

- Most Prominent Monument:
  Washington Monument (page 48)
- Most Stirring Sight:
  Lincoln Memorial (page 49)
- Best for American Nostalgia: **National Museum of American History** (page 52)
- Museum Worth Spending the Entire Day: **National Museum of African American History and Culture** (page 53)
- Best Place to Get Your Geek On: **National Air and Space Museum** (page 54)
- Best Place to See Historical Documents: **National Archives Museum** (page 52)

TOP RESTAURANTS

- Most Interesting Museum Café:
  Mitsitam Native Foods Café (page 61)

TOP ARTS AND CULTURE

- Best for Kids: **National Museum of Natural History** (page 64)
- Coolest Contemporary Art: **Hirshhorn Museum and Sculpture Garden** (page 63)
- Best for Art Lovers of All Kinds:
  National Gallery of Art (page 63)
- Most Sobering Reminder of the Past: **United States Holocaust Memorial Museum** (page 65)

TOP RECREATION

- Best Way to See the Cherry Blossoms:
  Tidal Basin Paddleboats (page 71)

GETTING THERE AND AROUND

- Metro lines: Blue, Green, Orange, Silver, Yellow
- Metro stations: Federal Center SW, L'Enfant Plaza, Smithsonian
- Major bus routes: DC Circulator National Mall

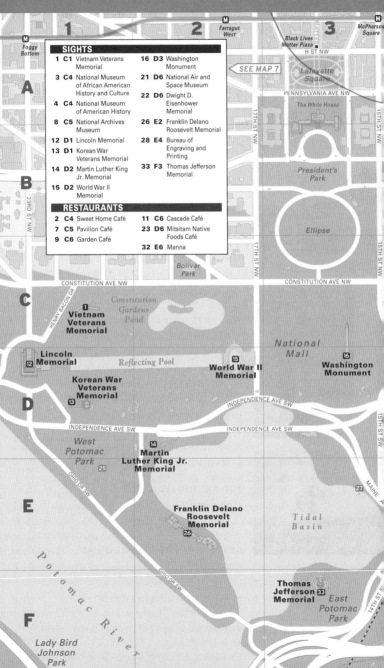

SIGHTS

1	**C1**	Vietnam Veterans Memorial	
3	**C4**	National Museum of African American History and Culture	
4	**C4**	National Museum of American History	
8	**C5**	National Archives Museum	
12	**D1**	Lincoln Memorial	
13	**D1**	Korean War Veterans Memorial	
14	**D2**	Martin Luther King Jr. Memorial	
15	**D2**	World War II Memorial	

16	**D3**	Washington Monument
21	**D6**	National Air and Space Museum
22	**D6**	Dwight D. Eisenhower Memorial
26	**E2**	Franklin Delano Roosevelt Memorial
28	**E4**	Bureau of Engraving and Printing
33	**F3**	Thomas Jefferson Memorial

RESTAURANTS

2	**C4**	Sweet Home Café
7	**C5**	Pavilion Café
9	**C6**	Garden Café
11	**C6**	Cascade Café
23	**D6**	Mitsitam Native Foods Café
32	**E6**	Manna

Foggy Bottom

Farragut West

Black Lives Matter Plaza

McPherson Square

H ST NW

SEE MAP 7

Lafayette Square

PENNSYLVANIA AVE NW

The White House

17TH ST NW

15TH ST NW

23RD ST NW

President's Park

Ellipse

17TH ST NW

15TH ST NW

Bolivar Park

CONSTITUTION AVE NW

CONSTITUTION AVE NW

HENRY BACON DR

Constitution Gardens Pond

Vietnam Veterans Memorial

National Mall

Lincoln Memorial

Reflecting Pool

World War II Memorial

Washington Monument

Korean War Veterans Memorial

INDEPENDENCE AVE SW

15TH ST SW

INDEPENDENCE AVE SW

INDEPENDENCE AVE SW

West Potomac Park

OHIO DR SW

Martin Luther King Jr. Memorial

MAINE A

Franklin Delano Roosevelt Memorial

Tidal Basin

OHIO DR SW

P o t o m a c   R i v e r

Thomas Jefferson Memorial

East Potomac Park

14TH ST S

Lady Bird Johnson Park

CHINATOWN

ARTS AND CULTURE

- **6** **C5** National Museum of Natural History
- **10** **C6** National Gallery of Art
- **17** **D4** United States Holocaust Memorial Museum
- **18** **D4** Freer Gallery of Art and Arthur M. Sackler Gallery
- **19** **D5** National Museum of African Art
- **20** **D5** Hirshhorn Museum and Sculpture Garden
- **24** **D6** National Museum of the American Indian
- **30** **E5** International Spy Museum
- **31** **E6** Museum of the Bible

RECREATION

- **5** **C4** Smithsonian Segway Tour
- **25** **E1** West Potomac Park
- **27** **E3** Tidal Basin Paddleboats

HOTELS

- **29** **E4** Mandarin Oriental Washington DC

SEE MAP 2

NEW YORK AVE NW

Metro Center

Freedom Plaza

PENNSYLVANIA AVE NW

FEDERAL TRIANGLE

Federal Triangle

National Museum of American History

National Museum of African American History and Culture

THE MALL

Smithsonian

Archives-Navy Memorial-Penn Quarter

National Archives Museum

CONSTITUTION AVE NW

John Marshall Place Park

PENNSYLVANIA AVE NW

SEE MAP 3

National Mall

MADISON DRIVE NW

JEFFERSON DRIVE SW

INDEPENDENCE AVE SW

National Air and Space Museum

Dwight D. Eisenhower Memorial

Bureau of Engraving and Printing

L'Enfant Plaza

VIRGINIA AVE SW

Federal Center SW

C ST SW

SCHOOL ST SW

E ST SW

VIRGINIA AVE SW

395

Benjamin Banneker Park

Jefferson Field

SEE MAP 8

SOUTHWEST WATERFRONT

Washington Channel

Town Center Park

0		300 yds
0		300 m

DISTANCE ACROSS MAP
Approximate: 2.2 mi or 3.6 km

© MOON.COM

NATIONAL MALL AND MEMORIALS WALK

TOTAL DISTANCE: 3.1 mi (5 km)
WALKING TIME: 1 hour and 15 minutes

For a history lesson on foot, head to the west side of the National Mall, where you'll find a maze of memorials set among idyllic grassy areas. It's possible to power through this walk in less than two hours, but it's better to budget up to three hours to fully take in the grandeur of the monuments (and take plenty of photos). To avoid crowds, try the walk in the early morning or dusk. Taking this walk during peak cherry blossom bloom, usually around late March to early April, should be on your travel bucket list—though you'll need to add at least one hour to your walking time to get around the Tidal Basin, which will be packed with tourists.

Start this walk at the corner of **17th Street NW and Constitution Avenue NW.** It's easily accessible by foot from downtown and Dupont Circle.

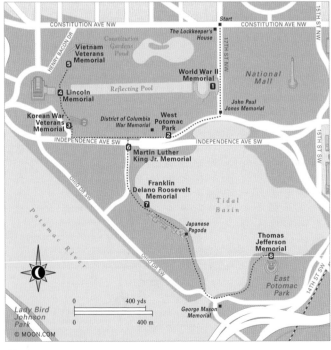

World War II Memorial

1 Walking south, you'll pass the **Lockkeeper's House** on your right, the small stone house for the lockkeeper who raised and lowered the C&O Canal lock, and the oldest structure on the National Mall. Walk two minutes down this block to approach the **World War II Memorial** on your right; you can't miss the 56 stone columns. You'll have a great view of the Washington Monument to the east and the Lincoln Memorial to the west, but keep walking southwest on the sidewalk along Homefront Drive SW. To your left is the **John Paul Jones Memorial,** a statue honoring the Revolutionary War hero considered the "Father of the U.S. Navy."

2 Homefront Drive runs into Independence Avenue SW. Keep heading west on Independence; you're in the heart of **West Potomac Park.** On the right you'll pass a circular, marble structure, the **District of Columbia War Memorial,** honoring the 499 Washington DC residents who died serving in World War I.

3 To see the Vietnam and Korean War Memorials, along with a closer look at the Lincoln Memorial, continue west on Independence Avenue SW for about five minutes. The **Korean War Veterans Memorial** will be on your right at the stoplight near David French Memorial Drive SW. Take in the 19 figures representing soldiers from all branches of the country's military. Get up close and you'll see for yourself the stunning detail imbued in each statue.

4 Take the path leading northwest to reach the **Lincoln Memorial.** Climb the steps to get an up-close view of the iconic statue of a seated Abraham Lincoln gazing toward the Reflecting Pool.

5 Next, take one of the paths headed northeast to reach the **Vietnam Veterans Memorial.** (If you get disoriented, look for rectangular gray signs pointing you toward major sights as well as tourist information and facilities.) Absorb the scale of the Vietnam War as you scan the 58,315 names of the Americans killed or missing in action that are engraved on the Memorial Wall. Retrace your steps to Independence Avenue, then head east until you reach West Basin Drive SW, about five minutes.

6 At West Basin Drive SW, cross the street to head south to the **Martin Luther King Jr. Memorial.** Keep walking south, through the "mountain of despair" to the "stone of hope," structures that represent a line from Dr. King's "I Have A Dream" speech. Stand as close as you can to the sculpture of MLK to feel the enormous impact he had on our nation, then walk back to the railing at the Tidal Basin to see him emerging from the mountains.

7 From here, continue walking south just under half a mile on the path around the Tidal Basin to reach the **Franklin Delano Roosevelt**

Franklin Delano Roosevelt Memorial

Memorial, where you can spend time exploring and taking photos of the life-size statues of FDR and First Lady Eleanor Roosevelt. Walk up the stone steps to enter the memorial at Room One, which represents Roosevelt's first presidential term, during the Great Depression. (Backtrack a bit to visit the Prologue Room, which was added later to accommodate a statue of FDR in a wheelchair. It's to the right by the visitor center once you're inside.) Continue south through the memorial, which guides you chronologically through each of Roosevelt's four terms and his death.

8 Exit the memorial on the south end to return to the Tidal Basin path. Look for the **Japanese Pagoda,** a 17th-century stone structure given to the United States by the mayor of Yokohama, Japan, in 1957. It symbolizes the friendship between the two nations. Keep along the asphalt path around the Tidal Basin for views of the Washington Monument and the Thomas Jefferson Memorial glimmering on the water. During cherry blossom season, this path is covered in pink blooms—and people. Cross the bridge at Ohio Drive SW and approach the **George Mason Memorial,** honoring a lesser-known Founding Father who did not sign the Declaration of Independence because it did not contain a bill of rights or abolish slavery. It's looking a little worse for the wear, but you can relax on the benches under the trellis, next to the bronze statue of George Mason. From here, walk east on East Basin Drive SW and turn left to approach the **Thomas Jefferson Memorial.** Walk counterclockwise around the memorial to approach the stone steps and enter the open-air memorial, where you'll see the 19-foot statue of Jefferson and quotations from his writings.

From here, you have options: Walk back to the east side of the National Mall for an afternoon at a museum, or go southeast to **East Potomac Park** and **Hains Point** for a scenic walk. If you do head to the park, stop at the **East Potomac Golf Course and Driving Range** for a bottle of water if you plan to walk the 1.8 mi (2.9 km) to Hains Point.

Sights

✪ Washington Monument

The Washington Monument dominates the horizon, but the tribute to George Washington is worth an up-close look. At 555 feet tall and comprising 36,000 stones, it's the world's tallest obelisk and the tallest structure in DC, excluding radio towers. Though it invites jokes about the Founding Fathers' Napoleon complexes, the enormity will nonetheless take your breath away.

Washington Monument

The monument to the first U.S. president took more than three decades to complete. Construction began on July 4, 1848; Congressman Abraham Lincoln was among those who attended the ceremony to lay the cornerstone. But construction was delayed due to a lack of funding and the Civil War. You'll notice the top two-thirds are a different color, because the original marble could not be matched when it was finally completed in 1888.

After being closed for renovations for three years, the monument reopened in September 2019 with a new, state-of-the-art elevator to zip visitors from the lobby, which features a statue of George Washington, to the observation deck and exhibits at the top in 70 seconds. Timed entry tickets are required for visitors ages 2 and up; reserve them online up to 90 days in advance at www.recreation.gov, though a limited number of same-day tickets are available starting at 8:30am at the visitor building in front of the monument on 15th Street NW.

MAP 1: 15th St. NW and Madison Dr. NW, 202/426-6841, www.nps.gov/wamo; grounds 24 hours daily, elevator access 9am-5pm daily except Independence Day and Christmas Day; timed entry tickets required, $1 fee/ticket for advance reservations

Lincoln Memorial

NEARBY:

- Appreciate iconic American objects at the National Museum of American History (page 52).
- Plan ahead to get an entry pass to the newest and best Smithsonian, the National Museum of African American History and Culture (page 53).
- See where paper currency gets printed at the Bureau of Engraving and Printing (page 55).
- Enjoy Southern and creole dishes at Sweet Home Café, in the Museum of African American History and Culture (page 61).
- Experience the United States Holocaust Memorial Museum, the most sobering reminder of the past (page 65).
- Explore the mall on foot or by Segway with Smithsonian National Mall Tours (page 70).

TOP EXPERIENCE

✪ Lincoln Memorial

"In this temple, as in the hearts of the people for whom he saved the Union, the memory of Abraham Lincoln is enshrined forever." *New York Herald Tribune* art critic Royal Cortissoz wrote these words, carved directly above the 19-foot sculpture of a seated President Lincoln inside the Lincoln Memorial, located in a former swampy area at the west end of the National Mall. The memorial was not completed until 50 years after Lincoln's assassination, but the awe-inspiring result was worth the wait—and it's most magnificent at night, after the crowds have dispersed and interior lights cast a dramatic glow on the 16th U.S. president as he gazes across the 2,029-foot-long Reflecting Pool, which stretches from the Lincoln Memorial to the Washington Monument.

THE SMITHSONIAN INSTITUTION MUSEUMS AND GALLERIES

National Air and Space Museum

There are more Smithsonian museums and galleries than most people can visit in one trip. This list outlines all of DC's Smithsonians and will help you choose the ones that are perfectly suited to your tastes, as well as give you the must-see exhibits at each spot.

NATIONAL MUSEUM OF AMERICAN HISTORY (PAGE 52)
Best for: Fans of American nostalgia and pop culture
Don't Miss: The Star-Spangled Banner; first ladies' dresses

NATIONAL MUSEUM OF AFRICAN AMERICAN HISTORY AND CULTURE (PAGE 53)
Best for: People looking to immerse themselves in a museum for an entire day
Don't Miss: History Galleries, including "Paradox of Liberty," about the slaves at Monticello; interactive lunch counter with stools from the 1960 Greensboro Woolworth sit-ins; Chuck Berry's Cadillac

NATIONAL AIR AND SPACE MUSEUM (PAGE 54)
Best for: Space geeks

Examine the symbolic details that architect Henry Bacon and sculptor Daniel Chester French thoughtfully placed throughout. As you climb the steps, you'll notice the 36 columns, which represent the 36 states in the Union when Lincoln died. Above the columns, 48 garland carvings represent the 48 states when the memorial was completed in 1922. These details symbolize his dedication to keeping the Union intact.

Inside, the texts of two of Lincoln's most important speeches are etched on either side of the statue: to the left, the 1863 Gettysburg Address, and to the right, the 1865 Second Inaugural

Don't Miss: Friendship 7, Lunar Module 2, Neil Armstrong's spacesuit

NATIONAL MUSEUM OF NATURAL HISTORY (PAGE 64)
Best for: Kids of all ages
Don't Miss: Hope Diamond and other gems; dinosaur fossils

HIRSHHORN MUSEUM AND SCULPTURE GARDEN (PAGE 63)
Best for: Lovers of cool contemporary art
Don't Miss: The latest temporary exhibition; Sculpture Garden

NATIONAL MUSEUM OF THE AMERICAN INDIAN (PAGE 68)
Best for: Those seeking a quiet, educational experience
Don't Miss: The tepee-like sculptures and native landscape on the grounds; the restaurant

FREER GALLERY OF ART AND ARTHUR M. SACKLER GALLERY (PAGE 65)
Best for: Asian art and decor aficionados
Don't Miss: Whistler's Peacock Room

NATIONAL MUSEUM OF AFRICAN ART (PAGE 67)
Best for: Admirers of traditional and contemporary African art
Don't Miss: Disney-Tishman Collection ceramics

NATIONAL PORTRAIT GALLERY (PAGE 90)
Best for: Those looking for a new view of American history
Don't Miss: The only complete collection of U.S. presidential portraits outside the White House; Amy Sherald's portrait of former first lady Michelle Obama

RENWICK GALLERY (PAGE 92)
Best for: American crafts and decorative arts buffs
Don't Miss: Larry Fuente's *Game Fish*; the gift shop

AMERICAN ART MUSEUM (PAGE 90)
Best for: American modern folk art enthusiasts
Don't Miss: Thomas Moran's massive paintings of the American West

NATIONAL POSTAL MUSEUM (PAGE 118)
Best for: Folks who want to kill some time near the U.S. Capitol
Don't Miss: William H. Gross Stamp Gallery; vintage mail planes

ANACOSTIA COMMUNITY MUSEUM (PAGE 224)
Best for: People who love getting off the beaten path
Don't Miss: Temporary exhibitions about local communities; film screenings and lectures

Address, which he delivered months before his death. The 60- by 12-foot murals above each speech depict Lincoln's values, with the Angel of Truth freeing slaves above the Gettysburg Address and uniting figures representing the North and the South above the Second Inaugural. (And if you're a grammar nerd, see if you can spot the spelling error in the Second Inaugural text.)

The most recent addition to the memorial was etched in 2003, on the 18th step below the top landing, marking the spot where Martin Luther King Jr. delivered his "I Have A Dream" speech on August 28, 1963.

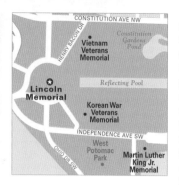

MAP 1: 2 Lincoln Memorial Circle NW, 202/426-6841, www.nps.gov/linc; 24 hours daily, rangers on duty 9:30 am-10pm daily except Christmas Day; free

NEARBY:

- Visit the Korean War Veterans Memorial and its extremely detailed figures representing soldiers from the three branches of the U.S. military (page 57).
- Take in the striking Martin Luther King Jr. Memorial, with its 30-foot carving of Dr. King (page 58).
- Pay your respects at the Memorial Wall at the Vietnam Veterans Memorial (page 59).
- Wander through West Potomac Park and see many of the national memorials (page 70).

✪ National Archives Museum

With the closing of the Newseum, the National Archives—the resting place of the Declaration of Independence, the U.S. Constitution, and the Bill of Rights—deserves a closer look. While the museum could, admittedly, use a bit of refurbishment, it nonetheless holds these precious founding documents with the reverence and security of the Sistine Chapel. (Every night, the documents are quickly lowered from the grand rotunda to a bomb-proof underground vault.) It's not as slick as some of the newer museums, but the text-heavy exhibits provide important information about the nation's founding and the history of rights, freedoms, and the rule of law.

MAP 1: Constitution Ave. NW between 7th St. NW and 9th St. NW, 202/357-5000, http://museum.archives. gov; 10am-5:30pm daily; free

✪ National Museum of American History

This Smithsonian has a heavy focus on American pop culture, technology, medicine, and media—but little examination of some of the more painful, and frankly shameful, aspects of American history. (Thankfully, the National Museum of the American Indian and the incredible National Museum of African American History and Culture cover those issues in detail.) Still, it's worth a visit to appreciate great American icons, offering educational but fun exhibits appropriate for all ages. If the museum is not too busy, you can hit the highlights in a couple hours, or spend more time digging into the best museum for American nostalgia.

The must-see exhibit is the Star-Spangled Banner, the 200-year-old flag that inspired Francis Scott Key to write the poem that would become the national anthem. This is the very flag that the U.S. troops raised after defeating the British at Fort McHenry in Baltimore during the War of 1812, turning the tide of the war. Today, the flag is kept in a climate-controlled chamber that still allows you to get a close look at the detail.

Other beloved exhibits include the first ladies' dresses, Julia Child's kitchen from her Massachusetts home, and the 26,000-square-foot America on the Move hall, containing historical trains and automobiles.

MAP 1: 1300 Constitution Ave. NW between 12th St. NW and 14th St. NW, 202/633-1000, http://americanhistory. si.edu; 10am-5:30pm daily; free

✪ National Museum of African American History and Culture

The newest and by far the best Smithsonian museum, the National Museum of African American History and Culture, deserves several days to fully explore the magnitude of information and artifacts contained in 12 exhibitions over five floors—but you'll likely only have entry passes for one day, so plan to spend the better part of a day here, if you can. Since the museum opened in September 2016, the timed entry passes have been snapped up almost as soon as they are released each month.

Beeline for the concourse level to tour the History Galleries. When you step off the elevator in the basement, you'll immediately sense the doom and terror one would have felt when being shackled in a slave ship to the New World; the low-ceilinged galleries are designed to feel this way. The horrifying facts of the journey, and what awaited the survivors, are described in overwhelming detail. Plan to spend at least two hours climbing the ramps

National Museum of American History

in the galleries from the Civil War through segregation and the civil rights movement to present day, alternately distraught by the treatment of African Americans by their fellow Americans and elated at the triumphs, culminating with the election of America's first black president.

After decompressing by the indoor rain-shower waterfall in the Contemplative Court, save time for the upper levels, which are dedicated to art and culture. Don't miss the celebratory Musical Crossroads, where you can see and hear African Americans' influence on music through the decades, with objects like Chuck Berry's red Cadillac as well as outfits worn by Marian Anderson, Michael Jackson, Whitney Houston, and Public Enemy.

MAP 1: 1400 Constitution Ave. NW between 14th St. NW and 15th St. NW, 844/750-3012, http://nmaahc.si.edu; 10am-5:30pm daily; free

National Air and Space Museum

✪ National Air and Space Museum

The soaring ceilings of the Smithsonian's National Air and Space Museum accommodate the world's largest collection of real aircraft and spacecraft, including the Wright brothers' 1903 plane and SpaceShipOne, the first private spacecraft in history to reach space and return, plus commercial and military aircraft.

Enter the museum at the Jefferson Drive entrance to get an immediate look at many of the must-sees in the Boeing Milestones of Flight Hall: *The Spirit of St. Louis,* which Charles Lindbergh flew on the first solo flight across the Atlantic Ocean in 1927; Mercury Friendship 7, in which John Glenn Jr. orbited Earth in 1962 during the Space Race with the Soviet Union; and Lunar Module 2, which was used for testing before the Apollo moon landing. This museum is extremely popular and crowded, especially during the summer; depending on your interest, you can see the ground floor's highlights in an hour or two, or geek out for half a day or longer.

When it's hot and sticky during DC's infamous summers, the museum is a great place to relax in the dark. The Albert Einstein Planetarium offers a free live show at 10:30am daily, while the immersive, five-story Lockheed Martin IMAX Theater shows several different films each day.

MAP 1: 600 Independence Ave. SW at 6th St. SW, 202/633-2214, http://airandspace.si.edu; 10am-5:30pm daily; free

NATIONAL MUSEUM OF AFRICAN AMERICAN HISTORY AND CULTURE ENTRY PASSES

National Museum of African American History and Culture

Since opening in September 2016, the Smithsonian's National Museum of African American History and Culture (1400 Constitution Ave. NW between 14th St. NW and 15th St. NW, 844/750-3012, http://nmaahc.si.edu; 10am-5:30pm daily; free) has welcomed more than 5 million visitors. While admission is free, timed entry passes are strongly recommended—and you'll need an alarm clock to get one.

If you're planning your trip at least three months in advance, check the museum's website to see when the next batch of passes will be released. The passes will be available on a certain date starting at 9am ET, and they're typically snapped up within a few hours.

A limited number of same-day passes are available. They are released online every day at 6:30am ET, and while they tend to go quickly, it's generally possible to snag them if you have a flexible schedule and you're not traveling in peak season. (In July, for example, we found same-day tickets for a hot Sunday afternoon, and more options in the middle of the week.) Depending on capacity, there are a limited number of walk-up passes available on weekdays only at 1pm at the entrance on Madison Drive.

If you're lucky enough to score a timed entry pass in advance, you don't need to show up more than a few minutes early, because you won't be permitted to go in before your entry time. If you're running late, don't panic; you can still enter after your time slot, though you may need to wait if the museum is already at capacity.

Bureau of Engraving and Printing

See, kids, money doesn't grow on trees—it's printed at the U.S. Treasury's Bureau of Engraving and Printing, which prints paper banknotes as well as other government documents, like official invitations and military commissions and awards. It's not to be confused with the United States Mint, which produces coins. During the week, tour the production floor via glass windows from a gallery above, where you can see money being printed—and destroyed. The 40-minute guided tours are free, but the required tickets are distributed first come, first served at the booth outside the bureau, so plan ahead if you want to visit. Large groups may make reservations for a tour.

Dwight D. Eisenhower Memorial

The capital's newest memorial, dedicated to the 34th president and general who led the Allies to victory in World War II, was unveiled in May 2020—but it almost didn't happen. For more than a decade, Eisenhower's descendants battled the memorial commission over the design from Frank Gehry, the architect most famous for the Walt Disney Concert Hall in Los Angeles and the Guggenheim in Bilbao, Spain. After more than $150 million and numerous revisions, the plans were finally approved. Set on four acres of parkland just southwest of the Capitol grounds, the memorial depicts Ike's life with bronze statues as well as scenes from the beaches of Normandy on D-Day, which he supervised as Supreme Allied Commander. It was officially dedicated on the 75th anniversary of VE Day, when the Nazis surrendered.

Franklin Delano Roosevelt Memorial

"The only thing we have to fear is fear itself." Spoken by President Franklin Delano Roosevelt during his first inaugural address in 1933, these words are carved in

Bureau of Engraving and Printing

commanding stone at the beginning of one of the National Mall's gems, the Franklin Delano Roosevelt Memorial, which tells the story of the 32nd president's impact on the nation. Many Washingtonians say this is their favorite memorial, a tranquil space for reflection away from the crowds (if you avoid cherry blossom season) and a memorial worthy of the president who championed national parks.

The memorial is set up like an outdoor museum, with "rooms" about FDR's presidency containing life-size statues of FDR and Eleanor Roosevelt (it's the only presidential memorial that includes a first lady). Stone walls with engraved quotations are interspersed with peaceful waterfalls. Each room covers one of his four terms: The Great Depression (1933-1937), The New Deal (1937-1941), The Second World War (1941-1945), and Legacy, about his final term, cut short when he died in 1945. The Prologue Room was added to the beginning of the memorial in 2001 to show FDR in his wheelchair, after the National Organization on Disability criticized the memorial for not accurately depicting Roosevelt as he was—paralyzed by polio.

Access the memorial, located on the west side of the Tidal Basin, from West Basin Drive SW or by walking through the Martin Luther King Jr. Memorial to the path along the Tidal Basin.

MAP 1: 400 W. Basin Dr. SW at Ohio Dr. SW, 202/426-6841, www.nps.gov/frde; 24 hours daily, visitors center and bookstore 9am-6pm daily; free

Korean War Veterans Memorial

The Korean War Veterans Memorial is dedicated to the American soldiers who helped South Korea fight North Korea from 1950 to 1953. On the west end of the National Mall, the memorial shows the human face of war, and it's even more stirring when you consider the United States' ongoing tensions with North Korea.

In the triangular memorial grounds, directly southeast of the Lincoln Memorial, stand 19 stainless steel figures representing soldiers from the Air Force, Army, Marines, and Navy, sculpted with striking detail by World War II veteran Frank Gaylord. If you get close enough, you'll see stunning detail that renders each figure into an individual. Be sure not to miss the three that are partially hidden in the trees.

On the south side of the triangle is a 164-foot-long black granite wall, with more than 2,500 images from the war etched on the surface. The triangle points to the **Pool of Remembrance,** where you'll find lists of the number of American and United Nations soldiers killed, wounded, missing in action, or taken prisoner during the war. Near the pool, another low wall has a simple but important reminder: "Freedom Is Not Free."

Korean War Veterans Memorial

MAP 1: 10 Daniel French Dr. SW at Independence Ave. SW, 202/426-6841, www.nps.gov/kowa; 24 hours daily; free

Martin Luther King Jr. Memorial

On the western banks of the Tidal Basin is the newest memorial on the Mall, the Martin Luther King Jr. Memorial, which was officially dedicated on August 28, 2011, the 48th anniversary of Dr. King's "I Have A Dream" speech. It's the first and only memorial on the National Mall dedicated to an African American, and the fourth dedicated to an individual who did not serve as U.S. president.

Martin Luther King Jr. Memorial

The centerpiece is a striking 30-foot carving of Dr. King, seemingly emerging from a block of stone, an incredible likeness created by Chinese master sculptor Lei Yixin. Behind the sculpture is a broken stone mountain, symbolizing a line from Dr. King's famous speech: "With this faith, we will be able to hew out of the mountains of despair a stone of hope." This is paraphrased on the side of the sculpture.

Surrounding the sculptures is a 450-foot-long granite wall inscribed with 14 of Dr. King's most memorable quotes, including one from his sermon at the Washington National Cathedral (3101 Wisconsin Ave. NW, 202/537-6200, www.cathedral.org) just four days before his assassination: "We shall overcome because the arc of the moral universe is long, but it bends towards justice." This metaphor originated with 19-century Unitarian minister Theodore Parker, and Dr. King used it several times in his sermons and speeches.

It's worth braving the crowds to pay your respects near the anniversary of Dr. King's death, April 4, because the cherry blossom trees that surround the memorial are often in full, glorious bloom.

MAP 1: 1964 Independence Ave. SW at W. Basin Dr. SW, 202/426-6841, www.nps.gov/mlkm; 24 hours daily; free

Thomas Jefferson Memorial

Thomas Jefferson was a complex man. On the one hand, the third U.S. president wrote the Declaration of Independence and led our nation to democracy. On the other, he owned more than 600 slaves, even while he was calling for equal rights to life, liberty, and the pursuit of happiness.

Designed in 1929 by John Russell Pope, who also designed the National Archives (Constitution Ave. NW between 7th St. NW and 9th St. NW, 202/357-5000, www.archives.gov) and the National Gallery of Art (Constitution Ave. NW between 3rd St. NW and 9th St. NW, 202/737-4215, www.nga.gov), this neoclassical memorial is inspired by the Pantheon in Rome. Jefferson loved this architectural style; similar columns and domes appear on Monticello, his estate in Charlottesville, Virginia, as well as the University of Virginia, which he founded in 1819.

Located on the southeast bank of the Tidal Basin, it's just far enough from the National Mall's most beaten paths to make it a little less crowded than the Lincoln Memorial during prime tourist season. Stand on the banks of the Tidal Basin to get the best photo op of the imposing, iconic structure from the outside, then go inside to see the 19-foot bronze statue of the man himself, surrounded by his words and looking toward the White House.

MAP 1: 701 E. Basin Dr. SW, adjacent to the Tidal Basin, 202/426-6841, www.nps.gov/thje; 24 hours daily, visitors center 9am-6pm daily; free

Vietnam Veterans Memorial

Visiting the Vietnam Veterans Memorial is an emotional experience. The focus is the **Memorial Wall**, comprising two 246-foot-long black granite walls carved with the names of the 58,318 Americans who were killed or missing in action during the long, controversial war. As you run your fingers over the sharply etched, seemingly infinite list of names, the shiny wall mirrors your reflection. The names are listed first by day of death or disappearance, then alphabetically within each day. Search for the location of a specific name at the Vietnam

Thomas Jefferson Memorial

Vietnam Veterans Memorial

Veterans Memorial Fund website (www.vvmf.org).

Amazingly, this poignant site is not the work of a venerable architect. The wall was the creation of Maya Lin, a 21-year-old architecture student at Yale University when she beat out more than 1,400 other applicants to have her design chosen for the memorial.

Two statues were added to the memorial grounds after the wall was built. *The Three Soldiers,* depicting three men—one white, one African American, and one Latino—looking at the wall, was added in 1984. The Vietnam Women's Memorial, showing three uniformed women helping a wounded soldier, was added in 1993 to honor the 265,000 women who served in Vietnam.

MAP 1: 5 Henry Bacon Dr. NW at Constitution Ave. NW, 202/426-6841, www.nps.gov/vive; 24 hours daily

World War II Memorial

Honoring the 16 million Americans who served during World War II and the 400,000 who died, the World War II Memorial sits on 7.4 acres of prime National Mall real estate, on the west side of the Washington Monument. The memorial's 56 stone pillars—one for each of the 48 U.S. states during the war, plus eight U.S. territories—are arranged in a circle around the Rainbow Pool, which was built in 1923 and incorporated into the memorial's design. Each pillar has a bronze and granite wreath, and between the pillars are detailed panels depicting various battles and scenes of soldiers preparing to go to war. By the entrance on 17th Street, two flagpoles emblazoned with the seals of each branch of the military welcome visitors.

From a distance, the memorial is massive. Inside, it's engulfing. In fact, some critics say the architecture is reminiscent of Fascist construction, its 17-foot utilitarian pillars feeling a little too similar to Albert Speer's Third Reich headquarters.

The memorial is not completely stone-cold. Look for the engravings of "Kilroy was here" graffiti, the bald cartoon man peeking over a fence.

American soldiers scribbled this everywhere they went, a sign for those who would come after them.

MAP 1: 1750 Independence Ave. SW at 17th St. SW, 202/426-6841, www.nps.gov/wwii; 24 hours daily

Restaurants

PRICE KEY

$	Entrees less than $15
$$	Entrees $15-25
$$$	Entrees more than $25

NATIVE AMERICAN

✪ Mitsitam Native Foods Café $$

Meaning "let's eat!" in the Delaware and Piscataway native language, Mitsitam at the National Museum of the American Indian is one of the most interesting of DC's museum cafés and a good choice for lunch on the National Mall since this museum is generally less crowded than the others in peak tourist season. The cafeteria-style restaurant serves seasonal native foods from across the Western Hemisphere, such as buffalo burgers and chili on fry bread from the Great Plains, pork *pibil* tacos from Mesoamerica, and salmon from the Northwest Coast, as well as soups and healthy veggie options. Beverages include beer, wine, and Mexican Coca-Cola, and the espresso bar (10am-5pm daily) serves coffee roasted by native peoples, as well as Mexican hot chocolate and snacks.

MAP 1: National Museum of the American Indian, 4th St. SW and Independence Ave. SW, 202/633-6644, www.mitsitamcafe.com; 11am-5pm Memorial Day-Labor Day, 11am-3pm daily early Sept.-late May

SOUTHERN AND SOUL FOOD

Sweet Home Café $

Nominated for the James Beard Best New Restaurant in 2017, Sweet Home Café at the National Museum of African American History and Culture is worth waiting in the long lunch line for if you're already inside the museum. Executive chef Jerome Grant prepares African American recipes from across the country, including tasty Southern and creole standards like shrimp and Anson Mills grits, and some say the best fried chicken in DC. But try something new, like the oyster pan roast inspired by Thomas Downing, a free African American who owned a famous oyster house in New York City and helped slaves traveling the Underground Railroad.

MAP 1: National Museum of African American History and Culture, 1400 Constitution Ave. NW, 202/633-6174, http://nmaahc.si.edu; 10am-5pm daily, serving lunch 11am-3pm daily

Mitsitam Native Foods Café

MEDITERRANEAN
Manna $$
Perhaps the healthiest museum restaurant in the city, the Museum of the Bible's fast-casual eatery is not, actually, fast—this museum is extraordinarily popular, especially near holidays—but worth the wait. Led by James Beard-winning local chef Todd Gray, the restaurant showcases the diversity of the Mediterranean: think flavorful flatbreads, falafel platters, Greek salad, and a filling vegan black-bean chili with za'atar pita chips.

MAP 1: Museum of the Bible, 400 4th St. SW, 866/430-MOTB, www.museumofthebible.org/museum/dining/manna; 11am-4pm daily

CAFÉS AND LIGHT BITES
Cascade Café $
Among the National Mall's limited options, you'll find the most choice at Cascade Café, the elegant food court at the National Gallery of Art's East Building. Set by the magnificent cascading waterfall, selections include reasonably priced make-your-own salads and grain bowls, sandwiches, pizzas, and locally sourced, free-range chicken, plus coffee, pastries, and beer and wine.

MAP 1: National Gallery of Art East Building, 4th St. NW and Constitution Ave. NW, 202/842-6679, www.nga.gov; 11am-3pm Mon.-Sat., 11am-4pm Sun.

Garden Café $$
Dine in the marble halls of the National Gallery of Art's West Building at Garden Café, the only table-service restaurant in a Smithsonian museum. Nestled among the exhibits, it's a lovely spot for a lunch or brunch date. Start with a glass of brut then share a cheese plate and French pastries or indulge in the weekend brunch buffet. Reservations are recommended.

MAP 1: National Gallery of Art West Building, 6th St. NW and Constitution Ave. NW, 202/842-6716, www.nga.gov; 11:30am-3pm Mon.-Sat., noon-4pm Sun.

Pavilion Café $

Grab a bite at Pavilion Café, which offers indoor and outdoor seating in the National Gallery of Art's Sculpture Garden. The menu features seasonal sandwiches, salads, soups, and pizzas, as well as coffee, pastries, beer, and wine. During Jazz in the Garden, held Friday evenings in the summer, the café serves hors d'oeuvres and grilled sandwiches as well as sangria and beer by the glass or pitcher. During the winter, later hours accommodate skaters at the ice rink.

MAP 1: National Gallery of Art Sculpture Garden, 7th St. NW and Constitution Ave. NW, 202/289-3360, www.pavilioncafe.com; 10am-4pm Mon.-Sat., 11am-5pm Sun. mid-Mar.-Memorial Day; 10am-6pm Mon.-Thurs., 10am-8:30pm Fri., 10am-6pm Sat., 11am-6pm Sun. Memorial Day-Labor Day; 10am-4pm Mon.-Sat., 11am-5pm Sun. Labor Day-mid-Nov.; 10am-7pm Mon.-Thurs., 10am-9pm Fri.-Sat., 11am-7pm Sun. mid-Nov.-mid-Mar.

Arts and Culture

MUSEUMS

✪ Hirshhorn Museum and Sculpture Garden

This Smithsonian museum dedicated to modern and contemporary art has some of the coolest art in town, with temporary exhibitions by of-the-moment artists like Yayoi Kusama and Ai Wei Wei. In addition to groundbreaking temporary exhibitions, the Hirshhorn is home to more than 12,000 paintings, sculptures, mobiles, and video installations by the likes of Hopper, Bacon, Miró, and Calder, as well as lesser-known artists. Don't miss the four-acre Sculpture Garden, which feels like a scene out of *Alice in Wonderland,* and take a walk around the circular building, a work of art itself by modern architect Gordon Bunshaft.

MAP 1: 7th St. SW and Independence Ave. SW, 202/633-4674, http://hirshhorn. si.edu; museum 10am-5:30pm daily, garden 7:30am-dusk daily; free

✪ National Gallery of Art

The National Gallery of Art has two distinct personalities and always something new on display. The resplendent original building, the West Building, is home to classic beauty: *Ginevra de' Benci,* Da Vinci's only painting on view in the Americas, plus Dutch masters, French impressionists, and more from the 15th to 19th centuries in a setting that transports you to Europe. The East Building, designed by I. M. Pei, is home to the cool crowd: Matisse, Picasso, Warhol, and Lichtenstein, plus Katharina Fritsch's bright blue

Hahn/Cock on the roof terrace. The Sculpture Garden has 17 major sculptures, and it hosts free jazz concerts on summer Friday evenings. MAP 1: Constitution Ave. NW between 3rd St. NW and 9th St. NW, 202/737-4215, www.nga.gov; 10am-5pm Mon.-Sat., 11am-6pm Sun.; free

✪ National Museum of Natural History

It's no surprise the National Museum of Natural History is the most-visited natural history museum in the world. After all, the big elephant, the big dinosaurs, and the big diamond—the Hope Diamond—all live in the building, making the museum a must-visit for families with children. But don't let the museum's popularity deter you; it's the size of 18 football fields, with more than 300,000 square feet of exhibition space, so there's plenty of room for everyone to enjoy the natural wonders inside.

In addition to the 14-foot elephant from Angola in the rotunda and the rare gems, highlights include human and animal mummies from Egypt and the high-tech Sant Ocean Hall, which will make you feel like you're deep underwater with some of the rarest specimens of the sea. In 2019, the fossil hall, called Deep Time, reopened with 700 specimens across 31,000 square feet, including the most complete *T. rex* skeleton in the world. If you want to explore a few exhibits, budget 3-4 hours minimum, especially during the summer, when there can be winding lines to view the jewels and other popular exhibits.

Hirshhorn Museum and Sculpture Garden

United States Holocaust Memorial Museum

MAP 1: 1000 Constitution Ave. NW at 10th St. NW, 202/633-1000, http://naturalhistory.si.edu; 10am-5:30pm daily; free

✪ United States Holocaust Memorial Museum

The United States Holocaust Memorial Museum must be experienced. The permanent exhibition, "The Holocaust," spans three floors; plan to take several hours to travel through the chronological timeline, from the rise of the Nazi Party to the horrifying treatment and murder of the Jews and, finally, to the liberation of the concentration camps and the end of World War II. You'll be amazed by the level of detail, the personal artifacts and first-hand accounts, and multimedia, although be prepared—it's challenging. The permanent exhibition is recommended for ages 11 and up. "Remember the Children: Daniel's Story," an exhibit about one family's experience during the Holocaust, told through the eyes of a young boy, is a better choice with young children or if you don't have time to explore the permanent exhibition, which requires 2-3 hours. Rotating exhibits cover other Holocaust topics or anti-Semitism and genocide in history and present day.

MAP 1: 100 Raoul Wallenberg Pl. SW between 14th St. SW and 15th St. SW, 202/488-0400, www.ushmm.org; 10am-5:20pm daily; free tickets for the permanent exhibition required Mar. 1-Aug. 31

Freer Gallery of Art and Arthur M. Sackler Gallery

Connected on the inside, the Smithsonian's Freer and Sackler Galleries showcase one of the most diverse collections of Asian art in the world—from Chinese jade and fine Persian books to contemporary Japanese prints and porcelain, as well as works from Egypt, Korea, India, Iran, Iraq, Pakistan, Syria, and Turkey. The highlight is

James McNeill Whistler's Peacock Room, an extravagant dining room he designed for a British shipping tycoon, which Charles Lang Freer purchased, shipped to the United States, and installed in his home in its entirety to showcase his impressive collection of Asian ceramics. The galleries are known for innovative cultural programming, like the annual Iranian Film Festival.

MAP 1: 12th St. SW at Independence Ave. SW, 202/633-4880, http://asia.si.edu; 10am-5:30pm daily; free

International Spy Museum

Bring out your inner James Bond at the International Spy Museum, the interactive, kid-friendly museum with the largest collection of spy artifacts like encryption machines, glasses that conceal cyanide pills, and lipstick and tobacco pipe guns. In 2019, the museum moved to a $162 million new building in L'Enfant Plaza—twice the size of the original downtown location—with new, state-of-the-art exhibits, such as one examining the mission to kill Osama bin Laden. The museum is connected to the food court in L'Enfant Plaza, with more than 40 quick-service restaurants and shops; we recommend Maizal (429 L'Enfant Plaza SW, #450, www.maizalstreetfood.com; 10:30am-7pm Mon.-Sat., $$), a local spot serving South American street food like arepas, tacos, tortas, and churros.

MAP 1: 700 L'Enfant Plaza, 202/393-7798, www.spymuseum.org; 10am-6pm daily; $24.95 adults 13-64, $19.95 seniors/military/law enforcement/intelligence community/college students, $14.95 children 7-12, free children 6 and under

National Museum of African Art

National Museum of the American Indian

Museum of the Bible

This $500 million museum opened in 2017 with controversy: funded by Hobby Lobby, the crafts store franchise at the center of a high-profile Supreme Court case about whether for-profit companies' health plans should be required to cover contraceptives, and the discovery that some of the artifacts intended for display had been illegally smuggled out of Iraq. But believers and nonbelievers alike will learn something from a visit to the 430,000-square-foot museum, which has neutral, scholarly exhibits on the Bible as a historical text and the impact it's had on the world. Even some of the more gimmicky exhibits, such as the village of Nazareth with live actors, are grounded in history. Don't miss lunch at Manna, the fast-casual Mediterranean restaurant—one of the healthiest dining options near the Mall.

MAP 1: 400 4th St. SW, 866/430-MOTB, www.museumofthebible.org; 10am-5pm daily; $24.99 adults, $19.99 seniors/military/first responders/ students, $14.99 ages 7-17, free for children 6 and under

National Museum of African Art

The only museum in the United States dedicated exclusively to African art, this smaller Smithsonian is an excellent choice when the others on the National Mall are packed. The collection spans the African continent, featuring traditional works, like rare ceramics from the Disney-Tishman Collection, one of the most important collections of West and Central African art, as well as contemporary paintings and video installations. Don't rush through the entryway; some of the works hanging there are believed to have spiritual powers, while others address the impact of social problems like the HIV/AIDS crisis on African communities.

MAP 1: 950 Independence Ave. SW, 202/633-4600, http://africa.si.edu; 10am-5:30pm daily; free

National Museum of the American Indian

It's not as thrilling as spacecraft or dinosaurs, but this Smithsonian explores a critically important piece of American history. In the five-story limestone building, learn about native culture and spirituality across the Western Hemisphere, as well as treaties between the United States and the American Indian Nations, told through the voices of American Indians, not occupiers. Plan to visit this quieter museum for lunch at Mitsitam Native Foods Café. The National Native American Veterans Memorial will be unveiled on the museum grounds in November 2020.

MAP 1: 4th St. SW and Independence Ave. SW, 202/633-6644, http://nmai.si.edu; 10am-5:30pm daily; free

Festivals and Events

Presidential Inauguration

Every four years, Washington DC puts political differences aside and comes together for the Presidential Inauguration. The bipartisan event includes the swearing-in ceremony at the U.S. Capitol and the parade on Pennsylvania Avenue, which are both open to the general public. Both events have free, public viewing areas, but you'll need tickets for the prime seats, which can be obtained through the Presidential Inaugural Committee (PIC) or your senator/representative. The PIC organizes the official inaugural balls, which may be attended by the First Family; information about the official balls as well as dozens of unofficial inaugural balls, concerts, and other special events is usually available several weeks after the November election.

National Mall/Citywide: Jan. 20 after a presidential election; costs vary by event

Independence Day

Celebrating Independence Day in the nation's capital will give you all the patriotic feels. The holiday begins with a mile-long parade (Constitution Ave. NW between 7th St. NW and 17th St. NW, www.july4thparade.com; 11:45am July 4; free) down Constitution Avenue, featuring bands from across the country as well as military units. In the evening, PBS hosts A Capitol Fourth (U.S. Capitol West Lawn, www.pbs.org/a-capitol-fourth; gates 3pm, concert 8pm-9:30pm July 4; free, no tickets required), the free concert on the West Lawn of the U.S. Capitol featuring celebrity musicians and military bands playing patriotic tunes. The concert builds anticipation for the spectacular fireworks display (National Mall, www.pbs.org/a-capitol-fourth; show begins at dark, approx. 9:15pm July 4; free, no tickets required), which can be viewed from the U.S. Capitol, National Mall, and anywhere you can see the Washington Monument.

Crowds begin forming very early in the day on the National Mall; plan to arrive at the concert shortly after the gates open at 3pm to stake out a spot closer to the stage, and stick around to enjoy the fireworks with the soundtrack of Tchaikovsky's "1812 Overture" and live canon fire at the conclusion of the concert.

Various locations: July 4; free

Smithsonian Folklife Festival

At the end of June, the Smithsonian Institution brings the museums outdoors. The part-fair, part-exposition, part-party is a celebration of unique world cultures, with musicians, artists, artisans, athletes, storytellers, and more showcasing specific countries, regions, or cultural identities on the National Mall morning until evening. The 2018 festival will feature food, fashion, and more from Africa, Armenia, and Catalonia, and the 2019 festival will highlight the social power of music.

National Mall: Between 7th St. and 12th St., 202/633-6440, http://festival. si.edu; late June-first week of July; free

Jazz in the Garden

It's a summer rite of passage for locals: Skip out of work early on Friday afternoons with a blanket and picnic for Jazz in the Garden, a series of free jazz concerts in the National Gallery's Sculpture Garden featuring American and international jazz musicians. Join them and relax among the gallery's modern and contemporary sculpture collection, enjoying snacks and beverages (including beer, wine, and sangria) from the Pavilion Café.

Independence Day Parade

National Mall: Pavilion Café at the National Gallery of Art Sculpture Garden, 7th St. NW and Constitution Ave. NW, 202/289-3360, www.nga.gov/jazz; Fri. mid-May-mid-Aug., weather permitting; free

National Cherry Blossom Festival

In March and April, the city celebrates the bloom of the cherry trees, a gift from Japan in 1912. The festival includes many free events: the parade, kite festival, Japanese street festival, fireworks, museum events, and, of course, the showcase of the magnificent pink and white blossoms around the Tidal Basin and National Mall. This is one of the busiest, most expensive times to visit DC, and it's tough to predict peak bloom, but if you catch it, you'll be glad you braved the crowds.

Citywide: 877/442-5666, www.nationalcherryblossomfestival.org; mid-Mar.-mid-Apr.; most headline events free and open to the public (some require tickets)

Recreation

TOURS

Smithsonian Segway Tour

The Smithsonian Institution partnered with professional tour operator Bike and Roll to offer the only tour departing from the National Mall. The 2.5-hour Monumental Experience (offered daily at 10am and 2pm) shows you the sights via Segway, covering 1,000 acres. Reservations are recommended.

MAP 1: National Museum of American History, 1300 Constitution Ave. NW between 12th St. NW and 14th St. NW, 202/384-8516, www.smithsoniansegwaytours.com; $10-49

PARKS AND TRAILS

West Potomac Park

Stretching from the Washington Monument west to Lincoln Memorial and southeast to the Thomas Jefferson Memorial, West Potomac Park includes many of the major national memorials in its grassy fields. In addition to getting a history lesson, you can kick around in the JFK Hockey Fields south of the Reflecting Pool, which are perfect for a game of Frisbee or soccer. The park includes the Tidal Basin, adjacent to the Franklin Delano Roosevelt Memorial and Martin Luther King Jr. Memorial, an artificial inlet of the Potomac River surrounded by the cherry trees gifted to the United States by Japan in 1912. The trail around it is approximately 2 mi (3.2 km); it's a gorgeous, albeit slow, walk during cherry blossom season. You can rent paddleboats from March to October. Visit the National Park Service website (www.nps.gov/nama) to learn about free, ranger-led tours, like "Obscure Memorials of the National Mall" and "African American History on Pennsylvania Avenue."

Tidal Basin paddleboats

MAP 1: National Mall from about 17th St NW west to the Lincoln Memorial and south to the Tidal Basin; 24 hours daily

BOATING
✪ Tidal Basin Paddleboats

There's no better way to spend a sunny day than paddleboating around the Tidal Basin, where you'll have an unobstructed view of several monuments. From March through October, rent one of the bright-blue paddleboats for two ($20/hour) or four ($30); if you can pedal your feet, you're good to go. During cherry blossom season (Mar.-Apr.), reserve your boat in advance online. This boat dock also offers adorable swan boats for two ($35/hour), which are equipped with motors so everyone can glide even if you aren't able to pedal. The dock is accessible via Maine Avenue SW, on the eastern shore of the Tidal Basin.

MAP 1: 1501 Maine Ave. SW, 202/ 479-2426, www. tidalbasinpaddleboats.com; 10am-6pm daily (last boat at 5pm) Mar.-Oct., weather permitting; $20-35/hour

Downtown and Penn Quarter

Map 2

Downtown is where the city's movers and shakers eat, work, and play . . . oh, yes, and the president of the United States lives here, too. It's the **ideal home base,** with easy access to the rest of the city by public transportation, as well as **beautiful hotels, fine restaurants,** and **historic cocktail bars** to enjoy at the end of a long day of sightseeing.

Downtown is home to Penn Quarter and **Chinatown,** the bustling home of the Capital One Arena and several theaters, as well as City-

CenterDC, a **luxury shopping** and dining development.

TOP SIGHTS
- Most Exclusive Address:
  The White House (page 76)

TOP RESTAURANTS
- Where Washington Has Always Met:
  Old Ebbitt Grill (page 81)
- Chef Changing Washington and
  the World: **Jaleo** (page 85)

TOP NIGHTLIFE
- Best Views: **POV** (page 87)
- Most Historic Venue:
  Round Robin Bar (page 87)
- Where the Cool Kids Hang:
  WILD DAYS (page 90)

TOP ARTS AND CULTURE
- Most Innovative Theater: **Woolly Mammoth
  Theatre Company** (page 92)

TOP SHOPS
- Most Special Gifts:
  Tiny Jewel Box (page 97)
- Best Official Souvenir: **White House
  Visitor Center Shop** (page 99)
- Best Shopping Experience:
  Apple Carnegie Library (98)

GETTING THERE AND AROUND
- Metro lines: Blue, Green,
  Orange, Red, Silver, Yellow
- Metro stations: Archives-Navy Memorial-
  Penn Quarter, Farragut North,
  Farragut West, Federal Triangle, Gallery
  Place-Chinatown, Judiciary Square,
  McPherson Square, Metro Center
- Major bus routes: DC Circulator
  Georgetown-Union Station, Woodley Park-
  Adams Morgan-McPherson Square Metro

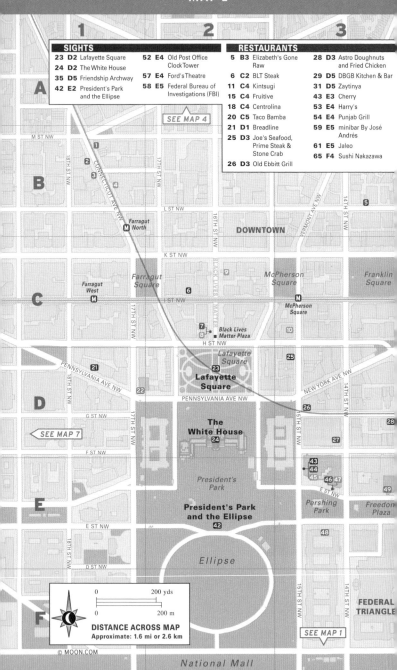

SIGHTS

- 23 **D2** Lafayette Square
- 24 **D2** The White House
- 35 **D5** Friendship Archway
- 42 **E2** President's Park and the Ellipse
- 52 **E4** Old Post Office Clock Tower
- 57 **E4** Ford's Theatre
- 58 **E5** Federal Bureau of Investigations (FBI)

RESTAURANTS

- 5 **B3** Elizabeth's Gone Raw
- 6 **C2** BLT Steak
- 11 **C4** Kintsugi
- 15 **C4** Fruitive
- 18 **C4** Centrolina
- 20 **C5** Taco Bamba
- 21 **D1** Breadline
- 25 **D3** Joe's Seafood, Prime Steak & Stone Crab
- 26 **D3** Old Ebbitt Grill
- 28 **D3** Astro Doughnuts and Fried Chicken
- 29 **D5** DBGB Kitchen & Bar
- 31 **D5** Zaytinya
- 43 **E3** Cherry
- 53 **E4** Harry's
- 54 **E4** Punjab Grill
- 59 **E5** minibar By José Andrés
- 61 **E5** Jaleo
- 65 **F4** Sushi Nakazawa

SEE MAP 4

M ST NW

18TH ST NW

CONNECTICUT AVE NW

17TH ST NW

16TH ST NW

VERMONT AVE NW

14TH ST NW

L ST NW

Farragut North M

DOWNTOWN

K ST NW

Farragut Square

McPherson Square

Franklin Square

Farragut West M

17TH ST NW

I ST NW

BLACK LIVES MATTER

M McPherson Square

H ST NW

Black Lives Matter Plaza

Lafayette Square

PENNSYLVANIA AVE NW

18TH ST NW

17TH ST NW

Lafayette Square

PENNSYLVANIA AVE NW

NEW YORK AVE NW

15TH ST NW

SEE MAP 7

G ST NW

The White House

F ST NW

14TH ST NW

President's Park

President's Park and the Ellipse

E ST NW

18TH ST NW

E ST NW

Pershing Park

Freedom Plaza

D ST NW

Ellipse

15TH ST NW

14TH ST NW

FEDERAL TRIANGLE

0   200 yds
0   200 m

DISTANCE ACROSS MAP
Approximate: 1.6 mi or 2.6 km

SEE MAP 1

© MOON.COM

National Mall

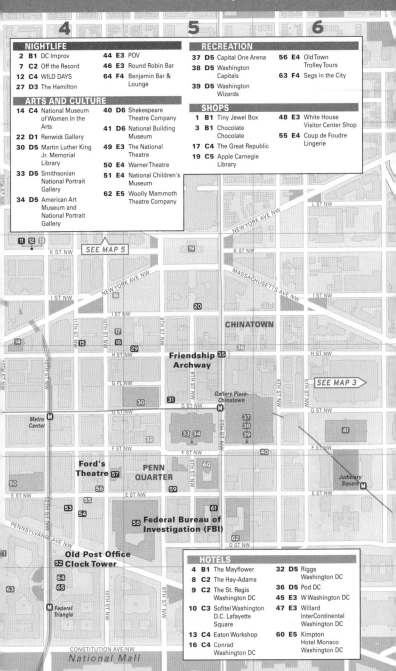

NIGHTLIFE

- 2 **B1** DC Improv
- 7 **C2** Off the Record
- 12 **C4** WILD DAYS
- 27 **D3** The Hamilton
- 44 **E3** POV
- 46 **E3** Round Robin Bar
- 64 **F4** Benjamin Bar & Lounge

ARTS AND CULTURE

- 14 **C4** National Museum of Women In the Arts
- 22 **D1** Renwick Gallery
- 30 **D5** Martin Luther King Jr. Memorial Library
- 33 **D5** Smithsonian National Portrait Gallery
- 34 **D5** American Art Museum and National Portrait Gallery
- 40 **D6** Shakespeare Theatre Company
- 41 **D6** National Building Museum
- 49 **E3** The National Theatre
- 50 **E4** Warner Theatre
- 51 **E4** National Children's Museum
- 62 **E5** Woolly Mammoth Theatre Company

RECREATION

- 37 **D5** Capital One Arena
- 38 **D5** Washington Capitals
- 39 **D5** Washington Wizards
- 56 **E4** Old Town Trolley Tours
- 63 **F4** Segs in the City

SHOPS

- 1 **B1** Tiny Jewel Box
- 3 **B1** Chocolate Chocolate
- 17 **C4** The Great Republic
- 19 **C5** Apple Carnegie Library
- 48 **E3** White House Visitor Center Shop
- 55 **E4** Coup de Foudre Lingerie

HOTELS

- 4 **B1** The Mayflower
- 8 **C2** The Hay-Adams
- 9 **C2** The St. Regis Washington DC
- 10 **C3** Sofitel Washington D.C. Lafayette Square
- 13 **C4** Eaton Workshop
- 16 **C4** Conrad Washington DC
- 32 **D5** Riggs Washington DC
- 36 **D5** Pod DC
- 45 **E3** W Washington DC
- 47 **E3** Willard InterContinental Washington DC
- 60 **E5** Kimpton Hotel Monaco Washington DC

NEW YORK AVE NW

MASSACHUSETTS AVE NW

SEE MAP 5

K ST NW

I ST NW

CHINATOWN

SEE MAP 3

Friendship Archway

Gallery Place-Chinatown

Metro Center

Ford's Theatre

PENN QUARTER

Judiciary Square

Old Post Office Clock Tower

Federal Bureau of Investigation (FBI)

Federal Triangle

PENNSYLVANIA AVE NW

CONSTITUTION AVE NW

National Mall

Sights

✪ The White House

America's most iconic home has served as the residence of every U.S. president except George Washington. Built in 1792-1800, the white neoclassical mansion made of painted sandstone includes the Executive Residence as well as the offices of the president in the West Wing, and reception rooms and the offices of the first lady in the East Wing. While George Washington oversaw the construction, John Adams was the first president to occupy it, writing in a letter to his wife, "I pray Heaven to bestow the best of blessings on this House, and all that shall hereafter inhabit it. May none but honest and wise men ever rule under this roof." (FDR had this line carved on the mantel in the State Dining Room.) Every first family has lived in the White House, with a few exceptions—like James Madison, who moved out after the British burned the structure in 1814, and Harry S. Truman, because the building was in disrepair and required its most extensive architectural renovation to date in 1949-1951.

Very little has changed since the 1950s, except the decor; First Lady Jackie Kennedy famously redecorated it with American antiques and artifacts to reflect the history

the White House

of the nation and the office, and she had the White House declared a museum to ensure the building and everything inside would be preserved for future generations.

There's an excellent photo op of the White House on Pennsylvania Avenue in Lafayette Square, a favorite gathering spot of protestors. Considered a part of the White House grounds, Lafayette Square provides a head-on view of the White House and North Lawn through a security fence. Usually, you can easily walk through the square and right up to the fence. However, the square is occasionally blocked off for high-level diplomatic events, such as a state dinner, or the inauguration, as it's part of the day's parade route.

Visit the White House Visitor Center (1450 Pennsylvania Ave. NW, 202/208-1631, www.nps.gov/whho; 7:30am-4pm daily), a few blocks away, to see nearly 100 artifacts and exhibits about the White House's history, architecture, and social events and shop official White House memorabilia.

As you're planning your trip to DC, you may be wondering how to get inside the White House. Before your trip, you can request a free, self-guided tour of the East Wing from your member of Congress's office (see *Touring the White House* on page 78 for more details).

MAP 2: 1600 Pennsylvania Ave. NW, 202/456-7041, www.whitehouse.gov

NEARBY:

■ Get an Instagram-worthy view of the White House from Lafayette Square (page 77).

■ Dine in the plush setting of Joe's

Seafood, Prime Steak & Stone Crab (page 83).

■ Soak in the old-school atmosphere at Old Ebbitt Grill as you devour a salad or sandwich (page 81).

■ Drink cocktails overlooking the White House and monuments at POV, a covered rooftop lounge (page 87).

■ Sip DC-inspired cocktails with movers and shakers at Off the Record (page 88).

■ Appreciate the collection of contemporary American craft at the Renwick Gallery (page 92).

Lafayette Square

Lafayette Square, on the north side of the White House, is named for French general Gilbert du Motier, Marquis de Lafayette, who helped the colonists defeat the British during the Revolutionary War. The park contains five statues: General Andrew Jackson, Lafayette, and other military leaders from France, Poland, and Prussia who aided the Continental Army during the American Revolution.

The park is surrounded by power players: the U.S. Treasury; the Eisenhower Executive Office Building, where many Executive

TOURING THE WHITE HOUSE

It's possible to get a glimpse inside the White House on a tour, but it requires planning ahead.

U.S. citizens must submit tour requests through the office of their senator or representative (www.senate.gov/senators/contact or www.house.gov/representatives/find). Requests should be submitted between three months and 21 days in advance. Submit your request as early as possible. If you want to see the holiday decorations in December, submit your request no later than September.

The free, self-guided tours are generally available 7:30am-11:30am Tuesday through Thursday and 7:30am-1:30pm Friday and Saturday, though they may be cancelled depending on the White House schedule and security concerns.

The tour takes approximately 30-60 minutes to complete. You won't have much choice of the day or time slot, but you will get to see the parlors that were meticulously restored by First Lady Jackie Kennedy as well as the State Dining Room. The tour also gives you a look at a few of the rooms in the East Wing and the ground floor of the residence, including the China Room, showcasing glassware used by First Families, and the East Room, with the iconic portraits of George Washington and John F. Kennedy. Secret Service agents stand ready to answer your questions about the building's history and artifacts. (If you want a tour of the West Wing, you generally need to have a friend in the White House to be admitted to the Oval Office, Press Room, and Rose Garden.)

For two days in the spring and fall, you can tour the White House gardens and grounds; check www.whitehouse.gov in early April and early October for tour dates and ticket information.

Tours for international visitors may be restricted. Contact your country's embassy in Washington for more information. Non-U.S. citizens may still schedule tours of the U.S. Capitol.

For more information on tours, contact the White House's 24-hour information hotline at 202/456-7041.

Branch employees work; and Blair House, the president's guest house for visiting dignitaries. St. John's Episcopal Church, where many U.S. presidents have worshipped since 1816, is to the north across H Street NW.

Don't be surprised if you run into a celebration or a peaceful protest here. The square is occasionally blocked off for security purposes.
MAP 2: Pennsylvania Ave. NW and H Street NW between 15th St. NW and 17th St. NW; 24 hours daily

President's Park and the Ellipse

President's Park is an 82-acre national park that includes must-see sights like the White House and Lafayette Square, as well as historic trails and public green spaces. Two of the park's trails allow access to many monuments and memorials north and south of the White House. Pick them up from the White House Visitor Center (1450 Pennsylvania Ave. NW, 202/208-1631, www.nps.gov/whho).

Inside President's Park, south of the White House, the Ellipse is a 52-acre circular park that's a popular meeting spot for events ranging from protests to official White House events. In 1932, President Calvin Coolidge lit the first national Christmas tree in the center of the Ellipse. Today, it continues to be the site for the National Christmas Tree Lighting, as well as the National Menorah and Christmas trees decorated for every state and U.S. territory.

MAP 2: Between 15th St. NW and 17th St. NW, H Street NW and Constitution Ave. NW, 202/208-1631, www.nps.gov/whho; 24 hours daily (hours may be limited for security purposes)

Federal Bureau of Investigation (FBI)

Inside the FBI headquarters, the FBI Experience is a 60- to 90-minute self-guided tour showcasing the history and mission of the agency, featuring real crime-solving equipment and artifacts from historic cases. But don't expect to just show up. U.S. citizens must contact their senator or representative (and foreign citizens should contact their country's embassy in DC) between four weeks and five months in advance to make a reservation. You'll be notified about two weeks before your requested date whether you've been cleared for the tour.

Even if you don't take the tour, it's worth passing by one of the most imposing—and one of the ugliest—buildings in DC. The J. Edgar Hoover Building, named for the agency's first director, received strong mixed reactions when it was completed in 1975. Many architecture critics considered the brutalist, "Orwellian" building a blight on the city, but others said the 2-million-plus-square-foot concrete structure was perfect for the agency tasked with capturing the most dangerous criminals.

MAP 2: 935 Pennsylvania Ave. NW, 202/324-3000, www.fbi.gov; tours 9am-3pm Mon.-Thurs. by reservation only; free

Ford's Theatre

During the Civil War, Ford's Theatre was a popular entertainment venue among Washingtonians, including President Abraham Lincoln, who attended the theater nearly a dozen times. And April 14, 1865, was his last time, when he was shot by John Wilkes Booth during a performance of *Our American Cousin*. The next morning, the president died in Petersen House, the boarding house across the street.

The theater was shuttered, but it reopened in 1968 and today shows American plays and musicals like *Ragtime* and *Death of a Salesman*. The highlight is the annual production of *A Christmas Carol*, which the theater has produced every holiday season since 1979.

The historic site offers 30- to 45-minute guided tours ($3) of the theater and Lincoln's private box, which has been carefully restored to look like it did on the night he died. Tour tickets include a self-guided tour of Petersen House and entrance to the on-site museum, which

Ford's Theatre

view from the Old Post Office Clock Tower

features exhibits about Lincoln's presidency and assassination. While same-day tickets may be available at the box office, it's recommended to reserve your timed entry tickets online in advance.

MAP 2: 511 10th St. NW, 202/347-4833, www.fords.org; tours 9am-4:30pm daily, box office 8:30am-5pm daily and until 8pm on performance days; tours $3

Friendship Archway

DC's Chinatown was established in the 1880s by Chinese residents around present-day Federal Triangle. They were later displaced by construction, and in the 1930s, the community moved northeast and eventually spanned G Street NW north to Massachusetts Avenue NW, between 5th Street and 8th Street NW. Alas, the 1968 riots caused an exodus to the suburbs, and the neighborhood continued to shrink through the 1990s with the construction of the massive Capital One Arena.

One of the most prominent landmarks of Chinatown is the Friendship Archway, an elaborate, 60-foot structure crossing H Street. Built in 1986, the colorful tiled archway incorporates elements of traditional Chinese architecture and symbolizes the friendship between Washington DC and Beijing. On the surrounding streets, a few residences house the bulk of the neighborhood's remaining Chinese community, as well as a dozen or so tired Chinese restaurants and shops (and Chinese characters on fast-food chains). During Chinese New Year, a traditional parade makes its way under the archway through what remains of the neighborhood.

MAP 2: H St. NW between 6th Street NW and 7th St. NW

Old Post Office Clock Tower

The Old Post Office has housed the D.C. General Post Office, federal offices, retail stores, and even a food court since 1899—and the grand Romanesque Revival structure with its 315-foot clock tower and soaring glass atrium has been slated for demolition a few times over the years. In 2013, several hotel companies bid on the chance to develop it into a luxury property—and Donald Trump won. You know the rest of the story—but you may not know the National Park Service maintains the clock tower, which has the second-highest view in the city topped only by the Washington Monument. Unlike the Washington Monument, however, the clock tower doesn't require advance tickets to access the platform with 360-degree views of the U.S. Capitol and monuments. If you don't care to take a peek at the reality show inside the hotel, you can access the clock tower by a separate entrance on 12th Street NW.

MAP 2: 1100 Pennsylvania Ave. NW, www.nps.gov/nama/learn/historyculture/old-post-office-tower.htm; 9am-5pm daily, last entry at 4:30pm; free

Restaurants

PRICE KEY

$	Entrees less than $15
$$	Entrees $15-25
$$$	Entrees more than $25

CLASSIC AMERICAN
✪ Old Ebbitt Grill $$

In 1856, innkeeper William Ebbitt founded a boarding house and saloon in the neighborhood, a favorite of Teddy Roosevelt and Ulysses S. Grant. While the saloon closed in the early 20th century, this restaurant honors the original, with mahogany wood and Victorian-style decor, as well as a few antiques salvaged from the Ebbitt of yore. Steps from the White House, it's beloved by federal employees and lobbyists, who fill the booths day and night for reliable sandwiches, salads, steaks, and snacks. The expansive menu will please the pickiest eaters, though locals will tell you to order the Orca Platter, the seafood tower with dozens of oysters, clams, shrimp, and crab, plus a whole lobster.

MAP 2: 675 15th St. NW, 202/347-4800, www.ebbitt.com; 7:30am-1am Mon.-Fri., 8:30am-1am Sat.-Sun., bars until 2am Sun.-Thurs., 3am Fri.-Sat.

NEW AMERICAN
minibar by José Andrés $$$

This avant-garde restaurant has two Michelin stars and serves 20-plus courses of whimsical dishes that look like science experiments, in which unconventional cooking

Old Ebbitt Grill

whimsical food at minibar in Penn Quarter

techniques, tools, and ingredients (like foam and liquid nitrogen) are employed. To reserve one of the 12 counter seats or the chef's table, purchase tickets on the website two months in advance. There are two seatings available each night, with arrival times at 5:30pm or 8pm. A counter seat costs $275 per person (not including beverages), while the chef's table for up to six is $565 per person. Next door, barmini (501 9th St. NW, 202/393-4451) is billed as a cocktail lab where you can enjoy a similarly creative take on cocktail flights ($95 pp) as well as an à la carte menu ($15 deposit pp) of cocktails, beer, wine, and snacks. Reservations for the bar are strongly recommended but not always required.

MAP 2: 855 E St. NW, 202/393-0812, www.minibarbyjoseandres.com; 5:30pm-1am Tues.-Sat.

Cherry $$

Opening after the hotel's $50 million renovation in 2019, Cherry makes the W Hotel a nightlife destination. Chef William Morris does simple food incredibly well on the wood-fired grill, highlighting local products. For dinner, we recommend sharing a few dishes; pair a few starters (baby gem salad, grilled avocado) and sides with the perfectly cooked steak seasoned with salt, pepper, and embers. The service is excellent, though the modern decor is a bit sterile; ask for a seat at the dining bar overlooking the grill—and have your nightcap upstairs at POV overlooking the White House.

MAP 2: 515 15th St. NW, 202/661-2442, www.cherrywdc.com; 6:30am-10pm Mon.-Fri., 7:30am-10pm Sat.-Sun.

STEAK AND SEAFOOD
BLT Steak $$$

While you have many options for steak downtown, BLT Steak is one of the best for atmosphere and food. The modern dining room and long bar are dark but inviting, and buzzy but not too loud. Make a reservation for lunch or dinner and enjoy perfectly cooked high-quality steaks, served sizzling on individual cast-iron skillets, or specials like American Wagyu and raw bar items.

MAP 2: 1625 I St. NW, 202/689-8999, www.bltrestaurants.com/blt-steak; 11:30am-2:30pm and 5:30pm-10:30pm Mon.-Thurs., 11:30am-2:30pm and 5:30pm-11pm Fri., 5:30pm-11pm Sat.

Cherry at the W

Joe's Seafood, Prime Steak & Stone Crab $$$

Whether you're wining and dining a client or a date, you can't go wrong with the DC outpost of this South Beach institution, where you can feel power pulsing through the shiny marble floors. Have an important conversation in one of the plush booths in the dining room—where you may very well spot a diplomat or hot-shot lobbyist—or flirt over champagne and a slice of house-made pie at the high-ceilinged bar.

Either way, the service and the seafood will be impeccable.

MAP 2: 750 15th St. NW, 202/489-0140, www.joes.net/dc; 11:30am-11pm Mon.-Thurs., 11:30am-midnight Fri.-Sat., 11:30am-10pm Sun.

PUBS
Harry's $

In the heart of downtown, Harry's is a reliable spot for late-night grub like buffalo wings, sandwiches, and really good burgers. The slightly grungy pub is located in the Hotel Harrington, a historic spot that's seen better days but remains easy on the wallet.

MAP 2: 436 11th St. NW, 202/624-0053, www.harryssaloon.com; 11am-1:30am Sun.-Thurs., 11am-2:30am Fri.-Sat.

FRENCH
DBGB Kitchen & Bar $$$

After cooking his acclaimed Lyonnaise cuisine around the world, famed French chef Daniel Boulud opened this restaurant in CityCenterDC in 2014. Standouts at this modern, boisterous bistro include house-made pâté and sausages, juicy burgers, and a garlic roasted chicken for two. Don't skip dessert: The baked Alaska will please a celebratory crowd, or you can do dessert like the French with an artisanal cheese plate.

MAP 2: 931 H St. NW, 202/695-7660, www.dbgb.com; 11:30am-10pm Mon.-Thurs., 11:30am-11pm Fri., 11am-11pm Sat., 11am-10pm Sun.

INDIAN
Punjab Grill $$$

Washington's new hotspot for Indian fine dining is one of the most beautiful restaurants in the city, with a lavish interior entirely designed and custom built in India—including hand-carved wall decor, a bar inlaid with mother of pearl, and a private dining room with more than 150,000 mirrors. Luckily, the delicious food matches the interior. Enjoy a mix of classic dishes and contemporary shareable plates, as well as plenty of vegetarian and vegan options, like a delicately battered broccoli with cheese and vegan "goat" biryani.

MAP 2: 427 11th St. NW, 202/813-3004, www.punjabgrilldc.com; 11:30am-10pm Mon.-Thurs., 11:30am-11pm Fri., 5pm-11pm Sat., 11am-9pm Sun.

ITALIAN
Centrolina $$$

Escape the hustle and bustle for superb house-made pasta in this cozy but posh restaurant. Start with a Negroni or Aperol spritz, then enjoy James Beard nominee Amy Brandwein's cooking: slurpy *tagliolini* (ribbon pasta), light and buttery chicken tortelloni, or wood-fired meats and fish. It's connected to a market (11am-9pm daily) where you can grab breakfast at the small counter and purchase fresh pasta and sauce, local produce, and Italian goodies.

MAP 2: 974 Palmer Alley, 202/898-2426, www.centrolinadc. com; 11:30am-2:30pm and 5pm-10pm Mon.-Thurs., 11:30am-2:30pm and 5pm-midnight Fri., 5pm-midnight Sat., 10:30am-2:30pm and 5pm-10pm Sun.

JAPANESE
Sushi Nakazawa $$$

Washingtonians agree that Jiro-trained Daisuke Nakazawa's omakase-only restaurant serves the most exquisite sushi in town. Michelin agreed, too, awarding the restaurant a star in the 2020 guide, one of just two Asian restaurants in the city with the honor. The 20-piece chef's choice menu is $120 pp in the contemporary dining room, $150 pp at the sushi bar, with sake or wine pairings from $65 pp—making it DC's most expensive sushi, too.

MAP 2: 1100 Pennsylvania Ave. NW, 202/289-3515, www.sushinakazawa. com; sushi counter 12-1pm, 6pm, 8:15pm Mon.-Thurs., 5pm, 7:15pm, 9:30pm Fri.-Sat., dining room 5pm-10:15pm Mon.-Sat.

MEDITERRANEAN
Zaytinya $$

José Andrés is behind this bustling meze restaurant, which provides a trip around the Mediterranean via small plates. Many of the dishes—hummus with ground lamb, *shish taouk* (marinated chicken shish kebab), and spanakopita—are made in the classic style, though there are often specials on offer, especially in the spring, when Greek Easter and the cherry blossoms provide inspiration for the menu. The modern dining room has glass windows, high ceilings, and an excruciating din on

Taco Bamba

pan con tomate and authentic jamón at Jaleo

busy nights; grab a seat at the bar for a more intimate, though still lively, experience.

MAP 2: 701 9th St. NW, 202/638-0800, www.zaytinya.com; 11am-10pm Sun.-Mon., 11am-11pm Tues.-Thurs., 11am-midnight Fri.-Sat.

MEXICAN
Taco Bamba $

This Chinatown taco shop near the convention center has a rock-music theme and soundtrack, but it's not a tourist trap. Enjoy tasty, inexpensive tacos ranging from standbys like carnitas and carne asada to more creative flavors like crispy cod and malt vinegar salsa. We recommend the Spicy 'Shroom, bursting with mushrooms, nuts, and goat cheese, even if you aren't vegetarian. Choose fast-casual takeaway or table service—or chef Victor Albisu's more upscale fare next door at Poca Madre (202/838-5300, www.poca-madredc.com).

MAP 2: 777 I St. NW, 202/289-7377, www.tacobamba.com; 8:30am-10pm Mon.-Thurs., 8:30am-11pm Fri., 10am-11pm Sat., 10am-10pm Sun.

SPANISH
✪ Jaleo $$

This tapas restaurant made José Andrés a culinary hero when he became the first chef to import prized *jamón ibérico* (Iberian ham), made from the black-footed pigs of Spain, to the United States—and with his work to feed victims of natural disasters, he's a humanitarian hero, too. And while new restaurants open in DC practically every week, the veteran Jaleo holds up. The *jamón* is a must, especially with tangy Manchego cheese and *pan con tomate* (grilled bread with tomato), as well as sautéed shrimp, spicy *patatas bravas* (fried potatoes), and *piquillo* peppers bursting with goat cheese. The sangrias and Spanish wines are noteworthy, but the tapas are best paired with a gin and tonic like you'd get on the coast in Spain. This colorful, energetic restaurant is good for groups who aren't afraid to share dishes. If you come with kids, try to get one of the glass-topped foosball tables.

MAP 2: 480 7th St. NW, 202/628-7949, www.jaleo.com; 11am-10pm Mon., 11am-11pm Tues.-Thurs., 11am-midnight Fri., 10am-midnight Sat., 10am-10pm Sun.

CAFES AND LIGHT BITES

Breadline $

A longtime favorite of nearby office workers who happily stand in line during the weekday lunch rush, Breadline serves filling made-to-order sandwiches and piadinas on bread baked in-house daily alongside famous fries fresh from the fryer. For a lighter lunch, choose from at least two daily soups and several salads, pastries, and coffee. Located steps from the White House and Renwick, the café has ample seating indoors and outdoors, or you can take your order to go to enjoy in Lafayette Park.

MAP 2: 1751 Pennsylvania Ave. NW, 202/822-8900, www.breadline.com; 7am-5:30pm Mon.-Fri.

VEGETARIAN AND VEGAN

Elizabeth's Gone Raw $$$

Elizabeth's Gone Raw proves raw vegan dining can be bold, flavorful, and filling. Founded by Elizabeth Petty, who turned to a raw vegan diet when she was diagnosed with breast cancer, the restaurant serves a seven-course plant-based tasting menu ($80 pp, wine pairing

additional $60 pp) featuring raw, vegan variations on pasta, ice cream, and even meat and shellfish made entirely with gluten-free, dairy-free, and seasonal ingredients. The townhouse-style restaurant is open Friday and Saturday nights only—it's a catering company and private-event venue the rest of the week—but you can usually get a reservation a week in advance.

MAP 2: 1341 L St. NW, 202/347-8349, www.elizabethsgoneraw.com; reservations 5pm-9pm Fri.-Sat.

Fruitive $

Trying to eat healthier? Try Fruitive, serving organic, plant-based breakfast and lunch—think super-grain bowls and wraps, avocado toast, and an avocado cucumber sandwich with greens and a sprinkling of sea salt, as satisfying as it is clean. For something light on the go, try a "liquid meal" or bottled juice. Plan to grab and go or try to grab one of the handful of indoor counter seats or outdoor tables. There's a second location in Dupont Circle (1330 Connecticut Ave. NW, 202/836-7734).

MAP 2: 1094 Palmer Alley NW, 202/836-7749, www.fruitive.com; 7am-8pm Mon.-Fri., 9am-7pm Sat.-Sun.

BREAKFAST AND BRUNCH

Astro Doughnuts and Fried Chicken $

This fast-casual restaurant founded by two native Washingtonians who played for the Washington Capitals serves affordable comfort food close to the major sights. You don't have to choose between crispy fried chicken or a fresh-baked doughnut—just get your fried chicken sandwich on a savory doughnut. But save room: Many foodies consider the crème brûlée doughnut one of the best sweet treats in the city.

MAP 2: 1308 G St. NW, 202/809-5565, www.astrodoughnuts.com; 7:30am-5:30pm Mon.-Fri., 9am-5pm Sat., 9am-3pm Sun.

COFFEE AND TEA
Kintsugi $

Located inside the Eaton Hotel, Kintsugi is more millennial-friendly coworking space than coffee shop—and one of our favorite spots to catch up on work or meet a friend. The spacious, naturally lit café with plenty of comfy seating and vintage flair serves artisanal coffee, tea, and pastries as well as trendy ayurvedic beverages with turmeric and reishi mushroom.

MAP 2: 1201 K St. NW, www.kintsugi-dc.com; 6:30am-6pm Mon.-Fri., 7am-3pm Sat.-Sun.

Nightlife

COCKTAIL BARS AND LOUNGES
✪ POV

At this swanky bar and lounge on the covered roof of the W Washington D.C., a chic crowd enjoys DC-themed cocktails and a full food menu year-round with a perfect view of the White House and monuments. Reservations are recommended; reservations after 5pm require a minimum spend of $50 pp, and you'll need to spring for bottle service after 10pm on weekends.

MAP 2: 515 15th St. NW, 202/661-2437, www.povrooftop.com; 11am-midnight Sun.-Thurs., 11am-2am Fri.-Sat.

✪ Round Robin Bar

The bar at the Willard InterContinental has witnessed a lot of history since it was established in 1850. It's where Senator Henry Clay of Kentucky introduced the mint julep to DC in 1851—it remains the bar's signature cocktail—and famous customers have included Walt Whitman, Mark Twain, Buffalo Bill Cody, and many presidents, including Lincoln, Coolidge, Wilson, and Taft. Politicos, lobbyists, and tourists enjoy classic cocktails and bar bites day and night in the mahogany and leather bar with windows looking out to the city.

MAP 2: 1401 Pennsylvania Ave. NW, 202/628-9100, www.washington. intercontinental.com; noon-1am Mon.-Sat., noon-midnight Sun.

Benjamin Bar & Lounge

The Trump International Hotel's lobby lounge is where to spot DC's most powerful—and most infamous. (Who's that having drinks over there?) The palatial bar and lounge under the Romanesque Revival building's soaring ceiling has remarkably tasteful gold and blue velvet decor, making it one of the most beautiful bars in the city. Here, Cabinet Secretaries, First

POV

Family members, lobbyists, and gawkers from around the world get a taste of an extravagant lifestyle—like expensive wine served in crystal spoons and selections from a cart of fancy-looking pastries rolling around during happy hour on Friday evenings. The beverage selections are good, but, really, you go for the people watching. (Of note, in case you want to go or avoid it: on the first Tuesday of the month, staffers, campaign alums, and donors pack the bar.) It's one of the strangest tents in the Washington circus today and, whatever your politics, worth visiting for a potent cocktail served by friendly, hard-working staff. If you get hungry, try the much-Instagrammed "bacon on a clothesline," beloved by the regulars, though we prefer the cheddar burger after a long day of lobbying.

MAP 2: 1100 Pennsylvania Ave. NW, 202/695-1100, www. trumphotels. com/washington-dc/benjamin-bar-and-lounge; 7am-midnight Sun.-Wed., 7am-2am Thurs.-Sat.

Off the Record

Many off-the-record conversations between Washington reporters and their sources have taken place in the basement lounge of The Hay-Adams, a small, dimly lit space where friendly bartenders who have seen everything serve DC-inspired versions of classic cocktails. It's across the street from the White House, so it can be tough to get a seat during happy hour, but if you do, be careful, because the cocktails are very strong.

MAP 2: 800 16th St. NW, 202/638-6600, www.hayadams.com/washington-dc-bars; 11:30am-midnight Sun.-Thurs., 11:30am-12:30am Fri.-Sat.

HAPPY HOUR

Washington DC is all about who you know and—if you really want business to get done—how often you have a few drinks with them. When visiting the nation's capital, you can take the pulse of the city and the political climate by going to happy hour at one of the many restaurants offering after-work food and drink specials, like bites hearty enough to make dinner plus discounted (sometimes by half) cocktails, beer, and wine. And if you're lucky, you'll overhear well-oiled staffers exchanging snippets of political gossip, especially if you choose a location near the White House or House and Senate office buildings.

The Hay-Adams

If you don't mind saddling up to the bar, happy hour is the best way to try some of the city's best restaurants at a fraction of the price, too.

- Enjoy discounted appetizers and American wines while you try to spot Members of Congress at Charlie Palmer Steak (page 111).

- Lobbyists from the K Street firms indulge in food and drink specials and gossip from 5pm-7pm on weekdays at BLT Steak (page 82).

- Near the White House, Old Ebbitt Grill serves 1/2-price oysters to a boisterous crowd from 3-6pm and 11pm-close daily (page 81).

- If you can get a seat at the busy bar, Joe's Seafood, Prime Steak & Stone Crab is a glamorous spot for food and drink specials with high rollers from 2:30pm-6:30pm on weekdays (page 83).

- Night owls should head to Hank's Oyster Bar, where the raw bar items are half off from 10pm-midnight daily (page 133).

- The supper-club-style "cocktail party" at The Riggsby is one of the best, with $5 classic cocktails (including a champagne cocktail) and bites from 4pm-7pm daily (page 132).

- The Michelin-starred Sushi Taro offers an incredible deal from 5:30pm-7pm weekdays at the bar only: 1/2 price sushi and alcoholic drinks. Yes, it gets crowded (page 134).

- Craving a taste of Italy by the water? Officina has special prices on Aperol Spritzes, wines, and beers—plus free snacks!—in the café on weekdays from 4pm-6pm (page 221).

LIVE MUSIC

The Hamilton

Before Alexander Hamilton made pop-culture history, Washingtonians long enjoyed late-night entertainment in his namesake concert venue and restaurant. The main stage holds about 600 people in a mix of seated and standing-room areas for blues, country, rock, and cover bands. Performers have included Carbon Leaf; the Old 97's; Beatles, Bruce Springsteen, and Led Zeppelin cover bands; and many local bands. Tickets for main stage performances average $30, but the intimate loft bar has free shows on weekends. After the show, grab a bite in the huge on-site restaurant, which serves everything from burgers to vegan sushi our vegetarian friends love.

MAP 2: 600 14th St. NW, 202/787-1000, www.thehamiltondc.com; 11am-2am Mon.-Thurs., 11am-3am Fri.-Sat., 10am-2am Sun.

✪ WILD DAYS

Sure, you can find a better view, but the Eaton Hotel's rooftop lounge definitely has the coolest vibe. From happy hour to late, local artists and DJs mingle with buttoned-up lobbyists loosening their ties over cocktails, canned rosé, and tacos and guac. It gets absolutely packed before the intimate, free concerts, with hour-plus waits for a table—though you can feel free to grab standing room at the small but efficient bar or on the wrap-around deck.

MAP 2: 1201 K St. NW, 202/900-8419, www.wild-days-dc.com; 4pm-1am Mon.-Thurs., 4pm-2am Fri., 1pm-2am Sat., 1pm-1am Sun.

COMEDY CLUBS
DC Improv

One of the few dedicated comedy clubs in Washington DC, the DC Improv hosts major standup stars—Dave Chapelle, Ellen DeGeneres, and Jim Gaffigan have performed here—as well as local comedians in the intimate, basement space. The club has a full dinner menu and bar with a two-item minimum per ticket. Seats are allocated first come, first served, so arrive early if you want to be close to the front.

MAP 2: 1140 Connecticut Ave. NW, 202/296-7008, www.dcimprov.com; box office 10am-5pm Tues.-Fri., 10am-9pm Tues.-Fri. on days with shows, noon-9pm Sat.-Sun.

Arts and Culture

MUSEUMS
American Art Museum and National Portrait Gallery

Go for Amy Sherald's now-iconic Michelle Obama portrait (third floor), stay for inspiring Americana at the Smithsonian American Art Museum and Smithsonian National Portrait Gallery, which are collocated (and more or less mixed together) in one of DC's oldest buildings. Don't miss the portraits of every U.S. president, but take time to meet other influential Americans, too, like feminist author Louisa May Alcott, groundbreaking astronomer Edwin Hubble, and composer George Walker, the first African American to win the Pulitzer for music. The 17 portrait galleries are interspersed with the American Art Museum's collection, including the art commissioned by the U.S. government during the New Deal in the 1930s as well as Thomas Moran's massive, majestic National Park landscapes.

Louisa May Alcott bust by Frank Elwell at the National Portrait Gallery

MAP 2: 8th St. NW and F St. NW, 202/633-7970, http://americanart.si.edu and http://npg.si.edu; 11:30am-7pm daily; free

National Building Museum

This favorite museum among locals contains stimulating exhibits about architecture, construction, and urban planning, as well as a cool interactive gallery for kids ages 2-6. Located inside a breathtaking Italian Renaissance Revival structure, which was the headquarters of the U.S. Pension Bureau after the Civil War, the galleries—formerly offices for 1,000-plus pension employees—surround a soaring atrium with 75-foot Corinthian columns.

MAP 2: 401 F St. NW, 202/272-2448, www.nbm.org; 10am-5pm Mon.-Sat., 11am-5pm Sun.; $10 adults, $7 students, seniors, and children 3-18, free for children 2 and under

National Children's Museum

If your kids have already done the dinosaurs, the spaceships, and the American flag, there's a brand-new museum in town—the only one dedicated exclusively to young minds. Previously located at the National Harbor in Maryland, the National Children's Museum moved to a new home a hop, skip, and jump from the National Mall and White House. The 33,000-square-foot space has interactive exhibits for children of all ages, from areas for infants to an art and technology exhibit sponsored by Nickelodeon and featuring (virtual) slime, which nostalgic parents might even enjoy.

MAP 2: 1300 Pennsylvania Ave. NW, 202/844-2486, www.nationalchildrensmuseum.org; 9:30am-4:30pm daily; $10.95, free for children under 1

National Museum of Women in the Arts

Shockingly, Washington's National Museum of Women in the Arts is the only major museum in the world dedicated exclusively to women artists. It was founded by Wilhelmina Cole Holladay, a diplomat and art collector who was appalled by the lack of information about women artists in American art textbooks, and she made it her mission to support women artists. Rotating exhibitions draw from the collection of nearly 5,000 pieces by more than 1,000 female artists, including Mary Cassatt, Clara Peeters, and Frida Kahlo, as well as hundreds of lesser-known artists.

MAP 2: 1250 New York Ave. NW, 202/783-5000, www.nmwa.org; 10am-5pm Mon.-Sat., noon-5pm Sun.; $10 adults, $8 students and seniors, free for children 18 and under

Renwick Gallery

Showcasing the Smithsonian's collection of contemporary American craft and decorative arts, this small, niche museum displays pieces like glass works by Dale Chihuly, jewelry by Alexander Calder, and Larry Fuente's *Game Fish,* a large 3-D fish sculpture made with tiny toys and game pieces. The building is one of the most interesting elements of the museum—don't forget to look at the ceilings—and fashionistas will want to pop in specifically to visit the gift shop, selling unique jewelry and accessories by American craftsmen and women.

MAP 2: Pennsylvania Ave. NW at 17th St. NW, 202/633-7970, http://renwick.americanart.si.edu; 10am-5:30pm daily; free

THEATER, MUSIC, AND DANCE
✪ Woolly Mammoth Theatre Company

The Woolly Mammoth Theatre Company produces, hands down, the most innovative theater in DC. It's been making audiences laugh, think, and squirm since 1980. Especially memorable productions include the colorful *Marie Antoinette* for the Kardashian era, as well as *Arguendo,* which explained how the U.S. Supreme Court works, using the exact language of the oral arguments of *Barnes v. Glen Theatre Inc.,* in which exotic dancers in Indiana argued that a state law requiring them to wear G-strings and pasties violated the First Amendment. (Indiana won.) Woolly Mammoth is dedicated to premiering groundbreaking

Renwick Gallery

DC'S THEATER SCENE

Whether you want to see a Broadway-quality musical or the premiere of a quirky new play, DC's theater scene offers something for every taste. Whatever you see, it will be both creative and smart—like the city itself.

- Experience world-class music, dance, and opera at The John F. Kennedy Center for the Performing Arts (page 201) in Foggy Bottom.
- The avant-garde dramas and comedies produced by the Woolly Mammoth Theatre Company (page 92) in Penn Quarter will make you think and squirm.
- Shakespeare fans will appreciate opportunities to see both popular and obscure works from the Shakespeare Theatre Company (page 93) or Folger Theatre (page 119).
- History buffs might enjoy a play and a tour at Ford's Theatre (page 79), where President Lincoln was shot during a performance of Our American Cousin.

American works but also welcomes performers like Mike Daisey, best known for his controversial *The Agony and the Ecstasy of Steve Jobs*. All performances take place at the company's 256-seat courtyard-style theater, where there's not a bad seat in the house; check the website for postshow panel discussions and pay-what-you-can nights.

MAP 2: 641 D St. NW, 202/393-3939, www.woollymammoth.net; box office noon-6pm Wed.-Sun.; tickets $59-79

The National Theatre

John Wilkes Booth wasn't a stranger to President Abraham Lincoln when he shot him at Ford's Theatre on April 14, 1865. Lincoln saw his assassin perform the lead in Shakespeare's *Richard III* at the National Theatre two years prior. Today, the theater, which has operated continuously since 1835, hosts national tours as well as world premieres of shows before they head to Broadway, including *Show Boat* in 1927, *West Side Story* in 1957, and *Mean Girls*, based on the cult film of the same name, in 2017.

MAP 2: 1321 Pennsylvania Ave. NW, 202/628-6161, www.thenationaldc.org; box office noon-6pm Mon.-Fri. and two hours prior to showtime until 30 min. after showtime; tickets from $45

Shakespeare Theatre Company

The play's the thing at the Tony Award-winning Shakespeare Theatre Company, which has performed Shakespearean works as well as classic dramas and comedies since 1986. The beautifully staged productions are true to Shakespeare's text, with inspiration drawn from contemporary politics. The 2017 production of *Macbeth*, for example, was set in an occupied third-world country in the present day. The company has two downtown theaters: the 775-seat Sidney Harman Hall (610 F St. NW) and the smaller Michael R. Klein Theatre (450 7th St. NW).

MAP 2: Sidney Harman Hall, 610 F St. NW, 202/547-1122 or 877/487-8849, www.shakespearetheatre.org; box office noon-6pm Mon.-Sun. and until curtain; tickets $25-120

Warner Theatre

This downtown theater opened in 1924 as a venue for vaudeville and silent films, and in the 1930s and 1940s it welcomed major stars like Bob Hope, Duke Ellington, and Jerry Lewis. The dazzling red-and-gold, 1,847-seat theater hosts major music and comedy acts, national tours of Broadway musicals, and the Washington Ballet's beloved annual production of *The Nutcracker,* which is set in Georgetown and stars George Washington as the lead. (The George Washington nutcracker doll makes an excellent gift, too.) Founded by Mary Day in 1944, the Washington Ballet is a renowned company and school, performing beloved classics and innovative premieres at theaters around the city, including The John F. Kennedy Center for the Performing Arts and Warner Theatre.

MAP 2: 513 13th St. NW, 202/783-4000, www.warnertheatredc.com; box office 10am-4pm Mon.-Fri. and three hours prior to showtime until 30 min. after showtime; tickets from $39

LIBRARIES

Martin Luther King Jr. Memorial Library

DC's flagship library, the Martin Luther King Jr. Memorial Library in Chinatown, was the last building designed by modernist architect Mies van der Rohe. It was completed in 1972. Following a $208 million renovation, the library is scheduled to reopen in the fall of 2020 with a new reading room, art and conference spaces, a café, and more.

MAP 2: 901 G St. NW, 202/727-0321, www.dclibrary.org/mlk

Festivals and Events

Smithsonian Craft Show

The Smithsonian Craft Show brings together over 100 American craftsmen and -women (from over 1,000 applicants) to Washington DC for a public, juried show and sale, with ticket proceeds benefitting the Smithsonian Institution's museums and programs. From housewares and baskets to jewelry and wearable art, there's something for every taste.

Downtown: National Building Museum, 401 F St. NW, 888/832-9554, www.smithsoniancraftshow.org; late Apr.; $15-30 general admission, $250 preview night

Washington Auto Show

The biggest show in DC, and one of the top auto shows in the world, the Washington Auto Show is a local post-holiday favorite, with more than 600 new models and special events at the Walter E. Washington Convention Center from late January to early February.

Downtown: Walter E. Washington Convention Center, 801 Mt. Vernon Pl. NW, www.washingtonautoshow.com; late Jan.-early Feb.; $5-12

National Book Festival

The Library of Congress celebrates reading at this annual one-day event, featuring more than 100 authors and illustrators across genres who read, sell, and sign their books and participate in panel discussions.

Downtown: Walter E. Washington Convention Center, 801 Mt. Vernon Pl. NW, 202/707-5000, www.loc.gov/bookfest; early Sept.; free

National Christmas Tree and Pathway of Peace

Since 1923, the POTUS has lit the National Christmas Tree on the Ellipse near the White House, and no holiday season in DC is complete without a nighttime visit to see the display. Surrounding the main tree, the Pathway of Peace features 56 trees decorated for each U.S. state and territory, as well as live entertainment, refreshments, and cheer.

Downtown: 202/796-2500, www.thenationaltree.org; early Dec.-Jan. 1; free

Downtown Holiday Market

Skip the big box stores on Black Friday and head to the Downtown Holiday Market, several blocks of regional vendors selling items for everyone on your list, from jewelry and accessories to art and housewares to local food gifts. The market also features live music across many genres, along with bites and beverages.

Downtown: 8th St. NW and F St. NW, www.downtownholidaymarket.com; Black Friday-Dec. 23; free

A Christmas Carol

For 35 years, Ford's Theatre has presented Charles Dickens's A Christmas Carol during the holiday season, making a trip to the historic theater a holiday tradition for Washington region families. The festive production tells the story of Ebenezer Scrooge and the Ghosts of Christmas Past, Present, and Future with colorful sets, joyful music, and a diverse cast.

Downtown: Ford's Theatre, 511 10th St. NW, 202/347-4833, www.fords.org; mid-Nov.-late Dec.; $32-105

The Washington Ballet's The Nutcracker

Tchaikovsky's beloved holiday ballet gets a Washington DC twist, set in a Georgetown mansion in 1882 and starring General George Washington in the title role as he fights the Rat King, King George III. From late November through Christmas Eve, there are performances in several area theaters, including The Warner Theatre.

Downtown: 202/362-3606, www.washingtonballet.org; late Nov.-late Dec.; $30-130

Recreation

TOURS

Old Town Trolley Tours

Catch an open-air, motorized trolley for a breezy way to see the White House, the National Mall, and Capitol Hill. The tours are narrated by entertaining drivers and cover more than 100 major sights at 25 stops in 90 minutes. You can hop off to explore and hop back on another trolley, which run approximately every half hour. Purchase tickets and start the tour at the Washington Welcome Center (1000 E St. NW, 202/347-6609; 8:30am-9pm daily), a tourist information center and souvenir shop across from Ford's Theatre. If you already have tickets, pick up the trolley at any stop along the route. It's also possible to transfer trolleys for a tour of Arlington National Cemetery.

MAP 2: 1000 E St. NW, 844/356-2603, www.trolleytours.com; 9am-5pm daily; $49-148 adults, $33-60 children 4-12, free for children 4 and under, advance purchase discounts available online

Segs in the City

This tour operator offers several options for seeing the sights on Segways, including two-hour guided tours around downtown or the monuments and a sunset tour with time for reflection in the Franklin Delano Roosevelt Memorial and Lincoln Memorial. If you don't mind stares from locals, this is the quickest way to tour the monuments and memorials up close with an engaging, knowledgeable guide. Or, rent your own Segway ($35/hour, $150/ five hours) to tour at your own pace. Tours depart outside the Ronald Reagan Building and International Trade Center and include a training session, helmet, and map.

MAP 2: 1300 Pennsylvania Ave. NW, 800/734-7393, www.segsinthecity.com; 9am-9:30pm daily weather permitting; $40-80 pp, ages 16 and up

SPORTS ARENAS
Capital One Arena

Since 1997, the Capital One Arena has packed the 20,000 seats for

Old Town Trolley Tours

sporting events and major concerts. In addition to being the place to see performers like Lady Gaga, Celine Dion, and Jay-Z, it's also the home of several professional sports teams, including the NBA's Washington Wizards and the NHL's Washington Capitals, as well as the Arena Football League's Washington Valor (202/661-5005, www.washingtonvalor.com), which plays from April to August. The Georgetown University Hoyas (202/687-4692, www.guhoyas.com) men's basketball team plays here, too. Tickets for all events are available at Ticketmaster outlets, including the arena box office.

MAP 2: 601 F St. NW, 202/628-3200, tickets 800/745-3000, http://capitalonearena. monumentalsportsnetwork.com; box office 10am-5pm Mon.-Fri., 10am to event start time Sat.-Sun.

SPECTATOR SPORTS
BASKETBALL
Washington Wizards

National Basketball Association (NBA) followers may remember when DC's franchise was called the Washington Bullets, a controversial choice considering the city's high crime rate in the 1980s and 1990s. The franchise rebranded to the Washington Wizards in 1997, though there's been a movement among longtime fans to change it back. The team hasn't won a final since the Bullets days, but they did win a division title in 2017. The Wizards play home games from October to April at the Capital One Arena (601 F St. NW); single game tickets are readily available via Ticketmaster and the arena box office.

MAP 2: 601 F St. NW, 202/661-5050, www.nba.com/wizards; tickets from $19

ICE HOCKEY
Washington Capitals

Founded in 1974, DC's National Hockey League (NHL) team has won two Stanley Cup championships, including one in 2018, and 10 divisional titles. Caps fans are loud and loyal; catch an exciting match from October to April at the Capital One Arena (601 F St. NW). Tickets are available via Ticketmaster and the arena box office, but plan ahead—the team sold out every home game in 2018-2019 for the ninth straight season.

MAP 2: 601 F St. NW, 202/266-2277, www.nhl.com/capitals; tickets from $39

Shops

CLOTHING, SHOES, AND ACCESSORIES
✪ Tiny Jewel Box

Since 1930, Tiny Jewel Box has been the choice of U.S. presidents and first ladies for fine jewelry and diplomatic gifts. Secretary of State Madeleine Albright purchased many of her colorful pins here, and First Lady Michelle Obama gave a gift to her predecessor that was designed by Tiny Jewel Box. Occupying the

Apple Carnegie Library

and M Street NW, it stocks international brands like Cartier and
Rolex, as well as designers like
David Yurman, who was discovered by owner Jim Rosenheim in
1977. You'll also find one-of-a-kind
and vintage pieces, or you can work
with the welcoming staff to create a
custom design.

Tiny Jewel Box

MAP 2: 1155 Connecticut Ave. NW,
202/393-2747, www.tinyjewelbox.com;
10am-5:30pm Mon.-Sat.

Coup de Foudre Lingerie

This pretty boutique in Penn
Quarter stocks the finest lingerie
from Paris, including Chantelle,
Lise Charmel, and Simone Pérèle,
as well as hip, lower-priced brands
like Commando and Hanky Panky.
Meaning "bolt of lightning," a
phrase used to describe love at first
sight in French, Coup de Foudre has
warm staff who will make you feel
comfortable during your bra fitting
and offer personalized suggestions
if you're shopping for a special gift.
MAP 2: 1001 Pennsylvania
Ave. NW, 202/393-0878, www.
coupdefoudrelingerie.com; 11am-6pm
Mon.-Sat.

GIFTS AND HOME
✪ Apple Carnegie Library

When you approach the beaux
arts Carnegie Library—DC's first

public library funded by philanthropist Andrew Carnegie—you'd never know you're looking at an Apple Store. Look closely, however, and you'll notice the iconic logo on iPhone-shaped marble stones on the facade before you enter this gleaming monument to the technology titan that's forever changed our daily lives. Yes, it's first and foremost a store, designed to take more of your cash for the next must-have gadget. But we can't criticize them too much because they've done an absolutely breathtaking job restoring this historic landmark, retaining the original layout of the library—for example, displaying children's products and games in the library's original children's room. Even if you don't need an iPad or Apple Watch, it's worth a visit to take a free guided tour of the building—the first unsegregated building in DC—and explore the DC History Center, with the Historical Society of Washington DC's collection of artifacts, maps, and photos. And if you are in the market for a new product, this is the place to shop, because Apple's brought in some of its most knowledgeable and friendly staff from across the country.

MAP 2: 801 K St. NW, 202/609-6400, www.apple.com/retail/carnegielibrary; 9am-9pm Mon.-Sat., 11am-7pm Sun.

✪ White House Visitor Center Shop

The flagship gift shop inside the White House Visitor Center stocks a large selection of official White House merchandise: cuff links and jewelry (including flag lapel pins), home and office decor like calendars and presidential busts, fine art, and

White House Visitor Center Shop

books. You can also buy every White House Christmas ornament since 1981 and Easter Egg Roll commemorative eggs. Another, smaller shop, the White House History Shop (1610 H St. NW, 202/218-4337), has a similar inventory and frequently hosts signings with authors of books about White House history.

MAP 2: 1450 Pennsylvania Ave. NW, 202/208-7031, www.whitehousehistory. org; 7:30am-4pm daily

The Great Republic

Did visiting the museums inspire you to add some Americana to your home or office? In CityCenterDC, The Great Republic sells authentic American antiques like rare maps and flags from the country's early days, books (including signed copies), and hand-carved eagles meant for hanging over your desk. Yes, they're expensive, but you're welcome to browse, or shop lower-priced, new items like made-in-America leather goods and cuff links.

MAP 2: 973 Palmer Alley NW, 202/682-1812, www.great-republic.com; 10am-8pm Mon.-Sat., 11am-6pm Sun.

GOURMET FOOD AND DRINKS

Chocolate Chocolate

This tiny, friendly shop sells a tasty souvenir: White Houses, Capitol domes, and monuments made from milk, dark, and white chocolate. The walls are packed with artisanal American, Belgian, and Swiss chocolate brands and self-serve gummies and chocolates, while small-batch house truffles and nostalgic candies, like vanilla buttercreams and mint meltaways, twinkle in the glass case.

MAP 2: 1130 Connecticut Ave. NW, 202/466-2190, www.chocolatedc.com; 10am-6pm Mon.-Fri., 11am-4pm Sat.

BEST SOUVENIRS

White House Christmas ornament from the White House Visitor Center Shop

Don't bother with the FBI sweatshirts and caps hawked by street vendors around the National Mall, and take home one of these only-in-Washington souvenirs or local products instead.

WHITE HOUSE MEMORABILIA

The official White House Christmas ornament is a bipartisan piece of Americana that the White House Historical Association has designed every year since 1981 to benefit the preservation of White House art and artifacts. Every year, a new design honors a president or significant anniversary, like the bicentennial of the presidency or the laying of the White House cornerstone. You can purchase it at the White House Visitor Center Shop (page 99) and the White House History Shop (page 99). The shops also sell other memorabilia, like cuff links and flag lapel pins and reproductions of presidential busts, too.

FOOD AND DRINK

Noteworthy artisan food and beverage companies have made their mark on the city. For cocktail enthusiasts, a bottle of Green Hat Gin, made by New Columbia Distillers (page 255) and available at liquor stores around town including Batch 13 (page 169), will remind you of evenings in DC's historic bars. With its newsprint-style label, it looks cool on your bar cart, too.

While many stores stock DC-themed barware, the Lincoln Memorial-themed growler jugs available at brewery DC Brau (3178 Bladensburg Rd. NE, 202/621-8890, http://dcbrau.com) stand out. Pair them with a six-pack of the brewery's The Public Pale Ale for a great gift.

For a wide selection of "Made in DC" products, ranging from Gordy's Pickle Jar pickles to Embitterment cocktail bitters to kitchen items featuring the DC flag, be sure to stop by Salt & Sundry (page 168), Union Kitchen Grocery (page 169), Hill's Kitchen (page 122), and Shop Made in D.C. (page 143).

BOOKS

For readers, there's no better souvenir than a signed book by a DC author. Check the lineup of author events at stores like Politics and Prose (page 230) or Kramerbooks (page 142). And don't forget to get your Reader Identification Card from the Library of Congress (page 108).

Capitol Hill and Atlas District
Map 3

In addition to being the location of two of the three branches of government, Capitol Hill is home to **cozy restaurants** and **dive bars,** where you can enjoy reasonably priced meals and get the legislative gossip during happy hour.

In the nearby Atlas District, **trendy restaurants, cafés,** and **bars** line popular **H Street NE,** where you'll mix with hipsters and millennials for a casual night out.

TOP SIGHTS

- Best Place to See History in the Making: **U.S. Capitol** (page 106)

TOP RESTAURANTS

- Best Place to Spot a Senator: **Charlie Palmer Steak** (page 111)

TOP NIGHTLIFE

- Quintessential DC Dive: **Tune Inn** (page 116)
- Most Welcoming Pub: **Mr. Henry's** (page 118)

TOP SHOPS

- Coolest Local Market: **Eastern Market** (page 123)
- Best Gifts for Chefs: **Hill's Kitchen** (page 122)

GETTING THERE AND AROUND

- Metro lines: Blue, Orange, Red, Silver
- Metro stations: Capitol South, Eastern Market, Union Station
- Major bus routes: DC Circulator Union Station-Navy Yard, DC Circulator Potomac Ave Metro-Skyland via Barracks Row, DC Streetcar H/Benning

NEW YORK AVE

1 PIERCE ST

2

1

3

4TH ST NW

395

L ST NW

L ST NE

Story
Park

L ST NE

2ND ST NE

3RD ST NE

4TH ST NE

5TH ST NE

6TH ST NE

A

K ST NE

K ST NE

NEW JERSEY AVE NW

NORTH CAPITOL ST

I ST NE

SEE MAP 2

H ST NE

DC STREETCAR

7

MASSACHUSETTS AVE NW

H ST NW

3RD ST NW

395

G ST NW

G PL NE

1ST ST NE

G ST NE

B

G ST NW

F ST NW

1ST ST NW

NEW JERSEY AVE NW

3

F ST NE

F ST NE

5TH ST NE

Union
Station
4

**Union
Station**
5

Judiciary
Square
M

E ST NW

17

16

6

E ST NE

Columbus
Circle

LOUISIANA AVE NW

Lower
Senate
Park

1ST ST NE

MASSACHUSETTS AVE NE

D ST NE

C

C ST NW

3RD ST NW

395

15

Upper
Senate
Park

DELAWARE AVE NE

2ND ST NE

3RD ST NE

4TH ST NE

C ST NE

Stanton
Park

6TH ST NE

CONSTITUTION AVE NW

CONSTITUTION AVE NE

PENNSYLVANIA AVE NW

**Supreme Court of
the United States**
20

A ST NE

5TH ST NE

D

**National
Mall**

SEE MAP 1

Capitol
Reflecting
Pool

**U.S.
Capitol**
18

**CAPITOL
HILL**

EAST CAPITOL ST

**Library of
Congress**
19

21

A ST SE

MARYLAND AVE SW

22

INDEPENDENCE AVE SW

INDEPENDENCE AVE SE

3RD ST SW

1ST ST SW

SOUTH CAPITOL ST

1ST ST SE

2ND ST SE

PENNSYLVANIA AVE SE

24

26
27
28

Seward
Square

E

C ST SW

WASHINGTON AVE SW

C ST SW

25

4TH ST SE

5TH ST SE

6TH ST SE

Federal
Center SW
M

D ST SW
M

2ND ST SW

395

D ST SW

Spirit of
Justice Park

NEW JERSEY AVE SE

Capitol
South
M

23

Folger
Park

3RD ST SE

D ST SE

E ST SW

E ST SW

E ST SE

Marion Park

F

0   300 yds

0   300 m

DISTANCE ACROSS MAP
Approximate: 1.6 mi or 2.6 km

G ST SW

DUDDINGTON PL

VIRGINIA AVE SE

695

F ST SE

SOUTH CAROLINA AVE SE

5TH ST SE

Garfield
Park

SEE MAP 8

SIGHTS

- **5** **B3** Union Station
- **18** **D2** U.S. Capitol
- **19** **D2** Library of Congress
- **20** **D2** Supreme Court of the United States

RESTAURANTS

- **7** **B3** Ethiopic
- **10** **B5** Thamee
- **14** **B5** Maketto
- **15** **C1** Charlie Palmer Steak
- **24** **E3** Pete's Diner
- **26** **E3** Good Stuff Eatery
- **27** **E3** We, the Pizza
- **30** **E4** Market Lunch
- **33** **E4** Acqua Al 2
- **35** **E4** Bullfrog Bagels
- **39** **F4** CHIKO
- **40** **F4** Ambar
- **41** **F4** Pineapple and Pearls
- **42** **F4** Rose's Luxury

NIGHTLIFE

- **9** **B4** Copycat Co.
- **12** **B5** H Street Country Club
- **13** **B5** Hill Prince
- **23** **E2** Bullfeathers
- **28** **E3** Tune Inn
- **29** **E3** Mr. Henry's
- **32** **E4** Harold Black

ARTS AND CULTURE

- **2** **A5** Logan Fringe Arts Space
- **4** **B2** National Postal Museum
- **11** **B5** Atlas Performing Arts Center
- **21** **D3** Folger Theatre
- **22** **E1** U.S. Botanic Garden

RECREATION

- **6** **B2** DC Ducks

SHOPS

- **1** **A3** REI Washington DC Flagship
- **8** **B4** Solid State Books
- **31** **E4** Eastern Market
- **34** **E4** Capitol Hill Books
- **36** **E4** East City Bookshop
- **37** **E4** Labyrinth Games & Puzzles
- **38** **E4** Hill's Kitchen
- **43** **F4** Summit to Soul

HOTELS

- **3** **B2** Phoenix Park Hotel
- **16** **C2** Liaison Capitol Hill
- **17** **C2** Kimpton the George
- **25** **E3** Capitol Hill Hotel

© MOON.COM

Sights

TOP EXPERIENCE

✪ U.S. Capitol

While this imposing white neoclassical dome is visible for miles, rising 288 feet into the Washington skyline, the U.S. Capitol, where Congress makes laws—or not, but who's keeping track?—is worth seeing up close.

If you plan ahead, it's relatively easy to take the free, 45-minute guided tour of the Capitol, either by contacting the office of your senator or representative or by reserving tickets online through the U.S. Capitol Visitor Center (1st St. SE and E. Capitol St. NE, 202/226-8000, www.visitthecapitol.gov). (For more information on tours, see *Booking a Tour of the Capitol* on page 108.)

The tour is the only way to see some of the Capitol's historic areas that are still in use. The highlight is the rotunda, the 96-foot-wide circular room under the dome that connects the House and Senate sides of the Capitol. Look up to see the magnificent fresco *The Apotheosis of George Washington,* painted by Italian artist Constantino Brumidi in 1865, depicting the first president as a god-like figure. (Want to go a little higher? It's possible to tour the top of the dome, if you're accompanied by a member of Congress. You'll climb 300 spiraling steps to get an up-close look at the dome and

rotunda of the U.S. Capitol dome

an expansive view from an exterior walkway. It's hard to nab a spot, but it's worth asking when you request a tour of the Capitol.)

The tour also takes visitors directly underneath the rotunda, to the crypt, with 40 Doric columns supporting the dome and a star marking the spot from which the city's quadrants and streets are laid out. The architects intended for George Washington to be buried under the star, though he chose to remain at home at Mount Vernon. Another stop is the statuary hall, where Congress hosts the luncheon for the newly inaugurated president. It contains 35 statues from the Capitol's collection of 100 influential Americans, two from every state; the remainder are located throughout the rotunda, crypt, and visitor center.

The visitor center, underneath the Capitol's east plaza, is open to the public and contains historical artifacts and exhibits about the history of Congress. The visitor center has two gift shops on the upper level with exclusive Capitol merchandise, as well as a large cafeteria (8:30am-4pm Mon.-Sat.) on the lower level, where you can try the famous Senate Bean Soup, which has been served in Senate dining rooms every day since the early 1900s.

All visitors must pass through airport-style security to enter the visitor center; expect waits up to 45 minutes during peak tourist season. Leave yourself plenty of time—your tour won't wait for you. (Tip: Visit the Capitol after you've toured the Library of Congress. From the LOC, there's an underground tunnel leading to the U.S. Capitol Visitor

Center, with lines that are often shorter than at the main entrance.)

The Capitol is nestled in a 58-acre park between Constitution Avenue NW and Independence Avenue SE at 1st Street, though the entire U.S. Capitol grounds cover about 270 acres. On the west side of the Capitol, explore the verdant grounds and see the dome and Capitol Reflecting Pool. To access the grounds, head southwest on Delaware Avenue NE through the Lower and Upper Senate Parks, and just keep heading toward the dome. **MAP 3:** U.S. Capitol Visitor Center, 1st St. SE and E. Capitol St. NE, 202/226-8000, www.visitthecapitol.gov; 8:30am-4:30pm Mon.-Sat.; grounds 24 hours daily

NEARBY:

- Get yourself a Reader Identification Card and cozy up in the Main Reading Room of the Library of Congress (page 108).
- Visit the Supreme Court of the United States, where you can even watch oral arguments if court is in session (page 109).
- Sink your teeth into a burger from Good Stuff Eatery (page 111).

BOOKING A TOUR OF THE CAPITOL

It's much easier to schedule a tour of the U.S. Capitol than the White House, though you'll still want to plan ahead. There are two options for public tours.

Option 1: Schedule a free, guided tour through the U.S. Capitol Visitor Center online (www.visitthecapitol. gov), up to three months in advance. Generally, the 45-minute tours depart every 10 minutes during opening hours. Schedule your tour at least a few weeks in advance, especially if you're traveling in the spring and summer, but same-day passes are sometimes available at the information desk on the visitor center's lower level. On the tour, you'll see the crypt, rotunda, and statuary hall.

U.S. Capitol Visitor Center

Option 2: Contact your senator or representative to schedule a tour led by a staff member or intern in the office. Visit www.senate.gov/senators/contact or www.house.gov/representatives/find for contact information, and contact the office as far in advance as possible. While these tours may be harder to get, they have advantages, including smaller groups as well as the possibility of seeing some areas of the Capitol that are not usually open to the public. In addition, the office can get you passes to enter the Senate or House gallery to see Congress in action. (International visitors can inquire about gallery passes at the House and Senate Appointment Desks in the visitor center.)

For more information, including details on exhibits at the visitor center and items you cannot bring through security, visit www.visitthecapitol.gov.

- Head to friendly Pete's Diner for breakfast or lunch (page 114).
- Hang out with the locals at Tune Inn, one of DC's last remaining dive bars (page 116).
- Stop into Bullfeathers for a cold beer and listen in on political gossip (page 117).
- Attend one of Shakespeare's plays at Folger Theatre (page 119).

Library of Congress

For voracious readers, there's no better souvenir than the Library of Congress Reader Identification Card, your key to the largest library in the world. You can register for your card in person with government identification; it will provide access to the library's Main Reading Room, where you can read, write, reflect, or dig into some of the 150 million books, recordings, photographs, and other materials in the collections with the help of the expert librarians.

Even without the card, you can visit the library's public rooms and exhibits, which occupy three buildings. Most of the must-see exhibits are located in the Thomas Jefferson Building, the magnificent main structure completed in 1897, and the entrance to the complex; it connects to the James Madison Memorial Building and the John Adams Building, which contain specialized reading rooms.

Library of Congress

Free, one-hour **guided tours** (hourly on the half hour, 10:30am-3:30pm Mon.-Fri., 10:30am-2:30pm Sat.) of the Thomas Jefferson Building are available, or you can download a self-guided tour booklet or pick one up at the information desks inside. Thomas Jefferson Building highlights include the handwritten Giant Bible of Mainz (circa 1452-1453), the first map to use the word "America" (circa 1507), and a replica of Jefferson's personal library, containing the 6,000-plus books he sold to the government after the British burned the Library of Congress in 1814. To see what else is on view from the library's collections, visit www.loc.gov/exhibits.

From the Library of Congress, you can access the **U.S. Capitol Visitor Center** (1st St. and E. Capitol St. SE) via underground tunnel. This entry to the U.S. Capitol often has a shorter wait time than the main entrance.

MAP 3: 10 1st St. SE, 202/707-8000, www.loc.gov; 8:30am-4:30pm Mon.-Sat.

Supreme Court of the United States

The Supreme Court of the United States is the highest authority on the law in the land, and yet even today, you can't watch the proceedings on television. (Who says newspapers are obsolete?) If you're visiting Washington DC while court is in session, you can watch the oral arguments in person at 10am and 1pm. (Check online for the court calendar.) Two lines for first-come, first-served seating at the 10am argument begin forming around 8am, earlier for major, headline cases; you can choose to wait for seating for the entire argument, or to pop in for three minutes.

Even when court is not in session, the building is open to the public via the main steps. While the Supreme Court does not offer guided tours, you can nonetheless take advantage

Supreme Court of the United States

of 30-minute, docent-led lectures about the Supreme Court and the architecture of the building, available every 30 minutes 9:30am-3:30pm on weekdays when court is not in session, and after court adjourns at 3pm when in session. You're free to explore most of the first and ground floors, where you'll find busts of every former chief justice, as well as special exhibits.

MAP 3: 1 1st St. NE, 202/479-3030, www.supremecourt.gov; 9am-4:30pm Mon.-Fri., visitor access may change when court is in session

Union Station

If you're traveling to Washington DC via Amtrak, you'll pass through Union Station, the city's major railroad station, which opened in 1908.

The three-level transportation hub (and Amtrak's second-busiest station in the country) is worth a visit to explore the beaux arts architecture designed by Daniel Burnham, architect of the Flatiron Building in New York City. On the outside, you'll recognize the neoclassical arches reminiscent of the Arch of Constantine in Rome. Inside the 96-foot-high Main Hall, beautifully restored again in 2012-2016 following an earthquake, soaring white granite arches inlaid with 23-karat gold leaf welcome about 40 million visitors and travelers each year.

In addition to providing access to Amtrak, Metro, local and national bus services, and several city tours, including DC Ducks (866/754-5039, www.dcducks.com; $28-42), Union Station contains dozens of casual and fast-food restaurants and shops on the departures level as well as in the basement food court.

MAP 3: 50 Massachusetts Ave. NE, 202/289-1908, www.unionstationdc.com; food court 6am-9pm Mon.-Fri., 9am-9pm Sat., 7am-6pm Sun., retail 10am-9pm Mon.-Sat., noon-6pm Sun.

Union Station

Restaurants

PRICE KEY

$	Entrees less than $15
$$	Entrees $15-25
$$$	Entrees more than $25

CLASSIC AMERICAN
Good Stuff Eatery $

Don't feel guilty giving in to your burger craving. Spike Mendelsohn, of the fourth season of Bravo's *Top Chef*, along with his restaurateur family, founded this fast-casual chain committed to supporting local farms. Sink your teeth into the best burgers in DC—like the Prez Obama Burger (farm-raised beef topped with Roquefort and bacon) or the Michelle Melt (made with free-range turkey)—as well as hand-cut fries and a toasted marshmallow shake that tastes like the real thing. Get your fix at the Capitol Hill flagship or in Georgetown (3291 M St. NW, 202/337-4663).

MAP 3: 303 Pennsylvania Ave. SE, 202/543-8222, www.goodstuffeatery.com; 11am-10pm Mon.-Sat.

NEW AMERICAN
Pineapple and Pearls $$$

Critics have bestowed many accolades upon this fine-dining establishment by Aaron Silverman. It's one of three regional restaurants to earn two stars from Michelin. The $325-per-head, 13-course tasting menu and beverage pairing is served in the understated dining room or at the chef's counter, or you can dine at the bar for $150 pp (beverages not included). The coveted reservations are released on the first of the month for the following month; they're readily available early in the week, or a few weeks in advance for Saturday night. Nearby, Little Pearl (921 Pennsylvania Ave. SE, 202/618-1868, www.littlepearldc.com; 8am-2:30pm, 5:30pm-10pm Tue.-Sat., 8am-2:30pm, 5:30pm-9pm Sun.) serves a more casual $49 pp dinner menu as well as à la carte snacks, light bites, and cocktails.

MAP 3: 715 8th St. SE, 202/595-7375, www.pineappleandpearls.com; reservations from 5pm-9:30pm daily, phone line noon-4pm Tue.-Fri.

Rose's Luxury $$$

It's tough to get a table at the (generally) no-reservations Rose's Luxury, an Aaron Silverman Michelin-starred restaurant that's credited with making DC a dining destination. However, the casual but creative American cuisine is worth the inevitable wait in line to put your name on the list; you can also try for a limited number of same-day reservations at 9am daily or reserve group dinners or special events in advance. Dine with fellow foodies and order several plates to share, including at least one pasta.

MAP 3: 717 8th St. SE, 202/580-8889, www.rosesluxury.com; 5pm-10pm Mon.-Sat.

STEAK AND SEAFOOD
✪ Charlie Palmer Steak $$$

Want to dine like the movers and shakers of Capitol Hill? Head to this white-tablecloth restaurant just a few blocks from the Capitol.

The elegant dining room is packed with lobbyists who lunch on USDA-certified Angus steaks and local seafood—and you'll likely spot a member of Congress or two, as well. Whatever your politics, you can't go wrong when choosing the wine, because every bottle on the extensive list is American.

MAP 3: 101 Constitution Ave. NW, 202/547-8100, www.charliepalmer.com; 11:30am-10pm Mon.-Fri., 5pm-10:30pm Sat.

Charlie Palmer Steak

ASIAN
CHIKO $$

Starving after a day of sightseeing? You can't do much better for the price than CHIKO'S extremely filling, extremely flavorful Chinese-Korean bowls ($15-18). The Orange-ish Chicken, with crispy chicken and candied mandarins, is tasty; there are tons of options for vegetarians and gluten-free diners, too. The better deal, however, is the reservations-only kitchen counter, where just a few diners each night can enjoy an extravagant tasting

menu inspired by royal dynasties for $55 pp. The Capitol Hill location serves dinner only, but lunch is available at the second location in Dupont Circle (2029 P St. NW, 202/331-3040; 11am-10pm Sun.-Thurs., 11am-11pm Fri.-Sat.).

MAP 3: 423 8th St. SE, 202/558-9934, www.chikodc.com; 5pm-10pm Sun.-Thurs., 5pm-midnight Fri.-Sat.

Maketto $$

Maketto—part restaurant, part café, and part store—is the cool kid on H Street NE, with clean, minimalist spaces and lots of natural light. The ground floor restaurant serves Cambodian and Taiwanese fare—noodle soups, rice bowls, pork *bao* (stuffed buns), and fried chicken—for lunch and dinner, as well as Sunday dim sum brunch. Upstairs, the naturally lit café buzzes morning to evening with locals on their laptops, enjoying Vigilante Coffee, snacks, and the much-Instagrammed matcha latte, served in a picture-perfect ceramic bowl. Before you leave, browse an edited selection of streetwear and accessories from labels like Comme des Garçons and Adidas designer collaborations at the retail shop by the entrance.

MAP 3: 1351 H St. NE, 202/627-0325, www.maketto1351.com; 7am-10pm Mon.-Thurs., 7am-11pm Fri.-Sat., 7am-5pm Sun.

BALKAN
Ambar $$

Think you've tried every international flavor in DC? Ambar offers something unique: authentic Balkan cuisine, with a focus on simply prepared but high-quality meats and

Ambar

vegetables. (It really is authentic; the sister restaurant is in Belgrade, Serbia.) Choose from dozens of small plates, including charcuterie and cheeses, spreads and flatbreads, and grilled meat and seafood—or try them all with unlimited small plates and house cocktails for $49 per person during dinner or $39 per person during brunch. The beverage list features wines from Armenia, Croatia, Macedonia, and Slovenia, among others, plus cocktails and flights using *rakia*, a fruit brandy popular in Eastern Europe.

MAP 3: 523 8th St. SE, 202/813-3039, www.ambarrestaurant.com; 11am-2pm and 4pm-10pm Mon.-Thurs., 11am-2pm and 4pm-11pm Fri., 10am-11pm Sat., 10am-10pm Sun.

BURMESE
Thamee $$

Burma or Myanmar? There's no debate. This cool kid of the dining scene is one of the best reasons to head to the Atlas District—and it's the only full-service restaurant in DC serving the cuisine of the diverse Southeast Asian country. Led by a mother-daughter duo, the cozy, minimalist spot showcases authentic but modern street food you'd find in the markets of Yangon/Rangoon, like crispy wonton cups, noodles, and whole steamed fish or sugarcane duck to share. Bonus: The bill includes a 4 percent "wellness charge" to cover health insurance for the employees.

MAP 3: 1320 H St. NE, 202/750-6529, www.thamee.com; 5:30pm-10pm Mon., 5:30pm-10pm Wed.-Fri., 10:30am-2:30pm, 5:30pm-10pm Sat.-Sun., closed Tue.

ETHIOPIAN
Ethiopic $$

The H Street Corridor's Ethiopic ably competes with the restaurants in Shaw's Little Ethiopia by offering classic cooking with an elegant ambience more suitable for finer dining. Named for the group of languages spoken in Ethiopia and Eritrea, the restaurant is known for the superb quality of meat used in the *tibs* (sautéed meat, usually beef or lamb) and *kitfo* (spicy minced beef usually served raw), as well as their selection of Ethiopian beers and wines.

MAP 3: 401 H St. NE, 202/675-2066, www.ethiopicrestaurant.com; 5pm-10pm Tues.-Thurs., noon-10pm Fri.-Sun.

ITALIAN
Acqua Al 2 $$$

Ask any Hill rat, including House Minority Leader Nancy Pelosi, where to find the best Italian food in DC, and they'll point you to this cozy, brick-walled Eastern Market eatery inspired by a restaurant in Florence of the same name. (Yes, there's a chance you'll see Pelosi when you visit.) Can't decide between rigatoni or a perfectly cooked strip steak with arugula? Go with a group and try a few *assaggios*, chef's tastings of 3-5 salads, pastas, steaks, or desserts, to sample the best of the menu.

MAP 3: 212 7th St. SE, 202/525-4375, www.acquaal2.com; 5:30pm-10:30pm Mon., 11:30am-2:30pm and 5:30pm-10:30pm Tues.-Thurs., 11:30am-2:30pm and 5:30pm-11:30pm Fri.-Sat., 11:30am-2:30pm and 5:30pm-10:30pm Sun.

BREAKFAST AND BRUNCH
Bullfrog Bagels $

The house-baked bagels and bialys at Bullfrog Bagels are slightly pricier than your average bagel shop, starting at $3 for one with plain cream cheese and going up to $8-plus for house-smoked salmon or Baltimore-style beef brisket. But the ingredients are fresh and the sandwiches are filling fuel for a day browsing the nearby Eastern Market artisans. The tiny shop has a line on weekends, but it moves quickly; there's plenty of seating upstairs, including a few chairs on the sunny balcony overlooking the market. There's another location nearby on H Street NE.

MAP 3: 317 7th St. SE, 202/494-5615, www.bullfrogbagels.com; 7am-2pm Mon.-Fri., 8am-2pm Sat.-Sun.

Market Lunch $

Since 1979, this Eastern Market counter-service vendor has been serving some of the best crab cakes in DC—along with breakfast plates and Benedicts, burgers, and yummy blueberry buckwheat pancakes, all prepared with locally sourced ingredients. Make sure you have money before you get in the long, snaking line during Sunday brunch hours, because it's cash only. Enjoy your food at the communal table (if you don't mind dining surrounded by people waiting in line) or take it to one of the tables in the market's North Hall.

MAP 3: 225 7th St. SE, 202/547-8444, www.marketlunchdc.com; 7:30am-2:30pm Tues.-Fri., 8am-3pm Sat., 9am-3pm Sun.; cash only

Pete's Diner $

An easy walk from the sights on Capitol Hill and the National Mall, Pete's is perhaps the most authentic diner in the District. Former Speaker of the House John Boehner visited almost every morning for eggs and sausage served by the friendly staff; Hill staffers and

food trucks near the Washington Monument

Washington has the third-highest cost of living in the United States—and it's getting more and more expensive to dine out, as Michelin-starred tasting menus can top $150 per person and $15 cocktails are the norm. However, it's possible to enjoy DC's culinary scene on a budget, without sacrificing flavor or a local experience.

Some of DC's most famous flavors are among the best budget eats. Ben's Chili Bowl (page 153) is a late-night must, but you can go anytime for the $6 half-smoke (spicy half-pork/half-beef sausage) with chili, $7.50 salad bowl, and cheap, hearty breakfasts. For something lighter, José Andrés's local chain Beefsteak (page 135) serves veggie bowls under $10, plus the beefsteak tomato "burger" for $5.

For a higher-end but still budget-friendly option, Busboys and Poets (page 158) serves clean, sustainable meals in several locations, with sandwiches and salads ranging $10-15, less for breakfast. A burger, fries, and shake at Good Stuff Eatery (page 111) will set you back $15-20, but you won't be hungry for a while. Pizzas start at $9 at 2 Amys (page 245). If you want a crab cake, head to Market Lunch (page 114), the Eastern Market counter where the $16 platter comes with two sides.

When sightseeing, food trucks are some of your best options for a reasonably priced gourmet lunch. You'll find the largest gatherings of trucks around the major museums daily, as well Farragut Square, L'Enfant Plaza, and Union Station. For the truck list and daily map, visit www.foodtruckfiesta.com.

residents continue to fill the counter and booths for cheap breakfast platters and pancakes, as well as grilled cheese, patty melts, and simple salads at lunch. Skip your usual Starbucks; Pete's has great coffee, too.

MAP 3: 212 2nd St. SE, 202/544-7335; 6am-3pm Mon.-Fri., 7am-3pm Sat.-Sun.

PIZZA
We, the Pizza $

Whether you order by the slice ($4) or whole pie, your purchase at this fast-casual pizza joint helmed by *Top Chef*'s Spike Mendelsohn supports community organizations that provide nutritional and educational services to local families. You can't go wrong with cheese or pepperoni, but

For the Greek in Us, cooked Sicilian-style in a cast-iron skillet and topped with feta and veggies, is a fresh alternative. Pair your pie with a homemade soda or $5 beer.

MAP 3: 305 Pennsylvania Ave. SE, 202/791-0168, www.wethepizza.com; 11am-10pm daily

Nightlife

COCKTAIL BARS AND LOUNGES
Copycat Co.
Tired of bartenders getting too creative with your cocktail? Go to Copycat Co. for a long drinks list that draws from the canon of classic cocktail recipe books, as well as for Chinese street food dishes like pot stickers, skewers, and pork *bao* (stuffed buns), which are served until late. Thanks to its industrial, ground-floor kitchen and counter, along with a moody upstairs bar with jade accents and dark lighting, you'll feel like you've been transported to a hip, hidden spot in Hong Kong. Owner Devin Gong is a former bartender at José Andrés's Barmini.

MAP 3: 1110 H St. NE, 202/241-1952, www.copycatcompany.com; 5pm-2am Sun.-Thurs., 5pm-3am Fri.-Sat.

Harold Black
Harold Black is a sleek, intimate speakeasy with a few rules—like no flash photography if you want to Instagram your drink, and a note on the menu encouraging you to keep your voice down. But don't worry, you don't need a secret password to enter; just make a reservation online via OpenTable. Located above Acqua Al 2, this slightly hidden lounge features cocktails inspired by the classics, plus snacks like cheese, charcuterie, and sandwiches.

MAP 3: 212 7th St. SE, no phone, www.haroldblackdc.com; 5:30pm-12:30am Tues.-Thurs., 5:30pm-1:30am Fri.-Sat.

Hill Prince
Named for the winner of the 1950 Preakness Stakes, Hill Prince is just a bar—in the best way. You won't find expensive, gimmicky drinks or a complicated reservation system; rather, the brick-walled row house and courtyard with a hint of equestrian decor has a perfectly simple menu of classic cocktails and an interesting selection of beer, wine, and snacks, with everything priced $10 or less. Expect a lively crowd ages late-20s to 40s on weekends.

MAP 3: 1337 H St. NE, 202/399-1337, www.hillprince.com; 5pm-midnight Tues.-Thurs., 5pm-late Fri., 3pm-late Sat., 3pm-10pm Sun.

SPORTS BARS AND DIVES
✪ Tune Inn
It's one of DC's remaining true dive bars, and an institution: Tune Inn has been serving beer and beloved pub grub to Capitol Hill's bigwigs and residents since 1947. While prices have increased since the bar

Mr. Henry's

opened, the skinny space with walls full of memorabilia and taxidermy remains many locals' favorite spot for cheap pitchers of beer and fried food, including fried pickles, fried mushrooms, and a beer-battered burger.

MAP 3: 331 Pennsylvania Ave. SE, 202/543-2725; 8am-2am Sun.-Thurs., 8am-3am Fri.-Sat.

Bullfeathers

Hill staffers and lobbyists are known for making deals and getting involved in scandals at Bullfeathers, named for President Teddy Roosevelt's favorite expression of frustration. Located close to the House of Representatives offices on Capitol Hill, this modern pub is a good place to stop for a cold beer ($4-12) after visiting the Capitol or Library of Congress. While you're unlikely to see members of Congress downing martinis at lunch these days, you are likely to hear political gossip from House staffers.

MAP 3: 410 1st St. SE, 202/484-0228, www.dcbullfeathers.com; 11am-11pm Mon.-Fri., noon-8pm Sat.

H Street Country Club

If you'd like to burn off the beers as you're drinking them, H Street Country Club has an indoor, nine-hole mini golf course ($9 pp per round) as well as shuffleboard and Skee-Ball. This spot draws a young crowd for happy hour specials, like $5 margaritas and two tacos for $3. While the DC-themed golf course provides the atmosphere in this grubby hangout, it also boasts the largest roof deck in the neighborhood, a good spot for those tequila specials in nice weather.

MAP 3: 1335 H St. NE, 202/399-4722, www.hstreetcountryclub.com; 4pm-1am Mon.-Thurs., 4pm-3am Fri., 11:30am-3am Sat., 11:30am-1am Sun.

LGBTQ

✪ Mr. Henry's

Since 1966, Mr. Henry's has been a Capitol Hill institution, a pub where everyone is welcome—including, and especially, the gay community. Founded by Henry Yaffe, Mr. Henry's has operated continuously with few changes to the decor or menu, until new management added healthier options in 2014. The pub launched the career of Roberta Flack, a local teacher who sang in the upstairs lounge. In addition to reliable pub fare and happy hour specials, enjoy jazz, bluegrass, and soul upstairs several nights a week.

MAP 3: 601 Pennsylvania Ave. SE, 202/546-8412, www.mrhenrysdc. com; 11:15am-midnight Mon.-Fri., 10am-midnight Sat.-Sun.

Arts and Culture

MUSEUMS

National Postal Museum

If you think a postage stamp museum sounds boring, you've never visited the Smithsonian Institution's National Postal Museum, which has one of the largest collections of postal paraphernalia in the world, including the world's first postage stamp. The exhibitions examine the history of mail and the impact of the U.S. Postal Service on American communities—much more influential than you might think. The William H. Gross Stamp Gallery is visually stunning. The building originally housed Washington DC's main post office for nearly a decade, and now it contains several vintage mail planes, coaches, and trucks.

MAP 3: 2 Massachusetts Ave. NE, 202/633-5555, http://postalmuseum.si/ edu; 10am-5:30pm daily; free

United States Botanic Garden

Located on the grounds of the U.S. Capitol, the United States Botanic Garden is an oasis loved by locals looking for an escape from a rough work day on Capitol Hill. The living museum is one of the oldest botanical gardens in North America, established by Congress in 1820, and one of the largest, with 65,000 plants for study and display. Inside, plants are organized by climate (Tropics, Mediterranean, Southern Exposure) as well as type; the walkway between Medicinal Plants and World Deserts is home to fascinating poisonous specimens. Outside, the National Garden highlights regional plants, while idyllic **Bartholdi Park** (dawn-dusk daily) features a fountain designed by Frédéric Auguste Bartholdi, who designed the Statue of Liberty.

MAP 3: 100 Maryland Ave. SW, 202/225-8333, www.usbg.gov; 10am-5pm daily; free

THEATER, MUSIC, AND DANCE

Atlas Performing Arts Center

H Street NE between 2nd Street NE and 15th Street NE has been nicknamed the Atlas District due to the Atlas Performing Arts Center. The

United States Botanic Garden

art deco movie theater was built in 1938, although the theater and the neighborhood were devastated during the 1968 riots. Following a complete restoration, the theater reopened in 2006 with 59,000 square feet of performance, rehearsal, and office space; the neighborhood has since experienced significant growth. Today, the center showcases theater, music, dance, and film, with a focus on cross-cultural performances as well as fringe works.

MAP 3: 1333 H St. NE, 202/399-7993, www.atlasarts.org; box office 11am-2pm, 3-pm-6pm Mon.-Fri. and two hours before events; tickets from $30

Folger Theatre

Since 1991, the Folger Theatre has performed the Bard's beloved plays as well as lesser-known works. Recent productions have included *Antony and Cleopatra* and *The Winter's Tale*. The 250-seat Elizabethan-style theater regularly hosts music performances, poetry readings, and lectures as well. The theater is also home to the **Folger Shakespeare Library** (10am-5pm Mon.-Sat., noon-5pm Sun.; free), which boasts the world's largest collection of the Bard's works. Serious fans will want to explore the library's exhibits, which include one of the first editions of Shakespeare's plays on display with a digital touch screen to allow you to look inside the precious 15th-century manuscript, as well as books, playbills, and Renaissance art, costumes, and instruments.

MAP 3: 202 E. Capitol St. SE, 202/544-4600, box office 202/544-7077, www.folger.edu; box office noon-5pm Mon.-Sat. and one hour before events; tickets $35-80

Logan Fringe Arts Space

After taking over venues throughout the city for nearly a decade, DC's annual Fringe Festival got a permanent home in the Atlas District in

2015. The Logan Fringe Arts Space is one of the city's most innovative arts venues, with a modern, 200-seat theater, art gallery, indoor bar, outdoor beer garden, and more. The **Capital Fringe Festival** (admission $7, tickets $17) takes place every July, but you can see encores of popular shows as well as other cutting-edge theater, music, and dance performances throughout the year.

Folger Theatre

MAP 3: 1358 Florida Ave. NE, 866/811-4111, www.capitalfringe.org

Festivals and Events

Capital Fringe

For more than a decade, DC's Fringe Festival has enticed audiences to all corners of the city for more than 100 performances, often news-driven and thought-provoking, with many by local artists. The festival is headquartered at Capital Fringe's new Atlas District venue, Logan Fringe Arts Space, which has a black box theater and bar.

Atlas District/Citywide: 1358 Florida Ave. NE, 866/811-4111, www. capitalfringe.org; July; festival button $7, tickets $17/show, multi-show passes $30-320

H Street Festival

Get to know the vibrant Atlas District during the H Street Festival, covering 11 blocks of H Street NE northeast of Union Station. The festival features several stages showcasing local musicians, fashion, and family-friendly entertainment, as well as the neighborhood's diverse flavors.

Atlas District: www.hstreetfestival. org; mid-Sept.; free

Recreation

TOURS

DC Ducks

Climb aboard a DC Duck, part tour bus and part boat, for a unique tour of the city by land and water with an entertaining captain to guide you. Departing from Union Station, the tour covers the major sights in 90 minutes, including the U.S. Capitol and the monuments and museums on the National Mall, before plunging into the Potomac River. The vehicles are restored amphibious military carriers, which were once used to carry supplies to ships at Pearl Harbor during World War II. Tours operate daily from mid-March through October, except Memorial Day, Independence Day, and the Marine Corps Marathon in October.

MAP 3: 50 Massachusetts Ave. NE, 866/754-5039, www.dcducks.com; $42 adults, $32 children 12 and under, discounts available online

Shops

BOOKS

Capitol Hill Books

This two-story Eastern Market bookstore is crammed floor to ceiling with used and rare books of all kinds—but don't expect to get lost in the stacks browsing alone, because it's impossible to avoid contact with other people, especially on Sundays when the market is busy. The fiction books are mostly alphabetical by author; others are organized by category, with a Mystery Room, Business Closet, Beats Corner, and foreign language books in the bathroom.

MAP 3: 657 C St. SE, 202/544-1621, www.capitolhillbooks-dc.com; 10am-8pm Mon.-Fri., 9am-8pm Sat., 9am-7pm Sun.

East City Bookshop

The service is excellent at this independent bookstore, where the chatty staff can make suggestions or place special orders. And many books have notes scribbled by staff members so you can find a recommended new read. The selection spans politics and history to bestsellers and children's books, with many already-signed copies by authors who have visited the store for readings and book signings.

MAP 3: 645 Pennsylvania Ave. SE, 202/290-1636, www.eastcitybookshop.com; 10am-8pm Mon.-Sat., 11am-6pm Sun.

Solid State Books

If you'd rather find your next book than spend your evening at crowded, trendy bar, Solid State Books has all the books you've been wanting to read—and it's open until midnight

Hill's Kitchen

the National Park Service experts in the Adventure Station (noon-7pm daily), or meet fellow runners. The store has a 1,052-square-foot La Colombe (7am-7pm daily), the Philadelphia-based coffee roastery known for draft lattes.

MAP 3: 201 M St. NE, 202/543-2040, www.rei.com; 10am-9pm Mon.-Sat., 11am-7pm Sun.

Summit to Soul

This small Barracks Row shop stocks an impressive selection of high-end athletic apparel and accessories for women and men. In addition to apparel by Beyond Yoga, Onzie, and Spiritual Gangster, browse water bottles, yoga mats, sunscreen—everything you might need for an impromptu bike ride or yoga class.

MAP 3: 727 8th St. SE, 202/450-1832, www.summittosoul.com; 11am-7pm Tues.-Fri., 10am-6pm Sat., 11am-5pm Sun.

on weekends. The independent shop and coffee bar stocks the latest bestsellers, with an eye to what left-of-center urbanites are reading. Check the website for author readings and book club events; book club selections are 10 percent off until the meeting date.

MAP 3: 600 H St. NE, 202/897-4201, www.solidstatebooksdc.com; 8am-10pm Sun.-Thurs., 8am-midnight Fri.-Sat.

OUTDOOR GEAR
REI Washington DC Flagship

The Beatles played their first concert in the United States in DC's Uline Arena, which was the site of inaugural balls and major speeches and athletic events throughout history. Now, the building is the DC flagship location of REI. Even without the history, the 51,000-square-foot store is a destination, where you can learn skills like bike maintenance and adjustment or knot tying, plan an excursion to one of the national parks with help from

HOME AND GIFTS
✪ Hill's Kitchen

Hill's Kitchen is a destination for edible goodies either made in the District or inspired by DC's flavors: Embitterment cocktail bitters, True grenadine and tonic syrup, Gordy's Pickle Jar pickles and brine, and Uncle Brutha hot sauce, which was originally sold at Eastern Market before going national. This row house near Eastern Market is the place to pick up U.S. state and monument cookie cutters and dish towels, and anything else you might need for your kitchen.

MAP 3: 713 D St. SE, 202/543-1997, www.hillskitchen.com; 10am-6pm Tues.-Sat., 10am-5pm Sun.

Labyrinth Games & Puzzles

This quirky store sells classic and unique games, puzzles, and mazes for every interest under the sun. (I was intrigued by Marrying Mr. Darcy, a *Pride and Prejudice* card game in which you must attend events and improve your character to find a suitor.) The exceptionally friendly staff is happy to tell you about any game in stock, as well as the store's weekly game nights and tournaments.

MAP 3: 645 Pennsylvania Ave. SE, 202/544-1059, www. labyrinthgameshop.com; 10am-10pm Tues., 10am-9pm Wed., 10am-10pm Thurs.-Fri., 9am-9pm Sat., 10am-6pm Sun.

MARKETS

✪ Eastern Market

Eastern Market is the longest-running public market in DC. The market building, completed in 1873, has survived riots and fire, and remains an important part of local life as well as a destination for excellent food, shopping, and people-watching, especially on weekends, when it's buzzing with activity. The historic building includes South Hall, from which merchants sell produce, meat, dairy, flowers, and prepared food and baked goods, as well as North Hall, now an events space with picnic tables and an area for kids to run around. On Saturdays and Sundays, dozens of local farmers and artisans set up stands surrounding the building's exterior to sell antique and refinished furniture, art and photography, jewelry, produce, and snacks. Spend a few hours on a beautiful weekend afternoon enjoying brunch—try the crab cakes or blueberry pancakes at Market Lunch, or a strudel from the bakery—then browsing the vendors for unique souvenirs. For a one-of-a-kind piece of contemporary Americana, look for artist Robert Jaxson around 7th Street and C Street SE, who paints brightly colored American and DC flags and jazz scenes on pieces of wood.

MAP 3: 225 7th St. SE, 202/698-5253, www.easternmarket-dc.org; indoor market 7am-7pm Tues.-Fri., 7am-6pm Sat., 9am-5pm Sun., outdoor market 7am-6pm Sat., 9am-5pm Sun.

Dupont Circle

Map 4

Washington comes together at Dupont Circle, the traffic circle and urban park where a mix of locals—intellectuals, activists, young families, and the homeless—congregate to have a bite, play chess, protest injustice, or even say their wedding vows. The spokes of the circle lead to **abundant dining and nightlife options,** The Phillips Collection and niche galleries, and the historic center of the city's **gay culture,** with beloved gay bars and events like Capital Pride in June and the High Heel Drag Race at Halloween. With several hotels set on leafy, residential streets, blocks from the grand foreign embassies, Dupont Circle is the ideal base for experiencing DC like a local.

TOP RESTAURANTS

- Best Late-Night Dining:
  Annie's Paramount Steak House (page 133) and **Hank's Oyster Bar** (page 133)
- Best Breakfast on the Go:
  Bagels Etc. (page 135)

TOP NIGHTLIFE

- Best Place to Party During Pride:
  JR's Bar (page 137)

TOP ARTS AND CULTURE

- Oldest Modern Art Museum:
  The Phillips Collection (page 137)

TOP SHOPS

- Best Bookstore: **Kramerbooks** (page 142)
- Best Place to Buy Local:
  Shop Made in DC (page 143)

GETTING THERE AND AROUND

- Metro lines: Red
- Metro stations: Dupont Circle
- Major bus routes: DC Circulator Dupont Circle-Georgetown-Rosslyn

WYOMING AVE NW

KALORAMA HEIGHTS

24TH ST NW

23RD ST NW

COLUMBIA RD NW

TRACY PL NW

CALIFORNIA ST NW

PHELPS PL

LEROY PL NW

A

BANCROFT PL NW

SIGHTS
5	**B2**	Spanish Steps	
24	**D4**	Dupont Circle	

RESTAURANTS
3	**A5**	Lauriol Plaza	
4	**A6**	Henry's Soul Café	
7	**B3**	Bistrot du Coin	
8	**B5**	Dupont Market	
9	**B5**	The Riggsby	
16	**C6**	Annie's Paramount Steak House	
20	**D3**	Bagels Etc.	
27	**D6**	Hank's Oyster Bar	
29	**D6**	Little Serow	
30	**D6**	Sushi Taro	
35	**F4**	The Palm	

NIGHTLIFE
2	**A5**	Larry's Lounge	
6	**B3**	McClellan's Retreat	
17	**D2**	Bier Baron Tavern	
28	**D6**	JR's Bar	
37	**F5**	Heist Night Club	
39	**F6**	Quill	

ARTS AND CULTURE
11	**C3**	Hillyer Art Space	
12	**C3**	Studio Gallery	
13	**C3**	The Phillips Collection	
15	**C5**	National Museum of American Jewish Military History	
18	**D3**	The Society of the Cincinnati Anderson House	
26	**D4**	Dupont Underground	

SHOPS
14	**C4**	Tabletop	
22	**D4**	Second Story Books	
23	**D4**	Kramerbooks	
31	**E4**	Shop Made in DC	
32	**E4**	Proper Topper	
33	**E4**	Jenni Bick Custom Journals	
36	**F5**	Betsy Fisher	
38	**F5**	Brooks Brothers	

HOTELS
1	**A3**	Washington Hilton	
10	**B5**	The Kimpton Carlyle	
19	**D3**	The Fairfax at Embassy Row	
21	**D3**	The Embassy Row Hotel	
25	**D4**	The Dupont Circle Hotel	
34	**E5**	Tabard Inn	
40	**F6**	The Jefferson	

B

Spanish Steps 5

PHELPS PL

KALORAMA

22ND ST NW

21ST ST NW

FLORIDA AVE NW

HILLYER PL NW

C

MASSACHUSETTS AVE NW

FLORIDA AVE NW

22ND ST NW

HOPKINS ST NW

CHIKO

P ST NW

D

O ST NW

NEWPORT PL NW

E

0	150 yds
0	150 m

DISTANCE ACROSS MAP
Approximate: 1.1 mi or 1.8 km

Rock Creek

SEE MAP 7

N ST NW

25TH ST NW

24TH ST NW

23RD ST NW

WEST END

22ND ST NW

21ST ST NW

NEW HAMPSHIRE AVE NW

WARD PL NW

Duke Ellington Park

F

© MOON.COM

DUPONT CIRCLE WALK

TOTAL DISTANCE: 1.6 mi (2.6 km)
WALKING TIME: 40 minutes

Any tour of Dupont Circle must include the circular park that lends its name—but the neighborhood is so much more than a traffic circle. Travel beyond the spokes to explore the rich history of this northwest DC neighborhood, and get to know the eclectic residents: diplomats, aristocrats, and even homeless chess players.

1 Start with carbs. **Bagels Etc.** has the closest thing you can get to a New York bagel in DC. The cash-only shop is cheap and fast; if you don't want breakfast, get a deli sandwich or pizza bagel. Take it to go, and walk east on P Street NW for about two blocks toward Dupont Circle.

2 Go to the center of **Dupont Circle** to eat on one of the benches surrounding the beaux arts fountain, a memorial to Admiral Samuel Francis Du Pont. On the northeast side of the circle, watch chess

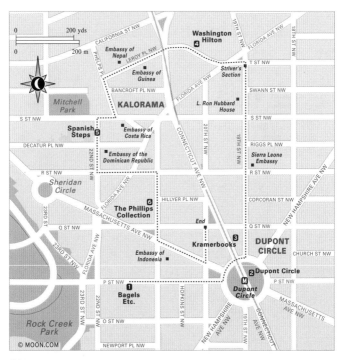

experts play—and don't be offended if you're asked to pay a small fee, because that's how some of the players make their living.

3 Head north toward Starbucks and walk half a block up Connecticut Avenue NW to **Kramerbooks.** Everyone has shopped here—including Monica Lewinsky, whose purchases were subpoenaed by Kenneth Starr to determine if she had bought gifts for President Bill Clinton. After you've browsed a bit, continue northwest to Q Street NW, where you'll turn east (right), then take a quick left to head north on 19th Street NW. Walk north about four blocks, passing the **Sierra Leone embassy.** You'll approach the **L. Ron Hubbard House** on your left, where its namesake lived when he founded the Church of Scientology in 1955.

4 Keep heading north for six blocks. The area from 19th Street eastward to 16th Street was once called **Strivers' Section.** This is where upper-middle-class African Americans, including Frederick Douglass and Langston Hughes, lived at the turn of the 20th century. Turn left at T Street NW. The **Washington Hilton** looms ahead. The curving, concrete, brutalist structure is nicknamed the Hinckley Hilton, because it's where John Hinckley Jr. shot President Reagan in 1981. Today, it's the location of the White House Correspondents' Association Dinner.

5 Continue west to Connecticut Avenue, then cross the street to Leroy Place NW and pass the **embassies of Guinea and Nepal.** Turn south (left) on Phelps Place NW and walk about two blocks; the **embassy of Costa Rica** will be ahead. Turn west (right) on S Street NW, then take a quick left to go south on 22nd Street NW. Keep your eyes peeled for the **Spanish Steps.** Meander down them and continue south on 22nd Street NW, past the **embassy of the Dominican Republic.**

6 When you reach R Street NW, turn east (left) and continue two blocks to 21st Street NW and turn south (right). You'll run into **The Phillips Collection,** America's first modern art museum, a great stopping point for a few hours. When you're ready to leave Dupont Circle, take 21st Street NW south for just over a block to Massachusetts Avenue NW toward the **Indonesian embassy,** also called the Walsh-McLean House for the wealthy owners. (How wealthy, you ask? *Washington Post* heir Edward McLean once purchased a special gift for his wife, Evalyn Walsh—the Hope Diamond.) If you're taking the Metro, walk 1.5 blocks to Q and 20th Streets NW to the station entrance. A quote from Walt Whitman's poem "The Wound-Dresser" envelops you as you enter. It was carved in the station's stone entrance in 2007 to recognize the AIDS crisis, which particularly affected this historic gay neighborhood.

Sights

Dupont Circle

Built in 1871 to honor Union Navy rear admiral Samuel Francis Du Pont, Dupont Circle is the heart of one of DC's most prestigious neighborhoods. At the center is a classical white marble fountain designed by beaux arts architect Henry Bacon and sculptor Daniel Chester French, best known for creating the Lincoln Memorial.

The park is an important rendezvous point for residents, protesters, yogis, young professionals with bagel and newspaper in hand, homeless men and women, and groups mingling over chess games at the permanent boards on the northeast side of the circle. The spokes lead to neighborhood must-sees: majestic embassies on Massachusetts Avenue, dining and shopping on Connecticut Avenue, and, during Capital Pride in June, a party on P Street.

On Sundays, head to 20th Street for the **Freshfarm Dupont Circle Market** (20th St. NW between Massachusetts Ave. and Hillyer Pl., www.freshfarm.org/dupont-circle; 8:30am-1:30pm year-round), where residents shop for local produce, meat, dairy, baked goods, and more. The market is small but robust, with options for picnics (everything from breakfast tacos and pizzas to dumplings and gourmet popsicles) and tasty souvenirs.

Dupont Circle fountain

Spanish Steps

MAP 4: Intersection of Massachusetts Ave. NW, Connecticut Ave. NW, New Hampshire Ave. NW, P St. NW, and 19th St. NW

Spanish Steps

For urban-planning geeks, Dupont Circle's Spanish Steps are worth a stop. The steps were built in 1911 during the City Beautiful movement, an urban architecture philosophy in which city planners built beautiful spaces in the inner cities of DC, Chicago, Cleveland, and Detroit to promote virtue and civic engagement. Inspired by the Spanish Steps in Rome, the steep, stone staircase leading to a small fountain is an idyllic place to enjoy your coffee and scroll through your iPhone camera roll. But, don't tell too many of your friends—Dupont Circle locals like to believe the steps, which are hidden among the embassies and homes around 22nd Street, are a secret spot. **MAP 4:** 22nd St. NW and Decatur Pl. NW

Restaurants

PRICE KEY

$	Entrees less than $15
$$	Entrees $15-25
$$$	Entrees more than $25

CLASSIC AMERICAN
The Riggsby $$

From the outside, The Riggsby at The Carlyle looks like an unassuming hotel restaurant, but inside, it's a gem. The elegant dining room with an inviting bar is our go-to for casual business meals, where you can enjoy James Beard winner Michael Schlow's supper club favorites, like roast chicken, classic Caesar salads, and raw bar selections. The bar has one of the best happy hours in town, with $6 classic cocktails served in vintage-style Nick and Nora glasses (4pm-7pm Mon.-Fri.).
MAP 4: 1731 New Hampshire Ave. NW, 202/787-1500, www.theriggsby.com; 7am-10:30pm Mon.-Fri., 8am-10:30pm Sat.-Sun.

STEAK AND SEAFOOD
The Palm $$$

The Palm is the place to be seen at lunch, especially for the politicos, journalists, and talking heads whose caricatures are painted on the walls. And you'll spot many who go nearly every day for the consistent seafood cocktails, steak salads, and burgers, along with the latest gossip in the bustling dining room.

The Riggsby

MAP 4: 1225 19th St. NW, 202/293-9091, www.thepalm.com; 11:30am-10pm Mon.-Thurs., 11:30am-10:30pm Fri., 5:30pm-10:30pm Sat., 5pm-9pm Sun.

✪ Annie's Paramount Steak House $$

After opening in 1948, this family-owned steakhouse "gained a reputation as a safe place for gay men, many of whom worked for the government and risked losing their jobs and going to jail if their sexuality were discovered," wrote long-time Washington food critic David Hagedorn when Annie's Paramount won the James Beard Foundation's America's Classics Award in 2019. Today, Annie's remains 17th Street's Cheers, where the neighborhood's gay community, office workers, and families enjoy hearty, affordable meals in a congenial atmosphere. Go early for steak-and-eggs breakfasts, go late for burgers or large salads—and go anytime on the weekends, because it's open 24 hours Friday through Sunday evening.

MAP 4: 1609 17th St. NW, 202/232-0395, no website; 10am-11pm Mon.-Thurs., 10am-midnight Fri., 24 hours Sat., midnight-11pm Sun.

✪ Hank's Oyster Bar $$

For more than a decade, Dupont Circle residents have been frequenting this neighborhood spot for market-fresh seafood, comfort-food suppers, and excellent cocktails. The brunch is particularly good, especially the shrimp and grits on the sunny patio—but the best time to go is 10pm-midnight, when the raw bar is half off. You'll find a similar menu on Capitol Hill (633 Pennsylvania Ave. SE, 202/733-1971) and at The Wharf (701 Wharf St. SW, 202/817-3055).

MAP 4: 1624 Q St. NW, 202/462-4865, www.hanksoysterbar.com; 11:30am-1am Mon.-Thurs., 11:30am-2am Fri., 11am-2am Sat., 11am-1am Sun.

FRENCH
Bistrot du Coin $$

The District is home to several flashy bistros, but Bistrot du Coin is one of the most authentic—albeit with friendlier service than you'll find on the Champs-Élysées. You can't go wrong with *le steak maison* (steak served with fries and Béarnaise sauce), but the large menu is full of bistro standards like salade Niçoise, *boeuf bourguignon* (beef stew in red wine sauce), cassoulet, and gooey *tartines* (open-faced sandwiches). Grab a big round table with your friends after happy hour—they're open late and don't mind noise.

MAP 4: 1738 Connecticut Ave. NW, 202/234-6969, www.bistrotducoin.com; 11:30am-midnight Mon.-Wed., 11:30am-1am Thurs.-Fri., noon-1am Sat., noon-midnight Sun.

SOUTHERN AND SOUL FOOD
Henry's Soul Café $

Henry's Soul Café has been baking the best sweet potato pie in the region since 1968. The tiny storefront is best for takeout—there are only a few stools—but you can order ahead online on your way to a picnic in Meridian Hill Park (16th St. and W St. NW). The menu features Southern favorites like lip-smacking barbecue chicken and ribs, as well as traditional soul food recipes like chitterlings, served with sides and a choice of bread (get the cornbread). Don't forget a slice of the pie.

MAP 4: 1704 U St. NW, 202/265-3336, www.henryssoulcafe.com; 11:30am-8:30pm Tues.-Sat., 11am-5pm Sun.

JAPANESE
Sushi Taro $$$

A favorite of Japanese diplomats, the Michelin-starred Sushi Taro offers some of the most authentic (and pricey) Japanese dinner experiences, featuring specialties like *suppon*, the soft-shell snapping turtle soup believed to have medicinal properties, for $100pp, or personalized chef's tasting menu at the sushi counter starting at $180pp. On a budget? The restaurant offers an à la carte menu—or, go for one of DC's best lunch deals, the $15 bento box.

MAP 4: 1503 17th St. NW, 202/462-8999, www.sushitaro.com; 11:30am-2pm and 5:30pm-10pm Mon.-Fri., 5:30pm-10pm Sat.

MEXICAN
Lauriol Plaza $$

Before DC's dining scene boomed, Lauriol Plaza was THE hot spot for 20-somethings to enjoy group dinners with "swirls" (frozen flavored margaritas) and long wait times before wild nights in nearby bars. Now, the large restaurant with a seasonal patio and roof deck caters to a calmer, more family-oriented crowd—and we had no problem walking in during prime dinner hour on St. Patrick's Day. In a city packed with trendy taco spots, Lauriol Plaza's simple, comforting tacos, enchiladas, and fajitas hit the spot—and fill you up without

Bagels Etc.

breaking the bank, with most entrees under $20. And while lots of things have changed, luckily, those potent pitchers of swirls have not.

MAP 4: 1835 18th St. NW, 202/387-0035, www.lauriolplaza. com; 11:30am-11pm Mon.-Thurs., 11:30am-midnight Fri.-Sat., 11am-11pm Sun.

THAI
Little Serow $$$

Try Johnny Monis's cooking at Little Serow. The no-reservations foodie favorite serves a northern Thai set menu for $54 per person. Line up by 4pm to put your name on the list for the evening. The restaurant accommodates only parties of four or fewer. Is it worth it? Absolutely, if you like seafood and a lot of spice.

MAP 4: 1511 17th St. NW, no phone, www.littleserow.com; 5:30pm-10pm Tues.-Thurs., 5:30pm-10:30pm Fri.-Sat.

DELIS
Dupont Market $

Want to grab a sandwich before gallery-hopping? Pop by this tiny deli for some of the best made-to-order, New York deli-style sandwiches in town—oddly, hard to find in DC. Enjoy on the small patio in the heart of a residential neighborhood if the weather's nice, or plan to take your order to go. The deli is packed floor to ceiling with beverages, snacks, and other essentials if you want to stock your hotel room, too.

MAP 4: 1807 18th St. NW, 202/797-0222, no website; 8am-10pm Mon.-Sat., 8am-9pm Sun

BREAKFAST AND BRUNCH
✪ Bagels Etc. $

Don't let the line snaking out the door on weekend mornings deter you, because this cash-only shop makes the best bagels in DC. You can't go wrong with a classic bacon-egg-cheese rapidly cooked to order, though the health conscious who drop by after their bike rides in nearby Rock Creek Park will find sprouts on everything wheat bagels as well.

MAP 4: 2122 P St. NW, 202/466-7171, www.bagelsetc.net; 6am-4pm Mon.-Sat., 6am-3pm Sun.

Nightlife

COCKTAIL BARS AND LOUNGES
McClellan's Retreat

The Civil War is an unusual theme for a bar, but this casual neighborhood lounge named for Union commander George B. McClellan works. Why? The drinks and atmosphere are simply good. Order one of the thoughtful house cocktails, which are prepared by lantern light at the wooden bar, or indulge in the extensive selection of whiskey, rye, and bourbon.

MAP 4: 2031 Florida Ave. NW, 202/265-6270, www.mcclellansretreat. com; 4pm-2am Mon.-Fri., 5pm-2am Sat.-Sun.

Quill at The Jefferson

Quill

If you want to impress your date, you could do worse than the sexy lounge at The Jefferson. You'll find older, well-heeled business and media types sipping seasonal cocktails at the golden-hued bar or gathered around the piano. To seal the deal, ask for a booth in one of the private rooms located just outside the bar.

MAP 4: 1200 16th St. NW, 202/448-2300, www.jeffersondc.com; 11am-midnight daily

CRAFT BEER
Bier Baron Tavern

This is the bar for beer connoisseurs. With over 50 drafts on tap, including limited release and seasonal selections, as well as more than 500 bottles, even well-traveled drinkers will find something new, especially on the lengthy "cellar" menu with vintage beers from around the world. It's an ideal spot to while away the hours on a rainy day and enjoy live comedy or trivia nights.

MAP 4: 1523 22nd St. NW, 202/293-1887, www.inlovewithbier.com; 4pm-midnight Sun.-Thurs., 4pm-2am Fri., 3pm-2am Sat.

DANCE CLUBS
HEIST

Don't let the velvet rope deter you—the bouncers will let you in, as long as you're willing to pay the hefty cover charge or make a reservation for bottle service. The beautiful, blingy, intimate venue recently won Lounge of the Year at the Nightclub & Bar Awards in Las Vegas, the first venue in Washington DC to earn the title. The club attracts young 20-somethings and bachelor/bachelorette parties and, occasionally, NBA stars and musicians looking to party after their concerts.

MAP 4: 1802 Jefferson Pl. NW, 202/688-0098, www.facebook.com/HEISTDC; 10pm-2am Tues.-Thurs., 10pm-3am Fri.-Sat.

GAY AND LESBIAN BARS
✪ JR's Bar

Located in the heart of DC's historic gay neighborhood, JR's Bar attracts a mix of local gay men of all ages, who pack this casual corner bar for happy hour specials like all-you-can-drink for $15. The bar has something for everyone, whether you prefer the popular showtunes night with live cabaret or mingling with the young professional kickball teams. The large, covered patio is packed during Capital Pride in June, when rainbow flags cover the street.

MAP 4: 1519 17th St. NW, 202/328-0090, www.jrsbar-dc.com; 4pm-2am Mon.-Thurs., 4pm-3am Fri., 1pm-3am Sat., 1pm-2am Sun.

Larry's Lounge

Follow the neon rainbow sign to Larry's Lounge, which has remained one of the neighborhood's essential dive bars, gay or straight, since before the area was covered in nightlife options. You won't find Edison bulbs or a fancy cocktail menu here, but you will enjoy reasonably priced beer, wine, and mixed drinks, on either a red vinyl bar stool or the dog-friendly patio.

MAP 4: 1840 18th St. NW, 202/483-1483, http://larryslounge-hub. com; 4pm-2am Mon.-Thurs., 4pm-3am Fri.-Sat., 2pm-2am Sun.

Arts and Culture

MUSEUMS
✪ The Phillips Collection

In a city full of free museums, The Phillips Collection is worth the admission fee. The nation's first modern art museum was founded in 1921 by banker and arts patron Duncan Phillips to showcase his collection of now-well-known works by Cézanne, Diebenkorn, O'Keeffe, and Van Gogh, to name a few. The showcase piece is Renoir's *Luncheon of the Boating Party* (1880-1881), depicting the artist's chic Parisian friends, but the arresting Rothko Room is a wonderful spot to get lost in thought. On the first Thursday of every month, a stylish crowd packs the intimate museum for Phillips After 5, featuring tours, entertainment, and a cash bar.

MAP 4: 1600 21st St. NW, 202/387-2151, www.phillipscollection.org; 10am-5pm Tues.-Sat., noon-6:30pm Sun.; $10-12 adults, $8-10 students and seniors, free for members and children under 18, permanent collection only free Tue.-Fri.

National Museum of American Jewish Military History

This small museum has an important mission: to document and preserve the stories of Jewish Americans who have served in the U.S. military, particularly the 550,000 who served during World War II. The displays draw from the museum's collection of more than 5,000 artifacts, as well as extensive archival materials. Hours are rather limited; it's worth checking the website for the calendar of guided tours and discussions with authors and historians.

MAP 4: 1811 R St. NW, 202/265-6280, www.nmajmh.org; 9am-5pm Mon.-Fri., by appointment Sun.; free

The Society of the Cincinnati Anderson House

In 1783, Continental Army officers formed the Society of the Cincinnati, dedicated to remembering the American Revolution. Named for Cincinnatus, the Roman statesman known for his civic virtue, the group supported soldiers and their families, and today it collects artifacts from the period. It's headquartered in **Anderson House,** the former home of American diplomat Larz Anderson and his wife, Isabel. This is your chance to explore an Embassy Row mansion and see how wealthy Washingtonians lived back in the day, as much of their original decor is on display, along with swords and firearms and an extensive collection of Revolutionary art.

MAP 4: 2118 Massachusetts Ave. NW, 202/785-2040, www. societyofthecincinnati.org; 10am-4pm Tues.-Sat., noon-4pm Sun.; free

GALLERIES
Hillyer Art Space

Tucked in an alley off Florida Avenue, Hillyer Art Space might introduce you to your new favorite artist; this contemporary gallery showcases fascinating works by emerging local and international artists who deserve a big break. Expect to see something new each

The Phillips Collection

Dupont Underground

time you visit, because the gallery debuts exhibitions on the first Friday of every month to coincide with **First Friday Dupont** (www.firstfridaydupont.org, 6pm-8pm first Fri. of the month), in which artsy young things pack about a dozen neighborhood galleries for happy hour receptions and special events.

MAP 4: 9 Hillyer Ct., 202/338-0325, www.hillyerartspace.org; noon-5pm Mon., noon-6pm Tues.-Fri., noon-5pm Sat.-Mon.; free, donations suggested

Studio Gallery

Located on a leafy residential street, Studio Gallery is the gallery for artists. Founded in 1956 by sculptor Jennie Lea Knight, whose work can be seen at the **Smithsonian American Art Museum** (8th St. and F St. NW, 202/633-7979, http://americanart.si.edu), the two-story gallery and outdoor sculpture garden showcase contemporary works with a focus on DC-based artists.

The gallery debuts several exhibitions every month during **First Friday Dupont** (www.firstfridaydupont.org, 6pm-8pm first Fri. of the month), with receptions that will make you feel like a local art scene insider.

MAP 4: 2108 R St. NW, 202/232-8734, www.studiogallerydc.com; 1pm-6pm Wed.-Fri., 11am-6pm Sat.; free

CULTURAL CENTERS
Dupont Underground

Before cars, buses, and the Metro, Washingtonians got around by a network of underground streetcars, which were powered for decades by horses, then electric cables. The streetcars were shut down in 1962, and the stations and tunnels, like the one under Dupont Circle, were for the most part closed. In 2016, however, the Dupont Circle station was unsealed and given a new life as a contemporary arts space. The 75,000-square-foot space has been cleaned up—although it's still

139

a bit creepy—and now hosts exhibits and events. You can schedule a private tour of the tunnels, or check the website for public events; recent Underground happenings have included contemporary art and graffiti exhibits, music performances, and a fashion show. Tickets are required to enter the space.

MAP 4: 1527 New Hampshire Ave. NW, no phone, www.dupontunderground. org; hours for tours, exhibitions, and special events vary; $15

Festivals and Events

Passport DC

Learn some diplomatic secrets when the Embassy Row mansions open to the public for a month of open houses and cultural events. Highlights include the Around the World Embassy Tour, when more than 40 embassies from Afghanistan to Zimbabwe open their doors for one day, and the EU Open House, when the European Union members invite you to experience their arts, culture, and food.

Dupont Circle: Embassy Row, www.culturaltourism.org; May 1-31; free

Dupont-Kalorama Museum Walk

While they usually charge admission fees, the independent museums, historic homes, and galleries in Dupont Circle and Kalorama

Capital Pride Parade

welcome the public free of charge for one weekend in June. In addition to the exhibits, enjoy family-friendly activities, arts and crafts, and entertainment all weekend long.

Dupont Circle: www. dupontkaloramamc.com; early June; free

Capital Pride

The highlight of one of the largest pride events in the United States is the celebratory Saturday afternoon parade through Dupont Circle, featuring more than 180 floats, entertainers, and supporting groups; after, the historic gay neighborhood is a massive party as paradegoers continue the celebration into the evening.

Dupont Circle: www.capitalpride.org; early-mid-June; free

High Heel Drag Queen Race

There's only one place to be the Tuesday before Halloween: 17th Street in Dupont Circle, where more than 100 costumed drag queens race—in high heels, no less—by the neighborhood's popular gay bars. JR's Bar started the event in 1986, and it's grown to be a must-attend event, with hundreds of thousands of spectators gathering for happy hour several hours before the 9pm race.

Dupont Circle: 17th St. between P St. NW and S St. NW; Tues. before Halloween; free

Shops

CLOTHING, SHOES, AND ACCESSORIES

Betsy Fisher

Busy Washington women who don't want to sacrifice style for professionalism shop at Betsy Fisher for designer ready-to-wear for all occasions. You'll find dresses, separates, and shoes to take you from work to cocktails to the PTA meeting, from labels like Elie Tahari, Max Mara, and Nicole Miller, as well as lesser-known designers, with regular trunk shows of new wares.

MAP 4: 1224 Connecticut Ave. NW, 202/785-1975, www.betsyfisher.com; 10am-7pm Mon.-Fri., 10am-6pm Sat., 1pm-5pm Sun.

Brooks Brothers

Sure, you can shop at this American retailer online, but if you're in the market for a new suit, get style inspiration from the lobbyists and lawyers who pop in between meetings to browse the sales. After all, Brooks Brothers has real DC street cred—the company has dressed 40 U.S. presidents, including President Lincoln, who was assassinated in his Brooks Brothers coat embroidered with the phrase "One Country, One Destiny."

MAP 4: 1201 Connecticut Ave. NW, 202/659-4650, www.brooksbrothers. com; 10am-7pm Mon.-Fri., 10am-5pm Sat., noon-5pm Sun.

Kramerbooks

Proper Topper

If you need an outfit for a horserace in the Virginia countryside, Proper Topper has you covered, literally. The tiny store has a selection of hats and fascinators at a variety of price points, as well as pretty dresses from labels like Tracy Reese. And the store always has the perfect gift, too, from mugs and cookbooks to candles and coasters to dainty DC flag jewelry.

MAP 4: 1350 Connecticut Ave. NW, 202/842-3055, www.propertopper.com; 10am-7pm Mon.-Fri., 10am-6pm Sat.

BOOKS

✪ Kramerbooks

Even an e-reader devotee will walk out of Kramerbooks with a shopping bag, because management seems to know exactly which books you wanted to read. This is DC, so politics, history, biography, and Washington life and culture dominate the shelves (including this book!), but you'll also find fiction and nonfiction bestsellers. It's one of locals' favorite spots to pick up new books by their friends, or their political foes; even President Obama dropped by with his daughters for Small Business Saturday in 2011. The café and bar serves seasonal breakfast, lunch, dinner, and late-night bites.

MAP 4: 1517 Connecticut Ave. NW, 202/387-1400, www.kramers.com; 7:30am-1am Sun.-Thurs., 7:30am-3am Fri.-Sat.

Second Story Books

Since 1973, Second Story Books has been providing Washington area readers with used books, boasting one of the largest collections of rare and collectible books, manuscripts, maps, and prints in the world. On most days, carts outside the store have an eclectic mix of sale books selling for as little as $2 each.

MAP 4: 2000 P St. NW, 202/659-8884, www.secondstorybooks.com; 10am-10pm daily

HOME AND GIFTS

Jenni Bick Custom Journals

Jenni Bick has been selling her gorgeous journals out of her home in Martha's Vineyard since 1990, but her flagship store is located in this city full of writers and dreamers. The store is a treasure trove for lovers of the written word, offering Jenni Bick's own leather journals, which can be embossed with initials or a phrase, as well as rainbows of notebooks by Moleskine and Leuchtturm1917, fine pens and pencils, and letterpress cards.

MAP 4: 1300 Connecticut Ave. NW, 202/721-0246, www.jennibickdc.com; 10am-7pm Mon.-Sat., noon-6pm Sun.

✪ Shop Made in DC

Located right off Dupont Circle, this store and café opened in 2017 to celebrate the growing number of artisans in Washington DC. It's small but stocks a tightly curated selection of excellent gifts and souvenirs, all, of course, made in the District. Merchandise might include "I'm Woke" baby onesies, DC-themed tees by District of Clothing, accessories made from upcycled bicycle parts by BicycleTrash, and lots of greeting cards and art prints. The café inside the shop features Bullfrog Bagels and Compass Coffee. There are additional locations in Georgetown (1242 Wisconsin Ave. NW; 10am-8pm Mon.-Sat., 10am-7pm Sun.) and District Wharf (10 District Sq. SW; 10am-8pm daily).

MAP 4: 1330 19th St. NW, no phone, www.shopmadeindc.com; 10am-8pm Mon.-Fri., 11am-6pm Sat.-Sun.

Tabletop

Specializing in quirky but stylish home accessories and gifts, Tabletop is the place to shop for your hard-to-buy-for friend, or to pick up a souvenir for yourself. The DC dish towels, baby onesies, and neighborhood map prints are worth the visit, but the shop also stocks Jonathan Adler and Marimekko home decor, kitchen supplies, jewelry, kids' toys and books, plus unique wrapping paper and greeting cards in case you're en route to a party.

MAP 4: 1608 20th St. NW, 202/387-7117, www.tabletopdc.com; 11am-7pm Mon.-Sat., 10am-5pm Sun.

U Street, Shaw, and Logan Circle

Map 5

The historic center of the city's **African American arts and culture** for much of the 20th century, U Street and Shaw are home to the African American Civil War Memorial and Howard University, as well as several restored institutions along "Black Broadway," like **The Howard Theatre** and **The Lincoln Theatre.** These neighborhoods, along with nearby Logan Circle, have become the **trendy hub** for **nightlife** and culture, as the city's young professionals with disposable income fill the **restaurants, cocktail bars,** and nightclubs that have exploded here in the last two decades.

TOP RESTAURANTS

- Essential Local Flavor:
  Ben's Chili Bowl (page 153)
- Best Ethiopian:
  Dukem Ethiopian Restaurant (page 155)
- Hub for Activists:
  Busboys and Poets (page 158)

TOP NIGHTLIFE

- Best Chance to Dance All Night:
  Black Cat (page 161)
- Best Live Music Venue:
  9:30 Club (page 161)
- Sunday Funday:
  Nellie's Sports Bar (page 163)

TOP ARTS AND CULTURE

- Where to Find DC's Underground Art
  Scene: **DC Alley Museum** (page 163)
- Best Venue to Experience Go-Go:
  The Howard Theatre (page 164)

TOP SHOPS

- Join a Movement: **The Outrage** (page 167)
- Where to Impulse-Buy Something
  Great: **Salt & Sundry** (page 168)
- Most Likely to Make You Wish You'd Brought
  a Truck: **Miss Pixie's** (page 168)
- Best Edible Purchases:
  Union Kitchen Grocery (page 169)

GETTING THERE AND AROUND

- Metro lines: Green, Yellow
- Metro stations: Shaw-Howard U, U Street/
  African-Amer Civil War Memorial/Cardozo
- Major bus routes: DC Circulator
  Woodley Park-Adams Morgan-
  McPherson Square Metro

SEE MAP 6

SIGHTS
1 **A5** Howard University
16 **C4** African American Civil War Memorial and Museum

RESTAURANTS
2 **B3** Maydan
3 **B4** Florida Avenue Grill
5 **C3** Busboys and Poets
9 **C3** The Wydown
10 **C3** Taqueria Nacional
11 **C3** Lupo Verde
13 **C3** Ben's Chili Bowl
15 **C4** Dukem Ethiopian Restaurant
21 **C5** Calabash Tea & Tonic
32 **D3** Pearl Dive Oyster Palace
33 **D6** ANXO Cidery & Pintxos Bar
34 **E3** Le Diplomate
40 **E4** Chercher
43 **E5** Compass Coffee
45 **F4** San Lorenzo
46 **F4** Buttercream Bakeshop
49 **F4** The Dabney

NIGHTLIFE
6 **C3** The Gibson
7 **C3** Marvin
14 **C4** U Street Music Hall
17 **C4** Nellie's Sports Bar
18 **C4** 9:30 Club
20 **C5** Flash
22 **C5** Right Proper Brewing Co.
24 **C5** El Techo
25 **D3** Black Cat
35 **E3** New Vegas Lounge
39 **E4** Maxwell Park
41 **E5** Dacha Beer Garden
50 **F4** Columbia Room

ARTS AND CULTURE
12 **C3** The Lincoln Theatre
23 **C5** The Howard Theatre
36 **E3** Studio Theatre
37 **E3** Transformer
48 **F4** Long View Gallery
51 **F4** DC Alley Museum

SHOPS
4 **B4** Cherry Blossom Creative
8 **C3** GoodWood
19 **C5** Lettie Gooch
26 **D3** Current Boutique
27 **D3** Batch 13
28 **D3** The Outrage
29 **D3** Miss Pixie's
30 **D3** Shinola
31 **D3** Salt & Sundry
42 **E5** Grand Cata
47 **F4** Union Kitchen Grocery

HOTELS
38 **E3** Kimpton Mason & Rook Hotel
44 **F3** Washington Plaza Hotel

0   300 yds
0   300 m

DISTANCE ACROSS MAP
Approximate: 1.7 mi or 2.7 km

SEE MAP 4

© MOON.COM

4   **5**   **6**

11TH ST NW
EUCLID ST NW
SHERMAN AVE NW
9TH ST NW
GEORGIA AVE NW

Upper Quad

Howard University
1
HOWARD PL NW

6TH ST NW

Banneker Park

McMillan Reservoir

COLLEGE ST NW
4TH ST NW

BARRY PL NW

FLORIDA AVE NW
3
10TH ST NW
11TH ST NW

BRYANT ST NW
BRYANT ST NW
ADAMS ST NW
FLAGLER PL NW
2ND ST NW
W ST

9TH ST NW
8TH ST NW

W ST NW
5TH ST NW
4TH ST NW

K. C. Lewis Park

V ST NW
4
V ST NW
V ST NW
OAKDALE PL NW
3RD ST NW
V ST NW

18
V ST NW

LeDroit Park

ELM ST NW

14 U Street
M
15
U ST NW
16 Civil War Memorial
17
19

U ST NW
U ST NW
LEDROIT PARK
U ST NW
THOMAS ST NW

African American Civil War Memorial and Museum

20

VERMONT AVE NW

T ST NW
Anna J. Cooper Circle

22 23
21
24

RHODE ISLAND AVE NW
2ND ST NW

WESTMINSTER ST
10TH ST NW

S ST NW
FLORIDA AVE NW

7TH ST NW
33

FRENCH ST NW
M Shaw-Howard University

Harrison Park

R ST NW
NEW JERSEY AVE NW
4TH ST NW
3RD ST NW

Shaw Park

SHAW
WARNER ST NW

Florida Ave Playground

Q ST NW
41
8TH ST NW
Q ST NW
MARION ST NW

TRUXTON CIRCLE

43
42

RHODE ISLAND AVE NW
P ST NW
P ST NW
P ST NW
P ST NW

COLUMBIA ST
Kennedy Park
Bundy Field

39
10TH ST NW
11TH ST NW
6TH ST
8TH ST NW
40
45

5TH ST NW
NEW JERSEY AVE NW

N ST NW
N ST NW

46 47
48
51 49
50

Convention Center

M Mt Vernon Square-7th St-Convention Center
RIDGE ST NW
MORGAN ST NW
KIRBY ST NW
3RD ST

SEE MAP 2

M ST NW

MOUNT VERNON SQUARE
NEW YORK AVE NW

U STREET AND SHAW WALK

TOTAL DISTANCE: 1.8 mi (2.9 km)
WALKING TIME: 35 minutes

Take a walk through U Street and Shaw, a center of African American life and culture for much of the 20th century, and the childhood home of Duke Ellington, who later played at the jazz clubs around U Street, known as "Black Broadway." The neighborhood was decimated during the riots in April 1968, after the assassination of Martin Luther King Jr. The neighborhood eventually began to rebuild. Today, you'll find rejuvenated landmarks like The Howard Theatre and markers for the self-guided African American Heritage Trail, as well as booming growth and development, with new restaurants and shops popping up seemingly every day.

To experience the joy of the neighborhood, take this walk on a weekend afternoon, when locals flock to the streets for late brunches that turn into early cocktails and dinner. If you're taking the Metro to the neighborhood, the starting point of the walk, Ben's Chili Bowl, is directly across the street from the 13th Street and U

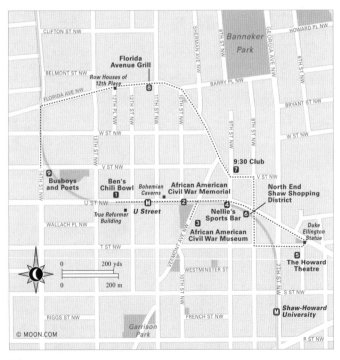

Street entrance of the U Street/African-Amer Civil War Memorial/
Cardozo Metro station.

1 The tour begins at one of the must-visit restaurants in DC: **Ben's Chili Bowl,** which stayed open late to serve half-smokes (spicy half-pork/half-beef sausages, served on buns and smothered in chili) to law enforcement and activists following the 1968 race riots. Have a bite at the old-fashioned counter, or at least peek at the walls covered with photos of famous diners visiting the restaurant, including President Obama. And don't miss the mural on the outside wall; it was redone in June 2017 to add Harriet Tubman, Dave Chappelle, and the Obamas.

2 Head east on U Street, busy with brunchers and shoppers and fitness fanatics on a weekend afternoon. On the right before 12th Street, look for the **True Reformer Building,** the classical revival and Romanesque building designed in 1903 by John Anderson Lankford, the first registered African American architect in Washington DC. Now the headquarters of the Public Welfare Foundation, the building originally housed organizations that helped African Americans set up businesses and access social services in the early 1900s. Keep walking east to 11th Street to **Bohemian Caverns,** DC's oldest jazz club, which operated for 90 years before it closed in 2016. Turn north onto 11th Street NW to see the gorgeous blue and purple mural depicting jazz legends (on the north

African American Civil War Memorial

Howard Theatre

side of the building). Return to U Street, then walk 1.5 blocks toward Vermont Avenue. Enter the plaza on your right at the Metro station to view the **African American Civil War Memorial.**

3 Continue southwest on Vermont Avenue to tour the **African American Civil War Museum,** across the street from the memorial. This museum is packed with educational displays about African Americans who fought in the Civil War. History buffs could easily spend a few hours diving in. If you have relatives who served in the Civil War, look up your family tree in the museum's registry.

4 Double back to U Street NW and walk two short blocks east to **Nellie's Sports Bar,** where a crowd has likely gathered on the roof if the weather's nice. On weekends, this popular gay bar is a hot spot from brunch into the evening. Head south on 9th Street NW, the heart of Shaw and DC's Little Ethiopia.

5 Walk south one block on 9th Street, then go east on T Street NW for about three short blocks to reach **The Howard Theatre.** The box office is open Tuesday through Sunday. If one of DC's go-go bands is on the schedule, be sure to get tickets to hear Washington's home-grown music tradition, which was popularized by the late Chuck Brown in the 1970s and 1980s. Half a block northeast of the theater at T Street NW and Florida Avenue NW, the 20-foot stainless steel **Duke Ellington statue** pays homage to the musician, who grew up in Shaw and began his career in the jazz clubs of "Black Broadway."

6 Walk northwest on Florida Avenue NW three blocks to 9th Street. You'll notice shiny new buildings as you enter the **North End Shaw shopping district,** which has several niche, high-end apparel, accessories, and beauty retailers.

7 When you're done shopping, head north on 9th Street NW two blocks to approach the **9:30 Club** at the corner of 9th and V Street NW. It looks like a nondescript warehouse from the outside, but this is the city's top music venue, rated one of the best in the country by *Rolling Stone*. The box office is open Monday through Friday, plus weekends when there's a show. Check the lineup, because if something catches your eye, a show at the 9:30 Club is must-experience nightlife.

8 Turn back the way you came on V Street NW and veer slightly northwest on Florida Avenue NW. Enjoy this quiet, mostly residential area, and walk for about four long blocks (10 minutes) to reach **Florida Avenue Grill** at the corner of Florida and 11th Street NW. If you didn't eat at Ben's, you can stop for a hearty meal at the oldest soul food restaurant in the world. Otherwise, continue west for another 2.5 blocks on Florida Avenue and peek at the rainbow of **row houses** on 12th Place.

9 Continue west along Florida Avenue for two long blocks (about five minutes) to reach 14th Street NW. Turn south on 14th Street, where you'll have a plethora of options for a cocktail or, if you're ready to eat, a late lunch or early dinner. At 14th Street NW and V Street NW, stop at neighborhood icon **Busboys and Poets,** where you can eat, drink, and shop in the on-site bookstore specializing in books about social justice issues and DC life and history.

To get back to the Metro and your starting point, walk another block south on 14th Street and go east on U Street for one long block (about four minutes). Or continue south on 14th Street, where the options for shopping and nightlife continue for six bustling blocks all the way to Logan Circle. Highlights include **Le Diplomate** and **Pearl Dive Oyster Palace,** as well as **Miss Pixie's** and **Salt & Sundry** for cool housewares and local souvenirs.

Sights

African American Civil War Memorial and Museum

The small but moving African American Civil War Memorial honors the 200,000 African Americans who served in the Union Army and Navy during the Civil War. Located in the heart of one of DC's historic African American neighborhoods and "Black Broadway," the center of African American arts and culture in the 20th century, the memorial includes a nine-foot bronze sculpture of several soldiers with the names of those who served on the walls surrounding it. Across the street from the memorial, the informative African American Civil War Museum (1925 Vermont Ave. NW, 202/667-2667, www.afroamcivilwar. org; 10am-5pm Mon., 10am-6:30pm Tues.-Fri., 10am-4pm Sat., noon-4pm Sun.) tells the stories of these soldiers through photographs, stories, and artifacts, and allows descendants of those who served to register and research their family members.

MAP 5: Vermont Ave. at 10th St. and U St. NW, 202/426-6841, www.nps.gov/afam; 24 hours daily

Howard University

Generations of black leaders have graduated from Howard University, the top-ranked historically black university founded in 1867. The university is named for Union Army general Oliver Otis Howard,

African American Civil War Memorial

Howard University

who led the Freedman's Bureau and helped freed blacks assimilate after the Civil War. The list of prominent graduates is a who's who of trailblazers in government, law, education, and the arts, including the first African American Supreme Court justice, Thurgood Marshall, civil rights activist Stokely Carmichael, U.S. Senator Kamala Harris, Sean "Puffy" Combs, and author Toni Morrison, as well as local icons like former DC mayor Adrian Fenty and Ben Ali, founder of Ben's Chili Bowl. The campus has played an important role in the black community

of DC. Even as early as the 1940s, Howard students organized sit-ins around the segregated city.

Located just northeast of Shaw's growing business and nightlife center, the campus has several points of interest, including the Gothic Andrew Rankin Memorial Chapel, built in 1894-1895, where renowned preachers, activists, and political leaders including Frederick Douglass, Martin Luther King Jr., and JFK have spoken. Howard continues to bring distinguished speakers to the campus, though the public Sunday service has outgrown the chapel and now congregates in the 1,500-seat Cramton Auditorium. Howard University Homecoming is another popular event, with a parade, fashion show, and parties at bars and clubs citywide every October. Prospective students may tour the campus at 10am, noon, and 2pm Monday through Friday when classes are in session.

MAP 5: 2400 6th St. NW, 202/806-6100, www.howard.edu

Restaurants

PRICE KEY

$	Entrees less than $15
$$	Entrees $15-25
$$$	Entrees more than $25

CLASSIC AMERICAN
✪ Ben's Chili Bowl $

Ben's Chili Bowl has been serving its famous chili half-smokes for 60 years—including during the 1968 race riots, when the restaurant got special permission to stay open late

to ensure activists and law enforcement had something to eat while they worked to restore the neighborhood. Today, celebrities, politicians, and locals drop by for the spicy half-pork/half-beef sausages, served on buns and smothered in beef or vegetarian chili. This brightly lit, counter-serve diner has traditional hot dogs, burgers, and great milk shakes, too, along with breakfast

PRESIDENTIAL PICKS

If you see people with dark suits and earpieces crowding the doorway of one of these hot spots, keep your eyes peeled, because the town's top VIP may be chowing down nearby.

The Obamas enjoyed dining at some of DC's most exclusive restaurants, including Komi, Fiola Mare (page 196), and, on more than one occasion, Cafe Milano (page 195), a favorite of Washington power players and Hollywood celebrities. And days before he took office, Barack Obama stopped by Ben's Chili Bowl (page 153), which memorialized him in their mural on the outside wall. (Other famous diners at the late-night spot known for half-smokes include former

Ben's Chili Bowl

French president Nicolas Sarkozy and his wife Carla Bruni, Anthony Bourdain, and many DC politicians.)

Other longtime favorites of White House occupants continue to welcome VIPs, staffers, and lobbyists today. Old Ebbitt Grill (page 81), just a few blocks from the White House, hosted McKinley, Grant, Johnson, Cleveland, Teddy Roosevelt, and Harding. In 1953, Senator John F. Kennedy proposed to Jackie Bouvier in booth 3 at Martin's Tavern (page 194), which has served every POTUS from Truman to George W. Bush. The Palm (page 132), where caricatures of its most famous regulars adorn the walls, opened after United Nations ambassador George H. W. Bush urged his favorite New York steakhouse to open a location in DC.

While Donald Trump rarely dines outside his own properties, his daughter Ivanka and her husband Jared Kushner are known for frequenting—no surprise here—Fiola Mare and Cafe Milano, as well as Logan Circle hotspot Le Diplomate.

items. There's another location on H Street NE.

MAP 5: 1213 U St. NW, 202/667-0909, www.benschilibowl.com; 6am-2:30am Mon.-Thurs., 6am-4am Fri., 7am-4am Sat., 11am-midnight Sun.

SEAFOOD
Pearl Dive Oyster Palace $$

Part of chef Jeff Black's local restaurant empire known for sustainable seafood, Pearl Dive Oyster Palace serves Gulf Coast flavors in a rustic hangout in the heart of Logan Circle. There are several types of oysters on offer, but try the Old Black Salt Oysters, a salty

variety Black helped to develop in Chincoteague, Virginia; they're best enjoyed at the bustling outdoor bar counter on 14th Street.

MAP 5: 1612 14th St. NW, 202/319-1612, www.pearldivedc.com; 5pm-10pm Mon., 5pm-11pm Tues.-Thurs., 11am-11pm Fri.-Sat., 11am-10pm Sun.

SOUTHERN AND SOUL FOOD
The Dabney $$$

Jeremiah Langhorne cut his teeth at the critically acclaimed McCrady's in Charleston before opening The Dabney, where reservations are snapped up quicker than you can say "Michelin star." (It has one.) The young, Virginia-born chef showcases the best of the Mid-Atlantic—soft-shell crabs and catfish, local produce, Anson Mill grits—in a rustic-chic row house in Shaw. Reservations are available at noon two weeks in advance of the date, by phone or online.

MAP 5: 122 Blagden Alley NW, 202/450-1015, www.thedabney. com; 5:30pm-10pm Tues.-Thurs., 5:30pm-11pm Fri.-Sat., 5pm-10pm Sun.

Florida Avenue Grill

Florida Avenue Grill $

The oldest soul food restaurant in the world, Florida Avenue Grill was founded in 1944 by Lacey C. Wilson Sr., a shoeshine on Capitol Hill who saved his tips to pursue his dream of opening a restaurant that would be open to everyone, especially the black community. The old-fashioned diner is still in the original spot, having survived the 1968 riots, and serves soul food favorites like fried chicken, ribs, pig's feet, and fried Atlantic croaker, as well as all-day breakfast.

MAP 5: 1100 Florida Ave. NW, 202/265-1586, www.floridaavenuegrill. com; 8am-9pm Tues.-Sat., 8am-4:30pm Sun.

ETHIOPIAN

✪ Dukem Ethiopian Restaurant $$

Ask any local who loves Ethiopian cuisine—whether they're a lobbyist or a taxi driver—where to get the best *doro wat* (chicken stew) and *kitfo* (steak tartare), and they'll tell you this casual corner restaurant near the heart of DC's Little Ethiopia. Don't let the grungy interior deter you, because you'll enjoy friendly service and plentiful, flavorful, authentic food that you'll eat exclusively with *injera* flatbread and your hands.

MAP 5: 1114-1118 U St. NW, 202/667-8735, www.dukemrestaurant. com; 9am-midnight Sun.-Thurs., 9:30am-1am Fri.-Sat.

Chercher $$

A newer mainstay of DC's Little Ethiopia, Chercher has been awarded a Michelin Bib Gourmand for serving "excellent food at a reasonable price." Named for Ethiopia's West Hararghe, a mountainous province known for agriculture, the cozy and casual restaurant is known for high-quality traditional beef dishes as well as a standout vegan platter that will feed a group for under $20.

MAP 5: 1334 9th St. NW, 202/299-9703, www.chercherrestaurant.com; 11am-11pm Mon.-Sat., noon-11pm Sun.

FRENCH

Le Diplomate $$$

Stephen Starr's Le Diplomate looks like the France Pavilion at Epcot in Disney World, but that doesn't stop the crowds from packing the large, festive dining room and patio tables every night of the week for gourmet,

LITTLE ETHIOPIA

Dukem Ethiopian Restaurant

In the 1970s and 1980s, thousands of Ethiopians fled civil war to Washington DC, building the largest Ethiopian community outside Africa. While skyrocketing rents have led to many moving to suburbs like Silver Spring, Maryland, and Alexandria, Virginia, dozens of Ethiopian businesses remain in Adams Morgan and Shaw, and the area around 9th Street and U Street NW is known as Little Ethiopia, home to restaurants like Dukem Ethiopian Restaurant (page 155) and Chercher (page 155). Today, Ethiopian food is an essential part of the District's culinary landscape.

No, the server didn't forget your fork. Instead of utensils, the family-style dishes are traditionally served with *injera*, a spongy, nutrient-dense, gluten-free flatbread used to scoop meats, vegetables, and spices from a communal platter. (Many restaurants will provide utensils if you ask.)

Ethiopian cuisine is often spicy, served with *berbere*, a dark red mixture of chilies, garlic, and a host of other spices, which you can add to taste. If it's too hot, ask for a side of homemade cottage cheese.

The must-try dishes for a newbie include *doro wat*, a spicy chicken stew, and *tibs*, sautéed beef or lamb. If you love steak tartare, try the *kitfo*, spicy minced raw beef. (Dukem will cook it, if you prefer.) And don't forget to order a colorful vegetarian platter, which usually includes lentils, peas, carrots, and greens.

if a bit pricey, bistro classics. The decadent brunch with its own dessert menu is perfect for a Sunday funday celebration; the Burger Américain is considered one of the best in DC.

MAP 5: 1601 14th St. NW, 202/332-3333, www.lediplomatedc. com; 5pm-11pm Mon.-Thurs., noon-midnight Fri., 9:30am-midnight Sat., 9:30am-11pm Sun.

ITALIAN
Lupo Verde $$

A personal favorite for casual dinners or late-night snacks and Peronis, Lupo Verde is a neighborhood bistro with lots to love: intimate tables set in brick-walled nooks, consistently good service, and an authentic menu featuring the cheese and charcuterie of your Italian holiday dreams. You can't go wrong with the homemade pastas with seasonal ingredients—and during truffle season, you can add a rather heaping portion for $10—but we're especially fond of sharing the Med-style steak with market vegetables and a side of polenta.

MAP 5: 1401 T St. NW, 202/827-4752, www.lupoverdedc.com; 5pm-11pm Mon.-Wed., 5pm-2am Thurs., 5pm-3am Fri., 10:30am-3am Sat., 10:30am-2am Sun.

San Lorenzo $$

This pretty but unassuming Shaw restaurant serves an authentic and simple Tuscan-style menu—and the best pasta you'll find within walking distance from the Convention Center, if not the entire city. The portion sizes are, appropriately, on the small side, allowing you to sample the breadth of antipasti, pasta, and a meat or fish course if you're particularly hungry; try the delicate squash blossoms stuffed with goat cheese, followed by the revelatory pappardelle with rabbit ragu.

MAP 5: 1316 9th St. NW, 202/588-8954, www.sanlorenzodc.com; 5:30pm-10:30pm Mon.-Thurs., 5pm-11pm Fri.-Sat., 5pm-9:30pm Sun.

MEDITERRANEAN
Maydan $$

Tucked in an alley next to the Manhattan Laundry building, Maydan's sultry environment and phenomenal food will transport you to Beirut or Tangier. The Mediterranean, Middle Eastern, and North African flavors are inspired by Rose Previte's travels (and her mother's Lebanese cooking): flavorful spreads with bread, grilled meat and fresh vegetables, and cooling cocktails and wines to cut the spice.

Le Diplomate

If you don't mind the smoke lingering on your clothes, eat at the bar to watch the action on the showpiece grill. To find Maydan, look for the large, unmarked wooden door.
MAP 5: 1346 Florida Ave. NW, 202/370-3696, www.maydandc.com; 5pm-11pm Mon.-Sat., 5pm-10pm Sun.

MEXICAN
Taqueria Nacional $
You'll find the best tacos in DC on a side street in the 14th Street Corridor, but don't take my word for it. Both *Bon Appétit* and the Mexican embassy have praised this casual taqueria, known for authentic tacos, quesadillas, and tostadas made with locally sourced, farm-fresh ingredients. (Seriously, you might see the farmer when he brings the pork delivery.)
MAP 5: 1409 T St. NW, 202/299-1122, www.taquerianacional.co; noon-10pm Mon.-Wed., noon-11pm Thurs.-Fri., 10am-11pm Sat., 10am-9pm Sun.

SPANISH
ANXO Cidery & Pintxos Bar $$
DC's first cidery is more than a bar; it's an authentic Basque restaurant, too, with a full menu of *pintxos* (snacks) like salty anchovies imported from Spain, as well as a tender rib-eye for two, one of the best steaks in the city simply prepared with olive oil and sea salt. If you have the choice, reserve a place at the nine-seat dining bar instead of a table so the bartenders can pair your meal with ANXO's ciders made in the District in Brightwood Park followed by calvados or apple brandy flight for dessert. Reservations are recommended for the second-floor dining room; the ground-floor bar

by the huge cider barrels is first come, first served.
MAP 5: 300 Florida Ave. NW, 202/986-3795, www.anxodc.com; 5pm-11pm Mon., 5pm-midnight Tue.-Thurs., 5pm-1am Fri., 10am-1am Sat., 10am-midnight Sun., kitchen closes two hours prior to closing

Busboys and Poets

CAFÉS AND LIGHT BITES
✪ Busboys and Poets $
Inspired by Langston Hughes, who worked as a busboy in a Washington hotel in the 1920s, Busboys and Poets is where progressive activists meet for breakfast before a march, where artists and poets ruminate on political and cultural issues, and where locals enjoy good, affordable food made with organic, hormone-free, and fair-trade ingredients. This busy, casual restaurant is covered in art inspired by its progressive, community-focused mission. Choose from standard dining tables or cozy couches where you can have coffee or tea while you work on your laptop. After your meal, enjoy

a poetry reading or browse the on-site bookshop specializing in social justice issues and DC life and history. In addition to the 14th and V flagship, there are several other locations throughout the city.

MAP 5: 2021 14th St. NW, 202/387-7638, www.busboysandpoets.com; 7am-midnight Mon.-Thurs., 7am-1am Fri., 8am-1am Sat., 8am-midnight Sun.

Buttercream Bakeshop

BAKERIES

Buttercream Bakeshop $

The cupcake craze jumped the shark years ago, but Buttercream Bakeshop is the exception; the almond cupcake with raspberry jam and creamy Chambord frosting will entice even those who claim they don't like sweets. The tiny storefront also sells baked-from-scratch cakes (whole or by the slice), cookies, bars, pies, and fritters, plus breakfast items and Compass Coffee. Grab one of a few stools or take your treats to go.

MAP 5: 1250 9th St. NW, 202/735-0102, www.buttercreamdc.com; 7am-2pm Mon., 7am-7pm Tues.-Thurs., 7am-8pm Fri., 8am-8pm Sat., 9am-7pm Sun.

COFFEE AND TEA

The Wydown $$

An espresso drink and snack could set you back $15 at this hip coffee shop, but you won't feel ripped off by the smiling staff. The drip coffee is brewed to order, and the matcha latte with almond milk is one of DC's best. Pair it with a pastry or raw, organic juice by District Juicery—but plan to take it to go, because the shop is tiny. There's a more spacious outpost in the **Atlas District** (600 H St. NE, 202/846-7986; 7am-10pm Tue.-Sat., 7am-7pm Sun.-Mon.).

MAP 5: 1924 14th St. NW, 202/507-8411, www.thewydown.com; 6:30am-7pm Mon.-Fri., 7am-7pm Sat.-Sun.

Calabash Tea & Tonic $

Trying to lose weight or cure a stomachache? Get pregnant? Fall in love? This Shaw café brews teas and tonics for dozens of ailments, organized by type (herbal, green, oolong, chai, etc.) with detailed descriptions of the flavors and properties on the menu board, plus *kombucha* (sweetened, fermented tea) on tap, organic coffee, and vegan snacks. The colorful café has hippie vibes and space to lounge or work.

MAP 5: 1847 7th St. NW, 202/525-5386, www.calabashdc.com; 9am-8pm Tue.-Sat., 9am-6pm Sun.

Compass Coffee $

If you haven't found your perfect cup, try this local chain founded by two former Marines who developed an easy-to-decipher matrix with nine bean blends organized by flavor profile and roast darkness. The shops brew single-origin roasts, espresso drinks, and nitro cold brew, too. The Shaw roastery and flagship has lots of space to work and relax. This growing chain has many locations citywide, including one in Chinatown (650 F St. NW, no phone).

MAP 5: 1535 7th St. NW, no phone, www.compasscoffee.com; 7am-8pm daily

Nightlife

COCKTAIL BARS AND LOUNGES

✪ Columbia Room

For a new spin on the cocktail experience, Columbia Room offers a three-course ($79 per person) or five-course ($108 per person) creative cocktail tasting paired with substantial snacks. Advance tickets are almost always required and can be reserved one month in advance; mixology classes are also available. If you prefer to drink à la carte, the bar's inviting Spirits Library, with leather chairs, serves riffs on the classics, while the outdoor Punch Garden has punches and bottled cocktails; seating for both is first come, first served.

MAP 5: 124 Blagden Alley NW, 202/316-9396, www.columbiaroomdc. com; 5pm-12:30am Tues.-Thurs., 5pm-1:30am Fri.-Sat.

The Gibson

It's not so secret anymore now that you can make a reservation online, but this speakeasy is worth visiting for cleverly named cocktails in a dark, moody space. Look for the unmarked black door to the left of Marvin. If there's space, you'll be shown to a bar stool or candlelit booth, but you won't be allowed to stand at the bar, so make a reservation a few days in advance to guarantee a seat.

MAP 5: 2009 14th St. NW, 202/232-2156, www.thegibsondc. com; 6pm-2am Mon.-Thurs., 6pm-3am Fri.-Sat., 6pm-midnight Sun.

Marvin

It's been around since 2007, but the roof deck at Marvin remains one of the best. The spacious deck and the snug indoor lounge adjacent attract a young, attractive crowd all weekend long, though it's a slightly older and more chill crowd on Sundays. Open year-round, it's known for Belgian beers but has a full bar and snacks, too. The ground-floor restaurant serves food inspired by Marvin Gaye's time spent in Washington DC and Ostend, Belgium—think fried chicken and waffles as well as *moules frites* (mussels and fries).

MAP 5: 2007 14th St. NW, 202/797-7171, www.marvindc.com; 5pm-2am Mon.-Thurs., 5pm-3am Fri.-Sat., 4pm-2am Sun.

CRAFT BEER
Dacha Beer Garden

When you find Liz Taylor, you've reached Dacha Beer Garden. A huge mural of the actress overlooks this outdoor beer garden located in a corner lot in Shaw, serving American, Belgian, and German craft beers as well as a few cocktails, wine, and seasonal bites. It's best on lazy summer afternoons, but it is open year-round, weather permitting; check the Facebook page to confirm the hours.

MAP 5: 1600 7th St. NW, 202/350-9888, www.dachadc.com; 4pm-10:30pm Mon.-Thurs., noon-midnight Fri., 11am-midnight Sat., 11am-10:30pm Sun., hours may vary seasonally

Right Proper Brewing Co.

One of the best places to try a new beer is at this no-reservations brewpub near The Howard Theatre, where there's almost always something new that's been made on-site. Right Proper has a constantly changing selection of their own beers and other craft varieties, plus a full bar and classic American food, like burgers, ribs, and wood-grilled fish and meats, as well as bar snacks. Enjoy in the industrial-chic pub (think Edison bulbs and exposed brick) or on the front patio.

MAP 5: 624 T St. NW, 202/607-2337, www.rightproperbrewing.com; 11:30am-11pm Mon.-Thurs., 11:30am-midnight Fri.-Sat., 11:30am-10pm Sun.

WINE BARS
Maxwell Park

Brent Kroll spent nearly a decade as sommelier at some of DC's best restaurants before opening this unstuffy wine bar in 2017. It might take you some time to decide what you want to order, because the menu changes monthly, with about 50 wines by the glass to fit a theme (like "anything but pinot grigio" or "unique bubbles from around the world")—but the helpful staff knows the wines inside and out and can guide you if needed. And while wine rules here, don't ignore the original cocktails.

MAP 5: 1336 9th St. NW, www.maxwellparkdc.com; 5pm-late daily

LIVE MUSIC
✪ Black Cat

Since 1993, Black Cat has been one of the best places to dance the night away. The 7,000-square-foot main stage has hosted Arcade Fire, Death Cab for Cutie, The Killers, Moby, and Rancid, among others. Don't miss theme parties like Eighties Mayhem and The Cure vs. The Smiths, which bring mixed crowds to dance the night away. And bring cash, because the venue doesn't take credit cards for cover at the door or drinks.

MAP 5: 1811 14th St. NW, 202/667-4490, www.blackcatdc.com; box office 6:30pm-midnight Mon.-Fri., 7pm-midnight Sat.-Sun., club hours vary depending on the show; tickets $0-25

✪ 9:30 Club

Named one of the top nightclubs in the world by *Rolling Stone* and *Billboard,* 9:30 Club is, simply put, an institution. The club opened in a tiny building in Chinatown in 1980; despite having a capacity of 200, it welcomed Nirvana, R.E.M., and the Red Hot Chili Peppers to the stage. Facing competition from larger venues, the owners moved the club to the much larger current venue, a 1,200-capacity club, which feels much more intimate when local bands like Thievery Corporation return for much-awaited, sold-out shows.

MAP 5: 815 V St. NW, 202/265-0930, www.930.com; box office noon-7pm Mon.-Fri., noon-11pm Mon.-Fri. on show nights, 6pm-11pm Sat. on show nights, 6pm-10:30pm Sun. on show nights; tickets $10-40

New Vegas Lounge

New Vegas Lounge

Open since 1971, New Vegas Lounge is the home of the Out of Town Band, a local, seven-piece rhythm and blues band that performs the best of Motown plus party hits on weekend nights. The small venue can get hot and crowded with 20- and 30-somethings; arrive early to grab one of the few tables, but be prepared to stand up and dance after midnight.

MAP 5: 1415 P St. NW, 202/483-3971, www.newvegasloungedc.com; 9pm-late Fri.-Sat.; cover $10

DANCE CLUBS

El Techo

Yes, it's the roof deck of a nondescript taco shop (Rito Loco)—but it's also where DC's coolest DJs play for a stylish crowd in the open air. Enjoy cheap and authentic tacos, ceviche, and tasty margaritas at a café table in the center of the action, or just grab a tequila shot and dance the night (or Sunday Funday) away to deep house, chill, disco, and Latin tracks.

MAP 5: 606 Florida Ave. NW, 202/836-4270, www.ritoloco.com/el-techo; 5pm-11:30pm Mon.-Thurs., 5pm-1:30am Fri., noon-1:30am Sat., noon-10pm Sun.; check the Facebook page for DJs and events

Flash

Feel the music in this intimate, two-level dance club that brings chart-topping international electronic DJs to Washington, including house and techno stars who spend their summers in music hubs like Ibiza. Flash is open every Friday and Saturday night until late; check the schedule for other events during the week, including Sunday afternoon sessions.

MAP 5: 645 Florida Ave. NW, 202/827-8791, www.flashdc.com; 8pm-4am Fri.-Sat., other days and times vary; cover $10-20

U Street Music Hall

Founded by one of the top local DJs, Will Eastman, U Street Music Hall is the club for music lovers, with a state-of-the-art sound system and plenty of space to dance on the cushioned dance floor. The come-as-you-are club hosts top electronic DJs and artists, as well as local performers.

MAP 5: 1115 U St. NW, 202/588-1889, www.ustreetmusichall.com; hours vary based on calendar; tickets $10-30

LGBTQ
✪ Nellie's Sports Bar
Named for the owner's great grandmother and great-great grandmother, this U Street institution is the ideal place to pop into for a bucket of beers and the big game, or plan your week around trivia night or the all-you-can-eat brunch with drag performers, which usually sells out in advance. After, soak up the sun on the expansive rooftop into the evening. The crowd varies depending on the day of the week, but everyone is always welcome.

MAP 5: 900 U St. NW, 202/332-6355, www.nelliessportsbar.com; 5pm-1am Mon.-Thurs., 3pm-3am Fri., 10:30am-3am Sat., 10:30am-1am Sun.

Arts and Culture

MUSEUMS
✪ DC Alley Museum
"This used to be an alley filled with artists, weirdos, and punks," said local artist Bill Warrell upon the opening of the DC Alley Museum in Shaw's Blagden Alley. Now, with the Convention Center across the street and some of the city's hippest restaurants and bars in the surrounding blocks, Blagden Alley isn't exactly counterculture, but it's worth a visit nonetheless to catch a glimpse of what remains of the city's underground arts scene. Tucked behind the businesses along 9th Street, the alley is home to several colorful garage-door murals commissioned by the city government, including "A System of Politics and Art" by Warrell, who was a leader in the DC underground art and music scene of the '70s and '80s, as well as "Windswept Mandala" by Cita Sadeli Chelove, which highlights musicians who've had an impact on the city. It's also the home of Lisa Marie Thalhammer's much-Instagrammed "LOVE" rainbow mural, which covers four garage doors.

MAP 5: Blagden Alley NW between M and N Sts. NW and 9th and 10th Sts. NW, www.dcalleymuseum.com; accessible 24 hours daily; free

GALLERIES
Long View Gallery
At 9,000 square feet, Long View Gallery in Shaw is the largest contemporary gallery in DC, showcasing about 10 exhibitions per year from a roster of more than two dozen local and international artists. Examples include Chris Stephens, a James Madison University professor who paints Shenandoah Valley landscapes, and Sondra N. Arkin, curator of the DC City Hall Art Collection, whose recent abstract works are made with ink, wax, and wire. Each exhibition opens with an evening party, a fun way to meet artsy locals. With exposed brick walls and lofty ceilings, the gallery is frequently rented for weddings and

DC Alley Museum

private events; call ahead to confirm it's open before you go.

MAP 5: 1234 9th St. NW, 202/232-4788, www.longviewgallerydc.com; 11am-6pm Wed.-Sat., noon-5pm Sun.; free

Transformer

This tiny, storefront gallery in Logan Circle has championed emerging artists since 2002, with half a dozen or so exhibitions of contemporary works per year. Recent shows have featured Iranian American women artists and local artists exploring what it means to live a hyperlocal, sustainable lifestyle. This is a good place to find new works to add to your collection from the gallery's FlatFile, which contains more than 200 small photos, paintings, drawings, and prints by DC artists priced $500 or less.

MAP 5: 1404 P St. NW, 202/483-1102, www.transformerdc.org; noon-6pm Wed.-Sat. during exhibitions or by appointment; free

THEATER, MUSIC, AND DANCE

✪ The Howard Theatre

The Howard Theatre opened in 1910 and quickly became an important part of "Black Broadway," Washington's center of African American arts, culture, and business. For the first half of the 20th century, it was one of the nation's largest venues for black performers including Duke Ellington, Ella Fitzgerald, Marvin Gaye, and The Supremes. After the 1968 riots, the theater and many businesses around it shuttered. In 2012, it reopened after a $29 million renovation, adding modern club-style lighting, sound, and decor as well as a flexible space for 600-capacity seated shows or 1,000-capacity standing shows. Recent performers range from Wale and Lil' Kim, to gospel and jazz, to DC's top go-go bands.

BUST LOOSE: THE GO-GO SOUND

While Washington DC in the 1970s was a time of turmoil in the aftermath of the 1968 riots and the subsequent flight of white and middle-class black families to the suburbs, one thing did flourish: go-go. The upbeat, uniquely DC musical genre is classified as funk, with strong soul, salsa, and Latin and African percussion influences, a precursor to the hip-hop sound of the 1980s. The typical show relies heavily on audience participation, with call-and-response elements and danceable music, which would "go and go and go" without stopping for 40 minutes to an hour, giving the genre its name.

The Howard Theatre

The style was popularized by Chuck Brown, known as "The Father of Go-Go," a DC icon who performed his signature sound until shortly before his death in 2012, though in the '70s and '80s, there were many popular go-go bands drawing crowds at dance clubs in DC and nearby Maryland suburbs. Of course, most go-go attendees went to dance—it's impossible not to—but as violent crime increased in the 1980s in DC, so too did violent incidents at go-go clubs, and city officials and police worked to shut down the scene. "If you have a black-tie event, you don't have any problem. But if you bring go-go in, you're going to have problems," said a police commander during a 2005 hearing to shut down one of the remaining go-go venues.

The fate of the go-go parallels the story of gentrification, and today, the go-go of Chuck Brown's heyday can only be found at clubs outside the District. However, it's possible to hear some of the legendary go-go bands from the '70s and '80s for special events at theaters, concert halls, and museums citywide, including The Howard Theatre. For a throwback go-go experience, look for shows by the Chuck Brown Band, as well as Rare Essence, founded in 1976; Trouble Funk, founded in 1978; and Experience Unlimited (E.U.), founded in 1975 and one of the few to achieve mainstream fame outside DC, with their song "Da Butt," featured in Spike Lee's 1988 film *School Daze.* Don't be surprised if you recognize some of the songs—notably Brown's "Bustin' Loose," which topped the Billboard R&B chart in 1979 and was sampled in Nelly's 2002 "Hot in Herre."

JAZZ CAPITAL

Washington-born Edward "Duke" Ellington spent much of his youth in Shaw, the center of African American arts and culture from the turn of the 20th century through the early 1960s, where jazz legends like Ellington, Billie Holiday, John Coltrane, Ella Fitzgerald, Louis Armstrong, and Miles Davis, to name a few, performed in theaters along U Street NW, known as "Black Broadway." While many of the jazz clubs of yore have closed—most recently, one of Ellington's haunts, Bohemian Caverns at 11th and U—DC's jazz tradition continues in theaters and venues citywide.

The Lincoln Theatre

In the U Street Corridor and Shaw, The Howard Theatre (page 164),

which opened in 1910, and The Lincoln Theatre (page 166), in 1922, both welcomed some of these jazz greats and remain good spots to see local and national jazz musicians as well other genres (including DC's other music tradition, go-go).

The John F. Kennedy Center for the Performing Arts (page 201) in Foggy Bottom has a robust jazz calendar exploring the diversity of the genre, including the jazz greats as well as modern collaborations, like a 2017 concert featuring jazz pianist and composer Jason Moran with rapper Q-Tip. Nearby in Georgetown, enjoy jazz nightly in Blues Alley (page 199), a nightclub were Dizzy Gillespie and Wynton Marsalis have performed.

In the summer, enjoy jazz outdoors during Jazz in the Garden (page 63), weekly free jazz concerts on Friday evenings in the National Gallery of Art's Sculpture Garden, and citywide during the DC Jazz Festival (page 227) in July.

MAP 5: 620 T St. NW, 202/803-2899, www.thehowardtheatre.com; box office noon-6pm Mon.-Sat. and 9:45am-close on show days; tickets from $25

The Lincoln Theatre

After opening in 1922, The Lincoln Theatre was an important cultural center on "Black Broadway" as a place for African Americans to enjoy theater and socializing during segregation. In its heyday, it showcased everything from vaudeville to jazz greats to televised boxing matches. It fell into disrepair after the riots but was fully restored to its former glory in 1993, with seats for more than 1,000 for concert tours ranging from

Lauryn Hill to Natalie Merchant, as well as comedy and film screenings. MAP 5: 1215 U St. NW, 202/888-0050, www.thelincolndc.com; box office 1pm-7pm or until headliner begins Mon.-Fri., 1pm until headliner begins Sat.-Sun. on show days; tickets $25-65

Studio Theatre

You can truly connect with the actors at Logan Circle's Studio Theatre, which produces memorable, thought-provoking contemporary theater, including U.S. and world premieres, on four stages, each with 225 or fewer seats. See productions that address hot-button cultural and political issues, like *The*

Apple Family Plays, Richard Nelson's series following a liberal American family in New York during significant political events.

MAP 5: 1501 14th St. NW, 202/332-3300, www.studiotheatre.org; box office noon-6pm or curtain time Tues.-Sun.; tickets from $52

Shops

CLOTHING, SHOES, AND ACCESSORIES

✪ The Outrage

March over to The Outrage to get your resistance-themed gear, including tees, tanks, totes, leggings, baby onesies, jewelry, art, and much more with activist slogans—think "Families Belong Together" and "It's My Body, It's My Choice" as well as designs celebrating gay pride and Supreme Court Justice Ruth Bader Ginsberg. The proceeds from every item sold benefit organizations like Planned Parenthood, the American Civil Liberties Union, and The Malala Fund.

MAP 5: 1722 14th St. NW, 202/885-9848, www.the-outrage.com; 9am-8pm Mon.-Thurs., 10am-8pm Fri.-Sat., 10am-6pm Sun.

Current Boutique

This consignment shop sells cast-offs from the neighborhood's pretty young things, who pack the dressing rooms on weekends to try on gently used pieces for work or a night at the nearby bars. It's not uncommon to find new-with-tags items on the racks, where stock tends toward youthful, feminine labels (Kate Spade, Milly). At the front, find a selection of new, trendy dresses, blouses, and rompers from lesser-known labels, mostly under $200.

MAP 5: 1809 14th St. NW, 202/588-7311, www.currentboutique. com; noon-8pm Mon.-Fri., 11am-8pm Sat., 11am-6pm Sun.

Lettie Gooch

A longtime favorite of neighborhood fashionistas, this boutique is a must-stop shop for trendy but affordable fashion from emerging womenswear brands you won't find elsewhere in DC. The personable staff will help you pick out easy, colorful dresses, tops, and funky fashion jewelry to help you stand out at your casual office job or brunch at the beer gardens in Shaw.

MAP 5: 1921 8th St. NW, 202/332-4242, www.lettiegooch.com; noon-7pm Mon.-Fri., 11am-7pm Sat., noon-6pm Sun.

Shinola

In 2013, Central Union Mission, DC's oldest homeless shelter for men, sold its grand building at the corner of 14th and R for $7 million and moved to a new facility by Union Station. And Shinola, which sells watches assembled in Detroit with top-of-the-line watch parts from Switzerland, moved in. In the polished store, studio lights shine from the lofty ceilings to highlight the watch collection for men and women as well as luxe leather goods, journals made with sustainable paper, and sleek, hand-assembled bicycles.

MAP 5: 1631 14th St. NW, 202/470-0200, www.shinola.com; 11am-8pm Mon.-Sat., 11am-7pm Sun.

HOME AND GIFTS

✪ Miss Pixie's

Inside Miss Pixie's pink doorway is a treasure trove of vintage and re-purposed furniture, art, and home accessories in superb condition, crammed into every corner of the store. They'll arrange delivery if you find the perfect piece; in between desks and dining sets, lighter travelers will find easier-to-pack souvenirs, including flawless vintage glassware, books and comic books, and piles of DC postcards.

MAP 5: 1626 14th St. NW, 202/232-8171, www.misspixies.com; 11am-7pm daily

✪ Salt & Sundry

It's impossible to leave Salt & Sundry without buying something, because the small shop is jam-packed with the most lovely things: stunning cookbooks and linens, funky jewelry by local designer Rachel Pfeffer, an adorable selection of DC-themed baby books and bibs, and local food and beverage fixings like Embitterment cocktail bitters. Another store is located inside Union Market (1309 5th St. NE, 202/556-1866).

MAP 5: 1625 14th St. NW, 202/621-6647, www.shopsaltandsundry.com; 11am-7pm Mon.-Fri., 10am-7pm Sat., 10am-6pm Sun.

Cherry Blossom Creative

Many shops around town specializing in local products sell the gorgeous, full-color map illustrations of DC neighborhoods made by Cherry Blossom Creative, the design studio that has created logos and collateral for many local businesses. The boutique stocks maps of dozens of neighborhoods, including the ones in this guide, printed on 100-pound Ecosilk paper, as well as elegant notebooks by local brand Appointed and stationery.

MAP 5: 2128 8th St. NW, 202/319-2979, www.cherryblossomworkshop.com; noon-8pm Wed.-Sun.

Miss Pixie's

GoodWood

Fans of Anthropologie will appreciate GoodWood, which has been selling exquisitely curated vintage and antique home furnishings in the U Street Corridor since 1994. The dimly lit store has a free-spirited but still sophisticated vibe, filled with boho-chic womenswear and accessories from international labels like Almatrichi of Spain and Beautiful Stories of Iceland. On wooden tables and shelves, find candles, fragrances, and beauty products you'll want to keep on your counter.

MAP 5: 1428 U St. NW, 202/986-3640, www.goodwooddc.com; noon-7pm Mon.-Sat., noon-5pm Sun.

Union Kitchen Grocery

GOURMET FOOD AND DRINKS

✪ Union Kitchen Grocery

Many local chefs and food companies partially owe their success to Union Kitchen, an incubator of sorts to mentor more than 50 food businesses and connect them with resources, including commercial kitchen space and storage. Union Kitchen Grocery is like a gourmet bodega, stocking more than 200 local brands, such as Capital Candy Jar, Capital Kombucha, and Vigilante Coffee, as well as grocery and pantry items. There's another location near Union Station (538 3rd St. NE; 7:30am-9pm daily).

MAP 5: 1251 9th St. NW, no phone, www.unionkitchendc.com; 7am-10pm Mon.-Fri., 8am-10pm Sat.-Sun.

Batch 13

This two-level spirits shop stocks more than 1,000 types of small-batch and craft beers and wine as well as small-batch, even obscure, liquors, including local varieties like Green Hat Gin and Republic Restoratives. In other words, don't go here for rail liquor—or rail-liquor prices—but for something entirely unique. On weekends, the store offers free tastings, with discounts on the products in the tasting.

MAP 5: 1724 14th St. NW, 202/483-0214; 2pm-10pm Mon.-Tues., noon-10pm Wed.-Thurs., noon-11pm Fri.-Sat., noon-6pm Sun.

Grand Cata

Specializing in Latino wines, this well-organized shop sells wine and liquor from the Caribbean, Central America, and South America, including the usual suspects (Chile) and less-familiar regions (Uruguay), as well as heritage regions like Spain and Portugal. The charming owners and employees know wine extremely well; don't hesitate to ask for recommendations for something unique and in your price range, because they have a large selection of wines under $20.

MAP 5: 1550 7th St. NW, 202/525-5702, www.grandcata.com; noon-8pm Sun.-Mon., 11am-9pm Tues.-Sat.

Adams Morgan

Map 6

With a large immigrant population, Adams Morgan has historically been one of DC's most **ethnically diverse** neighborhoods and a center for social activism. It's known for a young, **rowdy bar scene,** but it's also the place to go for good, affordable **ethnic food** and **neighborhood restaurants, live music** and **dive bars,** and community-focused **shops.**

Nearby, **Columbia Heights** draws locals to **Meridian Hill Park** and **hipster bars** on weekends. For a different side of DC, **Mount Pleasant** offers **small-town charm** and cheap Mexican and Latin American food.

TOP RESTAURANTS

- Best Crab Cake:
  Johnny's Half Shell (page 175)
- Most Impressive Fare:
  A Rake's Progress (page 174)
- Mount Pleasant's Top Destination:
  Ellē (page 175)

TOP NIGHTLIFE

- Great for Whiskey Lovers:
  Jack Rose Dining Saloon (page 178)
- Best Dive: **Dan's Café** (page 180)

TOP RECREATION

- Coolest City Park:
  Meridian Hill Park (page 183)

TOP SHOPS

- Best Vintage Shop:
  Mercedes Bien Vintage (page 184)

GETTING THERE AND AROUND

- Metro lines: Green, Red, Yellow
- Metro stations: Columbia Heights,
  Woodley Park-Zoo/Adams Morgan
- Major bus routes: DC Circulator
  Woodley Park-Adams Morgan-
  McPherson Square Metro

1

PORTER ST NW

2

MONROE ST NW

3

17TH ST NW

A

Rock Creek

ADAMS MILL RD NW

BEACH DR NW

18TH ST NW

PARK RD NW

LAMONT ST NW

19TH ST NW

Lamont
Park

**MOUNT
PLEASANT**

17TH ST NW

KILBOURNE PL NW

B

Smithsonian National
Zoological
Park

KENYON ST NW

IRVING ST NW

HOBART ST NW

**LANIER
HEIGHTS**

Rock

Creek

HARVARD ST NW

C

CATHEDRAL AVE NW

ADAMS MILL RD NW

SUMMIT PL NW

18TH ST NW

ONTARIO RD NW

15

16

**WOODLEY
PARK**

D

Walter Pierce
Park

ONTARIO PL NW

LANIER PL NW

10

COLUMBIA RD NW

14

BEACH DR NW

CALVERT ST NW

EUCLID ST NW

ONTARIO RD NW

17TH ST NW

11　12　13

BILTMORE ST NW

19

20

E

CONNECTICUT AVE NW

19TH ST NW

MINTWOOD PL NW

17

18

**ADAMS
MORGAN**

21

CHAMPLAIN ST NW

22

KALORAMA RD NW

BELMONT RD NW

20TH ST NW

Kalorama
Park

BELMONT RD NW

23

18TH ST NW

24

F

Rock Creek
Park

ASHMEAD PL NW

KALORAMA RD NW

KALORAMA RD NW

26

CHAMPLAIN ST NW

WYOMING AVE NW

27

19TH ST NW

28

CALIFORNIA ST NW

FLORIDA AVE NW

**KALORAMA
HEIGHTS**

WYOMING AVE NW

COLUMBIA RD NW

SEE MAP 4

SEATON ST NW

18TH ST NW

29　31

30

VERNON ST NW

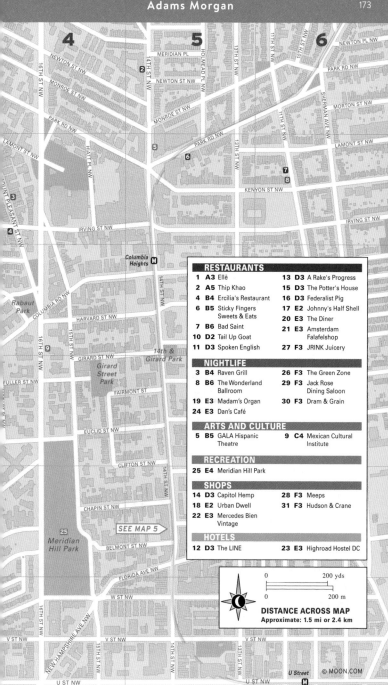

RESTAURANTS

1	**A3**	Ellé	13 **D3**	A Rake's Progress
2	**A5**	Thip Khao	15 **D3**	The Potter's House
4	**B4**	Ercilia's Restaurant	16 **D3**	Federalist Pig
6	**B5**	Sticky Fingers Sweets & Eats	17 **E2**	Johnny's Half Shell
7	**B6**	Bad Saint	20 **E3**	The Diner
10	**D2**	Tail Up Goat	21 **E3**	Amsterdam Falafelshop
11	**D3**	Spoken English	27 **F3**	JRINK Juicery

NIGHTLIFE

3	**B4**	Raven Grill	26 **F3**	The Green Zone
8	**B6**	The Wonderland Ballroom	29 **F3**	Jack Rose Dining Saloon
19	**E3**	Madam's Organ	30 **F3**	Dram & Grain
24	**E3**	Dan's Café		

ARTS AND CULTURE

5	**B5**	GALA Hispanic Theatre	9 **C4**	Mexican Cultural Institute

RECREATION

25	**E4**	Meridian Hill Park

SHOPS

14	**D3**	Capitol Hemp	28 **F3**	Meeps
18	**E2**	Urban Dwell	31 **F3**	Hudson & Crane
22	**E3**	Mercedes Bien Vintage		

HOTELS

12	**D3**	The LINE	23 **E3**	Highroad Hostel DC

SEE MAP 5

0   200 yds
0   200 m

DISTANCE ACROSS MAP
Approximate: 1.5 mi or 2.4 km

© MOON.COM

Restaurants

PRICE KEY

$	Entrees less than $15
$$	Entrees $15-25
$$$	Entrees more than $25

CLASSIC AMERICAN
The Diner $$

This Adams Morgan institution is one of the few DC restaurants open 24/7—but you won't sacrifice flavor for the convenience. Go for classic diner breakfasts (served day and night), a comforting grilled cheese with tater tots, fresh salads and veggie Reubens, or just a cup of coffee or boozy milk shake. The old-school diner is bright and bustling in the daytime, but darker and quieter at night, so you can linger over a cocktail on one of the retro stools overlooking the open kitchen. **MAP 6:** 2453 18th St. NW, 202/232-8800, www.dinerdc.com; 24 hours daily

NEW AMERICAN
✪ A Rake's Progress $$$

Meals are events at the hyperlocal, hyperseasonal showpiece restaurant in The LINE Hotel, led by the award-winning Spike Gjerde of Baltimore's Woodberry Kitchen. While presentation can border on pretentious—an earnest server might explain, for example, how your bourbon is served with water collected from a spring in West Virginia—you can't deny that everything's delicious.

The Diner

The menu changes at least weekly, using exclusively ingredients from the Mid-Atlantic region, like Chesapeake seafood and Virginia ham, while cocktails feature locally grown sorghum and herbs in lieu of nonindigenous citrus.

MAP 6: 1770 Euclid St. NW, 202/864-4190, www.thelinehotel.com/dc/venues; 6pm-10pm Wed.-Thurs., 6pm-11pm Fri.-Sat., 11am-3pm, 5pm-9pm Sun.

A Rake's Progress

✪ Ellē $$

Bakery by day, delightful restaurant by night—and the best reason to venture to Mount Pleasant, a neighborhood living up to its name north of Adams Morgan. Inspired by the space's previous occupant, Heller's Bakery, a destination for bread and pastries from 1928 to 2014, Ellē is a charming but modern spot for all-day dining. During the day, pop in for counter-service breakfast, lunch, coffee, and take-away baked goods. In the evening, enjoy a full-service dinner, with a light, creative menu balancing the exceptional breads and desserts with whole grains, kimchi, and seasonal vegetables.

MAP 6: 3221 Mt. Pleasant St. NW, 202/652-0040, www.eatatelle.com; kitchen 8am-3pm, 5:30pm-11pm daily; coffee and retail 7am-7pm daily

BARBECUE
Federalist Pig $

Does this Adams Morgan joint have the best 'cue in DC? The long line out the door and the fact that the tender cuts of brisket and pork spare ribs sell out almost every night strongly indicate yes. Go early, or place your takeout order in advance, to ensure your choice of wood-smoked meats and fresh vegetarian sides, or wrap your mitts around one of the big sandwiches, which local food critics adore. Seating inside is limited and cramped; grab a spot at one of the outdoor communal tables or take your meal to Meridian Hill Park, about a five-minute walk away.

MAP 6: 1654 Columbia Rd. NW, 202/827-4400, www.federalistpig.com; 5pm-9:30pm Wed.-Fri., noon until sold out Sat.-Sun.

STEAK & SEAFOOD
✪ Johnny's Half Shell $$

James Beard winner Ann Cashion has found a good home in Adams Morgan for her beloved seafood. Here, you'll find her superb Chesapeake Bay-style crab cakes, barbecue shrimp, and of course, oysters on the half shell. Don't let the foodies' accolades and exposed brick fool you into thinking this is a haughty hot spot; it's a friendly neighborhood restaurant through and through, with a big bar packed with regulars and staff who will make you feel like welcome guests

in the home of a friend who loves to cook and does it exceedingly well.
MAP 6: 1819 Columbia Rd. NW, 202/506-5257, www.johnnyshalfshell.net; 5pm-9pm Sun.-Thurs., 5pm-10pm Fri.-Sat., oyster bar from 4pm daily

FILIPINO
Bad Saint $$

Lovers of Filipino fare like *lumpia* (spring rolls) and chicken adobo rejoiced when the lauded Bad Saint started taking a limited number of reservations after several years as a no-reservations establishment. Didn't plan ahead? You can still line up outside to snag a seat at the teeny 24-seat restaurant, which was named one of the 13 most influential restaurants of the decade by *Food & Wine*.
MAP 6: 3226 11th St. NW, no phone, www.badsaintdc.com; 5:30pm-10pm Mon.-Thurs., 5:30pm-11pm Fri., 5pm-11pm Sat., 5pm-10pm Sun.

JAPANESE
Spoken English $$$

The best place to hang at a casual house party is in the kitchen, enjoying the host's delicious cooking right off the stove and trying some obscure sake they found on a recent trip to Japan while you get to know new friends. And that's Spoken English, Erik Bruner-Yang's unique concept in The LINE Hotel. Inspired by Japan's crowded, standing-room-only bars, the restaurant welcomes 15 diners every night to stand around two communal tables in the kitchen and enjoy inventive sharing plates, cocktails, sake, and conversation. Recognized by Michelin, the menu features adventurous skewers—think camembert cheese on

toast and turnips—and small plates, as well as chicken yakitori or a whole roast duck to share.
MAP 6: 1770 Euclid St. NW, 202/588-0525, www.spokenenglishdc.com; 6pm-midnight Tue.-Sat.

Amsterdam Falafelshop

LAOTIAN
Thip Khao $

After fleeing Laos during the Vietnam War as a child, Seng Luangrath lived in a refugee camp in Thailand, where she learned how to cook. She now runs this Michelin Bib Gourmand pick with her son, who graduated from the Culinary Institute of America and honed his craft at restaurants like minibar by José Andrés. Named for the baskets that hold sticky rice, this bright, modern restaurant serves flavorful cuisine, with many dishes coming with warnings about the spice.
MAP 6: 3462 14th St. NW, 202/387-5426, www.thipkhao.com; 5pm-10pm Mon., 5pm-10pm Wed.-Thurs., noon-3pm and 5pm-11pm Fri.-Sat., noon-3pm and 5pm-10pm Sun.

vegan cupcakes at Sticky Fingers Sweets & Eats

MIDDLE EASTERN
Amsterdam Falafelshop $

When feeding your late-night hunger pangs, skip the greasy pizza joints that line the Adams Morgan nightlife streets and opt for vegetarian-friendly falafel pitas and fries. Now a national chain, Amsterdam Falafelshop started in this Adams Morgan row house and remains one of Washington's top picks for cheap falafel and shawarma with fresh toppings. You can also get your falafel fix near 14th and U Streets NW (1830 14th St. NW) and L'Enfant Plaza (429 L'Enfant Plaza SW).

MAP 6: 2425 18th St. NW, 202/234-1969, www.falafelshop. com; 11am-midnight Sun.-Mon., 11am-2:30am Tues.-Wed., 11am-3am Thurs., 11am-4am Fri.-Sat.

SALVADORAN
Ercilia's Restaurant $

Mount Pleasant is known for Mexican and Latin American cuisine, including several joints serving traditional Salvadoran *pupusas*, which are corn tortillas stuffed with a combination of cheese, beans, and pork and fried golden and crispy. Try them at the long-standing Ercilia's, where they're just $2-4 each. The counter-service restaurant and carry-out spot serves tacos, fajitas, and chicken and shrimp platters, too, with most entrées around $10.

MAP 6: 3070 Mt. Pleasant St. NW, 202/387-0909, no website; 10am-10pm Sun.-Wed., 10am-11pm Fri.-Sat.

CAFÉS AND LIGHT BITES
The Potter's House $

Founded in 1960, The Potter's House is a nonprofit café and bookstore dedicated to social justice

177

issues—and you can feel good about your purchases, because the shop is known for paying workers above-average wages and offering a pay-what-you-can soup to the needy. In addition to coffee and tea, the café serves breakfast, sandwiches, and salads; stay a while and grab a book about current social and cultural issues, or hear guest authors and musicians.

MAP 6: 1658 Columbia Rd. NW, 202/232-5483, www.pottershousedc. org; 8am-8pm daily

VEGETARIAN AND VEGAN
JRINK Juicery $

If you aren't willing to give up your wellness routine while traveling, mark JRINK Juicery on your map, because their 100-percent-pure celery juice, pressed locally in Falls Church, Virginia, is the best bottled version in DC. In addition to cleanse kits and single bottles of juices, nut milks, and CBD-infused beverages, the shop sells made-to-order smoothies and bowls as well as other trendy wellness goodies. The Adams Morgan location is bright and spacious; others include Logan Circle (1630 14th St. NW, 202/459-7785) and Foggy Bottom (1922 I St. NW, 202/290-3193).

MAP 6: 1800 Wyoming Ave. NW, 202/415-2660, www.jrink.com; 8am-6pm Mon.-Fri., 10am-4pm Sat.-Sun.

Sticky Fingers Sweets & Eats $

Have your cake and eat it, too, sans milk and eggs. This vegan bakery serves tasty treats even nonvegans will love—after all, founder Doron Petersan won two seasons of the Food Network's *Cupcake Wars.* Try the famous sticky bun or moist cupcakes. The café also serves diner-style vegan sandwiches, burgers, and weekend brunch in a space inspired by retro diners.

MAP 6: 1370 Park Rd. NW, 202/299-9700, www. stickyfingersbakery.com; 8am-8pm Mon.-Thurs., 8am-9pm Fri., 9am-9pm Sat., 9am-8pm Sun.

Nightlife

COCKTAIL BARS AND LOUNGES
✪ Jack Rose Dining Saloon

It's all about the whiskey at Jack Rose Dining Saloon, a multilevel bar and restaurant known for its 2,500-bottle collection of whiskey and Scotch from around the world. Saddle up to the wooden bar, where you can have simple and hearty American fare, cocktails, and whiskey flights, including many rare bottles. When the weather's nice, the open-air terrace and separate tiki bar have their own menus of seasonally appropriate libations; enjoy half-price drinks at the tiki bar 5pm-9pm on Thursdays.

MAP 6: 2007 18th St. NW, 202/588-7388, www. jackrosediningsaloon.com; 5pm-2am Sun.-Thurs., 5pm-3am Fri.-Sat.

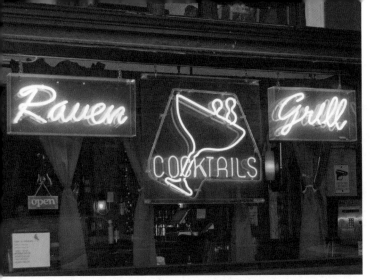

Raven Grill

Dram & Grain

This speakeasy-style bar is the place to expand your cocktail palate; tell the talented mixologists what you usually drink, and they'll steer you in the right direction. (We rarely deviate from a dirty martini but were pleasantly surprised by Stealing Tomatoes from the Garden of Eden, a light and savory vodka cocktail with fresh tomato water and mustard seed—seriously.) The regularly changing menu showcases atypical ingredients, like amaro, sherry, or anisette, though you can always order any classic. Reservations strongly recommended. Dram & Grain is located in the basement of The Imperial (202/299-0334, www. theimperial.com), a restaurant and raw bar.

MAP 6: 2001 18th St. NW, no phone, www.dramandgrain.com; 5pm-2am Wed.-Thurs., 5pm-3am Fri.-Sat.

The Green Zone

Created by a former World Bank employee inspired by his Middle Eastern heritage, The Green Zone mixes creative riffs on classic cocktails using Middle Eastern ingredients—like a shockingly potent frozen mint lemonade, similar to the traditional Lebanese beverage. In addition to cocktails, the menu features Turkish wine, Palestinian beer, and hummus, served in the bar decorated with lanterns that look like they came from the Grand Bazaar in Istanbul and a cheeky "Not WMD" sign on the keg.

MAP 6: 2226 18th St NW, no phone, www.facebook.com/thegreenzonedc; 5pm-2am Tue.-Thurs., 5pm-3am Fri.-Sat., 5pm-2am Sun.

LIVE MUSIC
Madam's Organ

Look for the mural of the well-endowed burlesque dancer to find live blues, bluegrass, country, and soul seven nights a week. (In fact,

179

DC'S OFFICIAL COCKTAIL

If you're visiting DC in the dead of summer, a refreshing **rickey** will cool you off better than any beer or rosé. Colonel Joe Rickey, a Confederate Army veteran turned well-connected Democratic lobbyist, was a frequent patron of Shoomaker's, a bar once located near the National Theatre, where he schmoozed and drank rye and water on ice. One summer day in 1883, according to legend, bartender George Williamson added half a lime to the mix, and the rickey was born, though today it's more commonly made with gin rather than rye or bourbon. (Some historians say Rickey asked for the lime, while others say he drank the cocktail with lemon, but either way, he's better known for his contribution to the American cocktail canon than anything he did in politics.)

gin rickey

In July 2011, the city council declared the rickey DC's official drink and the month of July "Rickey Month." While any decent bartender will be able to craft the simple highball, you'll find the drink on menus at bars across the city in July, when the DC Craft Bartenders Guild organizes an annual competition in which bartenders create their own takes. Rickey Month culminates in an all-you-can-drink championship event at one of the participating bars. For details on the competition and other cocktail events, visit the guild's Facebook page.

To make your own, simply combine half a lime; 2 ounces bourbon, rye, or gin; and sparkling water on ice.

The Madam is a bit controversial; the city government fined the owner because they claim the mural violates sign regulations.) The four-level establishment with five bars gets packed and sweaty on the weekends; if you need some fresh air, keep heading up to find space to lounge and a roof deck.

MAP 6: 2461 18th St. NW, 202/667-5370, www.madamsorgan. com; 5pm-2am Sun.-Thurs., 5pm-3am Fri.-Sat.; cover $5

Madam's Organ

SPORTS BARS AND DIVES

✪ Dan's Café

You won't find any frou-frou cocktails, hip DJs, or posh decor at Dan's Café—and that's why locals love it. Consistently named one of the top dive bars in the area, the family-owned establishment has been serving cheap beer and mix-your-own cocktails out of squeeze bottles to neighborhood regulars and rowdy 20-somethings since the 1940s. It's cash only, so come prepared—but you don't need more than $20 for the night.

MAP 6: 2315 18th St. NW, 202/265-9241; 7pm-2am Tues.-Thurs., 7pm-3am Fri.-Sat.

Raven Grill

This neighborhood dive has been serving cheap beer—really cheap, like $3 Natty Bohs—to Mount Pleasant residents since 1935. Its age shows, but that's what makes it unique in a city full of shiny establishments serving $15 cocktails and small plates. Come here for simple drinks (cash only), a full jukebox, and a diverse, relaxed crowd of regulars every night of the week.

MAP 6: 3125 Mt. Pleasant St. NW, 202/387-8411, no website; 4pm-2am Mon.-Tues., 2pm-2am Wed.-Thurs., 2pm-3am Fri.-Sat., 2pm-2am Sun.

The Wonderland Ballroom

Close your Tinder app and head to The Wonderland Ballroom in Columbia Heights, because this millennial paradise boasts that it's hosted nine weddings for couples who met here. During happy hour and until the wee hours on the weekends, 20- and 30-somethings crowd the bar filled with kitschy signs, the sweaty basement dance floor, and the beer garden for $3 Pabst Blue Ribbon and dance music.

MAP 6: 1101 Kenyon St. NW, 202/232-5263, www.thewonderlandballroom.com; 5pm-2am Mon.-Thurs., 4pm-3am Fri., 11am-3am Sat., 10am-2am Sun.

Arts and Culture

THEATER, MUSIC, AND DANCE

GALA Hispanic Theatre

Located in the circa-1920s Tivoli Theatre in Columbia Heights, this company has been showcasing Hispanic performing arts since the 1970s. Short for Grupo de Artistas LatinoAmericanos, GALA produces several classic and contemporary plays and musicals each year by writers from Spain, Latin America, and the United States, including many world premieres, in Spanish with English supertitles. The 265-seat theater also hosts an annual flamenco festival in November.

MAP 6: 3333 14th St. NW, 202/234-7174, www.galatheatre.org; box office 6:30pm-9pm Thurs.-Fri., 2pm-9pm Sat., noon-4pm Sun. during performance weeks; tickets from $30

CULTURAL CENTERS

Mexican Cultural Institute

The former embassy of Mexico is now home to a public educational institute showcasing Mexican arts and culture. The historical mansion is filled with spectacular

singers on Adams Morgan Day

murals painted by Roberto Cueva del Río in the 1930s and 1940s, depicting events like the Festival of the Flowers in Tehuantepec and Christopher Columbus's landing. The institute frequently hosts exhibits and events about Mexican art, cinema, music, and food; check the schedule on the website before visiting.

MAP 6: 2829 16th St. NW, 202/728-1628, www. instituteofmexicodc.org; 10am-6pm Mon.-Fri., noon-4pm Sat. during exhibitions; free

FESTIVALS AND EVENTS

Adams Morgan Day

DC's longest-running neighborhood festival, Adams Morgan Day showcases the diversity of the Northwest neighborhood, known for ethnic restaurants, iconic dives and music venues, and a progressive vibe. The one-day festival features live music and DJs, kids' games and crafts, and arts vendors, plus special deals at neighborhood restaurants, bars, and shops.

Adams Morgan: mid-Sept.; free

GALA Hispanic Theatre

Recreation

PARKS AND TRAILS
⭐ Meridian Hill Park

This 12-acre urban oasis has a storied history—and the longest cascading fountain in North America. Located on the United States' original prime meridian, 1.5 mi (2.4 km) due north of the White House, the park was the home of powerful Washingtonians, including John Quincy Adams, in the early capital days. The park has played important roles in the city's history, from serving as a camp for the Union Army to being a meeting place for civil rights rallies; when the surrounding neighborhoods burned in the 1968 riots after Martin Luther King Jr.'s assassination, Angela Davis called for the park to be named Malcolm X Park, which some longtime residents call it today. On weekends, locals lounge under statues of Dante, James Buchanan, and Joan of Arc, but the real party is at the top of the hill, where a drum circle has played every Sunday since the 1970s.

MAP 6: Between 15th St. NW and 16th St. NW, running from W St. NW north to Euclid St. NW; dawn-dusk daily; free

Joan of Arc statue by Paul Dubois in Meridian Hill Park

Shops

CLOTHING, SHOES, AND ACCESSORIES

✪ Mercedes Bien Vintage

Flawless treasures await at Mercedes Bien Vintage, on the second floor of an Adams Morgan row house. It's named after the owner, who will help you select items that suit your size and style; she carefully checks each piece before putting it on her well-organized racks, and prices are excellent considering the superb quality and fit. Most of the items are womenswear, though you'll also find pieces for men as well as shoes, jewelry, and accessories, mostly from the 1960s to 1990s. The shop is only open on weekends.

MAP 6: 2423 18th St. NW, 202/360-8481; noon-6pm Sat., noon-5pm Sun.

Meeps

This Adams Morgan mainstay feels more like a contemporary boutique than a vintage store, with edited and organized racks of on-trend, in-season clothing for men and women from the 1960s to 1990s. The items are labeled with the decade—and most are under $100. In the back, a costume room stocks more elaborate period pieces as well as new costume accessories.

MAP 6: 2104 18th St. NW, 202/265-6546, www.meepsdc.com; noon-7pm Sun.-Mon., noon-8pm Tues.-Sat.

HOME AND GIFTS

Capitol Hemp

The owners of Capitol Hemp have fought the nation's draconian cannabis laws and played a key role in decriminalizing possession of marijuana and cannabis plants for personal use in the District. Their accessible, brightly colored Adams Morgan shop sells pipes, vaporizers, cultivation equipment, and similar products, as well as ordinary household items made with industrial hemp, including nutritious food products as well as clothing and accessories.

MAP 6: 1770 Columbia Rd. NW, 202/846-1934, www.capitolhemp.com; 11am-6pm Sun.-Mon., noon-9pm Tues.-Sat.

Hudson & Crane

This hip furniture and home decor store, located where Dupont Circle meets Adams Morgan, is a

Mercedes Bien Vintage

must-stop for design inspiration. The store's nooks and shelves are filled with local gifts that are easier to pack than a couch, like city map glassware, Shrub District seasonal cocktail vinegars made in Northeast, and Ella B. candles, which have a scent for almost every major neighborhood in DC. There's another location at District Wharf (33 District Sq. SW, 202/322-7155).

MAP 6: 1781 Florida Ave. NW, 202/436-1223, www.hudsonandcrane.com; 11am-7pm Mon.-Sat., noon-6pm Sun.

Urban Dwell

If you can't find a cool souvenir or gift at Urban Dwell, it probably doesn't exist. The warm staff members will welcome you as you shop a vast assortment of whimsical DC and political-themed souvenirs and kitsch, ranging from lovely DC prints to Trump-themed toilet paper. The shop stocks luxury beauty products, ethical jewelry, fun office supplies, and baby gear and books, too.

MAP 6: 1837 Columbia Rd. NW, 202/558-9087, www.urbandwelldc.com; 11am-8pm Mon.-Tues., 11am-9pm Wed.-Fri., 10am-9pm Sat., 11am-6pm Sun.

Georgetown and Foggy Bottom

Map 7

Washington's rich and famous have always lived in Georgetown, but the quiet **cobblestone streets** with a college-town feel welcome more visitors lately thanks to several **fine restaurants** and **luxury hotels.**

Home to the U.S. Department of State and many government and hospital offices, Foggy Bottom is a quiet maze of concrete on weekends but well worth visiting to enjoy **world-class theater,** music, and dance at **The John F. Kennedy Center for the Performing Arts**

or drinks at **The Watergate Hotel,** with a mod design that will transport you to the neighborhood's heyday during the Nixon scandal.

TOP RESTAURANTS

- Best Way to Dine with DC's Elite:
  Cafe Milano (page 195)
- Most Romantic: **Fiola Mare** (page 196)
- Best Seasonal Menu:
  Blue Duck Tavern (page 193)

TOP NIGHTLIFE

- Best People-Watching:
  The Lounge at Bourbon Steak (page 198)
- Best Rooftop Bar:
  Top of the Gate (page 198)
- Best Spot for Jazz: **Blues Alley** (page 199)

TOP ARTS AND CULTURE

- Widest-Ranging Arts Venue:
  **The John F. Kennedy Center for
  the Performing Arts** (page 201)

TOP RECREATION

- Best City Hike:
  Theodore Roosevelt Island (page 202)

GETTING THERE AND AROUND

- Metro lines: Blue, Orange, Silver
- Metro stations: Foggy Bottom-GWU
- Major bus routes: DC Circulator
  Dupont Circle-Georgetown-Rosslyn,
  Georgetown-Union Station

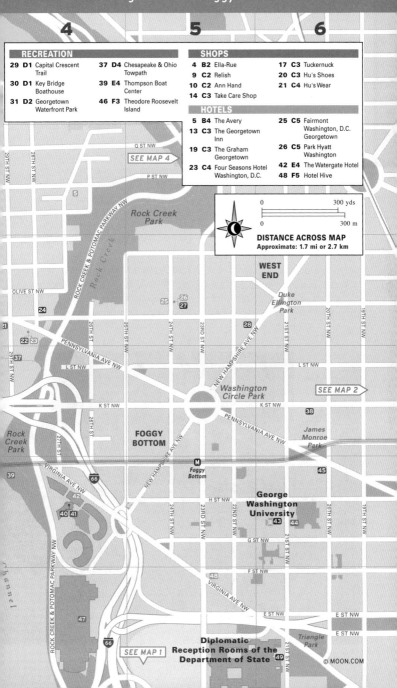

SEE MAP 4

Q ST NW
P ST NW

Rock Creek Park

0 — 300 yds
0 — 300 m

DISTANCE ACROSS MAP
Approximate: 1.7 mi or 2.7 km

WEST END

OLIVE ST NW

Duke Ellington Park

SEE MAP 2

L ST NW

K ST NW

Washington Circle Park

FOGGY BOTTOM

James Monroe Park

VIRGINIA AVE NW

Rock Creek Park

Foggy Bottom

George Washington University

H ST NW
G ST NW
F ST NW

VIRGINIA AVE NW

E ST NW
E ST NW

Triangle Park

SEE MAP 1

Diplomatic Reception Rooms of the Department of State

© MOON.COM

PENNSYLVANIA AVE NW

ROCK CREEK & POTOMAC PARKWAY NW

Sights

Diplomatic Reception Rooms of the Department of State

The U.S. Department of State is a sprawling complex in one of the swampiest parts of the city—hence the name Foggy Bottom. For the most part, it's closed to the public. However, you can tour the most splendid rooms in the building: the Diplomatic Reception Rooms, which are used for official meetings such as the signing of treaties or summits with foreign leaders. Located on the eighth floor of the State Department's headquarters, the rooms look like a colonial mansion and contain one of the finest collections of American art, furniture, and decorative arts, including some 5,000 objects from 1750 to 1825. Highlights include the desk on which Benjamin Franklin, John Jay, and John Adams signed the Treaty of Paris in 1783, ending the Revolutionary War, as well as silver made by Paul Revere and portraits of Jefferson, Franklin, Adams, and Henry Clay. You must register for the tour at least 90 days in advance on the U.S. Department of State website or through your member of Congress; the 45-minute guided tour is recommended for visitors age 12 and up.

MAP 7: 21st St. NW and C St. NW, 202/647-3241, http://receptiontours. state.gov; tours 9:30am, 10:30am, 2:45pm Mon.-Fri. by appointment

George Washington University

George Washington University

George Washington University breeds public servants, particularly in the postgrad programs in international affairs, business, and law, which are popular among young DC staffers who want to get ahead. Notable grads include senators, representatives, governors, diplomats, and media personalities, including General Colin Powell, U.S. Senator Harry Reid, First Lady Jackie Onassis Kennedy, and CNN's Dana Bash, to name a few. Founded in 1821 by an act of Congress and named for the president who hoped to establish a national university in the nation's capital, this private university is DC's largest, with 25,000 undergraduate and graduate students across three regional campuses, including the main campus in Foggy Bottom, just a few blocks from the White House and U.S. State Department. Places of note include The George Washington University Museum and The Textile Museum, which are open to the public daily, as well as The George Washington University Hospital, the most centrally located hospital for most visitors to DC, which is affiliated with the university's medical school. The Lisner Auditorium (730 21st St. NW, 202/994-6800, http://lisner.gwu.edu) is a 1,500-seat theater where you can attend discussions with politicians, authors, and media personalities ranging from Hillary Clinton to Alec Baldwin. Prospective students may register for a campus tour at the Admissions Welcome Center (800 21st St. NW, 202/994-6602).

MAP 7: 2121 Eye St. NW, 202/994-1000, www.gwu.edu

Georgetown University

Founded in 1789 by John Carroll, the first Catholic bishop in the United States, Georgetown University is the oldest Catholic and Jesuit institution of higher education in the nation. It's consistently ranked among the top universities, with a highly selective admissions process. Georgetown's elite alumni include President Bill Clinton (who lost his 1967 race for student council president), Supreme Court Justice Antonin Scalia, General John F. Kelly, and royals from Spain, Saudi Arabia, Jordan, and Greece.

The most iconic building on campus is the neomedieval Healy Hall, which looks like something out of the Harry Potter movies and bears the name of Patrick Francis Healy, the first African American president of a non-historically black college or university; Healy Hall was prominently featured in *The Exorcist,* the 1973 horror film based on the novel of the same name by William Peter Blatty, class of 1950. Sports fans may want to catch 1985 grad and former New York Knicks starter Patrick Ewing coaching the Georgetown Hoyas Division I men's basketball team, which has won several NCAA titles and plays home games at the Capital One Arena from November to March. Download a self-guided tour map (http://uadmissions.georgetown.edu) of the idyllic, 104-acre main campus, nestled on a hill high above the Georgetown shopping streets.

MAP 7: 37th St. NW and O St. NW, 202/687-0100, www.georgetown.edu

Old Stone House

Old Stone House

You might miss the unremarkable granite and fieldstone building entirely on your way to the boutiques or C&O Canal. However, the Old Stone House, smack in the middle of the M Street shopping district, is worth a stop for a snapshot of life in early Washington DC. Built in 1765, it's the oldest structure on its original foundation in the city. When the National Park Service purchased the house in 1953, then a used car dealership, it was thought to be the location where George Washington met with city planner Pierre Charles L'Enfant to discuss plans for the federal city; historians discovered the men actually met at a tavern a few blocks away, but the house had already been preserved and opened for tours. Take a guided tour of the inside to see how a middle-class family in the 18th century would have furnished their home, or stop for a shopping break in the Colonial Revival garden, a lovely spot to enjoy a treat from one of the neighborhood's excellent coffee shops.

MAP 7: 3051 M St. NW, 202/895-6000, www.nps.gov/places/old-stone-house. htm; house 11am-6pm daily, garden dawn-dusk daily; free

The Exorcist Stairs

Washington politics can be pretty frightening, but the most horrifying movie ever filmed in DC has nothing to do with political intrigue. In 1949, William Peter Blatty was attending Georgetown University when he heard a story in class about a real-life exorcism of a teen boy, which inspired him to write his bestseller The Exorcist. Many key scenes were filmed in Georgetown, notably the dramatic ending in which Father Damien Karras, momentarily possessed by the demon he has been trying to exorcise from Regan MacNeil, leaps out of the girl's bedroom window and tumbles down the steep staircase to his death. You can see the real house, and climb those terrifying steps, at the corner of Prospect Street NW and 36th Street NW. Don't try to count them, because you'll get a different number every time.

MAP 7: 3600 Prospect St. NW, 24 hours daily; free

Restaurants

PRICE KEY

$	Entrees less than $15
$$	Entrees $15-25
$$$	Entrees more than $25

CLASSIC AMERICAN

America Eats Tavern **$$**

José Andrés's casual, family-friendly restaurant celebrates American history with recipes from across the country, giving you details about where and when the recipe was created on the menu, which will please even picky palates. The menu is heavy on meat and barbecue—St. Louis-style pork ribs and Kansas-style beef brisket, fried chicken, a half-smoke hot dog inspired by Coney Island—but don't skip over tasty lighter options, like shrimp and grapefruit from the 1931 edition of The Joy of Cooking, and the original Hollywood-style Cobb salad.
MAP 7: 3139 M St. NW, 202/450-6862, www.americaeatstavern.com; 4pm-10pm Mon., 4pm-11pm Tue.-Thurs., 10am-midnight Fri.-Sat., 10am-10pm Sun.

NEW AMERICAN

✪ Blue Duck Tavern **$$$**

Blue Duck Tavern feels like a cozy neighborhood restaurant—albeit with destination-worthy, Michelin-starred cuisine in a chic atmosphere. The restaurant is warm and rustic, but modern—just like the menu, which features locally sourced,

America Eats Tavern

seasonal meats and produce cooked in the open kitchen. The brunch is one of the best; celebrate anything, or nothing at all, with the pecan sticky buns and a bottle of champagne on the patio.

MAP 7: 1201 24th St. NW, 202/419-6755, www.blueducktavern. com; 6:30am-10:30pm Sun.-Thurs., 6:30am-11pm Fri.-Sat.

Blue Duck Tavern

1789 $$$

This restaurant recognizes an important year in Washington history: 1789, the year Georgetown University was established and the United States Constitution came into force. Located in a Federal period townhouse near the top of *The Exorcist* stairs, the six dining rooms and more casual bar are decorated with historical American treasures and prints. The seasonal dishes, like fish, duck, and venison paired with produce from local farms, are served à la carte or in a five-course tasting menu ($105pp); the bar serves lower-priced bar bites, too.

MAP 7: 1226 36th St. NW, 202/965-1789, www.1789restaurant.com; 5pm-10pm Sun.-Thurs., 5pm-11pm Fri.-Sat.

STEAK AND SEAFOOD
The Prime Rib $$$

So many restaurants come and go in Washington, but this relic of the '70s and '80s with black leather booths, leopard-print carpet, and live piano music is as good as ever. Popular for both two-martini power dinners and date nights, The Prime Rib serves large portions of steaks, chops, and seafood alongside old-school steakhouse dishes like oysters Rockefeller, creamed spinach, and key lime pie—with warm service that will make you feel like one of the K Street regulars.

MAP 7: 2020 K St. NW, 202/466-8811, www.theprimerib.com; 5pm-10:30pm daily

PUBS
Martin's Tavern $$

To enjoy a family meal or to watch the big game in historical surroundings, Georgetown residents choose the cozy wooden booths at this warm tavern, which has welcomed U.S. presidents and members of Congress since 1933—including John F. Kennedy, who proposed to Jacqueline Bouvier in booth 3 in 1953. The reasonably priced pub menu features Irish favorites, a nod to the founder, William S. Martin, who immigrated to the United States from Galway in the 1890s.

MAP 7: 1264 Wisconsin Ave. NW, 202/333-7370, www.martinstavern.com; 11am-1:30am Mon.-Thurs., 11am-2:30am Fri., 8am-2:30am Sat., 8am-1:30am Sun.

DAS Ethiopian Cuisine

ETHIOPIAN
DAS Ethiopian Cuisine $$

If you're new to Ethiopian food, DAS Ethiopian Cuisine in Georgetown's shopping district is a good place to start. The smart, white-tablecloth dining room and sunny patio serve all the traditional dishes—like beef tartare *(kitfo), tibs* (sautéed meat), and hearty vegetable platters—but with utensils if you're unsure of how to eat with your hands. You'll get freshly baked *injera* bread with every order, too, in case you're a pro.

MAP 7: 1201 28th St. NW, 202/333-4710, www.dasethiopian.com; 5pm-10pm Mon.-Tue., 11am-10:30pm Wed.-Sun.

INDIAN
Rasika West End $$$

Try innovative Indian cuisine at the beloved Rasika, which comes from the Sanskrit word for "flavors." Start with a cocktail flavored with chili, cardamom, or masala chai in the light-filled bar, then move to the modern dining room for classic recipes with contemporary flair. The tandoori lamb chops are memorable, but the menu has plenty of options for vegetarians, too, including the must-try palak chaat, crispy spinach with a yogurt sauce. The West End location is sleek and modern; there's another, more classic and intimate location downtown (633 D St. NW, 202/637-1222) near the Woolly Mammoth Theatre Company.

MAP 7: 1190 New Hampshire Ave. NW, 202/466-2500, www.rasikarestaurant.com; 11:30am-2:30pm and 5:30pm-10:30pm Mon.-Thurs., 11:30am-2:30pm and 5pm-11pm Fri., 5pm-11pm Sat., 11:30am-2:30pm and 5pm-10pm Sun.

Bindaas $$

This design-driven and buzzy eatery serving Indian small plates is the one of the best restaurants near the World Bank and George Washington University Hospital—and a good spot for more casual Indian fare in a city packed with fine dining. The team behind Rasika cooks up shareable plates inspired by classic Indian street food, like Kolkata-style kathi rolls (meat or vegetable kebabs wrapped in bread), curries, rice lentil dosa, and a spicy fried chicken sandwich, along with inventive options like masala-spiced popcorn.

MAP 7: 2000 Pennsylvania Ave. NW, 202/516-4326, www.bindaasdc.com; 11:30am-10pm Mon.-Thurs., 11:30am-11pm Fri., 5pm-11pm Sat., 11am-9pm Sun.

ITALIAN
✪ Cafe Milano $$$

Since 1992, senators, cabinet secretaries, ambassadors, and even First Families have chosen buzzy Cafe Milano when they want to see and be seen during lunch or dinner. (In fact, it's the restaurant the Iranians plotted to blow up in 2011 while the Saudi ambassador was eating one of his frequent meals there.) Georgetown is no longer the hippest part of town, but the house-made pasta, simply prepared sea bass, and flavorful *panzanella* salad continue to attract movers, shakers, and visiting celebrities to the white-tablecloth dining room.

MAP 7: 3251 Prospect St., 202/333-6183, www.cafemilano. com; 11:30am-midnight Mon.-Tues., 11:30am-1am Wed.-Sat., 11am-11pm Sun., bar open late

✪ Fiola Mare $$$

Fiola Mare is such a good date night, even Barack and Michelle lingered for three hours when celebrating the former POTUS's 55th birthday. The sexy interior—dark hardwood, leather chairs, two marble bars—complements the superb seafood towers, caviar, lobster ravioli, and fresh fish, while a prosecco cocktail on the riverside patio will make you feel like you've escaped to Positano.

MAP 7: 3050 K St. NW, 202/628-0065, www.fiolamaredc.com; 4pm-9pm Mon., 11:30am-10pm Tues.-Sat., 11am-10pm Sun.

VEGETARIAN
Chaia $

Who says cheap tacos have to be junk food? Even nonvegetarians will like the fresh appeal of the seasonal, plant-based tacos at fast-casual eatery, which started as a farmers market stand. The tacos are just $3.75 apiece, or three for $11, and stuffed full of fresh produce; mushrooms, asparagus, kale, and collard greens are all on the menu, topped with fresh cheeses and flavorful sauces. There's a second location in Chinatown (615 I St. NW,

Rasika West End

202/290-1019; 11am-9pm Mon.-Fri., 10am-9pm Sat., 10am-5pm Sun.).

MAP 7: 3207 Grace St. NW, 202/333-5222, www.chaiadc.com; 11am-9pm Mon.-Fri., 10am-9pm Sat.-Sun.

Fiola Mare

BAKERIES
Baked & Wired $

A bohemian hideaway in what can be a stodgy neighborhood, Baked & Wired has the best cupcakes—much better than those by the famous cupcake shop up the street featured in the TLC reality show *DC Cupcake*. If it's in season, get the cherry blossom cupcake, a pink cake with real cherries and frothy frosting, though the classic yellow cake with chocolate frosting is an amped-up version of the childhood favorite. The small shop sells yummy baked goods (including excellent brownies and a wall of cookies) as well as coffee and a refreshing iced green tea.

MAP 7: 1052 Thomas Jefferson St. NW, 703/663-8727, www.bakedandwired. com; 7am-8pm Mon.-Thurs., 7am-9pm Fri., 8am-9pm Sat., 8am-8pm Sun.

Dog Tag Bakery $

Enjoy one of the famous fudgy brownies at Dog Tag Bakery and support men and women who have fought for our freedom. It's staffed by wounded military vets who take business classes at Georgetown University and put their education into practice by working in all areas of the shop, from the front of the house and the kitchen to the management office. The bakery has plenty of seating and serves breakfast and lunch, with coffee by Compass Coffee, a local roastery founded by two former Marines.

MAP 7: 3206 Grace St. NW, 202/407-9609, www.dogtagbakery.com; 7am-6pm Mon.-Fri., 8am-6pm Sat.-Sun.

Nightlife

COCKTAIL BARS AND LOUNGES

✪ The Lounge at Bourbon Steak

Come for the extensive cocktail menu, stay for the people-watching. You may find celebrities, social-ites, dealmakers, lonely hearts, and pretty young things looking to make connections at the long, dimly lit bar at the Four Seasons. If you get hungry, the burgers are good, or you can make your way to a table in the namesake restaurant, a pricey steak-house by Michael Mina.

MAP 7: 2800 Pennsylvania Ave. NW, 202/944-2026, www.bourbonsteakdc.com; 11:30am-midnight Mon.-Thurs., 11:30am-1am Fri., 2:30pm-1am Sat., 2:30pm-midnight Sun.

✪ Top of the Gate

With a 360-degree view of down-town, Georgetown, and Virginia, including several monuments, the sprawling, open-air rooftop bar at The Watergate Hotel is the best perch in the city—especially for happy hour, when the sun sets over the Potomac River. There's plenty of space to stand at the bar to enjoy re-freshing cocktails and champagne, or you can get a table, if you don't mind occasionally spotty service. Reservations are recommended on weekends, especially when the weather's nice; minimums for seats start at $25-40 per person or $300 for private groups.

MAP 7: 2650 Virginia Ave. NW, 202/322-6455, www.thewatergatehotel.com; 5pm-11pm Mon.-Thurs., 5pm-1am Fri., 1pm-1am Sat., 1pm-11pm Sun., April through autumn, weather permitting

The Lounge at Bourbon Steak

The Next Whisky Bar

"Show me the way to the next whisky bar," sang Jim Morrison of The Doors in 1967, the inspiration of the showstopper lounge on the main level of The Watergate Hotel. Take a seat in one of the red retro-style chairs, surrounded by 2,500 glit-tering whiskey bottles, and enjoy whiskey and bourbon cocktails and tastings with a psychedelic rock soundtrack.

MAP 7: 2650 Virginia Ave. NW, 202/827-1600, www.thewatergatehotel.com; 4pm-midnight Sun.-Thurs., 4pm-1am Fri.-Sat.

Blues Alley

cheese. No reservations are necessary; grab a plush velvet chair by the wood-burning fire and stay awhile.
MAP 7: 1035 31st St. NW, 202/965-2606, www.chezbillysud.com; 5pm-11pm Sun.-Thurs., 5pm-midnight Fri.-Sat.

LIVE MUSIC
✪ Blues Alley
Hidden in an alley off Wisconsin Avenue, this jazz club has been hosting some of the genre's greatest musicians since 1965, including Dizzy Gillespie, Ella Fitzgerald, Wynton Marsalis, and Sarah Vaughan, among many others, in the intimate space for about 125 guests. You can see live jazz performances—and sometimes, visiting celebrities in the audience—every night of the week.
MAP 7: 1073 Wisconsin Ave. NW, 202/347-4141, www.bluesalley.com; 6pm-12:30am daily; tickets $20-50, plus $12 food or beverage minimum pp

WINE BARS
Bar à Vin
There's no better retreat on a chilly evening than Bar à Vin, the dimly lit row house known for a broad list of French wines by the glass, as well as cocktails and noshes like house-made charcuterie and French

Arts and Culture

MUSEUMS
George Washington University Museum and the Textile Museum
For an academic look at the history of Washington DC, visit the largest university museum in the city. It features the Albert H. Small Washingtoniana Collection, which consists of 1,000 artifacts, including hand-drawn maps and a letter from George Washington to Congress describing the plans for the new capital. The museum is also home to more than 19,000 textiles from five continents, including carpets from Spain, Turkey, Egypt, and Iran, as well as ancient textiles from as early as 2500-3000 BC.
MAP 7: 701 21st St. NW, 202/994-5200, www.museum.gwu.edu; 11am-5pm Mon. and Fri., 11am-7pm Wed.-Thurs., 10am-5pm Sat., 1pm-5pm Sun., closed university holidays; suggested donation $8 adults, free for members, children, and GWU students, faculty, and staff

Tudor Place
The early days of the nation's capital come to life at Tudor Place,

The John F. Kennedy Center for the Performing Arts

the estate where six generations of Martha Washington's descendants lived from 1816 to 1983. Tour the restored neoclassical mansion, which is home to more than 15,000 decorative art pieces and artifacts from the Federal period—including the largest collection of objects from George Washington's life outside of Mount Vernon—as well as the 5.5 acres of lush gardens, which contain much of the original landscaping. Check the calendar for special holiday-themed events and garden tours.

MAP 7: 1644 31st St. NW, 202/965-0400, www.tudorplace.org; 10am-4pm Tues.-Sat., noon-4pm Sun., closed during January; $10 adults, $5 seniors, military, and students, $3 children 5-17, free for members and children under 5, $3 garden tour only

Dumbarton Oaks

In 1944, delegates from China, the Soviet Union, the United Kingdom, and the United States met at Dumbarton Oaks to create the United Nations Charter. Today, this tranquil estate high above the Georgetown shopping streets is home to former owners Mildred and Robert Woods Bliss's unparalleled collection of pre-Columbian and Byzantine art, as well as 16 acres of exquisite gardens and orchards designed by the country's first female landscape architect, Beatrix Jones Farrand. Take a guided tour, or simply enjoy some peace.

MAP 7: 1703 32nd St. NW, 202/339-6400, www.doaks.org; museum 11:30am-5:30pm Tues.-Sun. year-round, garden 2pm-6pm Tues.-Sun. Mar. 15-Oct. and 2pm-5pm Tues.-Sun. Nov.-Mar. 14; museum free, gardens free in winter and $10 adults, $8 seniors, and $5 children 12 and under Mar. 15-Oct.

GALLERIES
Book Hill Galleries

High on Wisconsin Avenue NW near Tudor Place, you'll find six fine art galleries for all tastes, ranging from locally made prints at the Washington Printmakers Gallery (1641 Wisconsin Ave. NW, 202/669-1497, www.washingtonprintmakers.com; 11am-6pm Thurs.-Sat., noon-5pm Sun., and by appointment), to Italian art and ceramics (and wine and authentic food) at Via Umbria (1525 Wisconsin Ave. NW, 202/333-3904, www.viaumbria.com; 11am-10pm Tue.-Sat., 11am-5pm Sun., and by appointment). Even if you're not in the market for fine art, the galleries welcome casual browsing; check the website for opening receptions and special events, including spring and fall art walks.

MAP 7: Wisconsin Ave. NW between O St. NW and Reservoir Rd., www.georgetowngalleries.com; hours vary by gallery

The REACH at the Kennedy Center

THEATER, MUSIC, AND DANCE

✪ The John F. Kennedy Center for the Performing Arts

Named for one of the nation's greatest advocates for the arts, the Kennedy Center showcases world-class music, theater, opera, dance, and comedy for all tastes and ages. One of the premier performing arts venues in the city, if not the country, it's home to the dazzling National Symphony Orchestra, which performs classical and contemporary works, as well as the Washington National Opera and Suzanne Farrell Ballet. The Kennedy Center holds a free performance every day of the year at 6pm in the Grand Foyer. Whatever you're there to see, arrive early to enjoy a pre-show drink at the Roof Terrace Restaurant (5pm-8pm before Concert Hall and Opera House evening performances, 11am-2pm most Sun.).

MAP 7: 2700 F St. NW, 202/467-4600, www.kennedy-center.org; box office 10am-9pm Mon.-Sat., noon-9pm Sun.; tickets $25-175

The REACH at the Kennedy Center

The first-ever expansion of the Kennedy Center since it opened in 1971, The REACH is a 72,000-square-foot campus on 4.6 acres dedicated to developing new art and art lovers with interactive experiences in a modern, LEED-certified space. As a sign of what's ahead, The REACH opened in 2019 with a 16-day festival chock full of free programing for all ages. Check the website for wide-ranging, inexpensive (around $20pp) or free events ranging from film screenings and art exhibits to contemporary music and comedy in a club-like space. Kids will love the Moonshot Studio, a free space to create and engage with art.

MAP 7: 2700 F St. NW, 202/467-4600, www.kennedy-center.org/reach; campus 10am-midnight daily, Moonshot Studio 10am-4pm Sat.-Sun.

Recreation

PARKS AND TRAILS

✪ Theodore Roosevelt Island

Located in the Potomac River at the DC-Virginia border, Theodore Roosevelt Island is a memorial to the 26th POTUS, a dedicated conservationist, and an idyllic spot to experience nature in the heart of the city. The island—which is indeed a real island, though it was cleaned up and landscaped by FDR's Civilian Conservation Corps—contains just over 2.5 mi (4 km) of easy trails through forests and swampland; you can also pick up the Mount Vernon Trail here. The island is located in DC but accessible only from Virginia. It's a 15-minute walk from the Rosslyn Metro station or a 20-minute walk from Georgetown over the Francis Scott Key Bridge; cross the footbridge at the parking lot to access the island.

MAP 7: Enter via the parking lot off the George Washington Memorial Parkway near the Francis Scott Key Bridge and Mount Vernon Trail, 703/289-2500, www.nps.gov/this; accessible 6am-10pm daily weather permitting; free

Capital Crescent Trail

The 11-mi (17.7-km), mostly paved Capital Crescent Trail is popular with joggers, cyclists, and even commuters who travel from the suburbs of Bethesda and Silver Spring to work in DC. The leafy but

Theodore Roosevelt Island

BICYCLE RENTALS

Capital Bikeshare station

For short-term or point-to-point rentals, Capital Bikeshare (877/430-2453, www.capitalbikeshare.com) makes it easy to find and acquire a bicycle. The program has more than 3,700 bikes at 440-plus stations in DC, Maryland, and Virginia. Look for the stations with their rows of shiny, cherry red bikes, use your credit card at the kiosk to get a code to unlock a bike, and pedal away. You can purchase a single trip up to 30 minutes for $2, a 24-hour pass for $8, or a 72-hour pass for $17; passes allow you to take unlimited 30-minute rides. Download the mobile app to see nearby stations and real-time availability.

For a longer ride, such as a day trip to Mount Vernon, or multiday rentals, Bike and Roll (202/842-2453, www.bikeandrolldc.com) has bicycles and equipment available at several locations; they'll also deliver bikes to your hotel.

The District of Columbia requires riders ages 16 and under to wear a helmet when riding a bike, scooter, or skateboard. For more information on bicycle rentals and trails, visit www.bikewashington.org.

well-maintained trail is one of the most traveled in the country, but it's rarely too crowded to enjoy. Take a 7-mi (11.3-km) bike ride to Bethesda, where you can break for lunch and still get back to DC in time to rest before dinner. Alternatively, stop at Fletchers Cove (4940 Canal Rd. NW, 202/244-0461) to switch to the water, or pick up the Chesapeake & Ohio Towpath, which runs parallel with the Capital Crescent Trail through Georgetown for about 3.5 mi (5.6 km).

MAP 7: Access via Water St. NW under Whitehurst Freeway, 202/610-7500, www.cctrail.org; 24 hours daily; free

Chesapeake & Ohio Towpath

The Chesapeake & Ohio Towpath follows the C&O Canal for 184.5 mi (300 km) from Georgetown to Cumberland, Maryland. Mile 0 is located at the canal's "watergate" near the famous hotel, but you can start your journey in Georgetown's shopping district. Look for the redbrick path at 29th Street south of M Street, and head east. If you're up for a long ride, follow the Capital Crescent

Chesapeake & Ohio Towpath

Trail through Georgetown, which runs parallel for about 3.5 mi (5.6 km), to Fletchers Cove (4940 Canal Rd. NW, 202/244-0461), where you can pick up the towpath to go to Great Falls (14 mi/22.5 km) or Harpers Ferry (60 mi/97 km).

MAP 7: Access from Thompson Boat Center or 29th St. NW at M St. NW, 301/739-4200, www.nps.gov/choh; 24 hours daily; free

Georgetown Waterfront Park

This 10-acre urban oasis is the perfect spot for a city picnic with a view of the Potomac River and major sights. The park has wide paved paths for cycling, skating, or jogging, and connects to several regional trails; there's ample green space as well as seating right on the riverbank. Children of all ages will enjoy features like the labyrinth and the fountain, which you're welcome to splash around in on a hot day.

MAP 7: 30th St. NW to 34th St. NW along the Potomac River, www.georgetownwaterfrontpark.org; 24 hours daily; free

BOATING

Key Bridge Boathouse

Rent a canoe, kayak, or paddleboard at the Key Bridge Boathouse and explore the Potomac River via the Georgetown Waterfront; prices range from $16 per hour for singles and $22-25 per hour for doubles. Just under the Francis Scott Key Bridge near the start of the Capital Crescent Trail, the boathouse offers 90-minute guided kayak tours of the monuments and major sights ($45) as well as stand-up paddleboarding ($55 pp), fitness and yoga classes ($10-40), and more.

MAP 7: 3500 Water St. NW, 202/337-9642, www.boatingindc.com; daily Apr. 15-Oct., hours vary

Thompson Boat Center

Thompson Boat Center

The slightly hidden boathouse by the Washington Harbor has everything you need for a day outdoors: kayaks ($16-22/hour), canoes ($25/hour), and paddleboards ($22/hour), so you can explore the Potomac River and Rock Creek, as well as bike rentals ($11/hour or $35/day). For a workout on the water, try sculling, which is rowing with two oars; certification is required.

MAP 7: 2900 Virginia Ave. NW, 202/333-9543, www.boatingindc.com; daily Apr. 15-Oct., hours vary

Georgetown Waterfront Park

Shops

CLOTHING, SHOES, AND ACCESSORIES

Ann Hand

Owned by the eponymous Georgetown power player, Ann Hand has been creating fine jewelry for policymakers, diplomats, and socialites since the 1980s, including custom-designed commissions for the White House. Here, pick up a commemorative flag or military lapel pin or the "Liberty Eagle" brooch famously worn by former Secretary of State Madeleine Albright, as well as jewelry, cuff links, and silk scarves with American imagery.

MAP 7: 3236 Prospect St. NW, 202/333-2979, www.annhand.com; 10am-4pm Mon.-Fri.

Ella-Rue

The stylish ladies of Georgetown take their (gently loved) cast-offs to luxury consignment boutique Ella-Rue, where you may find Chanel jackets, Tory Burch sheath dresses, and Manolo Blahnik pumps on the tightly packed racks, curated by the owner, who will help you find your desired look. The selections include party, professional, and casual clothing, but they're all high-end labels; many pieces have the original tags, and prices are fair for designer goods.

MAP 7: 3231 P St. NW, 202/333-1598, www.ella-rue.com; 10am-6pm Tues.-Sat., noon-5pm Sun.

Hu's Shoes

For the most luxurious, most covetable, most eat-ramen-for-a-month-to-own-them shoes in the city, run to Hu's Shoes, which has been adorning the feet of DC's most fashionable since 2005. In the luxe, minimalist shop, find brands you already love—Jimmy Choo, Manolo Blahnik, Fendi—plus new ones straight from New York, Paris, and Milan.

MAP 7: 3005 M St. NW, 202/342-0488, www.husonline.com; 10am-7pm Mon.-Sat., noon-5pm Sun.

Hu's Wear

Owned by a former graphic designer who decided to follow her passion for fashion, Hu's Wear, the sibling of Hu's Shoes across the street, is known for a tightly edited selection of staples fresh from the runways, from Altuzarra to Yigal Azrouel. The stock tends to be on the pricier

Hu's Shoes

side, though you'll find contemporary labels and denim, too.

MAP 7: 2906 M St. NW, 202/342-2020, www.husonline.com; 10am-7pm Mon.-Sat., noon-5pm Sun.

Relish

This Georgetown mainstay has been dressing well-dressed Washingtonians since 1996, with a fashion-forward selection that's current without being overly trendy. Here, you'll find clothing, shoes, and accessories from labels in the vein of Dries van Noten, Marni, and Simone Rocha, as well as emerging designers.

MAP 7: 3312 Cady's Alley NW, 202/333-5343, www.relishdc.com; 10am-6pm Mon.-Sat.

Tuckernuck

Get the fresh, all-American look, or a new wardrobe for your Nantucket vacation, at Tuckernuck, which started as an online boutique and opened a flagship in 2016 in Georgetown, the founder's hometown. In a space that looks like an upscale beach house, you'll find the prettiest, preppiest fashion of the season from labels like Rebecca Taylor, Shoshanna, and Jack Rogers—plus stuff for guys, too.

MAP 7: 1053 Wisconsin Ave. NW, 202/856-7260, www.tnuck.com; 10am-7pm Tues.-Sat., 11am-5pm Sun.

HEALTH AND BEAUTY
Take Care Shop

This ethereal shop decorated entirely in white is the destination for exclusively natural, organic, and plant-based skincare and beauty products, including buzzy brands like Herbivore Botanicals, May Lindstrom, Moon Juice, and Tata Harper, as well as local organic brand Skincando. Pick up a crystal or trendy jade face roller, or book a facial or makeup bag makeover before a night out.

MAP 7: 1338 Wisconsin Ave. NW, 202/717-2600, www.takecareshopdc.com; 11am-7pm daily

District Wharf, Navy Yard, and Anacostia

Map 8

Southwest Washington, just a quick Metro ride from the city center, is home to **The District Wharf.** Appealing to visiting foodies and fun seekers, this waterfront complex features several **mega restaurants, hotels,** and **entertainment venues.**

In Navy Yard, watch a game at **Nationals Park,** one of the greenest baseball stadiums in the country. Nearby, the **Anacostia Riverwalk Trail,** boating facilities, and green space make up for the neighborhood's lack of charm as **high-rise buildings** dominate the skyline.

On the other side of the river, **culturally rich** Anacostia is a neighborhood in transition. It boasts the Smithsonian's **Anacostia Community Museum,** which chronicles the city's history. Visit the **Frederick Douglass National Historic Site,** where the famed abolitionist once lived, or check out **art galleries** displaying the work of emerging artists.

TOP SIGHTS

- Hidden Black History Gem: **Frederick Douglass National Historic Site** (page 219)

TOP ARTS AND CULTURE

- Best Alternative to Broadway: **Arena Stage** (page 226)

TOP SPORTS AND ACTIVITIES

- Best Multiuse Trail: **Anacostia Riverwalk Trail** (page 227)
- Best Way to Enjoy America's Favorite Pastime: **Washington Nationals** (page 228)

GETTING THERE AND AROUND

- Metro lines: Green
- Metro stations: Navy Yard-Ballpark, Waterfront, Anacostia
- Major bus routes: DC Circulator Union Station-Navy Yard, Potomac Ave Metro-Skyland via Barracks Row

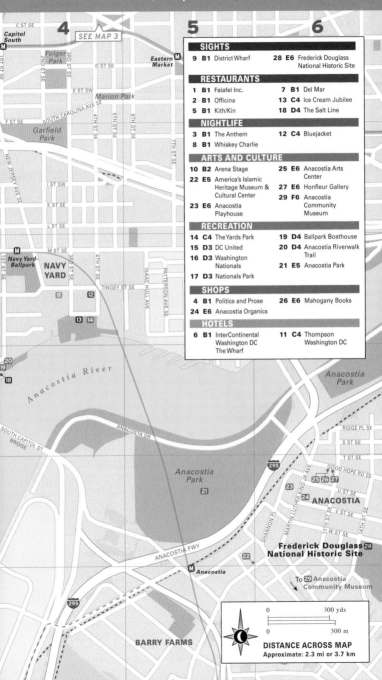

SIGHTS

9 **B1** District Wharf
28 **E6** Frederick Douglass National Historic Site

RESTAURANTS

1 **B1** Falafel Inc.
2 **B1** Officina
5 **B1** Kith/Kin
7 **B1** Del Mar
13 **C4** Ice Cream Jubilee
18 **D4** The Salt Line

NIGHTLIFE

3 **B1** The Anthem
8 **B1** Whiskey Charlie
12 **C4** Bluejacket

ARTS AND CULTURE

10 **B2** Arena Stage
22 **E5** America's Islamic Heritage Museum & Cultural Center
23 **E6** Anacostia Playhouse
25 **E6** Anacostia Arts Center
27 **E6** Honfleur Gallery
29 **F6** Anacostia Community Museum

RECREATION

14 **C4** The Yards Park
15 **D3** DC United
16 **D3** Washington Nationals
17 **D3** Nationals Park
19 **D4** Ballpark Boathouse
20 **D4** Anacostia Riverwalk Trail
21 **E5** Anacostia Park

SHOPS

4 **B1** Politics and Prose
24 **E6** Anacostia Organics
26 **E6** Mahogany Books

HOTELS

6 **B1** InterContinental Washington DC The Wharf
11 **C4** Thompson Washington DC

NAVY YARD WALK

TOTAL DISTANCE: 1.3 mi (2.1 km)
WALKING TIME: 30 minutes

This riverfront community was once the city's busiest port and the U.S. Navy's largest and longest-operating shipbuilding facility in the country, from 1799 until the 1960s. While shipbuilding activities have ceased, thousands of U.S. Navy administrative staff and federal employees work here today in the shadow of new apartment and condo buildings, restaurants, and Nationals Park. Here, you can pick up hiking trails or rent a boat, or just enjoy the view of the water; by the time you read this book, there's likely to be even more development, including more restaurants, bars, and shops, in this rapidly growing neighborhood.

The starting point for this walk is the **Navy Yard/Ballpark Metro station.**

1 When you get off the Metro, take the Department of Transportation exit to enter the heart of Navy Yard. Walk southeast (right) on

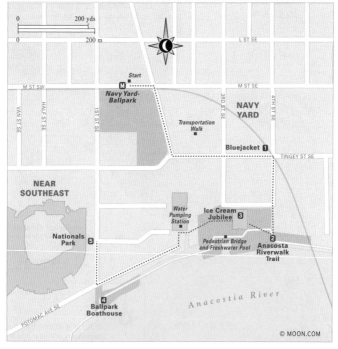

Anacostia Riverwalk Trail

New Jersey Avenue SE, with the 2.1-million-square-foot U.S. Department of Transportation on your left. After about a block and a half, turn left to enter the **Transportation Walk,** a two-block, outdoor museum about transportation milestones and leaders in America along the south side of the DOT's main building. Check out the old-fashioned gas pumps and a restored electrical substation, and informational signs about Sally Ride and the Lewis and Clark Expedition. Continue for just over a block to 4th Street SE, and go south (right). On your right, **Bluejacket** is a good place to stop for a beer and a bite in a former Navy Yard factory.

2 Cross Tingey Street SE and continue south on 4th Street SE. If beer isn't your cup of tea, you have several options on this block for refreshments, like District Winery, DC's first commercial winery which opened in 2017 with a tasting bar and full restaurant to much critical acclaim. Keep heading toward the Anacostia River to reach the **Anacostia Riverwalk Trail,** a 20-mi (32-km) paved riverside path that connects DC and Maryland. You'll soon be in the heart of Yards Park.

3 Head west along the boardwalk (part of the Anacostia Riverwalk Trail). If you want a snack, grab a locally made cone at **Ice Cream Jubilee** to enjoy on the grass. Cross the sculptural steel **pedestrian bridge,** or, if the weather is nice, dip your toes into the **freshwater pool** directly underneath the bridge, an area that's busy with families splashing around on hot days.

4 Keep heading west on the waterfront trail, which is busy with runners and cyclists year-round. You'll quickly come upon DC's historic **water pumping station,** the beaux arts structure that's been pumping wastewater since 1905. Today, it pumps 400 million gallons per day. After you check out the short exhibit about the DC Clean Rivers Project and

The Salt Line

The Yards Park

the work that goes into cleaning up the pollution in the river, keep walking west on the bridge to reach **Ballpark Boathouse,** where you can rent kayaks or canoes seasonally. If you didn't eat yet, our favorite Navy Yard restaurant, **The Salt Line,** is straight ahead and worth a stop for raw bar favorites on the water.

5 When you reach **Nationals Park,** head north on First Street SE, with the stadium on your left. If you want to get tickets to a ballgame, walk about three blocks to the main box office on N Street SE; otherwise, keep walking to M Street SE and head east one block to return to the Navy Yard-Ballpark Metro station. From here, the Green Line offers several choices for your next adventure: Go one stop south, where you can start the Anacostia walking tour on page 215. Take the Metro one stop north to the Waterfront station and check out the dining and entertainment options at the District Wharf. Or take a slightly longer ride: It's four stops to Gallery Place-Chinatown and the heart of downtown.

ANACOSTIA WALK

TOTAL DISTANCE: 1.4 mi (2.3 km)
WALKING TIME: 30 minutes

Among DC's neighborhoods, Anacostia has the most interesting and challenging history. It was incorporated in 1854 to be an affordable suburb for working-class families, but time—and the Civil War, segregation, and the 1968 riots after the assassination of Dr. Martin Luther King Jr.—brought turmoil and saw growth in drugs, gangs, and crime.

This has changed. Anacostia is a neighborhood in transition, one where residents, community organizations, and businesses are coming together to help Anacostia embrace the boom in DC while maintaining its historic character and culture. Note that some areas covered by this walking tour may feel desolate even during the day. You're advised to take the walk during the daytime and stick to the areas covered here unless you're familiar with the area.

This walk, which takes you through the Anacostia Historic District (listed on the National Register of Historic Places) to the Frederick

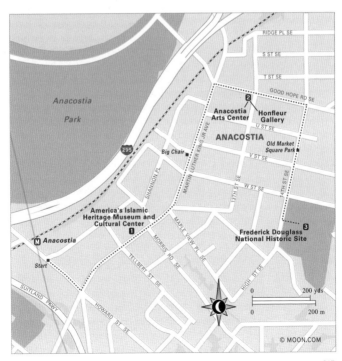

© MOON.COM

215

vintage Anacostia sign

Douglass National Historic Site, is a lovely way to learn about the neighborhood's rich history and bright future. The Anacostia Historic District is easily accessible by Metro; take the Green Line to **Anacostia Station** and exit at Howard Road.

1 From the Metro station, walk southeast on Howard Road for approximately one block, then head northeast on Martin Luther King Jr. Avenue SE. Along this route, you'll see several of the 20 numbered signs of the Anacostia Heritage Trail, which Cultural Tourism DC launched in 2015 to showcase the history of the community; get to know prominent African Americans who lived here, like John A. Moss, who escaped slavery and became the neighborhood's first lawyer; Solomon Brown, the first African American to work at the Smithsonian Institution; and, of course, Frederick Douglass. After about a block and a half, **America's Islamic Heritage Museum and Cultural Center** will be on the left. This museum has displays, rife with text and photographs, which traveled with the U.S. State Department before finding a permanent home in Anacostia. It's worth spending an hour or two here if you want to dig into the stories of American Muslims that you may not have known before.

2 Keep going northeast on Martin Luther King Avenue SE for about 2.5 blocks. You can't miss the 19.5-foot **Big Chair** on your left, a mahogany chair sculpture built in 1959 to advertise Curtis Bros. Furniture Company, an Anacostia business. Located between W Street SE and V Street SE, it's an iconic neighborhood landmark. Walk northeast another two blocks to Good Hope Road SE., past local businesses like **Anacostia Organics** and an outpost of **Busboys and Poets**. To your left at the intersection, a strip of buildings containing a drugstore and hydroponics supply shop sports the famous "Anacostia" neon sign. (If you were to keep heading north, you'd come to the 11th Street Bridge, which was part of John Wilkes Booth Jr.'s escape route after he assassinated President Abraham Lincoln.) From here, go east (right) on Good Hope Road SE for less than a block to get to the **Anacostia Arts Center** and **Honfleur Gallery.** In addition to housing art exhibitions, the Arts Center is a good place to stop for a cup of coffee or a snack and browse the boutiques that share the space.

the Big Chair

3 Walk east another block on Good Hope Road SE and head south on 14th Street SE. The median between U Street SE and V Street SE, surrounded by several churches, is **Old Market Square Park,** built in 1913; it's been an important community meeting spot for decades, though it was recently renovated with new benches and landscaping. Walk south on 14th Street SE another block, then go east on W Street SE. The **Frederick Douglass National Historic Site** is ahead high on the hill; pass by the stairs leading up to the mansion and start your tour in the visitors center.

4 To get back to the Metro, head west on W Street SE for about three blocks, then go south on Martin Luther King Jr. Avenue SE for four blocks to Howard Road SE. Turn north (right) onto Howard; the Metro station will be on your left in one block. If you haven't yet explored Navy Yard, take the Metro Green Line from Anacostia Station one stop north to Navy Yard/Ballpark Station, then follow the Navy Yard walking tour on page 212.

Sights

District Wharf

Since opening in October 2017, this 24-acre development—the largest new development in Washington DC in decades—has dramatically changed the landscape of Southwest's waterfront. This once-quiet stretch along the Potomac River, cut off from the city center by a major highway, is now a destination with three major hotels, four residence buildings, two office buildings, four recreation and transportation piers, and dozens of restaurants, bars, and shops, including some of the most influential names in dining and nightlife in DC.

District Wharf

This shiny, mile-long complex is not authentically cool, but it's impressive in scale—and when the newness wears off and the neighborhood finds its role in the rhythms of daily life in DC, District Wharf will surely become an essential part of the city. Already, there are reasons to visit, notably The Anthem (901 Wharf St., 202/888-0020, tickets 877/435-9849, www.theanthemdc.com), the 6,000-capacity club from the owners of the storied 9:30 Club. In addition, District Wharf has several much-hyped, multistory restaurants—providing dining options before or after a performance at nearby Arena Stage—including Del Mar (791 Wharf St. SW, 202/525-1402, www.delmardc.com), serving coastal Spanish cuisine by Fabio Trabocchi of Georgetown's Fiola Mare, and Kith & Kin (202/878-8566, http://kithandkindc.com), featuring Kwame Onwuachi's African-Caribbean fusion, as well as an outpost of Hank's Oyster Bar (202/817-3055, http://hanksoysterbar.com). And, of course, the piers provide recreation opportunities, including sailing lessons, rentals, and charters at DC Sail (202/547-1250, www.dcsail.org) and a seasonal ice-skating rink. For an authentic taste of the waterfront of yore, don't miss the Maine Avenue Fish Market, which opened in 1805 and remains the oldest continually operating fish market in the country. The open-air market has been incorporated into the west end of District Wharf, remaining an authentic choice for fresh seafood, including crabs, shrimp, oysters, and fish, which you can enjoy right on the water, or take home to prepare.

While District Wharf seems distant from the main tourist areas, it's actually quite convenient, less than 10 minutes by foot from the

Frederick Douglass National Historic Site

Waterfront and L'Enfant Plaza Metro stations, and less than 20 minutes by foot from the National Mall. A free shuttle (7th St. and Independence Ave. SW; 6:30am-11:30pm Mon.-Thurs., 6:30am-1am Fri., 9am-1am Sat., 9am-11pm Sun.) is available from the National Mall daily. From the Transit Pier, catch water taxis ($10-18 adults, $7-12.60 children) to Georgetown and Old Town Alexandria. Across the development, you'll find many quick-serve food and beverage kiosks as well as (a rarity!) public restrooms.

Phase II is expected to be completed in 2022.

MAP 8: Maine Ave. SW from 6th St. SW west toward L'Enfant Plaza, www. wharfdc.com; 24 hours/daily, individual merchant hours vary

TOP EXPERIENCE
✪ Frederick Douglass National Historic Site

While the National Museum of African American History and Culture has been getting so much attention, the National Park Service has been quietly preserving the legacy of one of the country's most important abolitionists—and you won't need to wait for hours to see it. Located in Anacostia, the Frederick Douglass National Historic Site is also known as Cedar Hill. It's the estate where Douglass lived from 1877, when he was appointed U.S. Marshall by President Rutherford B. Hayes, until his death in 1895. The tour of this restored Victorian mansion offers a glimpse of life at the turn of the 20th century. See rooms containing many of Douglass's personal belongings in the exact spots they would have been while he was alive, as well as artwork and photographs of the Douglass family. The home is only accessible by guided tour with a park ranger, who will point out fascinating artifacts and relate tidbits about the man who was born a slave and would eventually become a renowned (and mostly self-educated) abolitionist, author, and speaker. Tickets for the six daily, 30-minute tours are readily available if you reserve them online at least a few days in advance. Arrive early to catch the 19-minute film about Douglass, and when you finish the tour, take in the view from his porch, located high above the city on a 51-foot hill and offering expansive views all the way to the U.S. Capitol. MAP 8: 1411 W St. SE, 202/426-5961, www.nps.gov/frdo; 9am-5pm daily Apr.-Oct., 9am-4:30pm daily Nov.-Mar.; $1.50 for reserved ticket; reservations recommended

Restaurants

PRICE KEY

$	Entrees less than $15
$$	Entrees $15-25
$$$	Entrees more than $25

STEAK & SEAFOOD
The Salt Line $$

Our favorite restaurant in Navy Yard, the ballpark-adjacent restaurant and bar has Chesapeake Bay and New England-style seafood and lovely water views. Dine on clam chowder, East Coast raw bar items, and an addictive pimento cheese crab dip with Old Bay seasoning inside the pretty restaurant, or chill out with local beers and beachy cocktails on the riverfront patio, which gets packed before home games.

MAP 8: 79 Potomac Ave. SE, 202/506-2368, www.thesaltline. com; 4:30pm-midnight Mon.-Thurs., 4:30pm-1am Fri., 11am-1am Sat., 11am-midnight Sun.; patio hours vary seasonally

AFRO-CARIBBEAN
✪ Kith/Kin $$$

Yes, the all-day lobby restaurant in an otherwise ordinary modern hotel is worth visiting. Former Top Chef contestant Kwame Onwuachi (and author of Notes from a Young Black Chef) has found a home in the InterContinental in the Wharf, where he combines flavors of his African and Caribbean heritage with experience at the Culinary Institute of America and the acclaimed Eleven Madison Park in New York. In the glossy space with floor-to-ceiling windows and water views, try creative takes on braised oxtails, jerk chicken, and jollof rice, a traditional West African rice dish, as well as standard hotel breakfast fare.

entrée at Kith/Kin

The Salt Line

MAP 8: InterContinental Washington DC – The Wharf, 801 Wharf St. SW, 202/878-8566, www.kithandkindc.com; 6:30am-10:30pm Sun.-Thurs., 6:30am-11pm Fri.-Sat., bar bites in lounge to 11pm daily

ITALIAN
✪ Officina $$$

Michelin-worthy pasta, rooftop aperitivo, or pastry on the go? This three-story behemoth is like a trip to Italy—but we prefer the glam, all-day café with a marble bar, comfy leather stools, and huge windows opening onto the Wharf for an authentic café Americano you'll only find in Europe. Grab a fresh focaccia or house-made ice cream in the ground-floor market, which also stocks Italian pantry staples, or dine in the light-filled second-floor trattoria, which has an expansive menu of pasta, cheese and charcuterie, and meat and seafood. Officina also boasts DC's largest collection of Amari, Italian herbal liqueur, as well as a popular year-round roof terrace serving wine, cocktails, and bites.

MAP 8: 1120 Maine Ave. SW, 202/747-5222, www.officinadc.com; 11am-10pm Mon.-Thurs., 11am-midnight Fri.-Sat., noon-9pm Sun., market 11am-7pm Mon.-Wed., 11am-8pm Thurs.-Fri., 10am-8pm Sat., 10am-7pm Sun., terrace hours vary seasonally

MIDDLE EASTERN
Falafel Inc. $

Falafel Inc.'s vegetarian falafel, hummus, and bowls are not only good for you, but do good, too. For every $10 customers spend, the fast-casual restaurant feeds one refugee for a day through a partnership with the World Food Programme. And, somehow, the food's cheap, too—$3 pita sandwiches and zaatar fries and $4 bowls, made with locally sourced ingredients. There's another location in Georgetown (1210 Potomac St. NW, 202/333-4265, noon-10pm Mon.-Sat., noon-9pm Sun.).

221

MAP 8: 1140 Maine Ave. SW, 202/333-4265, www.falafelinc.org; 11:30am-8pm Mon.-Thurs., noon-9pm Fri.-Sat., noon-8pm Sun.

Del Mar

SPANISH
Del Mar $$$

Okay, so, the food's so expensive at the Fabio Trabocchi empire's Spanish restaurant, you'll wonder if the cured jamón and fresh lubina (branzino) flew business class on their way over from the Mediterranean. But we have to admit, it's almost as good as what you'd get at a posh beach club in Ibiza. If you're ready to spend for a very special occasion with water views (without the plane ticket to the Balearics), the authentic tapas and paella, uncommon raw bar selections, and gin and tonics with fresh herbs are worth your while.

MAP 8: 791 Wharf St. SW, 202/525-1402, www.delmardc.com; 4pm-9pm Mon., 11:30am-9pm Tue., 11:30am-10pm Wed.-Sat., 11:30am-9pm Sun.

DESSERT
Ice Cream Jubilee $

Close to Nationals Park, Ice Cream Jubilee scoops small-batch ice cream and sorbet made with local, natural ingredients. Try MarionBerry, a nod to DC's infamous former mayor, made with marionberry blackberries from Oregon and graham cracker crumbs; the seasonal menu may have flavors like Nats Red Velvet Cake during baseball season or maple rye pecan ice cream and cranberry sorbet in the winter. You can also get your fix in the U Street Corridor (1407 T St. NW, 202/299-9042).

MAP 8: 301 Water St. SE, 202/863-0727, www.icecreamjubilee.com; 11am-10pm Sun.-Thurs., 11am-11pm Fri.-Sat. summer, noon-9pm daily winter

Nightlife

COCKTAIL BARS & LOUNGES

Whiskey Charlie

Three words: go for sunset. The thrill of the jaunty bar on the 10th-floor rooftop of the Hilton Canopy at the Wharf is the panoramic view of Southwest Washington and the U.S. Capitol—seriously, you're as high as the dome. And unlike some of the other hotel bars with views, Whiskey Charlie is first come, first served—but it gets crowded on nice evenings and is frequently bought out for private events. If you can't get in, try The Watering Hole, the pool bar on the roof of the nearby InterContinental, which isn't quite as impressive but also not quite as well known.

MAP 8: Hilton Canopy Washington DC, 975 7th St. NW, 202/488-2500, www.whiskeycharliewharf.com; 3pm-midnight Mon.-Thurs., 3pm-1am Fri., 1pm-1am Sat., 1pm-midnight Sun.

CRAFT BEER

Bluejacket

With seating for 200 and beers for every palate, the industrial three-story microbrewery and restaurant inside a former Navy Yard factory is a good bet before or after a baseball game. On any given day, you'll find at least 20 of their own brews on tap, which are all made on-site, ranging from IPAs and sour ales to

The Anthem

authentic cask ales. Try a few four-ounce pours at the long, lofty bar, or reserve a spot on the brewery tour and tasting (7pm Fri., 3pm Sat.). The on-site restaurant, The Arsenal, serves traditional pub fare and hangover food, as well as a late-night menu for postgame snack attacks.

MAP 8: 300 Tingey St. SE, 202/524-4862, www.bluejacketdc. com; 11am-1am Sun.-Thurs., 11am-2am Fri.-Sat.

LIVE MUSIC
✪ The Anthem

This sleek District Wharf music venue opened in October 2017 with a sold-out show headlined by the Foo Fighters. With capacity for 6,000, it's bringing the big names—in addition to the Foo Fighters, Bob Dylan, Lorde, and The Killers performed in its first few months. The owners, who also run the iconic 9:30 Club (815 V St. NW, 202/265-0930, www.930.com), know how to put on a show. Despite the venue's large size, every show feels intimate due to a movable stage. Other features include premium, scalper-proof, reserved seat options at every show (including general admission shows), seven bars, and concessions from local businesses.

MAP 8: 901 Wharf St. SW, 202/888-0020, tickets 877/435-9849, www.theanthemdc.com; box office noon-7pm daily or until 9pm on show days

Arts and Culture

MUSEUMS
Anacostia Community Museum

Founded in 1967 as part of the Smithsonian Institution's effort to bring the arts to the Anacostia neighborhood, the museum about communities showcases art, photographs, documents, and other materials documenting life in Anacostia and surrounding neighborhoods. It's small, with three or four exhibits at any time, but they're thought provoking; recent ones have examined the experiences of Latino immigrants in major U.S. cities and the impact of the recent growth and development in Washington DC on various neighborhoods and populations. The museum has a robust schedule of free cultural events, including author talks, music performances, and film screenings. A bit off the beaten path, the museum offers free shuttle service from the Smithsonian's National Air and Space Museum and the Anacostia Metro station.

MAP 8: 1901 Fort Pl. SE, 202/633-4820, http://anacostia.si.edu; 10am-5pm daily; free

GALLERIES
Honfleur Gallery

Built in 2007, Honfleur Gallery was the first gallery developed by Action to Rehabilitate Community Housing (ARCH) Development Corporation, a nonprofit dedicated to providing access to arts, culture, and business services in Anacostia.

(The Anacostia Arts Center, another ARCH Development Corporation project, opened a year later.) Ever since, the gallery and neighborhood have become a burgeoning destination for diverse, contemporary art from around the world, with many of the gallery's artists hailing from DC. The gallery opens exhibits every few months, ranging from traditional mediums to photography to more experimental installations.

MAP 8: 1241 Good Hope Rd. SE, 202/365-8392, www.honfleurgallery. com; noon-7pm Wed.-Sat.; free

CULTURAL CENTERS
America's Islamic Heritage Museum & Cultural Center

The mission of this cultural center is more important than ever: to foster greater understanding of Islam in the United States. The text- and photo-heavy exhibits tell the story of the significant role of Islam in America from the 1500s—about 30 percent of slaves brought from Africa were Muslim—to modern day, including a look at Muslim American artists, musicians, and athletes, as well as Muslims who served in the military. If you're visiting during Ramadan, you can go to an *iftar*, the dinner to break the fast. These meals are often attended by Muslim government officials and embassy representatives. Check the website for the schedule and suggested donation.

MAP 8: 2315 Martin Luther King Jr. Ave. SE, 202/610-0586, www.aihmuseum. org; noon-5pm Tues.-Sun., $7 adults, $5 students and seniors

Anacostia Arts Center

Anacostia Arts Center

While off the beaten path, the Anacostia Arts Center is worth visiting to experience local art and support development in this historic and culturally rich neighborhood. The 9,300-square-foot building has five gallery and boutique spaces rented by local creatives, as well as a black box theater. Check the website for exhibit opening receptions, music and dance performances, and jazz brunches.

MAP 8: 1231 Good Hope Rd. SE, 202/631-6291, www. anacostiaartscenter.com; 10am-7pm Tues.-Sat, 10am-3pm Sun., hours and prices vary for special events

Arena Stage

THEATER, MUSIC, AND DANCE

✪ Arena Stage

Since opening in 1950, Arena Stage has had many "firsts" in theater history: It was one of the first non-profit theaters in the United States, the first regional theater to send a production to Broadway (*The Great White Hope,* about African American boxing champ Jack Johnson), and the first regional theater to win the Regional Theater Tony Award. With three performance spaces holding 200-680 people, Arena continues to debut American plays and revive classic American dramas and musicals—think *Oklahoma!* and *The Pajama Game.* Recent premieres include *Dear Evan Hansen,* which received nine Tony Award nominations after moving to Broadway in 2016, and *Sweat,* winner of the 2017 Pulitzer Prize for drama.

MAP 8: 1101 6th St. SW, 202/554-9066, www.arenastage.org

Anacostia Playhouse

In 2013, the Anacostia Playhouse opened in Historic Anacostia, to bring theater and nightlife to the neighborhood and spur development. In addition to producing performances, the Playhouse provides affordable performance space for emerging artists in the city. Recent performances have included a pay-what-you-can new works festival with the theme "Silenced Voices" and interactive puppet shows to introduce children to Shakespeare.

MAP 8: 2020 Shannon Pl. SE, 202/290-2328, www. anacostiaplayhouse.com

Festivals and Events

Martin Luther King Jr. Day

Dr. King had an enormous impact on Washington, which celebrates his birthday with several special events. Martin Luther King Jr. Day kicks off with the Memorial Peace Walk, where you can join government officials, media personalities, and community activists on a two-mile walk along Martin Luther King, Jr. Avenue in Southeast DC, one of the first streets in the country bearing his name. After, a parade follows the same route.

Anacostia: 2500 Martin Luther King Jr. Ave. SE, www.mlkholidaydc.org; third Mon. of Jan.; free

DC Jazz Festival

Originally named the Duke Ellington Jazz Festival in honor of perhaps the most influential musician from DC, the event showcases DC's jazz tradition, with performances at theaters, clubs, parks, and museums across the city by Grammy Award-winning headliners and local musicians. The major performances take place at The John F. Kennedy Center for the Performing Arts, The Yards in Navy Yard, and The Howard Theatre.

Navy Yard/Citywide: www.dcjazzfest. org; June; ticket prices vary

Recreation

PARKS AND TRAILS
✪ Anacostia Riverwalk Trail

The Anacostia Riverwalk Trail provides 12 (of a planned 20) mi (19.3 km) of safe, paved paths for walking, running, or biking along the Anacostia River, connecting neighborhoods including Anacostia, Capitol Hill, and Navy Yard to Bladensburg, Maryland, and 40 more mi (64 km) of trails. In addition to wildlife, you'll find conveniently located maps, benches, Capital Bikeshare stations, boating facilities, playgrounds, and more in the parks and communities along the trail.

MAP 8: Access via Diamond Teague Park, 99 Potomac Ave. SE, or via Anacostia Park, 1900 Anacostia Dr. SE; 24 hours daily

The Yards Park

Set on the Anacostia River, The Yards Park is 5.4 acres of green space and relaxing, waterfront views. The park frequently hosts events and festivals, including free concerts every Friday night in the summer. It's also an ideal stop during a bike ride along the Anacostia Riverwalk Trail; nap on a chaise lounge on the boardwalk, or grab a cone at nearby Ice Cream Jubilee.

MAP 8: 355 Water St. SE, www. capitolriverfront.org/the-yards-park; sunrise-2 hours after sunset daily

Anacostia Riverwalk Trail

BOATING
Ballpark Boathouse

Head to Ballpark Boathouse, located directly behind Nationals Park, to rent a kayak ($20/hour single, $25/hour double) or canoe ($25/hour) and catch a glimpse of the U.S. Capitol from the Anacostia River. Warning: The river isn't known for being the cleanest body of water in the city, so make sure you don't tip over.

MAP 8: 100 Potomac Ave. SE, 202/337-9642, www.boatingindc.com; Thurs.-Sun. and holidays May-Sept., hours vary

SPORTS ARENAS
Nationals Park

Completed in March 2008, the 41,546-seat Nationals Park is the first Leadership in Energy and Environmental Design (LEED) certified major stadium in the United States. With views of the U.S. Capitol and Washington Monument from some of the upper decks, the stadium's design was inspired by I. M. Pei's East Wing of the National Gallery of Art. In addition to seeing the Washington Nationals play home games here, you can see the modern stadium on a tour ($15-25 adults, $10-20 seniors, military, and children 12 and under) from April through November. The stadium also hosts major outdoor concerts like Paul McCartney and James Taylor.

MAP 8: 1500 S. Capitol St. SE, 202/675-6287, www.washington. nationals.mlb.com; box office 10am-30 minutes after the end of the game on Mon.-Sat. game days, 9am-30 minutes after on Sun. game days, 10am-5pm Mon.-Fri., 10am-3pm Sat. on nongame days

SPECTATOR SPORTS
BASEBALL
✪ Washington Nationals

Since 2005, many Washingtonians have adopted the Washington

FOOTBALL AT FEDEX FIELD

The Washington Redskins have invited controversy several times since the National Football League (NFL) franchise moved from Boston to DC in 1937. During the civil rights era, the owner came under fire for unabashedly refusing to hire black players. In 1962, it became the last team in the league to integrate, when the Kennedy Administration threatened to bar them from playing in their DC stadium, which was owned by the federal government. (Incidentally, the first black player drafted by the Redskins, Ernie Davis, was the first black player to win the Heisman Trophy.)

And, of course, the name is divisive. The current owner, and many fans, argue the name is important to the team's 80-year-plus history; the founding Washington Redskins team's head coach and four players were American Indian. And according to some national polls, a majority of self-identified American Indians aren't bothered by the name, though the National Congress of American Indians says otherwise. In 2017, the U.S. Supreme Court struck down a law banning offensive trademarks on the grounds of the law being a violation of the First Amendment—meaning the name can remain, at least legally.

Since 1997, the Redskins have played home games at FedEx Field in Landover, Maryland, about 40 minutes outside DC. This move possibly cost them the "home team advantage," as their only Super Bowl wins occurred when they played at Robert F. Kennedy Memorial Stadium in Southeast DC. The team is currently exploring new stadium options in DC, Maryland, and Virginia.

For information and tickets, visit www.redskins.com.

Nationals—and the whole city got on board when they won the 2019 World Series. Even if you don't root for the home team, seeing a Nats game during the April-October season is considered an essential activity for sports fans. Watch for the Presidents Race during the fourth inning, when bobblehead-style mascots George Washington, "Tom" Jefferson, "Abe" Lincoln, and Teddy Roosevelt race on the field (poor Teddy almost always loses, even when he's given a head start).

In addition to the usual hot dogs and peanuts, concession stands also sell popular local favorites like half smokes from Ben's Chili Bowl and beer by DC Brau. Single game tickets are readily available at the box office or online, though big weekend games sell out in advance. Starting 2.5 hours before the first pitch, you can purchase $5 grandstand seats for most games (one per person at the main box office only). These go quickly on weekends.

MAP 8: 1500 S. Capitol St. SE, 202/675-6287, www.mlb.com/nationals; tickets $5-150, discounts available for seniors, students, government employees, and active-duty military

SOCCER
DC United

Audi Field opened in 2018, finally giving DC United, Washington's Major League Soccer team (and the winningest in the country), the home they deserve. Blocks from

Nationals Park

Nationals Park, the 20,000-seat stadium is located at Buzzard Point, a new area of development where the Potomac River meets the Anacostia River. The team's fans are some of the most dedicated; expect a loud, raucous, but friendly experience. The regular season runs March to October; single game tickets are readily available via Ticketmaster, though popular matches toward the end of the season commonly sell out. **MAP 8:** 100 Potomac Ave. SE, 202/337-9642, www.dcunited.com; tickets $20-200

Shops

BOOKS

Mahogany Books

Focusing on books written by, for, and about people of the African Diaspora, Mahogany Books operated for 10 years online before opening its first brick-and-mortar location inside the **Anacostia Arts Center.** The shop sells fiction, non-fiction, children's and young adult books, as well as items with their slogan, "Black Books Matter," and frequently hosts authors for talks and signings. **MAP 8:** 1231 Good Hope Rd. SE, 202/844-2062, www.mahoganybooks.com; noon-7pm Tue.-Fri., 11am-7pm Sat., noon-4pm Sun.

Politics and Prose

Since opening in 1984, Upper Northwest's Politics and Prose has long been a favorite local shop to purchase books and meet authors, including many local political, media, and entertainment celebrities at the store's readings and signings that take place almost daily. (See *Where the Wonks Read* on page 231 for more about the original location.) The Metro-accessible, 2,300-square-foot location at the District Wharf is where you can find a curated selection of fiction, nonfiction, and children's books as well as cards, gifts, and other items. Check out the DC authors and books behind the register. **MAP 8:** 70 District Sq. SW, 202/488-3867, www.pollitics-prose.com; 10am-10pm daily

HEALTH & BEAUTY

Anacostia Organics

This 100-percent-minority-woman-owned medical cannabis dispensary—and the first east of the Anacostia River—is one of the latest signs of the development of Historic Anacostia. This dispensary feels more like a high-end spa, with bright white walls and chic decor and local art. The glass cases contain premium cannabis as well as health and wellness products. A medical cannabis card is required to enter the dispensary; the shop accepts cards from every U.S. state and Puerto Rico. **MAP 8:** 2022 Martin Luther King Jr. Ave. SE, 202/845-8574, www.anacostiaorganics.com; 11am-8pm Mon.-Sat., noon-5pm Sun.

WHERE THE WONKS READ

Everyone in Washington DC is shopping around a book. And when the author gets a publisher, there's one place in the city where they want to be: Politics and Prose (5015 Connecticut Ave. NW, 202/364-1919, www.politics-prose.com), the Upper Northwest independent bookstore known for its robust program of author talks and signings, including many by local newsmakers and newsbreakers. Almost every day, the store hosts well-attended events with U.S. senators, star reporters, and bestselling novelists. Events at the store are almost

Politics and Prose

always free and open to the public, though events with high-profile authors (Dan Rather, Patti Smith, Amy Tan) at other city venues often require advance tickets. For a uniquely DC experience, go to one of the store's evening book signings, then head to Comet Ping Pong, the "Pizzagate" restaurant just a few doors down, for pizza and beer.

The flagship is 15 minutes by taxi or car from Dupont Circle, and 1 mi (1.6 km) from the Van Ness-UDC Metro station. Other locations include The Wharf (70 District Sq. SW, 202/488-3867) and Union Market (1270 5th St. NE).

If you're looking for a book closer to the city center, locals' top picks include Capitol Hill's East City Bookshop (page 121), Dupont Circle's Kramerbooks (page 142), and Adams Morgan's The Potter's House (page 177), which also functions as a café. And don't miss the bookstores inside Busboys and Poets restaurants (page 158) for a curated selection focusing on social justice issues.

Greater Washington DC   Map 9

True to Pierre Charles L'Enfant's original plan, DC has **four quadrants** around the U.S. Capitol: Northeast, Southeast, Northwest, and Southwest. Many of the top attractions and neighborhoods for dining, shopping, and accommodations are centered around the White House and business districts in Northwest and the Capitol in Southeast, but there are destination sights, restaurants, and shopping in all four quadrants, ranging from **historic homes** and **parks** in Upper Northwest to the culinary delights of **Union Market** and **local distillers** in Northeast, to parks with water views in Southwest. And although not technically located in the District of Columbia, two of the top sights are just over the border in Virginia: **Arlington National Cemetery** and the **National 9/11 Pentagon Memorial,** both accessible by Metro.

TOP SIGHTS

- Most Moving Memorial: **National 9/11 Pentagon Memorial** (page 237)
- Best Place to Find Your Spirit Animal: **Smithsonian's National Zoo** (page 238)
- Where to Pay Your Respects: **Arlington National Cemetery** (page 236)

TOP RESTAURANTS

- Most Romantic: **Masseria** (page 245)
- Prettiest French Food: **Primrose** (page 244)

TOP ARTS AND CULTURE

- Most Opulent Historic Home: **Hillwood Estate, Museum & Gardens** (page 247)

TOP RECREATION

- Most Metro-Accessible Outdoor Excursion: **East Potomac Park and Hains Point** (page 251)
- Best Place to Connect with Nature: **U.S. National Arboretum** (page 251)

TOP SHOPS

- Coolest Local Liquor: **New Columbia Distillers** (page 255)

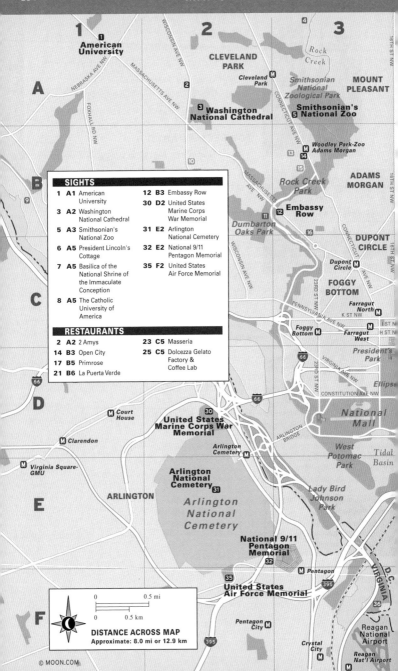

SIGHTS

1	**A1**	American University
3	**A2**	Washington National Cathedral
5	**A3**	Smithsonian's National Zoo
6	**A5**	President Lincoln's Cottage
7	**A5**	Basilica of the National Shrine of the Immaculate Conception
8	**A5**	The Catholic University of America
12	**B3**	Embassy Row
30	**D2**	United States Marine Corps War Memorial
31	**E2**	Arlington National Cemetery
32	**E2**	National 9/11 Pentagon Memorial
35	**F2**	United States Air Force Memorial

RESTAURANTS

2	**A2**	2 Amys
14	**B3**	Open City
17	**B5**	Primrose
21	**B6**	La Puerta Verde
23	**C5**	Masseria
25	**C5**	Dolcezza Gelato Factory & Coffee Lab

DISTANCE ACROSS MAP
Approximate: 8.0 mi or 12.9 km

0   0.5 mi
0   0.5 km

© MOON.COM

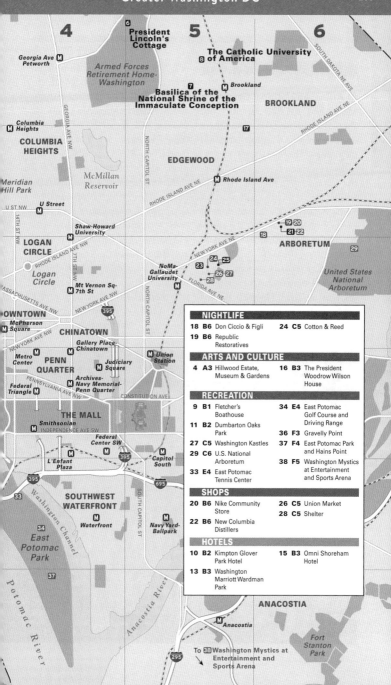

NIGHTLIFE

18 **B6** Don Ciccio & Figli
19 **B6** Republic Restoratives
24 **C5** Cotton & Reed

ARTS AND CULTURE

4 **A3** Hillwood Estate, Museum & Gardens
16 **B3** The President Woodrow Wilson House

RECREATION

9 **B1** Fletcher's Boathouse
11 **B2** Dumbarton Oaks Park
27 **C5** Washington Kastles
29 **C6** U.S. National Arboretum
33 **E4** East Potomac Tennis Center
34 **E4** East Potomac Golf Course and Driving Range
36 **F3** Gravelly Point
37 **F4** East Potomac Park and Hains Point
38 **F5** Washington Mystics at Entertainment and Sports Arena

SHOPS

20 **B6** Nike Community Store
22 **B6** New Columbia Distillers
26 **C5** Union Market
28 **C5** Shelter

HOTELS

10 **B2** Kimpton Glover Park Hotel
13 **B3** Washington Marriott Wardman Park
15 **B3** Omni Shoreham Hotel

Sights

✪ Arlington National Cemetery

More than 400,000 veterans and their immediate family members are buried at Arlington National Cemetery, the country's largest military cemetery, located across the Potomac in Arlington, Virginia. Inside, the seemingly endless sea of white headstones is a reminder of the high price of serving the country, a price that continues to be paid today.

After the security screening, stop by the welcome center for an introduction and map. There are dozens of memorials and historical sites to explore; plan to spend a minimum of 2-3 hours if you want to walk in the cemetery, and wear comfortable walking shoes and weather-appropriate clothing. Alternatively, you can take the official bus tour (866/754-9014, www.arlington-tours.com; $13.50 adults, $10 seniors, $6.75 children 3-11, free for children under 3, discounts for military/groups), which is operated by Old Town Trolley Tours (202/796-2606, www.trolleytours.com).

The two most prominent sites at Arlington are the Tomb of the Unknown Soldier, the memorial to unidentified American soldiers who died in battle, which is guarded 24/7 by the Army's 3rd U.S. Infantry Regiment, and President John

Arlington National Cemetery

F. Kennedy's gravesite, where a flame has been burning since he was buried on November 25, 1963; Jacqueline Kennedy Onassis was buried next to him in 1994.

Other notable locations include the gravesite of President William Howard Taft, the only person to serve as both president and chief justice of the Supreme Court, and Arlington House, the mansion once occupied by Confederate general Robert E. Lee. During the Civil War, the Union Army chose the site for the cemetery in part to ensure that Lee, who had resigned from the U.S. Army when Virginia seceded, could never again live in the mansion. Section 27 houses the graves of more than 3,000 former slaves who could not afford to buy burial plots, as well as about 1,500 African Americans who fought in the Civil War.

To find a specific grave, download the ANC Explorer app or visit http://ancexplorer.army.mil/publicwmv. The Arlington National Cemetery Metro station is located by the main entrance and welcome center. Paid parking is available in a garage at Memorial Avenue, but you cannot drive inside the cemetery unless you are attending a funeral. Arlington is an important historical site, but keep in mind it's also an operating cemetery, with funerals taking place Monday through Saturday. MAP 9: Entrance at Arlington Memorial Bridge and Memorial Ave. or Arlington National Cemetery Metro station (Virginia), 877/907-8585, www.arlingtoncemetery.mil; 8am-7pm daily Apr.-Sept., 8am-5pm daily Oct.-Mar.; free

NEARBY:

- Be inspired by the 16th president's legacy at the Lincoln Memorial, just across the Potomac (page 49).
- Pay your respects at the National 9/11 Pentagon Memorial (page 237).

✪ National 9/11 Pentagon Memorial

On September 11, 2001, at 9:37:46am, hijackers flew American Airlines Flight 77 into the Pentagon in Arlington, Virginia, killing the 59 passengers and crew on board as well as 125 people working in the U.S. Department of Defense headquarters.

Located on the southwest side of the building, where the plane hit, the National 9/11 Pentagon Memorial is accessible 24/7. The contemporary design is a place for calm reflection. The memorial consists of 184 cantilevered stainless steel and granite benches, representing the 184 individuals killed in the attack. Each bench has the name of one victim, and by looking at the name, you can determine where they died; if you see the Pentagon in your line of vision, the victim died in the building,

but if you see the sky, the person was a passenger on the flight. An illuminated pool of water is underneath each bench.

The memorial is surrounded by a wall that rises from 3 inches, representing the youngest passenger killed, age 3, to 71 inches, representing the oldest. Planted among the benches are 85 crape myrtles, which will provide a cooling canopy when they are fully grown. Dedicated and opened to the public on September 11, 2008, it was the first national 9/11 memorial completed in the United States.

Tours of the Pentagon are also available; reservations are required and must be booked 14-90 days in advance online (http://pentagon-tours.osd.mil). On the tour, you'll glean insight on the DOD's branches and activities, as well as see the indoor memorial near the crash site.

From the Pentagon Metro station, follow the signs to the memorial; visitor parking is not available at the Pentagon, but you may park at the nearby shopping mall, the Fashion Centre at Pentagon City, about a five-minute walk from the memorial through a pedestrian tunnel.

MAP 9: 1 N. Rotary Rd., Arlington (Virginia), 301/740-3388, www.pentagonmemorial.org; 24 hours daily, facilities 7am-10pm daily; free

✪ Smithsonian's National Zoo

Washington may be one of the only places in the world where even the zoo gets caught up in foreign policy. The Smithsonian's National Zoo has long been the home of giant pandas on loan from the People's Republic of China as part of a conservation program. However, the agreement for the two remaining pandas, Mei Xiang and Tian Tian, expires in December—and as of this writing, it's unclear whether China will renew the lease, or use them as leverage in the ongoing trade war.

Even if the pandas leave, the sprawling, 163-acre zoo is lovely to visit, especially with children in tow. Officially part of Rock Creek Park, the zoo is home to hundreds of animals, including fascinating primates in the Great Ape House, which love to stare at the humans outside the glass walls, and majestic lions, tigers, and elephants. In the American Trail exhibit, you can also see California sea lions and bald eagles.

National 9/11 Pentagon Memorial

In addition to the animals, attractions include a carousel ($3.50), a children's choo-choo train ($3), and animal demonstrations and feedings, as well as a free, two-hour guided tour of the highlights, which departs from the visitor center at 9:45am daily, no reservations required. The zoo is an outdoor park situated on hilly terrain, and many exhibits are outdoors, so wear comfortable walking shoes and weather-appropriate clothing. Refreshments are available for

lionesses at Smithsonian's National Zoo

purchase throughout the park, but you are welcome to bring your own food and nonalcoholic beverages; water is recommended if you're visiting during the summer. Plan to spend 2-3 hours minimum to see the major exhibits.

The zoo's main entrance is in residential Woodley Park, approximately 10 minutes by foot from both the Woodley Park-Zoo/Adams Morgan Metro station and Cleveland Park Metro station. There are two pedestrian- and bike-friendly entrances a short walk from Adams Morgan and Mount Pleasant, as well, where you can check out excellent ethnic restaurants and dive bars after your visit.

MAP 9: 3001 Connecticut Ave. NW, 202/633-4888, http://nationalzoo. si.edu; exhibit buildings 9am-6pm daily Apr.-Sept., 9am-4pm daily Oct.-Mar., grounds 8am-7pm daily; free

American University

In 1917, the U.S. government took over parts of the American University campus, located near Tenleytown, to train soldiers and begin extensive chemical weapons testing and research. The campus was divided into Camp American University, where construction crews found bombs and contamination underground as late as the 1990s, and Camp Leach, where military researchers developed camouflage techniques. Today, this private (and now bomb-free) university enrolls more than 13,000 undergraduate and graduate students; alumni of the Schools of International Service, Communication, and Public Affairs often go on to work in federal government, political management, or media, and several AU students receive the prestigious Presidential Management Fellowship every year. Of note, the **American University Museum at the Katzen Arts Center** (4400 Massachusetts Ave.

NW, 202/885-1300, www.american.edu/cas/museum) has 30,000 square feet of exhibition space for contemporary art exhibits featuring political art as well as works by DC artists. Prospective students may register for campus tours (www.american.edu/admissions) during the fall and spring semesters.

MAP 9: 4400 Massachusetts Ave. NW, 202/885-1000, www.american.edu

Basilica of the National Shrine of the Immaculate Conception

Walk in the pious footsteps of three popes, Mother Teresa, and one million annual pilgrims at the largest Roman Catholic church in North America. Serving The Catholic University of America and United States Conference of Catholic Bishops, the Byzantine-Romanesque structure honors the Virgin Mary in an enormous, uniquely American way, with 70 chapels and the largest collection of contemporary religious art in the world, including more than 75,000 square feet of mosaics. Close to the Brookland-CUA Metro station, the basilica offers free guided tours daily, along with six Masses and five hours of Confession; check the website for feast day schedules and special events.

MAP 9: 400 Michigan Ave. NE, 202/526-8300, www.nationalshrine.com; 7am-7pm daily Apr.-Oct., 7am-6pm daily Nov.-Mar.; free

Embassy Row

Crossing through several neighborhoods, Embassy Row is the stretch of Massachusetts Avenue NW lined with the stately international embassies and diplomatic missions where

Indonesian embassy

foreign ambassadors to the United States live and work. Beginning at Scott Circle, with the embassies of Australia and the Philippines, it heads northwest through Dupont Circle to the United States Naval Observatory, where the vice president lives. The buildings start getting really impressive just past the embassy of India in Dupont Circle, marked by a bronze Gandhi statue. The limestone Chinese embassy, designed by I. M. Pei, and imposing Japanese chancery building look like spy movie sets. Don't miss the former embassy of Iran (3003-3005 Massachusetts Ave. NW), known for some of the most lavish parties in Washington (think caviar, alcohol, and drugs, according to accounts by guests) before diplomatic ties were severed in 1980; the shuttered building is still owned by Tehran but maintained by the U.S. State Department. The embassies are generally closed to the public, but every May, they open their doors for Passport DC, when you can go inside dozens of the mansions to experience the countries' art, culture, and food.

MAP 9: Massachusetts Ave. NW from Scott Circle northwest to the United States Naval Observatory

President Lincoln's Cottage

The Old Soldiers' Home served as a refuge for wounded and retired military veterans, as well as a summer retreat for four U.S. presidents in the 19th century. President Lincoln loved it so much that he spent about a quarter of his presidency at the 34-room cottage on a secluded hill 3 mi (4.8 km) from the White House and found respite with his family from the stress of the Civil War. It's called "The Cradle of the Emancipation Proclamation" because he drafted his groundbreaking speech there.

Located in Petworth on the grounds of the still-operating Armed Forces Retirement Home, the cottage dives deeper into President Lincoln's ideas and presidency. Start at the visitor center, where you can explore exhibits about DC during the Civil War and Lincoln's experience at the Old Soldiers' Home, then depart on a lively, one-hour guided tour of the cottage, where you'll learn more about Lincoln's life and work. To protect the privacy of the retirement home's residents, you can only access the cottage by the guided tour, so advance tickets are recommended, especially on weekends.

MAP 9: 140 Rock Creek Church Rd. NW, 202/829-0436, www.lincolncottage.org; 9:30am-4:30pm daily.; $15 adults, $12 military ID, $7.50 members, $5 children 6-12, free for children under 6

The Catholic University of America

Founded in 1887 by a charter from Pope Leo XII, The Catholic University of America is the national university of the Catholic Church—and the only university in the country to have been visited by three popes, including Pope Francis in 2015. Catholic teachings and rituals are part of daily life on the Northeast DC campus, where the majority of the 6,000 undergraduate and graduate students identify as Catholic. In addition to schools for the arts and sciences, law, and business, among others, CUA has the only university music school in Washington DC, considered one of the top among Catholic colleges and universities, as well as the only school of Catholic canon law in the country. For visitors, the highlight is the **Basilica of the National Shrine of the Immaculate Conception,** the largest Roman Catholic church in North America, with the largest collection of contemporary religious art in the world. Prospective students may register for **campus tours** (www.catholic.edu/admission) at 10am and 2pm most weekdays and select Saturdays.

MAP 9: 620 Michigan Ave. NE, 202/319-5000, www.catholic.edu

United States Air Force Memorial

United States Air Force Memorial

You can't miss the three stainless steel spires rising 402 feet into the sky. This memorial is designed to look like the Air Force Thunderbirds, the branch's exhilarating demonstration jets, taking off in the bomb-burst formation. In this case, there are just three jets, instead of four, signifying the Missing Man Formation, used during funerals

in honor of the 54,000 airmen and airwomen who died in combat. Four eight-foot bronze statues of members of the Air Force Honor Guard stand near the spires. Two 56-foot-long granite walls name members who have received the Medal of Honor. Completed in 2006, it has a slick, postmodern design by James Ingo Freed, a contemporary of I. M. Pei. In the summer, the Air Force Bands perform free concerts at the memorial.

MAP 9: 1 Air Force Memorial Dr., Arlington, Virginia, 703/462-4093, www.airforcememorial.org; 9am-9pm daily Apr.-Sept., 8am-8pm daily Oct.-Mar.; free

United States Marine Corps War Memorial

Known as "Iwo Jima," the United States Marine Corps War Memorial is a monument to the Marines who have died in battle since 1775, though it depicts one iconic day in history: February 23, 1945. The staggering memorial is a bronze replica of the Pulitzer Prize-winning photograph of six U.S. Marines raising the second American flag on Mount Suribachi on Iwo Jima, Japan's island base for kamikaze attacks, which the United States had seized. Taken by the Associated Press's Joe Rosenthal, the photograph became one of the defining images of World War II—depicting the obscenely bloody battle in which more than 6,800 Americans and 23,000 Japanese died, including three of the soldiers pictured.

The American flag has flown at the memorial every single day since the dedication by President Dwight D. Eisenhower in 1954. Visit during

Washington National Cathedral

the summer to see one of the sunset parades, featuring the United States Marine Drum and Bugle Corps.

MAP 9: 1 U.S. Marine Memorial Circle, Arlington, Virginia, 703/289-2500, www.nps.gov/gwmp; 6am-midnight daily; free

Washington National Cathedral

During times of war, terror, and strife in the United States, Northwest's Washington National Cathedral has served has a gathering place for people of all faiths. And the cathedral's walls have witnessed quite a bit of consequential history since President William McKinley attended the first service in 1898—perhaps most notably, Reverend Dr. Martin Luther King Jr.'s last Sunday sermon on March 31, 1968, days before he was assassinated. Inside, 215 stained-glass windows mix with statues of historical figures, including Dr. King and past U.S.

presidents; on the outside, more than 1,000 gargoyles and grotesques keep watch, including some original to the building and others added later, like the Darth Vader gargoyle, added to the northwest tower on the "dark side" of the building in 1980. Tours of the highlights inside the cathedral are included with the price of admission; behind-the-scenes tours, gargoyle tours, and climbs up the 333-step Central Tower to see one of the highest views in the city are available for an additional fee. On Sundays, the cathedral holds worship services open to all, regardless of faith, with free admission.

MAP 9: 3101 Wisconsin Ave. NW, 202/537-6200, www.cathedral.org; 10am-5pm Mon.-Fri., 10am-4pm Sat., 8am-4pm Sun.; admission and highlights tour $12 adults, $8 children 5-17, students and teachers with ID, seniors, active military, and veterans, free for children under 5, free on Sun.

Restaurants

PRICE KEY

$	Entrees less than $15
$$	Entrees $15-25
$$$	Entrees more than $25

CLASSIC AMERICAN
Open City $$

This Woodley Park diner and coffee house is worth the Metro or Uber fare for a hair-of-the-dog brunch, especially if you'd like to visit the Smithsonian's National Zoo after. Steps from the Woodley Park-Zoo/Adams Morgan Metro and about a 10-minute walk from the zoo's main entrance, the family-friendly spot serves affordable breakfast all day, every day, plus a large menu of sandwiches, salads, pizza, and cocktails early until late.

MAP 9: 2331 Calvert St. NW, 202/332-2331, www.opencitydc.com; 7am-midnight Sun.-Thurs., 7am-1am Fri.-Sat.

FRENCH
✪ Primrose $$$

You'll be tempted to go to Primrose once for the Instagram-worthy interior, like the ostrich feather chandeliers and inviting aqua blue bar—but you'll go again and again for the elegantly prepared classic French dishes. (The roast chicken is so good you might ask them to spill the beans on their purveyor if you live in the area.) End your meal with

Primrose in Brookland

a divine cheese plate and calvados, or apple brandy, flight, and carry the warm glow into your evening.

MAP 9: 3000 12th St. NW, 202/248-4558, www.primrosedc.com; 5:30pm-10pm Mon.-Fri., 11am-2pm, 5pm-11pm Sat., 11am-2pm, 5pm-9pm Sun.

Masseria

ITALIAN
✪ Masseria $$$

Hidden among the warehouses around Union Market, Masseria is a destination. Nicholas Stefanelli's Michelin-starred cuisine is inspired by his childhood in Puglia, Italy's sunny, fertile heel, known for *burrata* cheese, orecchiette pasta, and farm-fresh ingredients. Neither the ingredients nor the pricey bill compare to the *masserias,* or country houses, in Bari or Brindisi, but Stefanelli does a fine job of making you forget you're in DC by the end of one of the rich four-, five-, or six-course meals ($92-135 pp). Go when the weather is nice for a romantic evening on the patio, with dreamy lighting and landscaping plus cozy couches for a nightcap. Make your reservation at least a few days in advance, a week or more for weekends or if you want to dine outside in the summer, though last-minute tables

are typically available if you're willing to dine early or late; lounge seating on the patio is first come, first served.

MAP 9: 1340 4th St. NE, 202/608-1330, www.masseria-dc.com; 5:30pm-9:30pm Tues.-Thurs., 5:30pm-10pm Fri., 5pm-10pm Sat.

MEXICAN
La Puerta Verde $$

Inside the namesake green door in the Hecht Warehouse in Ivy City, you'll find the most addictive guacamole in the District. The secret? The avocados are grilled. And the tacos, stuffed full of meat and fresh cilantro, are a steal at three for $9. Grab a stool at the festive tiled bar, and enjoy the food with a cold margarita or beer. The bar is surrounded by vibrant murals by Cita Sadeli, who has been creating street art in DC since the 1990s.

MAP 9: 2001 Fenwick St. NE, 202/290-1875, www.lapuertaverdedc.com; 5pm-10pm Wed.-Thurs., 5pm-11pm Fri., 11am-11pm Sat., 11am-10pm Sun.

PIZZA
2 Amys $

Head to Cathedral Heights, the quiet neighborhood near the Washington National Cathedral, for Washington's first, and very best, D.O.C.-certified pizzeria, meaning it follows the Italian regulations for Neapolitan-style pizza, guaranteed to be made in a wood-burning oven with San Marzano tomatoes and Fior di Latte or Bufala mozzarella, among other ingredients. This casual, subway-tiled restaurant with an open-air deck doesn't take reservations, but these pies are worth any wait. And, best of all, it's cheap—the D.O.C. Margherita is $13 and fills one, or it can easily satisfy two when combined with salad and homemade ice cream (or delicious cinnamon doughnuts during weekend brunch).

MAP 9: 3715 Macomb St. NW, 202/885-5700, www.2amysdc.com; 5pm-10pm Mon., 11am-10pm Tues.-Thurs., 11am-11pm Fri.-Sat., noon-10pm Sun.

DESSERT
Dolcezza Gelato Factory & Coffee Lab $

With more than half a dozen locations throughout the area, Dolcezza Gelato is the king of the cone, serving gelato and sorbet made with local, seasonal ingredients. Flavors range from standbys like Indonesian Vanilla Bean and Coffee & Cookies to more exotic ones like Virginia Peanut Butter, Black Sesame, and White Peach Prosecco. Visit the factory near Union Market, where you can try just-made treats as well as Stumptown coffee drinks in the roomy, industrial space with counter seating and communal tables. The gelato and sorbet are also sold at local grocery stores and restaurants.

MAP 9: 550 Penn St. NE, 202/333-4646, www.dolcezzagelato.com; 11am-7pm Fri.-Sun.

NIGHTLIFE

Nightlife

TASTING ROOMS AND DISTILLERIES
Cotton & Reed

You'll never want Captain Morgan again after trying the dry-spiced rum made with 17 botanicals at Cotton & Reed. Founded by former NASA employees Reed Walker and Jordan Cotton, DC's first rum distillery also produces a carefully crafted white rum and allspice dram. Try them all in the industrial tiki tasting room and bar near Union Market, which serves until late and regularly hosts public parties to celebrate new blends, or take a 30-minute tour, available at 1pm, 2pm, and 3pm on Saturday and Sunday, which costs $22 and concludes with a flight.

MAP 9: 1330 5th St. NE, 202/544-2805, www.cottonandreed.com; 4pm-midnight Mon.-Thurs., 4pm-2pm Fri., 2pm-2am Sat., noon-midnight Sun.

Don Ciccio & Figli

It's always aperitivo hour at Ivy City's Italian liqueur distillery—at least, when the tasting room's open on weekends. Francesco Amodeo creates more than a dozen liqueurs ranging from sweet and familiar cordials like limoncello to amari and bittersweet aperitivi, inspired by the liqueurs crafted by his grandfather on the Amalfi Coast. Try them all in the tasting room, then head to the intimate blue-hued **Bar Sirenis** for larger pours or cocktails like spritzes or Negronis.

MAP 9: 1907 Fairview Ave. NE, www.
doncicioefigli.com; tasting room
1pm-8pm Sat.-Sun.

Republic Restoratives

This growing, woman-owned distillery produced a limited-edition rye for November 2016: Rodham Rye, celebrating what they thought would be the election of the first female POTUS. Things didn't quite go as planned, but Pia Carusone and Rachel Gardner released it anyway. Visit their tasting room bar, which is built in a warehouse in the former B&O Railroad Yard in Ivy City and has lots of natural light and sleek wood finishes, where you can try refined cocktails made with their clean Civic Vodka or Borough Bourbon (made with Kentucky whiskey). Check their calendar of events for special tasting events, like yoga classes and brunch parties with local food vendors.

MAP 9: 1369 New York Ave.
NE, 202/733-3996, www.
republicrestoratives.com; 5pm-11pm
Thurs., 5pm-midnight Fri.,
noon-midnight Sat., 1pm-6pm Sun.

Arts and Culture

MUSEUMS AND GARDENS

✪ Hillwood Estate, Museum & Gardens

During the last two decades of her life, General Foods heiress and socialite Marjorie Merriweather Post lived on an estate near Rock Creek Park, where she hosted dinner parties for Washington's A-list and showed off her extravagant art collection, including 18th- and 19th-century French art, prerevolutionary Russian art and porcelain she purchased while living in the Soviet Union in the 1930s, and decorative objects like a gold chalice commissioned by Catherine the Great and nearly 100 Fabergé pieces. You can see these items and others on display in the home, lavishly decorated in 18th-century French style and the closest thing to Versailles in Washington DC. Wander through the home on your own, or take a guided tour with a docent who will tell you about Post's life and the objects on display, which, if you're lucky, will include some of her enviable designer wardrobe or jewels.

The home is set on 25 acres, including 13 acres of lush, formal gardens with carefully planned landscaping and private nooks; as with the house, you can stroll the gardens on your own (picnics are encouraged) or take one of the popular one-hour guided garden tours in the spring and fall.

MAP 9: 4155 Linnean Ave. NW,
202/686-5807, www.hillwoodmuseum.
org; 10am-5pm Tues.-Sun.; suggested
donation $18 adults, $15 seniors, $10
students, $5 children 6-18, free for
children under 6 and members

The President Woodrow Wilson House

When President Woodrow Wilson left the White House in 1921, he

Hillwood Estate

moved to posh Kalorama, where wealthy families and diplomats lived. He died a few years later, but his wife kept the house intact and eventually donated it to the National Trust for Historic Preservation. Get a look at life in the neighborhood's grand mansions during the early 20th century, and see artifacts from his historic presidency, when he led the nation through World War I.

MAP 9: 2340 S St. NW, 202/387-4062, www.woodrowwilsonhouse.org; accessible by tours only, days/hours vary; $10 adults, $8 seniors, $5 students and members of the National Trust for Historic Preservation, free for children 12 and under

Festivals and Events

Walkingtown DC

During one week in September, Events DC hosts more than 50 free walking tours around the District, allowing you to explore DC's culturally diverse neighborhoods with in-the-know volunteers. Whether you're interested in exploring presidential history, universities, street art, or areas of new development, there's a walking tour available.

Citywide: www.culturaltourismdc. org; mid-Sept.; free but registration recommended

Army Ten-Miler

The second-largest 10-mile race in the country, the Army Ten-Miler starts and finishes at the Pentagon, with several major monuments and memorials on the route. The race takes place in early October, but

registration opens in May and typically sells out in a couple days.
Citywide: www.armytenmiler.com; early Oct.; $75 fee

Marine Corps Marathon

Called "The People's Marathon," the Marine Corps Marathon draws runners from around the world in mid-October. It's the largest marathon in the world that does not offer prize money, opting instead to recognize the "honor, courage, and commitment" of runners. Registration is by lottery beginning in March.
Citywide: www.marinemarathon.com; mid-Oct.; $160 fee

Boo at the Zoo

Celebrate Halloween with creepy crawlies and terrifying beasts at the National Zoo's popular Halloween event for families. For three evenings, visitors can trick-or-treat at more than 40 stations throughout the zoo, meet zookeepers and their charges, and enjoy family-friendly entertainment.
Greater Washington: Smithsonian's National Zoo, 3001 Connecticut Ave. NW, 202/633-4888, http://nationalzoo. si.edu; mid-Oct.; $20 members, $30 nonmembers, free for children 2 and under

Zoolights

From Thanksgiving weekend through the New Year, the National Zoo is illuminated with more than 500,000 environmentally friendly holiday lights. From 5pm to 9pm, enjoy festive light shows set to music as well as holiday treats like hot chocolate, egg nog, and cookies while you shop for zoo-themed holiday gifts.
Greater Washington: Smithsonian's National Zoo, 3001 Connecticut Ave. NW, 202/633-4888, http://nationalzoo. si.edu; mid-Nov.-Jan.; free

Taste of DC

There are so many restaurants in DC, and so little time. At the city's largest culinary festival, you can try more than 65 area restaurants and food trucks, plus local beer and wine. The event features local artisans as well as live entertainment and cooking and mixology demos at the Robert F. Kennedy Memorial Stadium in Southeast.
Greater Washington: www. thetasteofdc.org; early Oct.; free admission to festival, tasting packages $10-50

Recreation

SPECTATOR SPORTS

Washington Kastles

The Washington Kastles team, DC's World TeamTennis franchise, has counted major stars like Venus and Serena Williams, Martina Hingis, and Sam Querrey on the team roster. And the team has lived up to the hype, becoming the first team in the league to play a perfect season (2009) and winning five subsequent championships. The Kastles play in July on their own court on the roof of **Union Market**. Single game tickets are readily available via Ticketmaster, though expect games with big tennis stars to sell out a week in advance.

MAP 9: 1309 5th St. NE, 202/483-6647, www.washingtonkastles.com

Washington Mystics

One of the first Women's National Basketball Association (WNBA) franchises, the Washington Mystics had a rocky first few seasons. But they made the 2018 WBNA Finals—and won their first championship in 2019. The Mystics play home games from May through September at the new, 4,200-seat **Entertainment and Sports Arena** (1100 Oak St SE, 202/470-4008, www.esaontherise.com), which opened in 2018. Single-game tickets are readily available via Ticketmaster and the arena box office.

Hains Point

MAP 2: 1100 Oak St. SE, 877/324-6671, http://mystics.wnba.com; tickets from $19

PARKS AND TRAILS

✪ East Potomac Park and Hains Point

If you want to get away and enjoy some time outdoors and still get back to your hotel with plenty of time to rest before dinner, head to this large man-made island in the Potomac River, a popular spot to run, bike, fish, picnic, or just toss a ball around in the wide open space within walking distance of the National Mall. At the tip of the island, Hains Point has playgrounds and picnic facilities with panoramic views of the water as well as Southwest DC and Ronald Reagan National Airport. In the middle, play at the East Potomac Golf Course and Driving Range and East Potomac Tennis Center. It's just over 4 mi (6.4 km) from the Jefferson Memorial around the entire perimeter and back; the golf and tennis clubs are the only places to get water or snacks on the island.

MAP 9: Ohio Dr. SW between E. Basin Dr. SW and Hains Pt., 202/426-6841; dawn-dusk daily; free

✪ U.S. National Arboretum

It's a park, it's a garden, it's a museum—it's the U.S. National Arboretum, the 446-acre living museum and horticultural research center in Northeast, where there's something new blooming every month. It's a bit of a hike from the city center through industrial, up-and-coming parts of the city (and 2 mi [3.2 km] from the closest Metro station, Stadium-Armory) but well

worth the visit to explore these off-the-beaten-path gardens, groves, monuments, and trails. While it's possible to take a taxi/ride-share and reach some of the must-see sights by foot, a car or bike will allow you to more easily explore the vast grounds. (There are several free parking lots inside the arboretum.) Either way, start your visit at the administration building and visitor center, where you can pick up a map, get advice on what's blooming, and see the magical Aquatic Garden as well as the National Herb Garden and the National Bonsai and Penjing Museum (10am-4pm daily). Other highlights include Mount Hamilton in the southwest corner of the arboretum, covered in brilliant azaleas in April and May, and fall foliage in October and November, as well as the National Capitol Columns, 22 Corinthian columns taken from the Capitol's East Portico in 1958, which feel almost alien in the vast meadow not far from the visitor center.

MAP 9: Entrance at 24th St. and R St. NE off Bladensburg Rd., 202/245-2726, www.usna.usda.gov; 8am-5pm daily; free

Dumbarton Oaks Park

Escape to the country without leaving the city. The 27-acre Dumbarton Oaks Park was originally part of the lovely estate and gardens at Dumbarton Oaks (1703 32nd St. NW, 202/339-6400, www.doaks. org), but it opened to the public as a national park in 1940. Beatrix Jones Farrand, a pioneering female landscape architect, designed the park to feel like the countryside, with dirt paths through naturalistic woodlands and wildflowers, worlds away from the hustle and bustle of DC. It's an idyllic place for a nature walk after exploring the nearby estate; while the two share a name, a fence blocks off the estate, which requires an admission fee, from the park, which is now managed by the National Park Service.

MAP 9: Entrance at Lovers' Lane at R St. NW and 31st St. NW, 202/333-3547, www.dopark.org; daily during daylight hours; free

Gravelly Point

This flat, grassy stretch adjacent to Ronald Reagan National Airport is the perfect place to while away the hours with a shockingly up-close view of planes landing a few hundred feet away. The open park is a favorite with families, who take picnics on weekend afternoons. Parking is limited; bike there from

Theodore Roosevelt Island via the Mount Vernon Trail, which you can take south to Alexandria, Virginia, and Mount Vernon.

MAP 9: Entrance at George Washington Memorial Parkway North, north of the Ronald Reagan National Airport, 703/289-2500, www.nps.gov/gwmp; daily 4am-10pm; free

BOATING
Fletcher's Boathouse

On the Potomac River at the meeting point of the Capital Crescent Trail and mile marker 3.1 of the C&O Towpath, this historical boathouse is where you can start an epic outdoor adventure. Choose a kayak ($20-25/hour), canoe ($25/hour), or rowboat ($25/hour or $50/day) and pick up some fishing tackle at the shop; stand-up paddleboards ($22/hour) are available, too. Or, rent

Corinthian columns at the U.S. National Arboretum

Rock Creek Park

Covering more than 2,000 acres of parkland and historic sites around Rock Creek in Northwest DC, Rock Creek Park is an oasis for outdoors enthusiasts. Created by Congress in 1890, it's one of the oldest national parks and includes Meridian Hill Park in Columbia Heights, the Old Stone House and Thompson Boat Center in Georgetown, and the Smithsonian's National Zoo.

To access trails and athletic facilities, head to the swath of parkland north of the zoo, roughly between Oregon Avenue NW/Broad Branch Drive NW and 16th Street NW. The park has two main hiking trails, which run from the DC-Maryland border at Beach Drive south toward the zoo. The Western Ridge Trail is 5.5 mi (8.9 km) one way, and the Valley Trail on the eastern border is 7 mi (11.3 km) one way; east-west trails connect them. The park has several picnic spots with grills, most of which are first come, first served.

The nature center (5200 Glover Rd. NW, 9am-5pm Wed.-Sun.; free) has a visitor center with kid-friendly exhibits (including live animals, beehives, and gardens) and the National Park Service's only operating planetarium, with free, regularly scheduled shows. The horse center (5100 Glover Rd. NW, 202/362-0117, www.rockcreekhorsecenter.com; 10am-6pm Mon.-Fri., 9am-5pm Sat.-Sun.) offers trail and pony rides, while the tennis center (16th St. and Kennedy St. NW, 202/722-5949, www.rockcreektennis.com; open daily, hours vary seasonally) has hard and clay courts available year-round, and hosts the Citi Open in July. The wooded golf center (6100 16th St. NW, 202/882-7332, www.golfdc.com/rock-creek-gc; open daily Mar.-Dec. including most holidays, hours vary seasonally) has a challenging 18-hole course and putting green.

The park is free and open daily during daylight hours; the nature center and horse center are closed Thanksgiving Day, Christmas Day, and New Year's Day. Parking is available at the nature center and at picnic areas near Beach Drive.

bikes ($11/hour or $35/day) to take one of the trails onward.

MAP 9: 4940 Canal Rd. NW, 202/244-0461, www.boatingindc.com; daily Apr.-Oct., hours vary

GOLF

East Potomac Golf Course and Driving Range

Play a round with a view of Southwest DC and the Washington Monument. Located in the middle of

East Potomac Park, this public golf club has one 18-hole course and two 9-hole courses, plus putting greens, a heated and covered driving range, and a mini golf course for the whole family to enjoy. The snack bar has cheap breakfast, lunch, and snacks, and the pro shop has you covered if you didn't bring your clubs.

MAP 9: 972 Ohio Dr. SW, 202/554-7660, www.golfdc.com; open daily, hours vary; greens fees $12-30 Mon.-Fri., $13-34 Sat.-Sun.

TENNIS

East Potomac Tennis Center

With five indoor courts plus 19 outdoor clay and hard courts, the East Potomac Tennis Center on the north end of East Potomac Park offers opportunities to play tennis year-round. Reservations are recommended, but walk-in courts and lessons are available; call the center or check the website for the schedule. Facilities include showers and lockers, and a pro shop sells gear and snacks.

MAP 9: 1090 Ohio Dr. SW, 202/554-5962, www.eastpotomactennis.com; 7am-10pm daily

Shops

CLOTHING, SHOES, AND ACCESSORIES

Nike Community Store

Located in the historic art deco Hecht Warehouse in up-and-coming Ivy City, the Nike Community Store does more than sell sneakers and workout pants. The brand's first community store on the East Coast has a mission to employ people who live within a 5-mi (8.1-km) radius and support athletic programs for local kids. This factory store has merchandise you might find at an outlet mall, with some good deals on apparel and gear for men and women; you can purchase merchandise from the store and Nike's website in a single transaction, and get your online order shipped to you for free.

MAP 9: 1403 New York Ave. NE, 202/529-1868, www.nike.com; 10am-8pm Mon.-Sat., noon-6pm Sun.

Nike Community Store

Shelter

This minimalist Union Market boutique has all the pretty things: jewelry from local and international designers, including delicate pieces featuring semi-precious stones by owner Mallory Shelter (pieces from $150 to $1,000 plus), along with chic housewares and stationery and crystals. The shop specializes in unique wedding jewelry, including engagement rings with alternative stones and vintage pieces.

MAP 9: 1258 5th St. NE, 202/548-0011, www.shopshelter.com; 11am-7pm Mon.-Sat., 11am-6pm Sun.

Union Market

GOURMET FOOD AND DRINKS

✪ New Columbia Distillers

DC's first distillery opened in 2011 and sells **Green Hat Gin,** inspired by George Cassiday, "The Man in the Green Hat" who provided bootleg liquor to Washington's elite during Prohibition. This distilled gin is perfect in the rickey, DC's official cocktail, and the rectangular bottles with a vintage-style label are made for Instagram. At the Ivy City distillery in a nondescript brick warehouse, you can purchase the classic gin and seasonal blends as well as take a free tour of the factory and, when the weather's nice, enjoy drinks in the garden.

MAP 9: 1832 Fenwick St. NE, 202/733-1710, www.greenhatgin.com; 1pm-8pm Sat., 2-6pm Sun.

Union Market

Union Terminal Market opened in Northeast in 1931, and for decades it was the center of food wholesale and distribution in the District. Over the years, however, the market declined. Eventually, the main market building reopened as Union Market, a bright, airy food hall with tons of space for food vendors and artisans. The market is leading the revitalization of this industrial part of town, serving as a home base for many food and beverage startups inside the main market building and surrounding warehouses.

Some advice: Go hungry. Union Market has about 40 vendors, permanent restaurants, and takeout stalls serving innovative cuisine, ranging from local pickles, fast-casual Ethiopian, and gluten-free Venezuelan arepas to an outpost of the kitchen supplies and gift store **Salt & Sundry** (202/556-1866, www.shopsaltandsundry.com), to Harvey's, the family-owned butcher and market mainstay that has been operating since 1931. If you'd like to stay awhile, have a bagel and egg cream at **Buffalo & Bergen** (202/543-2549, www.buffalobergendc.com), or try **Rappahannock Oyster Co.** (202/544-4702, www.rroysters.com). Outside the main building, one of DC's best Italian restaurants, **Masseria** (1340 4th St. NE, 202/608-1330, www.masseria-dc.com), is hidden among the warehouses and graffiti-filled alleys.

MAP 9: 1309 5th St. NE, 301/347-3998, www.unionmarketdc.com; 11am-8pm Tues.-Fri., 8am-8pm Sat.-Sun., vendor hours may vary

WHERE TO STAY

Hotels in Washington DC are notoriously expensive, especially around major events like the National Cherry Blossom Festival, Independence Day, and major conferences.

The Jefferson in Dupont Circle

Nonetheless, the District has more than 31,000 rooms and dozens of international hotel chains from high-end to budget brands, so while prices may increase astronomically during busy seasons, you can almost always find a room if you're willing to pay. Alas, the most historic and unique properties tend to be luxury properties, with rates to match. If you can swing it, they're worth the price, offering the chance to walk in the footsteps of policymakers of the past while enjoying views of the monuments. For those who can't afford the high-end digs, there are plenty of midpriced boutique hotels and a few pod-style properties offering lower-priced, tiny rooms in convenient locations.

Most properties are downtown, home to many of the historic hotels. While prices tend to be higher, you have many choices—and, you can walk or take public transportation almost everywhere. Dupont Circle and Georgetown/Foggy Bottom are hubs, as well, with many stately, quiet properties close to dining, nightlife, and shopping. Capitol Hill and Logan Circle have noteworthy, midpriced properties, but again, expect prices to rise to five-star levels during major events. If you're willing to venture away from the tourist centers to Woodley Park or even the suburbs, you can often find deals at Metro-accessible properties.

HIGHLIGHTS

✪ **BEST VIEW: The Hay-Adams** boasts views of the White House from many of its rooms (page 261).

✪ **MOST FASHIONABLE: Sofitel Washington DC Lafayette Square** is très chic, with French style and luxurious beds (page 264).

✪ **COOLEST ROOMS:** The guest rooms at the **Kimpton Hotel Monaco Washington DC** used to be offices; they have soaring ceilings and trendy decor (page 263).

✪ **BEST PLACE TO MEET LOCALS:** The social-media-ready **Eaton Workshop** has a coworking space and popular rooftop lounge steps away from the convention center (page 263).

✪ **MOST SCANDALOUS:** Famous for its role in more than one DC scandal, **The Mayflower** is a sophisticated hotel that embraces its long, storied history with photos and memorabilia of the infamous events (page 264).

✪ **BEST BASE FOR SEEING THE SIGHTS:** The **Liaison Capitol Hill** is a short walk from the U.S. Capitol and National Mall, and it has a resort-style rooftop pool for relaxing after a long day of sightseeing (page 266).

✪ **BEST FOR ROMANCE: The Jefferson** has everything you need for a romantic getaway: beautifully restored rooms with soaking tubs, a Michelin-starred restaurant, and a sexy lounge with discreet nooks for canoodling over cocktails (page 267).

✪ **BEST HOME AWAY FROM HOME: Kimpton Carlyle** offers art deco style with modern conveniences for business or pleasure travelers, who will appreciate up-to-date rooms and top-notch amenities on a quiet, residential street (page 267).

✪ **BEST POOL:** Designed by Morris Lapidus, **Washington Plaza Hotel** is an affordable option with a large, resort-style outdoor pool (page 270).

✪ **BEST PRESIDENTIAL SUITE: The Watergate Hotel** has two posh presidential suites with breathtaking view of the water and monuments (page 271).

✪ **BEST PLACE TO STAY FOR A BALLGAME:** The modern **Thompson Washington DC** is a calming space in Navy Yard (page 274).

✪ **BEST WITH KIDS:** Steps from the zoo, the **Omni Shoreham Hotel** is affordable luxury with a large, heated, outdoor pool (page 274).

PRICE KEY

$	Less than $150 per night
$ $	$150-300 per night
$ $ $	More than $300 per night

CHOOSING WHERE TO STAY

National Mall

While many must-see sights are located on the National Mall, hotels (as well as dining and nightlife) are limited. The Mandarin Oriental Washington DC and several budget-friendly chains are directly south of the Mall. However, other neighborhoods, including Downtown, Capitol Hill, and the District Wharf, are equally convenient while providing more choices in restaurants, bars, and accommodations.

Downtown and Penn Quarter

Whether you're visiting DC to party or to protest, you'll find convenient hotels downtown and in Penn Quarter at all price points, within walking distance to the National Mall and U.S. Capitol and accessible by several Metro lines and DC Circulator routes. It's the city's central business district and busiest on weekdays, but restaurants, bars, theaters, and shops keep the area lively on evenings and weekends, too.

Capitol Hill and Atlas District

With the Capitol dome in sight, Capitol Hill provides both proximity to power and quiet residential streets lined with casual pubs. Most of the neighborhood's hotels are within blocks of Union Station but walking distance to dining hot spots like Eastern Market and Barracks Row. It's a quick taxi or streetcar ride to the Atlas District, known for hip nightlife.

Dupont Circle

If you don't require a monument view, Dupont Circle's many hotels

The Mayflower

provide easy access to public transportation and the buzziest dining and nightlife, as well as the chance to get to know the quieter side of DC while exploring neighborhood restaurants, galleries, and boutiques on tree-lined streets. (Bonus: The major sights are not far, and you can even walk to them if you're feeling ambitious.)

U Street, Shaw, and Logan Circle

This part of town is where the city's young and fashionable spend their weekends brunching, shopping, and imbibing in the many cocktail bars, beer gardens, and nightclubs. The area is quiet on weekdays, and many restaurants don't open until the evening, but it's no matter; take the Metro or use a ride-sharing app to get to the sights, then return to explore the humming nightlife scene, stumbling distance from a few noteworthy hotels.

Adams Morgan

This ethnically diverse, residential neighborhood is a hub for good food and laid-back bars, but not hotels. You will find the luxury boutique hotel The LINE as well as a solid hostel; otherwise, you can utilize Airbnb—or stay elsewhere, like Dupont Circle, a quick walk or taxi ride away. Nearby, Columbia Heights and Mount Pleasant offer similar attractions.

Georgetown and Foggy Bottom

Home to college students and socialites, Georgetown has chic boutique hotels and a charming, historical atmosphere, with good restaurants and shopping on the brick-lined sidewalks as well as outdoor activities. However, it's not Metro accessible, so prepare to use taxis/ride-sharing apps or take the DC Circulator to Dupont Circle or downtown. Foggy Bottom is more convenient, with a few of the city's most luxurious (albeit expensive) hotels.

Navy Yard and Anacostia

These neighborhoods are experiencing some of the most rapid growth in DC—most notably, District Wharf, with dozens of restaurants and a few chain hotels at various price points. You'll find budget-friendly options around Nationals Park, a quick Metro ride to the business and tourism centers. There are no hotels east of the Anacostia River; stay elsewhere and take the Metro or a taxi to explore the Anacostia Historic District.

Greater Washington DC

Woodley Park is a mini hub for family-friendly hotels, steps from the Metro's Red Line as well as good dining and the zoo. And north of Georgetown up Wisconsin Avenue, Glover Park is a laid-back residential neighborhood minutes from shopping and dining, if you don't mind using ride-hailing apps heavily.

ALTERNATIVE LODGING OPTIONS

Washington DC is a transient town, with residents coming and going as their jobs change with the political winds, or to work on campaigns or U.S. State Department assignments, for example. As a result, short-term rentals are plentiful, with thousands of listings on sites like Airbnb

WHERE TO STAY IF . . .

YOUR MAIN GOAL IS TO SEE THE SIGHTS ON THE MALL:
District Wharf in Southwest DC, less than 10 minutes by foot from the National Mall, and a dining hub.

YOU ONLY HAVE ONE WEEKEND:
Downtown, because you're walking distance to both the major sights and the best dining and nightlife.

YOU'RE ON A BUDGET:
Penn Quarter or Dupont Circle. While hotels are expensive citywide, these neighborhoods have a few wallet-friendly deals if you plan ahead, plus lots of choices for dining and the ability to walk or take public transportation to the major sights.

YOU'RE SEEKING QUIET:
Woodley Park in Greater Washington DC, with several family-friendly hotels nestled near Rock Creek Park.

YOU WANT TO EAT, DRINK, AND PARTY:
U Street or Logan Circle, where you're a stone's throw from the hippest restaurants, cafés, bars, and nightclubs.

YOU WANT TO FEEL LIKE YOU'RE IN THE WASHINGTON DC OF MOVIES AND TELEVISION:
Capitol Hill, where hotels with DC-inspired details are steps from the top monuments and museums and offer scenic views of the halls of power.

(www.airbnb.com) and VRBO (www.vrbo.com) to allow you to experience the city like a local. More than two-thirds of these listings are private residences offering privacy at a lower price, especially in residential neighborhoods in Northwest and Capitol Hill.

When hotel prices are exceptionally high during major events or conferences, hotels near Ronald Reagan Washington National Airport are sometimes cheaper while still being Metro accessible and convenient to the city center; there are more than a dozen international chain hotels ranging from The Ritz-Carlton and Hilton to budget options in Crystal City and Pentagon City, Virginia. Similarly, there are chain hotels near Washington Dulles International Airport in Dulles and Herndon, Virginia, but these are 45-60

minutes from the city center in normal traffic, requiring a taxi ride or several changes on public transportation. Instead, consider staying in Alexandria, Virginia (see the *Day Trips* chapter), an easy Metro journey from DC, or Metro-accessible Maryland suburbs, like Bethesda, which is 15-20 minutes from Dupont Circle or Farragut North station, or downtown Silver Spring, 30 minutes from Gallery Pl-Chinatown station.

You can't pitch a tent on the National Mall—unless it's part of a public protest or demonstration and you get a permit from the National Park Service—but there are a few camping facilities in the region. Cherry Hill Park (800/801-6449, www.cherryhillpark.com) is the closest campsite, located in College Park, Maryland, approximately 30-40 minutes from DC by car and offering amenities including tent sites, RV hookups, laundry facilities, outdoor pools, and miniature golf. Between DC and Dulles, Lake Fairfax Park (703/471-5414, www. fairfaxcounty.gov) has tent and RV sites near the 18-acre lake, and next to Manassas National Battlefield Park, Bull Run Regional Park (703/631-0550, www.novaparks.

com) has cabins as well as campsites close to hiking trails, golf, and outdoor activities. Alternatively, you're within two hours from several national parks with camping facilities in Virginia and Maryland, including Shenandoah National Park; visit www.recreation.gov for information and reservations.

National Mall

Map 1

Mandarin Oriental Washington DC $$$

This luxurious but family-friendly hideaway is convenient to the major sights, boasting 373 well-appointed blue and silver rooms with city or water views. Empress Lounge (202/787-6148) in the lobby serves light meals, cocktails, and elegant high tea (by reservation), opening to a grassy lawn with space for the kids to run around. The tranquil, resort-style spa houses a 1,400-square-foot

fitness center and indoor pool (complimentary for hotel guests) and offers transformative massages and other treatments. You're about a 5-minute walk under a bridge to the District Wharf, and CVS and Starbucks are outside the front door. MAP 1: 1330 Maryland Ave. SW, 202/554-8588, www.mandarinoriental.com

Downtown and Penn Quarter

Map 2

✪ The Hay-Adams $$$

The next best option to staying at the White House is getting a room at The Hay-Adams—ideally, one of the suites with an unobstructed view of the White House. The 145-room historic hotel has been impeccably preserved, offering understated luxury that recalls a more civilized time in the capital. Enjoy impeccable service as well as a discreet basement bar,

Off the Record. The roof terrace, often booked for Washington's most exclusive events, boasts the best view in town. MAP 2: 800 16th St. NW, 202/638-6600, www.hayadams.com

Riggs Washington DC $$$

Blending historic architecture with a modern design sensibility—and the city's buzziest new cocktail bar—Riggs Washington DC is the capital's new grand hotel. Located in the former Riggs National Bank, the bank of 23 presidents (and a few major news headlines), the 1899 building has been completely refurbished with touches like Carrara marble and a few design nods to its history. **Café Riggs** (202/788-2800, www.caferiggs. com) is already a go-to for all-day French classics in a soaring space with marble columns, while acclaimed London-based mixologist Ryan Chetiyawardana's **Silver Lyan** (202/788-2799, www.silverlyan. com) serves inventive cocktails in the bank's former vault.

MAP 2: 900 F St. NW, 202/638-1800, www.riggsdc.com

The St. Regis Washington DC $$$

Two blocks from the White House, the St. Regis Washington DC exudes classic luxury, with 172 elegant guest rooms in warm hues and five-star service (personal butler optional). The presidential suite was refreshed to celebrate the hotel's 90th anniversary in 2016, and the grand lobby with its red and gold bar is a popular spot for afternoon tea, nightly champagne sabering, and the hotel's signature Bloody Mary with Old Bay.

MAP 2: 923 16th St. NW, 202/638-2626, www.stregiswashingtondc.com

Willard InterContinental Washington DC $$$

The term "lobbying" was coined at the Willard InterContinental by President Ulysses S. Grant, who was

The Hay-Adams

annoyed by the "lobbyists" bothering him in the lobby while he was trying to enjoy a drink; Dr. Martin Luther King Jr. finalized his "I Have A Dream" speech in the same lobby in 1963. These are just two of the countless significant events that have taken place at the stately, 335-room property. Even if you don't stay here, have a drink at the Round Robin Bar (202/628-9100) and peruse the History Gallery on the ornate ground floor.

MAP 2: 1401 Pennsylvania Ave. NW, 202/628-9100, www.washington.intercontinental.com

the lobby bar at The St. Regis Washington D.C.

W Washington DC $$$

The W Washington DC is best known for the rooftop lounge, POV (202/661-2419, www.povrooftop. com), where locals wait in line or reserve pricey tables for cocktails overlooking the monuments. It's located in the former Hotel Washington, which opened in 1918; today, many of the 317 rooms are small but modern. The tiny basement hideaway,

Bliss Spa (202/661-2416, www. blissspa.com), offers a full menu of luxurious treatments.

MAP 2: 515 15th St. NW, 202/661-2400, www.wwashingtondc.com

✪ Eaton Workshop $$

Near the convention center, Eaton Workshop is made for the social media era, with decor like trendy gold fixtures, vintage go-go concert posters, rare books in the 209 guest rooms and lobby, and lots of plants and natural light. And with a coworking space and radio station for left-of-center activists and "radicals," it's also a place to connect with like-minded locals who hang out in the public spaces. In addition to a wellness space with yoga and meditation classes, Eaton Workshop has several dining and drinking options, including good, expensive coffee at Kintsugi (www.kintsugi-dc.com), happening rooftop lounge WILD DAYS (202/900-8425, www.wild-days-dc.com) and cocktails in the "radical library." American Son (202/900-8416, www.american-son1978.com) serves American fare all day.

MAP 2: 1201 K St. NW, 202/289-7600, www.eatonworkshop.com

✪ Kimpton Hotel Monaco Washington DC $$

The Kimpton Hotel Monaco, in a neoclassical former post office, has some of the coolest architecture of any Washington hotel. Get swept away in the long hallways, swirling staircases, and marble surfaces throughout the property, which covers an entire city block. The 183 guest rooms used to be offices, so they have soaring ceilings; following the top-to-bottom renovation in 2015-2016, they're decorated with bold blue and purple decor and a five-foot lion's head mounted above the bed. Enjoy amenities like daily complimentary wine in the colorful lobby lounge. Dirty Habit (202/449-7095, www.dirtyhabitdc.com) serves global small plates and cocktails in an edgy, industrial space with a year-round patio.

MAP 2: 700 F St. NW, 202/628-7177, www.monaco-dc.com

✪ Sofitel Washington DC Lafayette Square $$

The Sofitel Washington DC Lafayette Square is très, très chic, with Parisian style fitting for its proximity to the park named for French general Lafayette, a key player in the Revolutionary War. The 237 guest rooms have black and white decor and luxurious, float-on-a-cloud beds, as well as white marble bathrooms with Lanvin toiletries. The renovated restaurant, Opaline Bar & Brasserie (202/730-8701, www.opalinedc.com), is a lovely choice for a glass of champagne.

MAP 2: 806 15th St. NW, 202/730-8800, www.sofitel-washington-dc.com

✪ The Mayflower $$

Get involved in a scandal at The Mayflower, where President Bill Clinton was photographed hugging Monica Lewinsky during a campaign event in 1996, and, infamously, where New York governor Eliot Spitzer (client no. 9) met Ashley Dupré. For those not looking for trouble, the Autograph Collection property is still a good choice to rest your head for business or pleasure, with 581 comfortable

Kimpton Hotel Monaco Washington DC

drinks at The Hay-Adams

Whether they're meeting a friend, a date, or a source, Washingtonians frequent the city's many hotel bars, known for strong cocktails, inviting ambience, and discreet bartenders. These are the top six.

- For the history: Round Robin Bar at the Willard InterContinental Washington DC
- For schmoozing a source: Off the Record at The Hay-Adams
- For only-in-Washington views: POV at W Washington DC
- For people-watching: Lounge at Bourbon Steak at the Four Seasons Hotel Washington DC
- For romance: Quill at The Jefferson
- For cool music and decor: The Next Whisky Bar at The Watergate Hotel

rooms with spacious bathrooms, plus a surprisingly large, state-of-the-art fitness facility. Explore the public spaces and the guest room floors, which have artifacts and plaques explaining the history of the hotel in a particular decade.
MAP 2: 1127 Connecticut Ave. NW, 202/347-3000,
www.themayflowerhotel.com

Conrad Washington DC $$

From the sleek glass facade to the minimalist decor, the new hotel in the CityCenterDC shopping district is like something you'd find in Hong Kong. The restaurant is hit or miss, but the 11th-floor rooftop bar is worth a stop for a cocktail. Book a calming suite with an electric fireplace and sweeping city views for an escape in the middle of everything.
MAP 2: 950 New York Ave. NW, 202/844-5900,
www.conradwashingtondc.com

Pod DC $

The Pod DC is definitely what you might call a crash pad. The 245 "micro" rooms measure about 150 square feet, but they're clean and well designed with private baths and amenities like free Wi-Fi, access to a fitness center, and a whiskey bar and late-night diner. It's steps from the Gallery Pl-Chinatown Metro, though not the nicest block in the neighborhood.

MAP 2: 627 H St. NW, 202/847-4444, www.thepodhotel.com

Capitol Hill and Atlas District

Map 3

✪ Liaison Capitol Hill $$

Literally steps away from the U.S. Capitol and a short walk from the monuments and museums on the National Mall, the Liaison Capitol Hill is the ideal base for sightseeing—especially during the summer, when you can enjoy the rooftop pool with resort-style cabanas and a bar featuring tropical cocktails, sangria, and snacks. The 343 modern guest rooms have super-comfortable beds, plus plenty of space to work or relax. Art & Soul (202/393-7777) serves comfort-food favorites for breakfast, lunch, dinner, and weekend brunch.

MAP 3: 415 New Jersey Ave. NW, 202/638-1616, www.yotel.com

Capitol Hill Hotel $$

Nestled between the Library of Congress and the neighborhood's best restaurants and bars, the Capitol Hill Hotel is your home away from home. The 152 suites are chic and spacious, and thoughtful amenities include self-service laundry, on-site bikes, and, for extended-stay guests, grocery service and discounts on meeting space. There's no restaurant or bar on-site, but every suite has a full kitchen or kitchenette, with a market in the lobby. It's pricey during the week and prime

travel seasons, but you can find good deals on suites on the weekend.

MAP 3: 200 C St. SE, 202/543-6000, www.capitolhillhotel-dc.com

Kimpton the George $$

This patriotic boutique hotel, in sight of the U.S. Capitol, is decorated with silhouettes of George and Martha Washington and other, clever details inspired by the first U.S. president throughout the hotel. The 139 smart guest rooms provide a zen-like environment with beige and blue decor as well as marble bathrooms; expect the usual amenities from Kimpton, including on-site bikes, yoga mats, and the daily wine hour in the recently renovated lobby. Bistro Bis (202/661-2700, www.bistrobis.com), a longtime favorite of U.S. Senate staffers and lobbyists, serves excellent French fare and cocktails.

MAP 3: 15 E St. NW, 202/347-4200, www.hotelgeorge.com

Phoenix Park Hotel $$

Do you have an early train home? Check in to Phoenix Park Hotel, directly across the street from Union Station. In November 2016, the hotel completed an $8 million renovation, revamping the public spaces and 149 guest rooms and suites, which have glam furniture and finishes. Many offer views of the U.S. Capitol. **The Dubliner** (202/737-3773, www. dublinerdc.com) serves classic pub fare, including Irish favorites like fish-and-chips and beef stew, from early morning until late.

MAP 3: 520 N. Capitol St. NW, 202/639-6900, www.phoenixparkhotel.com

Dupont Circle

Map 4

✪ The Jefferson $$$

The Jefferson is pure, discreet luxury. The beaux arts structure, built in 1923 as a premier residential building, was meticulously renovated in 2009. The result mixes the best of old and new: 99 beautiful guest rooms with patterns Thomas Jefferson brought to the United States from Paris, a tiny, practically private spa specializing in treatments using herbs grown at Monticello, and antique furniture, art, and books throughout the property. For a romantic weekend, dine at Michelin-starred **Plume** (202/448-3227, www.plumedc.com), the only Forbes five-star restaurant in DC, and canoodle over cocktails in the sexy lounge **Quill** before retiring to your suite's soaking tub.

MAP 4: 1200 16th St. NW, 202/448-2300, www.jeffersondc.com

The Dupont Circle Hotel $$$

Literally 3 minutes by foot from the Dupont Circle Metro station, The Dupont Circle Hotel is the ideal base for shopping, dining, and gallery-hopping. The 327 guest rooms are posh; expect muted but stylish decor and marble baths, plus hardwood floors in the suites. A multimillion-dollar renovation in 2019 brought midcentury modern design to the popular bar, as well as **The Pembroke** (202/448-4302, www.thepembrokedc.com) a much-needed finer dining option for the neighborhood.

MAP 4: 1500 New Hampshire Ave. NW, 202/483-6000, www.doylecollection.com

✪ The Kimpton Carlyle $$

This recently renovated Kimpton property is perfect for travelers who don't want to sacrifice style for convenience. The designer, Miami Beach artist Michele Oka Doner, kept many of the original art deco details—like the stunning marble floor in the entry—while adding modern touches, including her own art. The 198 refreshed rooms in blues and grays have sparkling marble and subway tile bathrooms; 56 have kitchenettes. The fitness center is spacious, though every guest room has a yoga mat and 24-hour yoga and Pilates channel on the giant television if you prefer to zen out in private; bikes are also available for guest use. Like all Kimptons, the hotel hosts a wine hour 5pm-6pm every evening in the Living Room, which displays contemporary art installations that rotate quarterly.

Don't miss **The Riggsby** (202/787-1500, www.theriggsby.com), serving supper club-style food and classic cocktails day and night.

MAP 4: 1731 New Hampshire Ave. NW, 202/234-3200, www.carlylehoteldc.com

The Embassy Row Hotel $$

Despite the prime location, walking distance from Georgetown, Adams Morgan, and the U Street Corridor, you may never want to leave The Embassy Row Hotel. The property is infused with a fresh dose of cool: a bright interior with eye-popping furniture; **Station Kitchen & Cocktails,** featuring a 24-hour snack pantry for guests; and the neighborhood's only rooftop pool, offering tropical drinks and spa treatments in the summer. The large hotel is also full of local flavor,

like cherry blossom wallpaper and **Compass Coffee** in the lobby.

MAP 4: 2015 Massachusetts Ave. NW, 202/265-1600, www.destinationhotels.com

The Fairfax at Embassy Row $$

Where Dupont Circle meets the foreign embassies stands a stately hotel that's been hosting politicians and diplomats since 1927. President Eisenhower had his first inaugural breakfast here, and Vice President Gore spent his childhood on the top floor while his father served as the U.S. senator from Tennessee. The hotel maintains historical character with modern updates, like cherrywood furniture and original crown molding in the 259 beige and green rooms with Frette linens. The lobby restaurant and bar, **The SALLY,**

The Jefferson

specializes in local small plates and cocktails.

MAP 4: 2100 Massachusetts Ave. NW, 202/293-2100, www.fairfaxwashingtondc.com

Washington Hilton

Washington Hilton $$

The Washington Hilton has welcomed every U.S. president since it opened in 1965—perhaps most infamously President Reagan, who was shot by John Hinckley Jr. while leaving the 1981 AFL-CIO luncheon. The massive brutalist structure is prepared for VIPs with amenities like a bulletproof carport and hidden passageway to DC's second-largest ballroom. The 1,000-plus guest rooms could use a refresh, but the conference hotel has everything you need for any kind of trip: a large gym with fitness classes, 11,000-square-foot sundeck and outdoor pool (with a view of the fireworks on July 4), and many business services. Big Bus Tour (www.bigbustours.com) stops at the hotel's doorstep, and the staff can provide curated itineraries to help you personalize your trip.

MAP 4: 1919 Connecticut Ave. NW, 202/483-3000, www.hilton.com

Tabard Inn $

Each of the 35 guest rooms at the Tabard Inn has a unique personality, just like the hotel itself, with lovely vintage furniture and decor. You don't stay here for high-tech conveniences; there are creaky staircases instead of an elevator, no televisions, and some rooms with shared baths. But you do stay here for a charming retreat in the heart of the city and for the unbeatable rates in this neighborhood. Have a cocktail in the cozy bar, a local favorite to hole up by the fire on winter nights.

MAP 4: 1739 N St. NW, 202/785-1277, www.tabardinn.com

U Street, Shaw, and Logan Circle

Map 5

Kimpton Mason & Rook Hotel $$

In the heart of the bustling nightlife district of Logan Circle, Kimpton's Mason & Rook Hotel is a great place to enjoy DC like the locals. The 178 rooms are huge, with modern decor and lots of space to work at the large desk or relax. There are several cool public spaces to enjoy, too, including Radiator (202/742-3150, www.radiatordc.com), with creative cocktails and outdoor fire pits, and a rooftop bar.

MAP 5: 1430 Rhode Island Ave. NW, 202/742-3100, www.masonandrookhotel.com

✪ Washington Plaza Hotel $

Did you really want to go to Miami instead? Book the Washington Plaza Hotel, designed by Morris Lapidus, the architect of the Fontainebleau in South Beach. It's a good compromise—walking distance to the White House, plus a large, resort-style outdoor pool with plenty of sun loungers and a bar. And the 340 clean, comfortable rooms, many with balconies overlooking the pool, are perfect for resting your head after a late night on U Street.

MAP 5: 10 Thomas Cir. NW, 202/842-1300, www.washingtonplazahotel.com

Adams Morgan   Map 6

The LINE $$$

Any chain property could have been a welcome addition to Adams Morgan, with its shortage of accommodations. But The LINE, which opened in 2017 in a renovated circa-1912 church, brings a lot of panache (if a little pretension). In the soaring lobby, a grand chandelier made from the church's organ pipes welcomes guests. The 220 guest rooms, which range from well-appointed king and queen rooms with custom furniture to apartment-style suites, boast works by local female artists and photographers as well as a small library in each. The restaurants and bars led by two James Beard Award-winning chefs elevate the neighborhood's options, too, especially A Rake's Progress, led by Spike Gjerde of Baltimore's Woodberry Kitchen, which tops the city's best dining lists for its uniquely local cuisine. Other options include Erik Bruner-Yang's Brothers and Sisters, which serves American fare with Asian influences from

The LINE

morning 'til late, and Spoken English (202/588-0525, www.spokenenglishdc.com), the 12-person, is a standing-room-only restaurant specializing in Asian street food and sake. In addition to standard 24-hour room service from Bruner-Yang's kitchen, guests can avail themselves of a roaming cocktail cart from 4pm to 7pm.

MAP 6: 1770 Euclid St. NW, 202/588-0525, www.thelinehotel.com/dc

Highroad Hostel DC $

This recently renovated hostel has amenities worthy of a boutique hotel—sleek decor, memory-foam mattresses, Netflix—at a fraction of the price. On a residential street off the bustling Adams Morgan business district, it has space for 92 guests, including cheap beds in shared dorm rooms, plus private rooms (all with shared baths), though the private room rates can run as high as hotel rooms during busy times. It's an easy walk, bike ride, or Uber anywhere you want to go, though the hostel encourages mingling on-site with dinners and social events.

MAP 6: 1804 Belmont Rd. NW, 202/735-3622, www.highroadhostels.com

Georgetown and Foggy Bottom

Map 7

✪ The Watergate Hotel $$$

The Watergate Hotel—yes, the one and the same complex as President Nixon's 1972 crime—reopened in 2016 following a complete renovation, with design that nods to the hotel's heyday in the '60s and '70s while still being thoroughly modern. Almost every one of the 336 sophisticated guest rooms and suites has views of the Potomac River, but the two 2,400-square-foot presidential suites are the best in the city, more like posh apartments than hotel rooms, with dark wood floors, a working fireplace, and a private

The Watergate Hotel

kitchen in case you invite guests to experience your breathtaking view of the water and monuments. If you want to leave your room—which would be surprising—unwind at three restaurants and bars, or the Argentta Spa, which has custom treatments, a state-of-the-art fitness center, and the original indoor pool.

MAP 7: 2650 Virginia Ave. NW, 844/617-1972, www.thewatergatehotel.com

The Avery $$$

You'll feel like you live in Georgetown at this luxe inn, a few blocks back from the main shopping drags. The 15 cheery guest rooms and suites are just a couple of years old; some have private patios, fireplaces, or soaking tubs. There's no on-site restaurant or fitness center, but the inn has complimentary breakfast and evening drinks—and there are plenty of options for dining and exercising in the neighborhood.

MAP 7: 2616 P St. NW, 202/827-4390, www.averygeorgetown.com

Fairmont Washington DC Georgetown $$$

With 413 spacious, elegant rooms—and exceptionally comfortable beds—plus countless amenities, this Fairmont outpost offers five-star service at a four-star price point. Everything sparkles—including the large courtyard, where you can enjoy dinner or drinks under the cherry trees. Keep your eyes peeled—former president Barack Obama has offices in the World Wildlife Fund next door, and Michelle frequents the SoulCycle across the street.

MAP 7: 2401 M St. NW, 202/429-2400, www.fairmont.com

Four Seasons Hotel Washington DC $$$

The contemporary brick Four Seasons Hotel is not the most attractive on the outside, but inside, it's five-star, five-diamond luxury. The 222 neutral rooms and suites—including the only bullet-resistant suite in DC—draw power players and celebrities, as does the spa and salon, known for primping first ladies and Hollywood stars. Michael Mina's Bourbon Steak (202/944-2026, www.bourbonsteakdc.com) has good food and even better people-watching.

MAP 7: 2800 Pennsylvania Ave. NW, 202/342-0444, www.fourseasons.com

Park Hyatt Washington $$$

In town for a big meeting? Unwind at the modern Park Hyatt Washington, conveniently located between Georgetown and downtown. There's plenty of room to work and relax in the 220 guest rooms and suites; you'll appreciate the clean, contemporary lines and spa-like bathrooms. The Michelin-starred Blue Duck Tavern (202/419-6755, www.blueducktavern.com) is excellent for breakfast, lunch, or dinner; the intimate bar is nice for a nightcap, but the tea cellar (202/419-6755) with more than 50 global varieties is especially soothing.

MAP 7: 1201 24th St. NW, 202/789-1234, www.washingtondc.parkhyatt.com

The Georgetown Inn $$

Visitors rave about the cozy Georgetown Inn, which provides historical charm reminiscent of when it first opened in 1962, along with modern amenities. Located in the center of the action near the neighborhood's best restaurants and attractions, the hotel's 96 rooms have classic decor with updated finishes; the affordable suites are perfect for families.

MAP 7: 1310 Wisconsin Ave. NW, 866/971-6618, www.georgetowninn.com

The Graham Georgetown $$

Named for Alexander Graham Bell, who lived in the neighborhood and taught at Georgetown University, The Graham Georgetown is a boutique hotel with 57 stylish guest rooms and suites. Meet young, fashionable locals at the hotel's two bars: The Alex, the basement speakeasy—ask for the passcode at the front desk—and The Observatory, the popular rooftop bar.

MAP 7: 1075 Thomas Jefferson St. NW, 855/341-1292, www.thegrahamgeorgetown.com

Hotel Hive $

The 83 rooms at DC's first micro-hotel may be small—they measure 125-250 square feet each, with a maximum occupancy of two people—but they're well designed and perfect for minimalist travelers on a budget. The hotel has the essentials—private bathrooms, Wi-Fi, charging stations, in-room amenities on request—as well as a popular pizza joint and rooftop bar serving local spirits and beers.

MAP 7: 2224 F St. NW, 202/849-8499, www.hotelhive.com

tea cellar at the Park Hyatt Washington

District Wharf, Navy Yard, and Anacostia   Map 8

✪ Thompson Washington DC $$

It's less than 10 minutes by foot from Nationals Park if you're staying for play, and a quick taxi ride to Capitol Hill if you're here for business. The Hyatt property's 225 guest rooms blend the neighborhood's industrial vibe with modern luxury in calming, neutral hues and hardwood floors, and many have oversized windows looking out to the Anacostia River. Maialino Mare (202/508-5249, www.maialinomare.com) brings Roman-style Italian via New York City, while Anchovy Social (202/249-6274, www.anchovysocial.com) has seafood snacks and cocktails with a view.

MAP 8: 221 Tingey St. SE, 855/949-1949, www.thompsonhotels.com

InterContinental Washington DC The Wharf $$

Located at the District Wharf, this hotel is sleek and luxurious, with amenities like a 5,000-square-foot spa and a rooftop infinity pool and bar overlooking the city. The 278 guest rooms have high-tech amenities, like smart TVs and touch-panel room controls; high rollers can book the two-level penthouse suite, featuring a wraparound balcony and offering panoramic views. Top Chef's Kwame Onwuachi's all-day restaurant Kith/Kin (202/878-8566, www.kithandkindc.com), elevates standard hotel fare with African and Caribbean flavors.

MAP 8: 801 Wharf St. SW, 202/800-0844, www.wharfintercontinentaldc.com

Greater Washington DC   Map 9

✪ Omni Shoreham Hotel $$

A quick walk from Smithsonian's National Zoo, the Omni Shoreham Hotel provides affordable, family-friendly luxury, plus games and amenities for the kids when you arrive. When you need a break from sightseeing, relax by the large, heated, outdoor pool set on 11 acres of gardens. Many of the 834 classically decorated rooms have views of nearby Rock Creek Park, and several on-site dining options mean you don't need to leave the property if the giant pandas wore you out.

MAP 9: 2500 Calvert St. NW, 202/234-0700, www.omnihotels.com

Kimpton Glover Park Hotel $$

This quietly elegant hotel has 154 up-to-date guest rooms, some with kitchenettes, in calming white with black accents. You're not close to the Metro, but you are a leisurely walk from Embassy Row and Georgetown. On the property, Casolare (202/625-5400, www.casolaredc.com), led by James Beard winner Michael Schlow, serves noteworthy Italian.

MAP 9: 2505 Wisconsin Ave. NW, 202/337-9700, www.gloverparkhotel.com

Washington Marriott Wardman Park $$

When the Wardman Park Hotel opened in 1918, it was the largest in the city. Langston Hughes was a busboy there before he became a famous poet. Now managed by Marriott, the hotel is massive, with more than 1,000 guest rooms and suites and frequent conferences, but it offers good value (and an outdoor pool) in a convenient location steps from the Metro and close to Rock Creek Park and the international flavor of Adams Morgan.

MAP 9: 2660 Woodley Rd. NW, 202/328-2000, www.marriott.com

DAY TRIPS

While you could spend weeks exploring Washington's museums and parks, you'll find worthwhile excursions nearby, from bustling cities to quiet coun-

schooner along Old Town
Alexandria waterfront

try towns—both with an abundance of history tracing back to the country's founding—to battlefields, spacecraft, innovative wineries, and destination dining. And outdoor enthusiasts will find much to love in the Mid-Atlantic, including some of the best spots for sailing and hiking in the country, less than two hours from DC's city center.

With a car, the region is your oyster—from the idyllic Chesapeake Bay (and famous blue crabs) in Maryland, to the bucolic Virginia countryside, to Shenandoah National Park, covering nearly 198,000 acres in the shadow of the Blue Ridge Mountains. Do you like the water? Cross the Chesapeake Bay Bridge to explore the Eastern Shore's humble small towns, and walk in the footsteps of Frederick Douglass and generations of shipbuilders, sailors, crabbers, and oyster canners. Do you prefer scrambling rocky peaks to find views of expansive valleys you'll only find in America? Head to Shenandoah National Park and Skyline Drive, where you can hike miles upon miles of trails and stay in rustic lodges—or, spend the night in luxe country inns, known for farm-to-table dining and local wine. (And foodies won't want to miss the spectacular Inn at Little Washington, which redefined farm-to-table dining and has three Michelin stars.)

Even without a car, you can find history and adventure. After a quick journey on the Metro, Civil War history and water views await in Old Town Alexandria; venture a little farther to explore George Washington's Mount Vernon, perhaps the region's best historic site outside of DC.

HIGHLIGHTS

✪ **BEST HISTORIC SIGHT: Mount Vernon,** George Washington's immaculately preserved Virginia estate and plantation, is reachable by car, boat, or bike from Washington DC (page 286).

✪ **BEST SPOT TO GET ON THE WATER:** Head to America's Sailing Capital to catch a boat tour or rent your own sailboat from **Annapolis Harbor and City Dock** (page 289).

✪ **BEST PLACE TO HAVE CRABS ON THE WATER:** Cross the Chesapeake Bay Bridge to **St. Michaels,** where you can crack Maryland's famous steamed blue crabs with an Old Bay Bloody Mary (page 300).

✪ **BEST EXCURSION WITH KIDS:** The National Air and Space Museum's **Steven F. Udvar-Hazy Center** has massive hangars with eye-popping airplanes and spacecraft, 45 minutes from DC near Dulles Airport (page 303).

✪ **BEST SCENIC DRIVE: Skyline Drive** is the destination, not the journey, especially when the leaves in Shenandoah National Park are changing in the fall (page 305).

✪ **BEST ROMANTIC GETAWAY:** Dinner at **The Inn at Little Washington** will be one of the most memorable (and probably most expensive) meals of your life (page 307).

✪ **BEST PLACE TO HIDE FROM A SCANDAL:** In America's Horse and Hunt Capital, **Historic Middleburg** has been a favorite hideaway for wealthy Washingtonians for decades (page 310).

Chesapeake Bay crabs

Day Trips

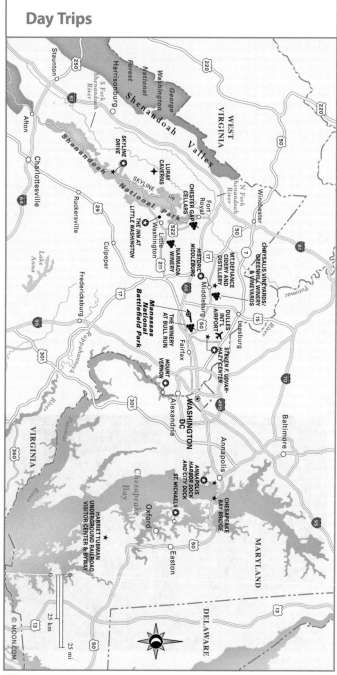

PLANNING YOUR TIME

If you have just half a day, or even a few hours, you can get to Alexandria quickly by Metro or boat; Old Town is 30 minutes by water taxi from the National Mall, allowing you to get a taste of the city's Civil War history, have dinner by the water, and still get back to DC for an early bedtime. Mount Vernon requires half a day, including travel time; give yourself a full day if you want to explore the estate at a more leisurely pace or take the round-trip bike journey from Theodore Roosevelt Island. Similarly, Annapolis requires half a day at minimum; it's possible to go for a crab cake lunch and get back to DC for evening cocktails, but why not spend a little more time exploring the sailing capital and its history? You'll need at least a full day to explore the Eastern Shore or Shenandoah National Park, but a weekend is better.

You can get to Alexandria and Annapolis by public transportation, taxi, or ride-sharing app—and it's better to take the Metro or a taxi to Alexandria rather than drive yourself—but you'll need a car to see the Eastern Shore or Virginia countryside. In some cases, such as taking the frightening drive over the Chesapeake Bay Bridge or, better yet, traveling part of Skyline Drive in Shenandoah National Park, the journey is a key part of the destination. Serious foodies can take car service to The Inn at Little Washington for dinner, or on a wine-tasting excursion, but doing both makes for a memorable weekend getaway. The Virginia countryside is most beautiful in the fall when the leaves change, while the Eastern Shore shines in the summer, but these times will be the most crowded, too. Shenandoah National Park is open year-round, but be aware that many facilities close beginning in November, and winter weather conditions can make hikes more difficult. Parts of Skyline Drive may be closed in inclement weather.

While DC, Maryland, and Virginia share borders, don't try to see all of these excursions in one trip. Choose one or two towns or sights, and luxuriate in the slower pace of life outside the District.

Alexandria

Southwest of DC on the Potomac River, Alexandria was an important colonial port city, included in the original boundaries of Washington DC but given back to Virginia in 1846. Today, many people who work in DC live in Alexandria. With its charming Old Town, friendly restaurants and bars, and a few important historic sites from the capital's earliest days, it's the ideal choice for an easy getaway, or even a relaxing place to stay when you want to visit DC.

OLD TOWN ALEXANDRIA

SIGHTS

African American Heritage Park

The nine-acre African American Heritage Park (500 Holland Ln., 703/838-4356, www.alexandriava. gov/blackhistory; dawn-dusk daily; free) opened in 1995, after archaeologists uncovered the graves of 26 Alexandrians who were buried in the Black Baptist Cemetery, founded in 1885 and located on the park's grounds. The park incorporates natural wetlands as well as three bronze trees sculpted by Jerome Meadows, inscribed with the words "Truths that Rise from the Roots Remembered" and the names

Old Town Alexandria

of African Americans who played a role in the city's development.

Alexandria National Cemetery

Explore Alexandria's Civil War history at the five-acre Alexandria National Cemetery (1450 Wilkes St., 703/221-2183, www.cem.va.gov/cems/nchp/alexandriava.asp; dawn-dusk daily; free). It was established in 1862 to bury soldiers who died around Alexandria, which was a strategically important camp and supply center for the Union Army. In just two years, however, the cemetery was full, and the government began to make plans to build a larger one in Arlington. In addition to the graves of more than 229 African American soldiers who fought in the Union Army, a memorial honors the four civilian men who drowned while chasing John Wilkes Booth after he killed President Lincoln.

Freedom House Museum

One of the largest slave trading companies in the country, Franklin & Armfield, was headquartered in Alexandria, selling more than 1,000 slaves annually during its most profitable years. After arriving at the Alexandria port, people were kept in the holding pens at the company's row house on Duke Street before being shipped farther south. The last slave trader to work for the company was James Birch, who was behind the kidnapping and sale of free black man Solomon Northup, as depicted in *12 Years a Slave*. In 1996, the Northern Virginia chapter of the National Urban League, the African American advocacy and educational organization, purchased the building. Now, it's the site of the

Freedom House Museum (1315 Duke St., 703/836-2858, www.alexandriava.gov/FreedomHouse; 10am-4pm Mon.-Fri., weekends and holidays by appointment; free), where you can learn about the slave trade that infested Washington DC and Virginia, which is not discussed enough.

Old Town Alexandria Waterfront

The main draw of a trip to Alexandria, the Old Town Alexandria waterfront has sparkling views of the Potomac River as well as dining, entertainment, and leisure activities, accessible via Strand Street at King Street or Prince Street. In addition to enjoying dockside dining at several restaurants and bars, you can catch a river cruise to see the National Mall from the water, as well as water taxis to Nationals Park, District Wharf, or Georgetown. The waterfront has several parks, including Founders Park (N. Union St., between Oronoco St. and Queen St.), a grassy stretch a quick walk from the marina.

The George Washington Masonic National Memorial

George Washington was a member of the Masons, one of the world's oldest and largest fraternal societies. Masons are committed to the ideals of brotherly love, truth, and relief, or charity—ideals that undoubtedly influenced the Founding Fathers, many of whom were Masons, too, in their quest for liberty and justice for all. (In fact, 9 of the 56 signers of the Declaration of Independence, and 13 of the 39 signers of the U.S. Constitution, were Masons.) The

Old Town Alexandria

Alexandria National Cemetery

To The George Washington Masonic National Memorial and King Street Metro Station

LORIEN HOTEL & SPA

To African American Heritage Memorial Park and Nick's Night Club

FREEDOM HOUSE MUSEUM AT THE NORTHERN VIRGINIA URBAN LEAGUE ★

ACME MID-CENTURY & MODERN ■

VERMILION

AUGIE'S

HANK'S OYSTER BAR ▼

THE HOUR
▼ KILLER E.S.P.

TAVERNA CRETEKOU ▼

BISHOP BOUTIQUE ■

To Pendleton Carryout Co. and The Birchmere

PRINCE

CAMERON

QUEEN

ST

DUKE

PATRICK

HENRY

KING

ST

WILKES

ALFRED

COLUMBUS

ST

ST

ST

ST

ST

WASHINGTON

WOLFE

ST ASAPH

PITT

ROYAL

FAIRFAX

LEE

UNION

PRINCESS

ST

ST

ST

ST

ST

ST

QUAY ST

ORONOCO

THE ALEXANDRIAN ●

Market Square

THE SHOE HIVE ■

THE CHRISTMAS ATTIC ■

THE OLD TOWN SHOP ■

THE LUCKY KNOT ■

ALEXANDRIA VISITOR CENTER

HOTEL INDIGO OLD TOWN ALEXANDRIA ●

HUMMINGBIRD ●

BIKE AND ROLL ■

THE STRAND

THE STRAND

VOLA'S DOCKSIDE GRILL & HI-TIDE LOUNGE ▼

TORPEDO FACTORY ART CENTER ★

OLD TOWN ALEXANDRIA WATERFRONT ★

To Mount Vernon Trail

Waterfront Park

Founders Park

Potomac River

© MOON.COM

0   200 yds
0   200 m

282

George Washington Masonic National Memorial

displays artifacts unearthed from Alexandria's history during excavations of the city.

RESTAURANTS

If the view is what you're after, try Vola's Dockside Grill (101 N. Union St., 703/935-8890, www.volasdockside.com; 11am-midnight Mon.-Thurs., 11am-1am Fri., 10am-1am Sat., 10am-midnight Sun.; $15-27), named for Alexandria's first female city manager, Vola Lawson, and enjoy casual seafood outdoors right on the Potomac River. The beachy, boozy brunch beverages (with $4 refills) paired with oysters or fish tacos will complete your vacation. For the very best seafood, however, locals will tell you to go to Hank's Oyster Bar (1026 King St., 703/739-4265, www.hanksoysterbar.com; 11:30am-midnight Mon.-Fri., 11am-midnight Sat.-Sun.; $18-32), an outpost of the Washington DC raw-bar favorite, serving fresh catches for lunch, dinner, and weekend brunch—plus oyster specials during happy hour (3pm-7pm daily) and a half-price raw bar from 10pm until closing.

For something more special, go to Vermilion (1120 King St., 703/684-9669, www.vermilionrestaurant.com; 11:30am-10pm Mon., 5:30pm-10pm Tue., 11:30am-10pm Wed.-Thurs., 11:30am-11pm Fri., 10:30am-11pm Sat., 10:30am-9pm Sun.), which has a $72pp four-course tasting menu with seasonal ingredients from local farms—which would probably cost twice the price in a hip DC neighborhood.

In the heart of the King Street shopping district, Taverna Cretekou (818 King St., 703/548-8688, www.tavernacretekou;

George Washington Masonic National Memorial (101 Callahan Dr., 703/683-2007, www.gwmemorial.org; 9am-5pm daily; $15 adults, free children 12 and under) honors the nation's first president, who served as Master of the Masons' Alexandria Lodge later in life. Tour the grandiose temple, inspired by the ancient lighthouse in Alexandria, Egypt, and get a peek inside the secret society at the center of many conspiracy theories.

Torpedo Factory Art Center

Founded in 1974, Torpedo Factory Art Center (105 N. Union St., 703/746-4570, www.torpedofactory.org; 10am-6pm Fri.-Wed., 10am-9pm Thurs.) is home to 160 resident artists, who open their studios to the public daily. Housed in a former torpedo plant right on the waterfront, the center has seven galleries to showcase contemporary and community art, as well as the Alexandria Archaeology Museum (10am-3pm Tues.-Fri., 10am-5pm Sat., 1pm-5pm Sun.; free), which

11:30am-2:30pm and 5pm-10pm Tues.-Fri., noon-10:30pm Sat., 11am-3pm and 5pm-9:30pm Sun.; $18-36) has been a local favorite for more than 40 years. Enjoy authentic, regional Greek food, wine, and atmosphere, with live music and dancing on Thursday evenings; the brick-patio garden is open seasonally.

The cozy **Killer E.S.P.** (1012 King St., 703/200-3200, www.killeresp. com; 9am-9:30pm Sun.-Thurs., 9am-11:30pm Fri.-Sat.) does indeed serve killer coffee, including espresso drinks made with Stumptown Coffee. Pop in for a shopping break and pair your coffee or tea with homemade gelato and sorbet, or a slice of sweet or savory pie, warmed on request by the friendly staff.

Pendleton Carryout Co. (807 Pendleton St., 571/970-2625, www. pendletoncarryoutco.com; noon-9pm daily) is a buzzed-about restaurant incubator for young chefs, food trucks, and market stalls thinking about making a move to brick-and-mortar establishments. The fast-casual establishment has recently featured cult-favorite southern-style biscuits, non-GMO pizza, and authentic dumplings.

NIGHTLIFE

Nightlife in Alexandria is pretty casual compared to DC, with many cozy restaurant bars, traditional pubs, and casual patios. For frozen drinks with a view, the **Hi-Tide Lounge at Vola's Dockside Grill** (101 N. Union St., 703/935-8890, www.volasdockside.com; 3pm-11pm Mon.-Thurs., 3pm-1am Fri., noon-1am Sat., noon-11pm Sun.) is a casual, indoor tiki bar with 1960s decor. For beer, hit the open-air beer garden with more than 70 on tap (as well as good mussels) at **Augie's** (1106 King St., 703/721-3970; 11am-midnight Sun.-Wed., 11am-1am Thurs.-Sat.).

Two nightclubs are worth the Uber fare outside of Old Town, or outside of the District, for that matter. Just 15 minutes from Old Town, **The Birchmere** (3701 Mt. Vernon Ave., 703/549-7500, www.birchmere. com; box office open 5pm-9pm on show nights) has hosted major rock, country, folk, and jazz performers since 1966, including Mary Chapin Carpenter, Emmylou Harris, and the Dave Matthews Band, among others. The 500-seat music hall has first-come, first-served seating and a full dinner menu; Flex Stage shows are standing-room only. And, about 20 minutes west of Old Town close to Red Lobster and a few self-storage centers, **Nick's Night Club** (642 S. Pickett St., 703/751-8900, www.nicksnightclub.com; 4pm-midnight Tues., 4pm-11:30pm Wed., 4pm-10:30pm Thurs., 4pm-1:30am Fri., 6pm-1:30am Sat.) is an authentic country bar, where a wide mix of folks from Virginia and DC go for live country music and cheap beer. This crowd knows their line dances; put on your cowboy boots and arrive by 7:45pm on Fridays and Saturdays for $10 lessons.

SHOPS

Old Town is one of the region's best shopping districts, with dozens of independent boutiques lining King Street and the side streets, from Henry Street west to the waterfront.

The Old Town Boutique District (www.oldtownboutiquedistrict. com) is heavy on women's apparel and accessories with colorful, contemporary styling, where the area's self-proclaimed fashionistas go for pretty dresses and shoes. **Bishop Boutique** (815-B King St., 571/312-0042, www.bishopboutique.com; 10am-7pm Mon.-Sat., 11am-6pm Sun.) is a tiny shop with big trends, carrying labels like Loeffler Randall, Joie, and L.K. Bennett, with shoe boxes stacked floor to ceiling. **The Shoe Hive** (127 S. Fairfax St., 703/548-7105, www.theshoehive.com; 10am-7pm Mon.-Sat., noon-5pm Sun.) has been selling delicious designer shoes by brands like Butter, Rag & Bone, and Stuart Weitzman since 2003, while **The Lucky Knot** (101-103 King St., 703/549-1797, www.theluckyknot.com; 10:30am-8pm Mon.-Sat., 11am-7pm Sun.) is the destination for jaunty men's and women's attire perfect for a day on the water, like Lily Pulitzer and Sperry Top-Sider.

No shopping spree is complete without a stop at **The Hour** (1015 King St., 703/224-4687, www.thehourshop.com; 11am-6pm Fri.-Sat., noon-5pm Sun.), selling authenticated, mint-condition vintage barware, glassware, and dining accessories, from the Prohibition era to the middle of the 20th century. Take home a set of like-new martini glasses and feel like Don Draper during cocktail hour. And if you need a cocktail table for your new set, **Acme Mid-Century & Modern** (1218 King St., no phone, www.acmemidcentury.com, 3pm-7pm Fri., 11am-6pm Sat., 11am-5pm Sun.) sells, as the name suggests, furniture and home decor from the mid-century and modern eras, including designers like Eames.

For souvenirs and gifts, **The Old Town Shop** (105 S. Union St., 703/684-4682, www.theoldtownshop.com; 10am-9pm daily) stocks Alexandria and DC souvenirs, including apparel, housewares, tchotchkes, and locally made products, such as gourmet food and Virginia peanuts. **The Christmas Attic** (125 S. Union St., 703/548-2829, www.christmasattic.com; 10am-5pm daily) has been selling high-end, collectible holiday decorations as well as everything you need to deck your halls since 1971.

WHERE TO STAY

It's not necessary to stay overnight in Alexandria—in fact, many people live in Alexandria and commute to DC daily—but there are several noteworthy hotels, ranging from boutique hotels with every amenity to budget-friendly chains. And, when rates are exorbitant in DC, such as during major events like an inauguration or large convention, hotels in Alexandria are sometimes slightly more affordable while still being a short Metro ride away from the capital.

For a luxurious stay blocks from the King Street Metro Station, check in to the **Lorien Hotel & Spa** (1600 King St., 703/894-3434, www.lorienhotelandspa.com; $169-270), a Kimpton property that was completely renovated in January 2017. The 107 guest rooms are decorated in calming light blue and white decor, providing respite following a day of sightseeing or a massage at the spa, the only hotel spa in Alexandria. **Brabo** (703/894-3440, www.braborestaurant.com; 5pm-10pm Mon.-Thurs., 5pm-11pm

Fri.-Sat., 11am-2:30pm and 5pm-9pm Sun.; $85) serves excellent Belgian American fare.

Just four blocks from the waterfront and across the street from city hall, The Alexandrian (480 King St., 703/549-6080, www.thealexandrian.com; $125-250) is an excellent choice for exploring Old Town with the family; it's about a 20-minute walk from the Metro. Part of Marriott's Autograph Collection, the hotel has 241 colorful guest rooms, including 11 recently renovated suites, as well as four-star amenities in a historic, Civil War-era building.

You can't get much closer to the water than the Hotel Indigo Old Town Alexandria (220 S. Union St., 703/721-3800, www.hotelindigooldtownalexandria.com; $150-250), which opened in May 2017. The 120 guest rooms are simple but cheerful and modern, with hardwood floors and city or water views. Hummingbird (703/566-1355, www.hummingbirdva.net; 6:30am-10pm Mon.-Thurs., 6:30am-11pm Fri., 7am-11pm Sat., 7am-9pm Sun.; $18-32) is already getting attention from DC food critics for the seafood and view.

INFORMATION AND SERVICES

For directions and tickets for sights, tours, and transportation, visit the Alexandria Visitor Center (221 King St., 703/746-3301, www.visitalexandriava.com; 10am-6pm Sun.-Wed., 10am-8pm Thurs.-Sat. Apr.-Sept.; 10am-5pm daily Oct.-Mar.), located in a historic former home near the city hall. Visit Alexandria (www.visitalexandria.com) has a wealth of information

about little-known sights, recreational activities, and the city's history.

TRANSPORTATION

It's easy to reach Alexandria from Washington DC. Many Alexandrians commute to DC daily, so you have several transportation options. Old Town is very walkable.

The King St-Old Town Metro station (1900 King St., www.wmata.com) serves the Blue and Yellow Lines of the Metro. From the station, walk or catch the free King Street Trolley (www.dashbus.com; every 10-15 minutes, 10:30am-10:30pm Sun.-Wed., 10:30am-midnight Thurs.-Sat.; free) to reach Alexandria's sights, restaurants, shops, and hotels.

Old Town is approximately 20-25 minutes by car from DC. Unless you're staying at a hotel with parking, take a taxi or ride-hailing service because parking can be limited.

Alternatively, you can take a water taxi (Ohio Dr. SW and West Basin Dr. SW, west side of the Tidal Basin, 877/511-2628, www.potomacriverboatco.com) from the National Mall to the Old Town Alexandria waterfront; the trip takes about 30 minutes. Round-trip tickets cost $28 for adults and $16 for children under 12. It's also possible to take a water taxi from District Wharf (round-trip tickets from $20 adults, from $14 children) to reach Alexandria.

✪ MOUNT VERNON

You'll step back in time when you arrive at George Washington's Mount Vernon (3200 Mount Vernon Memorial Hwy., 703/780-2000, www.mountvernon.org;

BIKING TO ALEXANDRIA

Old Town Alexandria is accessible by bicycle via the 18-mi (29-km) Mount Vernon Trail, which starts near Theodore Roosevelt Island and ends at George Washington's Mount Vernon. From DC, you can get on the trail near the entrance of the island, just under the George Washington Memorial Parkway in Rosslyn, and follow the parkway and the Potomac River south for approximately 7.5 mi (12 km) to Old Town. Stop for lunch and get back to DC in time for dinner, or continue onward another 10 mi (16.1 km) to Mount Vernon. The trail gets a little lost in the busy streets of Old Town; just keep riding south to the end of Union Street or Royal Street to pick the trail back up. The trail is paved or wooden boardwalks the entire ride, and mostly flat until right before you reach Mount Vernon; the trail can get very crowded on weekends, so prepare to dodge other bikers as well as hikers and joggers.

If you're already in Alexandria and want to bike to Mount Vernon or DC and back, there are several Capital Bikeshare (www.capitalbikeshare.com) stations in the city. Bike and Roll (1 Wales Alley between Union St. and Strand St., 202/842-2453, www.bikeandrolldc.com; 10am-6pm Tues.-Sun.) offers bike rentals (first two hours $16-30 adults, $10 children) and a package that includes a boat ride from Mount Vernon back to the Old Town waterfront; reservations are recommended.

9am-5pm daily Apr.-Oct., 9am-4pm daily Nov.-Mar., $20 adults, $19 seniors, $12 children ages 6-11, and free for children under 6), George and Martha Washington's Virginia estate and plantation, which has been immaculately preserved and restored—the farm even has some of the same breeds from Washington's time.

Mount Vernon

It's possible to power through your visit in a few hours, but you could easily spend a day or two exploring. Admission includes access to the mansion and museum, as well as the outside buildings and six acres of gardens and farm, including the tombs of George and Martha. For a more in-depth look at life on the estate, add one of a dozen specialty tours to your ticket, in which you'll meet Washington family members and employees (portrayed by actors).

If you have time, George Washington's Distillery and Gristmill (5513 Mount Vernon Memorial Hwy., www.mountvernon.org/the-estate-gardens/distillery; 10am-5pm daily Apr.-Oct.), where he produced flour, cornmeal, and whiskey, is worth a visit; shuttles are available from the estate. When he died, it was the largest distillery in America, and it continues to produce his whiskey today. Mount Vernon Inn Restaurant (703/799-6800, www.mountvernon.org/inn; 11am-5pm Mon., 11am-9pm Tues.-Fri., 10am-9pm Sat., 10am-5pm Sun.; $14-26) serves lunch, dinner, and weekend brunch, while a food court serves quick meals and snacks; nearby, the shops sell souvenirs including reproductions of estate items and the distillery's whiskey.

Open 365 days a year, including Christmas and New Year's Day, Mount Vernon is magical when decorated during the holiday season; special holiday events include candlelight tours and festivals.

INFORMATION AND SERVICES

George Washington's Mount Vernon (www.mountvernon.org) is the definitive resource for planning your visit to the estate, with history, virtual tours, and details on tours and special events. Purchase tickets online in advance for discounts; note that boat cruises from DC and Alexandria to Mount Vernon include admission.

TRANSPORTATION

There are several ways to get to Mount Vernon from DC and Alexandria.

By car, take the George Washington Memorial Parkway south toward Reagan National Airport/Mount Vernon, approximately 20 mi (32 km, 30-35 minutes) from DC and approximately 8 mi (12.9 km, 18-20 minutes) from Old Town Alexandria. There is ample free parking at the estate.

By Metro, take the Yellow Line to Huntington station (2501 Huntington Ave., www.wmata.com) and catch the southbound Fairfax Connector bus 101 (703/339-7200, www.fairfaxconnector.com), running about every 5-10 minutes daily; the bus ride is approximately 20 minutes from the station to the Mount Vernon entrance. This route is the least efficient, but it's the cheapest if you don't have a car.

Alternatively, you can take a boat from DC or Alexandria; choose this option if you'd like a scenic, albeit longer, journey. From DC, Spirit of Mount Vernon river cruises (866/302-2469, www.spiritcruises.com, round-trip tickets $49.95 adults, $43 children 6-11, free for children 5 and under; Tues.-Sun. from March to October) travel from the Southwest Waterfront directly to Mount Vernon; the journey takes approximately 90 minutes, departing DC at 8am and leaving Mount Vernon at 1:30pm. From Alexandria, Potomac Riverboat Company (877/511-2628, www.potomacriverboatco.com, round-trip tickets $50 adults, $44 children) offers 90-minute cruises, departing Old Town at 10:30am and leaving Mount Vernon at 4pm. Mount Vernon admission is included with both river cruises; reservations are strongly recommended.

You can bike to the estate via the Mount Vernon Trail, which links DC, Alexandria, and Mount Vernon. It's 18 mi (29 km) from DC to Mount Vernon, but the trip will not be too difficult for experienced riders. From Alexandria, it's just 8 mi (12.9 km) to the estate's entrance. (See *Biking to Alexandria* on page 287 for more information.)

Annapolis and Maryland's Eastern Shore

Annapolis is the state capital of Maryland, and the sailing capital of the country, a good choice to spend a day on the water and explore colonial history before you try Maryland's famous blue crab cake. Or, continue over the Chesapeake Bay Bridge to explore some of the Eastern Shore's most charming small towns; Easton, Oxford, and St. Michaels are close enough to one another to visit in one day, or you can make a relaxing weekend.

ANNAPOLIS
SIGHTS
✪ Annapolis Harbor and City Dock

Getting out on the water is a must when visiting "America's Sailing Capital," and City Dock (1 Dock St., Main St. at Compromise St.) is the place to do it. Head southeast on Main Street until you see the sailboats—you'll see a lot of them in the busy harbor.

After perusing the restaurants, pubs, and boutiques around the dock, take a boat cruise to see the Annapolis shoreline from the water. Enjoy a 40-minute, narrated tour on the circa 1973 river boat *Harbor Queen* (410/268-7601, http://cruisesonthebay.com; daily cruises Mar.-Oct.; $19 adults, $6 children 3-11, free for children 2 and under), or board one of the elegant Woodwind schooners (80 Compromise St., 410/263-7837, www.schoonerwoodwind.com; daily cruises Apr.-Oct.; $45-48 adults, $43-46 seniors, $31 children under 12), which offer daytime and sunset cruises as well as private charters.

To sail yourself, go to the Annapolis Sailing School (7001 Bembe Beach Rd., 410/267-7205, www.annapolissailing.com), where you can rent one of their Rainbows or take a class. Prefer to stay on dry land? Catch one of the races on Wednesday evenings at 6pm from

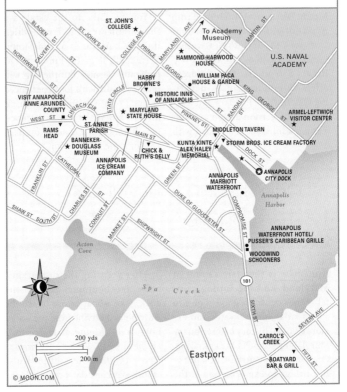

Annapolis

ST. JOHN'S
COLLEGE

BLADEN ST

NORTHWEST ST

CALVERT ST

ST. JOHN'S ST

COLLEGE AVE

PRINCE GEORGE ST

MARYLAND AVE

MARTIN ST

To Academy
Museum

HAMMOND-HARWOOD
HOUSE

U.S. NAVAL
ACADEMY

KING GEORGE ST

HARRY
BROWNE'S

WILLIAM PACA
HOUSE & GARDEN

STATE CIRCLE

CHURCH CIR

VISIT ANNAPOLIS/
ANNE ARUNDEL
COUNTY

WEST ST

HISTORIC INNS
OF ANNAPOLIS

EAST ST

ARMEL-LEFTWICH
VISITOR CENTER

MARYLAND
STATE HOUSE

PINKNEY ST

RANDALL ST

RAMS
HEAD

ST. ANNE'S
PARISH

MAIN ST

MIDDLETON TAVERN

STORM BROS. ICE CREAM FACTORY

BANNEKER-
DOUGLASS
MUSEUM

FRANKLIN ST

CATHEDRAL ST

CHICK &
RUTH'S DELLY

KUNTA KINTE-
ALEX HALEY
MEMORIAL

DOCK ST

ANNAPOLIS
ICE CREAM
COMPANY

GREEN ST

ANNAPOLIS
MARRIOTT
WATERFRONT

ANNAPOLIS
CITY DOCK

Annapolis
Harbor

CHARLES ST

CONDUIT ST

SHAW ST

SOUTH ST

MARKET ST

SHIPWRIGHT ST

DUKE OF GLOUCESTER ST

COMPROMISE ST

ANNAPOLIS
WATERFRONT HOTEL/
PUSSER'S CARIBBEAN GRILLE

WOODWIND
SCHOONERS

Acton
Cove

181

Spa   Creek

SIXTH ST

SEVERN AVE

0   200 yds

0   200 m

Eastport

CARROL'S
CREEK

FIFTH ST

BOATYARD
BAR & GRILL

© MOON.COM

May to September, or visit for one of biggest sailboat shows in the world, the **Annapolis Spring Sailboat Show** in April and the **United States Sailboat Show** (www.annapolisboatshows.com) in October.

Where Main Street meets Compromise Street at the traffic circle by the dock, the **Kunta Kinte-Alex Haley Memorial** pays tribute to Alex Haley, author of *Roots: The Saga of an American Family*. Haley's novel is based on his ancestor Kunta Kinte, who was captured in Gambia and brought to Annapolis in 1767, where he was sold as a slave.

Historic Annapolis

Founded by Puritans seeking religious freedom in 1649 and chartered as the capital of the colony of Maryland in 1708, Annapolis was a thriving center of politics, culture, and the tobacco and slave trade for the young nation. With more than 100 18th-century buildings still standing today, the city is a time capsule of colonial architecture, with important historic sites situated around State Circle near the harbor.

The centerpiece is the **Maryland State House** (100 State House Cir., www.msa.maryland.gov; 9am-5pm daily except Christmas Day and New Year's Day; free), the oldest state house in the country still in use. Here, the United States and Great Britain signed the Treaty of Paris in 1783, ending the Revolutionary War, and the Continental Congress met shortly after.

East of the State House, William Paca House & Garden (186 Prince George St., 410/990-4543, www.annapolis.org; 10am-5pm Mon.-Sat., noon-5pm Sun. Mar.-Dec.; $5-10 guided house and self-guided garden tours) is the home of the third governor of Maryland and one of the state's four signers of the Declaration of Independence, fully restored to its 18th-century glory. Nearby, Hammond-Harwood House (19 Maryland Ave., 410/263-4683, www.hammondharwoodhouse.org; noon-5pm Mon., Wed.-Sun. Apr.-Dec.; $10 adults, $8 seniors/students, $5 children) is another beautifully restored 18th-century mansion with an extensive collection of colonial furniture and fine art.

Founded in 1696 as the King William's School, St. John's College (60 College Ave., 410/263-2371, www.sjc.edu; admissions office 8:30am-5pm Mon.-Fri.) is one of the oldest educational institutions in the country. St. Anne's Parish (199 Duke of Gloucester St., 410/267-9333, www.stannes-annapolis.org; free tours at 10am on the first and third Mon. of the month, 12:30pm every Wed.) was founded in 1692 and named for Queen Anne, who signed the Establishment Act allowing Annapolis to build a state house, church, and school; the current structure west of the State

Annapolis Harbor

House on Church Circle was built in 1858-1859.

Finally, named for Maryland natives Benjamin Banneker and Frederick Douglass, the small Banneker-Douglass Museum (84 Franklin St., 410/216-6180, www.bdmuseum.maryland.gov; 10am-4pm Tues.-Sat.; free) highlights Maryland's African American history in the former Mount Moriah African Methodist Episcopal Church, built in 1875.

United States Naval Academy

Since 1845, the United States Naval Academy has trained generations of America's brightest sailors. Located on the Severn River at the site of former naval base, the campus provides an in-depth look at U.S. naval history. Start at the Armel-Leftwich Visitor Center (52 King George St., entrance at Prince George St. or Randall St., 410/293-8687, www.usnabsd.com; 9am-5pm daily Mar.-Dec., 9am-4pm Mon.-Fri. Jan.-Feb.; free, government identification required) to embark on a free guided tour, available daily though times vary depending on the season. Key sights include the chapel, with the iconic dome and crypt of Revolutionary War commander John Paul Jones, and Tecumseh, the rescued figurehead from the USS *Delaware*, which was intentionally sunk during the Civil War so it could not be taken over by Confederates. The U.S. Naval Academy Museum (118 Maryland Ave., 410/293-2108, www.usna.edu; 9am-5pm Mon.-Sat., 11am-5pm Sun; free, government identification required) showcases the history of the U.S. Navy and the academy.

RESTAURANTS

When dining in Annapolis, you must have Chesapeake Bay seafood—particularly the famous Maryland crab cakes. You'll find them, as well as other crab dishes, at any seafood restaurant in the Annapolis vicinity. The best ones boast lump crab meat with very little filler, and a lot of Old Bay seasoning—and while you'll find upscale entrées as well as casual sandwiches, they're best enjoyed on a dock with coleslaw and a cold beer.

Two blocks from the harbor, Chick & Ruth's Delly (165 Main St., 410/269-6737, www.chickandruths.com; 6:30am-11pm Sun.-Thurs., 6:30am-midnight Fri.-Sat.; $6-15) is something out of a Norman Rockwell painting, known for affordable breakfasts, sandwiches, and homemade pies as well as a daily recitation of the Pledge of Allegiance, at 8:30am on weekdays, 9:30am on weekends. While prices have increased since the deli opened in 1965, you'd be hard-pressed to find better than the half-pound jumbo lump crab cake for $14.95.

Or, have your crab with politicos at Harry Browne's (66 State Cir., 410/263-4332, www.harrybrownes.com; 11am-10pm Mon.-Sat., 10am-9pm Sun., lounge until 2am daily; $24-36). Directly across from the Maryland State House, the old-school restaurant is where legislators and lobbyists dine on crab cakes, cream of crab soup, and cocktails; the well-priced happy hour includes $7 snacks and $6 martinis and manhattans.

For dinner, head across the harbor to Eastport for a view of the Annapolis skyline and several restaurants and bars. Carrol's Creek Café (410 Severn Ave., 410/263-8102, www.carrolscreek.com; 11:30am-9pm Mon.-Thurs., 11:30am-10pm Fri.-Sat., 10am-8:30pm Sun.; $22-34) is a white-tablecloth restaurant on the water serving lunch, dinner, and Sunday brunch with views of Spa Creek, formerly Carrol's Creek, named for Charles Carroll, one of Maryland's signers of the Declaration of Independence. Boatyard Bar & Grill (400 4th St., 410/216-6206, www.boatyardbarandgrill.com; 7:30am-midnight Mon.-Fri., 8am-midnight Sat.-Sun.; $10-22) is a family-friendly restaurant with a yachty interior whose famous "no-filler" crab cake ranks among the best in the Annapolis area. (First Lady Michelle Obama supposedly said it was the best crab cake she'd ever had.)

If you want to try the Maryland tradition of cracking crabs, locals urge you to drive 15 minutes (4.2 mi/6.8 km) across the Severn River to Cantler's Riverside Inn (458 Forest Beach Rd., 410/757-1311, www.cantlers.com; 11am-midnight daily; $10-32) on Mill Creek. The steamed, hard-shell crabs are served by the dozen, half dozen, or per piece at market prices; other menu items include fresh fish and peel-and-eat shrimp, crab cake sandwiches, and burgers.

End your night with ice cream. Storm Bros. Ice Cream Factory (130 Dock St., 410/263-3376, www.stormbros.com; 11am-11pm Sun.-Thurs., 11am-midnight Fri.-Sat.) on the dock has been around since 1976; the cash-only shop has over 40 flavors, plus yogurt, sorbet,

and sherbet, starting at just $2.95 for a single scoop. On Main Street, Annapolis Ice Cream Company (196 Main St., 443/482-3895, www.annapolisicecream.com; noon-9pm Sun.-Thurs., noon-10pm Fri.-Sat.) is frequently named best in Annapolis for their more than 17 percent butterfat ice cream made in-house.

NIGHTLIFE

Leave the expensive cocktails and rooftops to Washington DC; nightlife in Annapolis is all about laid-back taverns and pubs. Established in 1750, Middleton Tavern (2 Market Space, 410/263-3323, www.middletontavern.com; 11:30am-1:30am Mon.-Sat., 10am-1:30am Sun.) served ale to several Founding Fathers; today, it's known for beer specials, bar snacks, and seafood, as well as live music on weekends.

Rams Head (33 West St., 410/268-4545, www.ramsheadtavern.com; 11am-2am Mon.-Sat., 10am-2am Sun.) is a casual spot to dine and drink until late, with a live music venue (www.ramsheadonstage.com; box office 9am-9pm daily) that seats 500 for folk, rock, country, and tribute bands. For drinks on the dock, Pusser's Caribbean Grille (80 Compromise St., 410/626-0004, www.pusser-susa.com; 6:30am-midnight Mon.-Thurs., 6:30am-2am Fri., 7am-2am Sat., 7am-midnight Sun.) serves boat drinks made with Pusser's Rum from the British Virgin Islands.

SHOPS

The downtown Annapolis shops are full of colorful, preppy, yacht-worthy clothing and accessories, Navy sweatshirts, and only-in-Maryland souvenirs—a crab mallet is the perfect gift for the cook. You'll find dozens of independent boutiques lining Main Street, between Church Circle and City Dock, and Maryland Avenue, between Prince George Street and State Circle. For fine art galleries, head to the Annapolis Arts District (www.annapolisarts-district.org), located on West Street between Westgate Circle east to Church Circle; from May through November, the Arts District comes alive for First Sundays (www.firstsundayarts.com), a street festival with dozens of artists and artisans, live music, and food. For the most up-to-date information on Annapolis shops, hours, and special events, check www.visitannapolis.org.

WHERE TO STAY

Stay right on the water at the Annapolis Waterfront Hotel (80 Compromise St., 888/773-0786, www.annapoliswaterfront.com; $250-400), the city's only hotel directly on the Annapolis Harbor. The Autograph Collection property has 150 guest rooms—some with waterfront balconies—and the entire hotel is decorated in a jaunty blue and white nautical style. Pusser's Caribbean Grille (410/626-0004, www.pussersusa.com; 6:30am-midnight Mon.-Thurs., 6:30am-2am Fri., 7am-2am Sat., 7am-midnight Sun.; $20-30) is on the property.

Historic Inns of Annapolis (58 State Cir., 410/263-2641, www.historicinnsofannapolis.com; $120-250) manages three charming properties in 17th- and 18th-century homes, updated with 21st-century amenities and elegant decor in the combined 124 rooms and suites. Governor Calvert House, where you check in, and Robert Johnson House are located on State Circle, while Maryland Inn is nearby on Church Circle; all three have access to a restaurant serving daily breakfast, an English-style pub, and 24-hour fitness center. These well-priced rooms book up in advance, especially during major events and busy wedding weekends in the spring and fall.

INFORMATION AND SERVICES

In the center of Historic Annapolis near Church Circle, Visit Annapolis & Anne Arundel County (26 West St., 410/280-0445, www.visitannapolis.org; 9am-5pm daily) can help you plan your trip to Annapolis and the surrounding area as well as provide brochures, maps, and event calendars. A satellite Visitor Information Booth is located at City Dock. The website has a wealth of information as well as mobile apps with up-to-date information and driving tours.

TRANSPORTATION

The best way to get from Washington DC to Annapolis is by car; the 30-mi (48-km) trip will take approximately 45-60 minutes depending on traffic. From downtown DC, head east on New York Avenue NW to U.S. 50 E to Maryland. Take exit 24/MD 70 S to get to the harbor and historic downtown area. There are several convenient parking garages, lots, and metered spaces; www.visitannapolis.org has maps and pricing details.

CROSSING THE BAY BRIDGE

Crossing the Chesapeake Bay Bridge, which connects Washington DC and Annapolis to the small towns and beaches of Maryland's Eastern Shore, is a rite of summer for many Washington locals. But, be warned—the bridge's soaring heights and seasonal traffic are not for nervous drivers. The dual-span, five-lane bridge is 4.3 mi (6.9 km) long and 190 feet above the windy bay at its highest, providing enough clearance for ocean-going ships to pass underneath. Part of U.S. 50 and the most efficient route over the bay, the bridge is one giant traffic jam on Friday afternoons and Saturday mornings during peak beach season.

To reach the bridge from Washington DC, just stay on U.S. 50 E for about 40 mi (64 km), or just under an hour. The bridge has a one-way toll eastbound; currently, it's $4 per car, or $2.50 per car with E-ZPass. During the summer, traffic is heaviest eastbound on Friday through Saturday evening, and westbound on Sunday. For more information, including traffic advisories and lane closures, call 877/229-7726 or visit www.baybridge.maryland.gov.

Can't handle the heights? **Kent Island Express** (410/604-0486, www.kentislandexpress.com) will drive your car over the bridge for you, 24 hours per day, seven days per week. Call one hour before you're ready to cross the bridge to arrange a meeting point; the service costs $30 one-way 7am-8pm daily; additional fees may apply outside of those hours.

While renting a car is recommended to explore Annapolis and the Chesapeake Bay, you can use ride-hailing apps like Uber and Lyft to get from DC to Annapolis and back; expect to pay $50-60 for a standard car and $160-180 for a black car each way during nonsurge periods.

It's possible to take public transportation to Annapolis, as well, but it's rather inconvenient. Take Amtrak or Metro Orange Line to **New Carrollton station** (4700 Garden City Dr., www.wmata.com), then catch the **Young Transportation Services bus 921** (www.ytsonline.net); bus hours are limited, so check the schedule online, and plan to use a ride-hailing service or take a taxi back to DC if you're having dinner in Annapolis.

It's very easy to walk around Annapolis and see the harbor, historic sights, and United States Naval Academy by foot. The free **Annapolis Circulator trolley** (every 20 minutes, 7:30am-11pm Mon.-Sat., 8am-8pm Sun.; free) runs from four of the parking garages around the city, hitting City Dock, Church Circle, and other key points of interest.

To get to the restaurants in Eastport, you can catch a **water taxi** from City Dock; taxis and ride-hailing services are readily available, as well.

EASTON
SIGHTS
Historic Easton

Once the capital of Maryland's Eastern Shore, Easton is the Talbot County seat, founded in 1661 and named for Lady Grace Talbot, sister of the second Lord Baltimore. Today, Easton is considered one of the "top small towns in America," with a population of about 16,000 and a historic district with quaint streets filled with 18th- and 19th-century architecture. **Talbot Historical Society** (30 S. Washington St.,

Easton

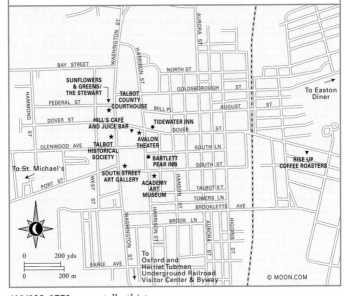

410/822-0773, www.talbothistory.
org; 10am-4pm Thurs.-Sat.; free)
manages a small museum in one of
the oldest buildings with exhibits
about the history and residents of
Easton and Talbot County, as well
as idyllic gardens, free to the public
daily during daylight hours.

Speaking of Talbot County's former residents, Frederick Douglass is
perhaps the most famous. The abolitionist's autobiography, *Narrative
of the Life of Frederick Douglass,* begins, "I was born in Tuckahoe, near
Hillsborough, and about 12 miles
from Easton, in Talbot County,
Maryland." In 2004, the Talbot
County Council voted to place a
statue of Douglass in front of the
Talbot County Courthouse—directly adjacent to *Talbot Boys,* the
controversial 1916 memorial to
84 Confederate veterans from the
county. In September, the town

celebrates Frederick Douglass
Day (www.frederickdouglassday.
com) with lectures by historians,
concerts, and family activities. For
one-hour driving tours exploring
Talbot County through his eyes,
visit www.frederickdouglassbirth-
place.org.

RESTAURANTS

Easton is an excellent spot to enjoy
café culture. Hill's Café and Juice
Bar (32 E. Dover St., 410/822-9751,
www.hillscafeandjuice.com; 8am-
3pm weekdays; $6-10), serves sim-
ple, healthy breakfasts, sandwiches,
salads, and juice, in the historic
Hill's Drug Store, founded in 1928.
Need caffeine after navigating the
traffic jam on the Bay Bridge? Rise
Up Coffee Roasters (618 Dover
Rd., 410/822-1353, www.riseupcof-
fee.com; 6am-7pm daily) has been

waking up the Eastern Shore with certified organic and fair-trade coffee since 2005. The Easton roastery is housed in a 1920s gas station; the company's food truck, Mad Eggs, serves breakfast and lunch sandwiches and healthy bowls, 6am-3pm. Sunflowers & Greens (11 Federal St., 410/822-7972, www.sunflowersandgreens.com; 11am-3pm Mon.-Sat.; $10-20) specializes in seasonal salads, with daily specials using local seafood and produce, served in an elegant sunlit space with a marble dining bar.

If you're sticking around for cocktails or dinner, don't miss The Stewart (3 Federal St., 410/793-4128, www.thestewart.com; 5pm-11pm Wed.-Sat.; $18-35), the cozy lounge serving comforting small plates like a braised short rib grilled cheese and sticky toffee pudding alongside an impressive collection of Scotch.

On U.S. 50 near Dunkin Donuts and several budget hotels, Easton Diner (8451 Ocean Gateway, 410/819-0535, www.eastondinermd.com; 6am-10pm daily; $7-15) is a good stop on your way out of the Eastern Shore, serving cheap but hearty breakfast, lunch, and dinner in a colorful, retro-style diner.

ARTS AND CULTURE

Easton is a surprising cultural hub. In a former 19th-century schoolhouse turned historical landmark, Academy Art Museum (106 South St., 410/822-2787, www.academyartmuseum.org; 10am-4pm Mon., 10am-8pm Tues.-Thurs., 10am-4pm Fri.-Sat., noon-4pm Sun.; $3 nonmembers, free children under 12, free on Wed.) is one of the

Eastern Shore's premier arts venues, with more than 1,400 works from 1850 to present day by the likes of Chuck Close, Gene Davis, Robert Rauschenberg, and Picasso as well as regional artists. In addition to rotating exhibits featuring works from the impressive permanent collection, the museum frequently shows works from the National Gallery of Art. Visit during First Friday, when Easton's galleries and shops open their doors until 7pm or 8pm on the first Friday of the month from April to December.

Built in 1922 as a movie theater, Avalon Theatre (40 E. Dover St., 410/822-0345, www.avalonfoundation.org; box office 11am-5pm Wed.-Fri. and two hours prior to every show) brings live blues, folk, jazz, and rock musicians to the Eastern Shore, with performances several nights a week in the renovated 380-seat art deco theater and 60-seat cabaret-style room.

In July, Plein Air Easton (410/822-7297, www.pleinaireaston.com) is the United States' largest juried festival of plein air painting, or landscape painting outdoors, bringing dozens of artists from around the world to compete and sell their works. And coinciding with the start of goose hunting season in November, the Waterfowl Festival (410/822-4567, www.waterfowlfestival.org; $15 adults, free for children 10 and under) showcases Talbot County's art and sportsmanship in what has become the most important economic and cultural event for Easton as well as a fundraiser for local conservation projects. During the festive, three-day event, see works by local artists, learn about goose hunting, fishing, and duck calling, and enjoy local food and beverage tastings.

WHERE TO STAY

Renovated in early 2020, Tidewater Inn (101 E. Dover St., 410/822-1300, www.tidewaterinn.com; $160-280) is an excellent base for a weekend exploring the Eastern Shore, with 92 clean and modern guest rooms, spa, and fitness center. It's walking distance to Easton's attractions and a quick drive to neighboring towns, but you may want to stick around and enjoy a relaxed dinner and drinks at Hunter's Tavern (410/822-4034, www.tidewaterinn.com; 7am-9pm Sun.-Thurs., 7am-10pm Fri.-Sat.; $28-38), the onsite restaurant with an expansive American menu.

One of the Chesapeake Bay's top-rated bed-and-breakfasts, Bartlett Pear Inn (28 S. Harrison St., 410/770-3300, www.bartlett-pearinn.com; $139-289) is ideal for a romantic getaway. Located in an 18th-century home, the inn has seven charming rooms with private baths, and it serves a superb breakfast.

INFORMATION AND SERVICES

The Talbot County Office of Tourism (11 S. Harrison St., 410/770-8000, www.tourtalbot.org; 8:30am-5pm Mon.-Fri., 10am-2pm Sat.) has all the information you need to plan your trip to Easton and the surrounding area, in-person in Easton or online. For the calendar of events and more information about dining, shopping, and accommodations, visit www.eastonmd.org or www.discovereaston.com.

TRANSPORTATION

By car, Easton is approximately one hour (42 mi/68 km) from Annapolis and 1.5-2 hours (70 mi/113 km) from Washington DC, depending on traffic.

From either city, take U.S. 50 East to the Chesapeake Bay Bridge. After crossing, continue on U.S. 50 E/Ocean Gateway about 25 mi (40 km), approximately 25 minutes. Veer right on MD 322. Turn left on Glebe Road, then continue on North Harrison Street into Easton's historic center. You should have no problem finding street parking or space in a lot near the Talbot Historical Society or Avalon Theatre; during events like the Waterfowl Festival, signs will direct you to parking lots.

While driving is the most convenient way to get to Easton, Greyhound (www.greyhound.com) buses run daily from Union Station in Washington DC to Easton and back; the bus stops at a gas station on U.S. 50, about 1 mi (1.6 km) from Easton's historic district.

Easton is just 10 mi (16.1 km) from both Oxford and St. Michaels, so you can easily explore all three towns in one day by car or bike.

OXFORD
SIGHTS
Historic Oxford

Founded in 1683, Oxford is the oldest town in Maryland, and one of the oldest in the country. Once an international shipping hub for tobacco trade on par with Annapolis, Oxford now has a population of just over

600. This sleepy boat town played an important role in the American Revolution as a vital port and home of several Founding Fathers and war heroes, including Robert Morris Jr., the first and only superintendent of finance (precursor to the treasury secretary), and Colonel Tench Tilghman, George Washington's aide de camp, who carried the message that the British Army had surrendered at Yorktown to the Continental Congress. Explore the history at the Oxford Museum (100 S. Morris St., 410/226-0191, www.oxfordmuseummd.org; 10am-4pm Fri.-Mon. Apr.-Nov.; free); it's tiny, but colonial history buffs may enjoy the artifacts and family heirlooms on display.

Then, take a ride on the Oxford-Bellevue Ferry (101 East Strand, 410/745-9023, www.oxfordbellevueferry.com; 9am-sunset daily Apr.-Oct., 9am-sunset Sat.-Sun. in Nov.), the oldest private ferry operating in the United States, which has connected Oxford to Bellevue across the Tred Avon River since 1683. There's not much on the other side; the attraction is the 10-minute, three-quarter-mile ride, a chance to get on the water without renting a boat. The ferry runs every 15-20 minutes daily from April to November; rates range from $6 round-trip for pedestrians to $22 round-trip for cars.

RESTAURANTS AND WHERE TO STAY

Oxford has several lovely inns with well-regarded restaurants. Founded in 1710, Robert Morris Inn (314 N. Morris St., 410/226-5111, www.robertmorrisinn.com; $145-240) claims to be the oldest in America, in the yellow house one block from the ferry. And while the age does show, the 35 rooms are lovingly maintained, and many have water views. The restaurant, Salter's Tavern (8am-10:30am, noon-2:30pm, 5pm-9pm Mon.-Sat., 8am-2:30pm and 5pm-9pm Sun., hours vary seasonally so call ahead to confirm; $19-32), is one of the best in the area, led by chef Mark Salter, who combines local seafood and produce with his experience cooking at some of the finest hotels in Europe.

For a beach vacation vibe, the Sandaway Suites & Beach (103 West Strand Rd., 1-888-SANDAWAY, www.sandaway.com; $279-359) offers the service and charm of a bed and breakfast, with 18 bright, modern, beach house-style suites and amenities like a business center and board games. Many of the suites have screened porches overlooking the sandy private beach with sun loungers available for guests only; the inn will also arrange delivery of boat and bike rentals.

For a casual meal, Doc's Sunset Grille (104 W. Pier St., 410/226-5550, www.docssunsetgrille.com; 11am-10pm Tues.-Sun., hours may vary seasonally; $10-30) is a beachy dockside restaurant and bar on the Tred Avon River with steamed crabs and live music on weekends.

For dessert, don't miss Scottish Highland Creamery (314 Tilghman St., 410/924-6298, www.scottishhighlandcreamery.com; open daily May-Sept., weekends Apr./Oct., hours vary) consistently ranked one of the top ice cream shops in the country.

INFORMATION AND SERVICES

For information on attractions, accommodations, and events in Oxford, visit www.portofoxford.com, www.oxfordmd.net, or the Talbot County Office of Tourism in Easton (11 S. Harrison St., 410/770-8000, www.tourtalbot.org; 8:30am-5pm Mon.-Fri., 10am-2pm Sat.).

TRANSPORTATION

By car, Oxford is approximately one hour (52 mi/84 km) from Annapolis and 1.5-2 hours (80 mi/129 km) from Washington DC, depending on traffic.

From either city, take U.S. 50 East to the Chesapeake Bay Bridge. After crossing, continue on U.S. 50 E/Ocean Gateway about 30 minutes to MD 322/Easton Parkway. Turn right on MD 322 and drive about 3 mi (4.8 km) to MD 333 S/Oxford Road/Peachblossom Road. Continue about 9 mi (14.5 km) over a few creeks to the center of Oxford. There is a public parking lot near the ferry dock, and the entire town is easily walkable.

Oxford is 10 mi (16.1 km) from Easton, and it's just under 20 mi (32 km) to St. Michaels—9 mi (14.5 km) if you take the Oxford-Bellevue Ferry.

✪ ST. MICHAELS
SIGHTS
Boat Cruises on the Miles River

Get to know Maryland's historic hub of shipbuilding and oyster harvesting during a boat cruise on the Miles River. Patriot Cruises (213 N. Talbot St., 410/745-3100, www.patriotcruises.com; daily in summer, weekends in off-season; $24.50-29.50 adults, $22 seniors, $12.50 children 12-17, $5 children 3-11, free for children under 3) offers 60- to 75-minute tours as well as cocktail cruises on summer Saturday evenings. Or, board the historic H.M. Krentz (213 N. Talbot St., 410/745-6080, www.oyster-catcher.com; daily Apr.-Oct.; $47.50 adults, $39 seniors, $33 military ID, $28 ages 7-20, $20 for children ages 2-6, free for children under 2), one of the few remaining skipjacks, the oyster dredge boats built specifically for use on the Chesapeake Bay in the late 19th and early 20th centuries. The Chesapeake Bay Maritime Museum (213 N. Talbot St., 410/745-2916, www.cbmm.org) offers cruises and summer boat rentals as well.

Chesapeake Bay Maritime Museum

Covering 18 acres on the banks of the Miles River, the Chesapeake Bay Maritime Museum (213 N. Talbot St., 410/745-2916, www.cbmm.org; 9am-5pm daily May-Oct., 10am-4pm daily Nov.-Apr.; $16 adults, $13 seniors/students/retired military, $6 children ages 6-17, free for children 5 and under and active military) catalogues the region's history, from the American Indian residents and settlement by English explorers to an in-depth look at the region's more modern industries of shipbuilding, oyster harvesting and canning, and crabbing. On campus, explore the working boatyard, where the museum preserves and restores dozens of Chesapeake Bay watercraft, as well as the circa 1879 lighthouse.

Born a slave in Dorchester County, Maryland, approximately 30 mi (48 km) south of Talbot County, Harriet Tubman would eventually escape and become one of the nation's most influential abolitionists, rescuing 70 people from the Eastern Shore via the Underground Railroad. With a car and a weekend, you can follow the journey of the woman called "Moses" and learn more about her life in Maryland.

Start at the **Harriet Tubman Underground Railroad Visitor Center** (4068 Golden Hill Road, Church Creek, 410/228-1000, www.harriet-tubmanbyway.org/visitor-center; 9am-5pm daily; free), which opened in 2017. The 10,000-square-foot center has interactive exhibits about Tubman's life and the Underground Railroad. From there, you can pick up the **Harriet Tubman Underground Railroad Byway**, a 125-mi (201-km), self-guided driving tour featuring 36 sites, including the **Bucktown Village Store** (4303 Bucktown Rd., Bucktown), where a slaveowner hit her in the head with a weight when she refused to help him tie up a runaway slave, and station houses, bridges, and river landings where she shepherded dozens of people to freedom. Download a map and audio tour at www.harriettubmanbyway.org/the-byway, or schedule a guided tour in advance with one of several operators.

The Harriet Tubman Underground Railroad Visitor Center is 96 mi (155 km) southeast of Washington DC via U.S. 50 (approx. two hours), and 27 mi (43 km) south of Easton/Oxford (approx. 35 minutes). Stop #1 on the Byway, the **Dorchester County Visitor Center** (2 Rose Hill Pl., Cambridge, 410/228-1000, www.visitdorchester.org; 8:30am-5pm daily), is closer—85 mi (137 km, 1.5 hours) from Washington DC and 15 mi (24 km, 20 minutes) from Easton/Oxford. Visit www.harriettubmanbyway.org/plan-your-visit for detailed itineraries, including suggestions for restaurants along the way.

St. Michaels Museum and Walking Tours

Located in three restored historical buildings, **St. Michaels Museum** (201 E. Chestnut St., 410/745-9561, www.stmichaelsmuseum.org; 1pm-4pm Fri., 10am-4pm Sat., 1pm-4pm Sun. May-Oct.; $3 adults, $1 children ages 6-17, free for children under 6) chronicles the history of the town. The buildings have small exhibits on everyday life and commerce in 19th-century St. Michaels; one, the Chaney House, was built by three free African American brothers who eventually bought their father's freedom. On Saturdays, the museum offers several guided walking tours, including one tracing Frederick Douglass's teenage years in the town before he escaped slavery.

RESTAURANTS

For a small town, St. Michaels has substantial dining options, ranging from elegant bistros to classic crab houses to quick-serve coffee shops and bakeries. Many restaurants are closed in the winter or take a short break before opening for the season in the spring, so call ahead in the off-season.

For a sophisticated dinner date, make a reservation at 208 Talbot (208 N. Talbot St., 410/745-3838, www.208talbot.com; 5pm-9pm Thurs.-Sun.; $13-36), where Eastern Shore native David Clark prepares top-rated local seafood in the white-tablecloth, brick-walled space. Bistro St. Michaels (403 S. Talbot St., 410/745-9001, www.bistrostmichaels.com; 4:30pm-8pm Mon.-Tue., Thurs., 4:30pm-9pm Fri., 10am-9pm Sat., 10am-1:30pm Sun.; $20-39) serves French favorites inspired by the Chesapeake Bay and made with local, sustainable ingredients.

Marylanders recount childhood memories of taking boats to The Crab Claw (304 Burns St., 410/745-2900, www.thecrabclaw.com; from 11am daily Mar.-Oct.; $15-30) for Maryland's famous steamed crabs, which opened in 1965 in a former clam- and oyster-shucking shed on the water. Order steamed crabs by the dozen or the piece, which are best enjoyed on the covered deck as you watch fishing boats bring in fresh catches for the restaurant.

Had enough seafood? Ava's Pizzeria & Wine Bar (409 S. Talbot St., 410/745-3081, www.avaspizzeria.com; 11:30am-9pm Sun.-Thurs., 11:30am-10pm Fri.-Sat.; $10-20) is frequently rated the best pizza on Maryland's Eastern Shore, with brick-oven pizza, pasta, and subs made with seasonal produce.

WHERE TO STAY

The most polished of the Eastern Shore's small towns, St. Michaels is home to the luxurious Inn at Perry Cabin (308 Watkins Ln., 410/745-2200, www.belmond.com/inn-at-perry-cabin-st-michaels; $515-860), the Belmond property on the banks of the Miles River. (Yes, the main reception in *Wedding Crashers* was filmed here.) The colonial mansion has 78 plush rooms and suites, an outdoor pool and acclaimed spa, and lots of resort activities. From the inn's dock, you can catch a boat cruise or embark on crabbing, fishing, or kayaking excursions.

St. Michaels has at least a dozen bed-and-breakfasts of various sizes and price points. The adults-only Five Gables Inn & Spa (209 N. Talbot St., 410/745-0100, www.fivegables.com; $140-195) has 20 rooms in three 19th-century homes, plus an Aveda spa, indoor pool, and thoughtful touches like bicycles and in-room fireplaces. One of the oldest homes in the town, Snuggery Bed & Breakfast (203 Cherry St., 410/745-2800, www.snuggery1665.com; $200-250) has just two suites but plenty of charm, with antique decor and an old-fashioned porch; enjoy a farmers market breakfast daily before exploring the town.

INFORMATION AND SERVICES

For information on attractions, accommodations, and events in St. Michaels, visit www.stmichaelsmd.org or www.townofstmichaels.com, or the Talbot County Office of Tourism in Easton (11 S. Harrison St., 410/770-8000, www.tourtalbot.

org; 8:30am-5pm Mon.-Fri., 10am-2pm Sat.). In addition to guided tours, the **St. Michaels Museum** (201 E. Chestnut St., 410/745-9561, www.stmichaelsmuseum.org; 1pm-4pm Fri., 10am-4pm Sat., 1pm-4pm Sun. May-Oct.) has information and self-guided walking tour maps.

TRANSPORTATION

By car, St. Michaels is approximately 1 hour (50 mi/81 km) from Annapolis and 1.5-2 hours (80 mi/129 km) from Washington DC, depending on traffic.

From either city, take U.S. 50 East to the Chesapeake Bay Bridge. After crossing, continue on U.S. 50 E/Ocean Gateway about 30 minutes to MD 322/Easton Parkway. Turn right on MD 322 and drive about 2 mi (3.2 km) to MD 33 W/St. Michaels Road. Take St. Michaels Road for about 9 mi (14.5 km) to the town center. There's ample public parking near the marina, and the entire town is easily walkable.

St. Michaels is 10 mi (16.1 km) from Easton, and it's just under 20 mi (32.2 km) to Oxford—9 mi (14.5 km) if you take the Oxford-Bellevue Ferry.

Shenandoah National Park and Vicinity

Skyline Drive is the 105-mi (169-km) scenic drive through Shenandoah National Park, which offers abundant hiking. Shenandoah makes a choice getaway from Washington DC.

I-66 is your gateway to Skyline Drive and Shenandoah National Park, which is especially glorious in the fall, and hundreds of miles of hiking trails and wilderness to explore. But don't miss the attractions along the way, including the lovely small towns of Middleburg and Little Washington—home to the famous, three-Michelin-star Inn at Little Washington, the ideal destination for a milestone birthday or anniversary—as well as wineries, horse racing, and even Civil War battlefields along the way. You can reach the Virginia countryside in one day,

but you won't want to head back to the hustle and bustle of DC after experiencing life in the shadow of the Blue Ridge Mountains.

WASHINGTON DC TO SHENANDOAH NATIONAL PARK
✪ STEVEN F. UDVAR-HAZY CENTER

Near Washington Dulles International Airport in Chantilly, Virginia, this outpost of the Smithsonian's National Air and Space Museum is the best excursion with kids, whether you go for the afternoon or make it your first stop on an adventure in the Virginia countryside. The **Steven F. Udvar-Hazy Center** (14390 Air and Space Museum Pkwy., 703/572-4118, http://airandspace.

Shenandoah Nat'l. Park

si.edu; 10am-5:30pm daily except Christmas Day; free admission, $15 parking) might be even more impressive than the museum in DC, with two massive hangars full of airplanes and spacecraft, including the space shuttle *Discovery*, a Concorde, and even American and German World War II planes. See a film at the IMAX theater, or check out the view from the observation tower. Visit the restoration hangar to see Smithsonian employees preserving aircraft for generations to come.

The center is approximately 45-60 minutes from DC by car and 90 minutes by public transportation. If driving, take I-66 W to exit 53B for Route 28 N and follow the signs to the center, or take I-495 W/Capital Beltway to Dulles Toll Road West/Route 26 and exit via Route 28 S/exit 9A. By Metro, take the Silver Line to Wiehle-Reston East and catch the Fairfax Connector bus 983 (703/339-7200, www.fairfaxconnector.com) directly to the center; the journey is approximately 1 hour and 30 minutes.

MANASSAS NATIONAL BATTLEFIELD PARK

On July 21, 1861, the Union and Confederacy met in Manassas, about 30 mi (48 km) from Washington DC, to fight the first major battle of the Civil War. The Union was expected to win handily, but the Confederates scraped by, giving Confederate general Thomas Jonathan "Stonewall" Jackson his nickname; 4,700 men died, an omen of things to come in America's bloodiest war. About one year later, the Second Battle of Bull Run left nearly 3,000 dead and countless wounded or missing.

Manassas National Battlefield Park (6511 Sudley Rd., 703/361-1339, www.nps.gov/mana; daily dawn-dusk; free) is a must-visit for history buffs and a good pit stop on the way to Shenandoah National Park. At the entrance, Henry Hill Visitor Center (8:30am-5pm daily except Thanksgiving Day and Christmas Day) has interactive maps and exhibits as well as park information; guided tours of both battles are available daily, or you can take a self-guided tour across 40 mi (64 km) of trails. Throughout the year, interpreters reenact both battles at Chinn Ridge (check the website for the schedule).

From Washington DC, take I-66 W to exit 47B, Route 234 N/Sudley Road. The visitor center is on the right.

EXPLORING THE PARK
✪ SKYLINE DRIVE

Whether it's your access point to an outdoor adventure in Shenandoah National Park or simply a leisurely drive to see the Blue Ridge Mountains and Virginia's storybook landscape, Skyline Drive (www.visitskylinedrive.org) is the most beautiful byway in the region. The Civilian Conservation Corps broke ground on the Depression-era infrastructure project in 1931; the full, 105-mi (169-km) route was completed in 1939. Today, the drive will take you to 500 mi (805 km) of hiking trails, horseback riding, and otherworldly caverns—or, you can just enjoy the drive. If you're going for the drive, you can't beat autumn, when the foliage changes to red and yellow and gold, but the views over the Shenandoah Valley from one of

the 75 scenic overlooks are beautiful any time of year.

There are four entrances to Skyline Drive; the Front Royal entrance is the closest to Washington DC and the best option if the drive itself or outdoor activities are your goal, though you can easily reach the Thornton Gap entrance and Luray Caverns via Little Washington.

The Shenandoah National Park entrance fee ranges from $25 per vehicle to $10 per individual, and the pass is good for seven days beginning the day of purchase; check www.nps.gov for free-fee days, though expect crowds.

LURAY CAVERNS

Luray Caverns (101 Cave Hill Rd., 540/743-6551, www.luraycaverns. com; tours from 9am daily, hours vary seasonally; from $30 adults, $25 seniors, $15 children ages 6-12, free children 5 and under) is a bit of a tourist trap, but for good reason. The caverns were discovered in 1878 but formed much earlier, when acid and water eroded layers of limestone and clay, creating huge rooms with golden-hued stalactites, stalagmites, and other amazing formations. Descend through a nondescript building for the one-hour, 1.25-mi (2.0-km) guided tour via lighted, paved path, in which you'll see the 47-foot column in Giant's Hall, the Great Stalacpipe Organ "playing" the formations, and even a lake. These are the largest caverns on the East Coast, and while it can get crowded, it's an impressive geology lesson and unique diversion when bad weather cancels outdoor plans.

Included with caverns admission,

Luray Valley Museum tells the story of the Shenandoah Valley's history from the earliest inhabitants to the 19th century, and the Car and Carriage Caravan Museum has one of the oldest working cars in the country, a Mercedes-Benz from 1892.

Luray is to the west of the park. To get there, head to the Thornton Gap entrance, approximately 80 mi (129 km) from DC via I-66 West to U.S. 211 West, through Little Washington.

SPORTS AND ACTIVITIES

Shenandoah National Park offers outdoor activities year-round, for all levels, whether you're an advanced, adventuresome hiker or just looking for a fun day exploring the great outdoors.

There are more than 500 mi (805 km) of hiking trails inside the park, with options suitable for families with children as well as the most advanced hikers, including 101 mi (163 km) of the Appalachian Trail. Old Rag Mountain is the park's most famous—as well as the most difficult and dangerous, as you must trek 9 mi (14.5 km) and complete a rock scramble to get to the summit. Considered the must-do hike in the Mid-Atlantic, it gets very crowded, especially on weekends. Before attempting the hike, you're advised to read about the trail conditions and tips on the National Park Service website.

From the Dickey Ridge Visitor Center near the Front Royal entrance, which is the closest to DC, you'll find the Fox Hollow Trail Hike, an easy, 1.2-mi (1.9-km) nature walk, as well as the Sneed Farm Loop Hike, a moderately challenging but still family-friendly 3.7-mi (6.0-km) loop. If the Appalachian Trail is on your bucket list, summit Mary's Rock, a moderate, 3.7-mi (6.0-km) round-trip hike that crosses part of the trail; you can access the trailhead from Thornton Gap close to Little Washington and Luray. For more information on Shenandoah hiking trails, including maps and directions, visit www.nps.gov/shen or either of the visitor centers.

The park is a popular spot for horseback riding, as well. Skyland Stables (Skyline Dr. mile 42.5, 877/847-1919) offers 1-hour and 2.5-hour guided trail rides on horseback or pony, daily April through November, weather permitting.

While you're in the park, keep your eyes peeled for the animals—if you're lucky, you'll see one of the famous black bears.

RESTAURANTS AND WHERE TO STAY

If you're looking for luxury, stay in Middleburg, closest to the Front Royal entrance, or Little Washington, near to the Thornton Gap entrance. If you're looking for a rustic experience with hiking trails outside your doorstep, Shenandoah National Park operates two family-friendly lodges, which are rated relatively high for rustic accommodations inside a park. Skyland Resort (Skyline Dr. mile 41.7-42.5; $100-210), built in 1888, has 178 motel-style rooms and cabins. It's close to Skyland Stables and several hikes, including Mary's Rock. On the National Register of Historic Places, Big Meadows Lodge

(Skyline Dr. mile 51.2; $100-185) has 25 rooms in the main lodge plus 75 cabins, some with valley views. Both have dining rooms serving breakfast, lunch, and dinner daily, as well as taprooms with a full bar and a quick-serve counter selling coffee and sandwiches; considering the lack of options inside the park, the restaurants have substantial variety and reasonable prices.

The National Park Service operates four campgrounds on Skyline Drive with space for tents, campers, and RVs; some are first come, first served while others accept reservations, and fees range $15-20 per night depending on the season. In addition, most of the park is open for camping if you prefer to rough it; a few areas around some of the more popular hiking trails, including Old Rag Mountain, are limited, so check with the National Park Service for details.

There are a few food stops along Skyline Drive, some with grocery and camping supplies, gift shops, gasoline, and shower facilities. For details on the resorts and other Skyline Drive facilities, visit www. goshenandoah.com.

INFORMATION AND SERVICES

There are two major visitor centers along Skyline Drive, with maps and information on hikes, activities, accommodations, and the history of the park. Dickey Ridge Visitor Center (Skyline Dr. mile 4.6, 9am-5pm daily early Apr. to late Nov.) is near the beginning of Skyline Drive near the Front Royal entrance. Harry F. Byrd, Sr. Visitor Center (Skyline Dr. mile 51, 9am-5pm daily

late Mar. to late Nov., 9am-5pm, Fri.-Sun. late Nov. to late Mar.) is farther along, just past Big Meadows Lodge. For more information, visit www. nps.gov/shen, www.skylinedrive. org, and www.goshenandoah.com.

TRANSPORTATION

Skyline Drive and Shenandoah National Park are approximately 1.5-2 hours (70 mi/113 km) from Washington DC. The Front Royal entrance is the start of Skyline Drive, and the closest entrance to DC, via I-66 W to VA-79/VA-55 W (this road has tolls). You can detour through Middleburg on your way to or from the entrance. You'll need a car to get to Skyline Drive, though, of course, you can hike or bike through the park.

Middleburg is approximately 45 minutes (30 mi/48 km) to Skyline Drive, and Little Washington is very close, about 20 minutes (12 mi/19.3 km) to Skyline Drive via the Thornton Gap entrance.

LITTLE WASHINGTON
SIGHTS
✪ The Inn at Little Washington

The Inn at Little Washington (Middle St. and Main St., 540/675-3800, www.theinnatlittlewashington.com), the sublime destination restaurant and inn, is perhaps the best reason to leave the District for the weekend. When visionary chef Patrick O'Connell opened the restaurant in a former garage in tiny Washington, Virginia, in the 1970s, entrées started at $4.95. Today, Washingtonians happily spend close to $1,000 for two for the three-star, four-course menus featuring produce and dairy from the inn's farm

The Winery at Bull Run

Virginia is the fifth-largest wine-producing region in the United States, and there are dozens of wineries 45-90 minutes from DC on the country roads to Shenandoah National Park. About 45 minutes from DC on the edge of Manassas National Battlefield Park, The Winery at Bull Run (15950 Lee Hwy./Rte. 29, Centreville, 703/815-2233, www.wineryatbullrun.com; 11am-7pm Sat.-Wed., 11am-8pm Thurs., 11am-10pm Fri.; $15 tasting) is a good introduction to the Virginia terroir with several award-winning wines, including fruit wines. As you head toward Shenandoah, Chester Gap Cellars (4615 Remount Rd., Front Royal, 540/636-8086, www.chestergapcellars; 11am-6pm Fri.-Sun. and most holiday Mondays) has some of the best views, 10 minutes from the Front Royal entrance of the park.

In Middleburg, Chrysalis Vineyards (39025 John Mosby Hwy., Middleburg, 540/687-8222, www.chrysaliswine.com; noon-6pm Mon.-Thurs., noon-8pm Fri.-Sat., noon-7pm Sun.; $15 tasting) is known for the Norton grape, the country's oldest native wine grape, which was bred in Richmond. Greenhill Winery & Vineyards (23595 Winery Ln., Middleburg, 540/687-6968, www.greenhillvineyards.com; noon-6pm Mon.-Thurs., noon-7pm Fri.-Sun. May-Sept., noon-6pm daily Oct.-Apr.; $14 tasting) has 100 percent Virginia wines and a tasting room set on 128 rolling acres of gorgeous countryside.

Little Washington Winery (72 Christmas Tree Ln., Washington, 540/987-8330, www.littlewashingtonwinery.com, 11am-6pm Thurs.-Sun.) produces some of the top-rated wines in Virginia, while Narmada Winery (43 Narmada Ln., Amissville, 540/937-8215, www.narmadawinery.com; 11am-5pm Mon., 11am-5pm Thurs.-Fri., 11am-7pm Sat., 11am-6pm Sun., hours vary seasonally) is known for some of the best food in the area, offering classic Indian dishes paired with their award-winning wines.

For something different, don't miss Mt. Defiance Cidery & Distillery (207 W. Washington St., Middleburg, 540/687-8100, www.mtdefiance.com; noon-6pm Tues.-Sun.; tasting prices vary), where you can try ciders and unique, apple-based liquors; a bottle of the surprisingly smooth apple brandy, one of the original American spirits, is a good souvenir.

Many wineries will arrange round-trip car service from Washington DC if you prefer not to drive.

To plan your Virginia wine tour, visit www.virginiawine.org or www.discovershenandoah.com/wineries.

and orchard, plus dessert or cheese from the charming mooing, clanging cow cart, just one of the many whimsical details.

If you can swing the pricey meal and one of the 24 refined rooms, it's worth it to stay the night, because they think of everything—from the keepsake menu and journal to help you remember your stay (as if you could ever forget), to the tasting of freshly pressed juices at breakfast, to a handwritten card from O'Connell if you're there for a special occasion. A decadent afternoon tea is included with the price of the room—though you may want to skip it so you don't spoil your appetite for the main event, and instead take the three-quarter-mile leisurely walk around the fields and gardens, where chickens, sheep, and a llama named Francesca live in splendor. And you can leave your phone in your room, because cell service is, blissfully, limited.

Historic Little Washington

There's not much to do in "Little" Washington, population just under 200—but that's entirely the point. In 1749, the young surveyor George Washington dropped by the town, which later became the first in the nation bearing his name. Today, The Inn at Little Washington houses **gift shops** (www.theinnatlittlewashington.com/tavern-shops; open daily) and a farmers market. **Little Washington Theatre** (291 Gay St., 540/675-1253, www.littlewashingtontheatre.com) has community theater, jazz, and even Smithsonian-sponsored concerts, and **Little Washington Wellness & Spa**

(261 Main St., 540/675-1031, www.littlewashingtonspa.com; 10am-6pm Thurs.-Mon., by appointment Tue.-Wed.) has a full menu of spa services and hair and beauty treatments. And the town has a smattering of shops and galleries, such as **R. H. Ballard Shop & Gallery** (307 Main St., 540/675-1411, www.rhballard.com; 10am-6pm Wed.-Mon.), a housewares shop and fine art gallery worth a stop.

WHERE TO STAY

The Inn at Little Washington (Middle St. and Main St., 540/675-3800, www.theinnatlittlewashington.com; $520-900) is simply the best, conveniently located to explore Shenandoah National Park. But if you can't get a room or want something a little more budget friendly, you aren't entirely out of luck, as there are several inns and bed-and-breakfasts within stumbling distance from dinner. The six modern rooms at **The White Moose Inn** (291 Main St., 540/675-3207, www.whitemooseinn.com; $425-625) are decorated in white with high-tech amenities and Molton Brown toiletries, while **Gay Street Inn** (160 Gay St., 540/316-9220, www.gaystreetinn.com; $279-329) has five homey guest rooms in a restored 1850s farmhouse.

INFORMATION AND SERVICES

Staff at **The Inn at Little Washington** (Middle St. and Main St., 540/675-3800, www.theinnatlittlewashington.com) are experts on the region and can provide directions to key sights and Shenandoah

Valley hikes, wineries, and other activities; the website has lots of information and links.

For more information on the surrounding area, visit the Rappahannock Historical Society (328 Gay St., 540/675-1163, www.rappahannockhistsoc.org; 11am-5pm Mon., Tues., and Thurs.) a block from the inn, or the Rappahannock County Visitors Center (3 Library Rd., 540/675-3153, www.rappahannock.com; 9am-5pm Fri.-Sat. and Mon. holidays, noon-5pm Sun., hours vary seasonally), less than 1 mi (1.6 km) east.

GETTING THERE

Little Washington is approximately 1.5-2 hours (about 70 mi/113 km) west of Washington DC, and a good base to explore Shenandoah National Park and nearby wineries. Take I-66 W to U.S. 29 S (exit 43A toward Gainesville/Warrenton). Continue on Route 29 S for 12 mi (19.3 km) to Warrenton, then turn right on U.S. 211 W. Stay on U.S. 211 W for 23 mi (37 km) to the town. While you don't need a car within Little Washington, you'll need one to get there and explore the surrounding area; if you want to go for dinner and back, the Inn at Little Washington can arrange car service for you, or contact Reston Limousine (703/478-0500, www.restonlimo.com).

Little Washington is about 20 minutes (12 mi/19.3 km) from the closest Skyline Drive entrance at Thornton Gap, via U.S. 211 W/U.S. 522 S, which will also take you to Luray Caverns in 35 minutes. It's one hour (36 mi/58 km) from

Middleburg, a great scenic route/detour on the way back to Washington DC.

MIDDLEBURG
SIGHTS
✪ Historic Middleburg

Founded in 1787 by Revolutionary War lieutenant colonel and politician John Leven Powell on a busy trading route from Alexandria, Middleburg is the "Nation's Horse and Hunt Capital," a retreat for wealthy Washingtonians for decades (including JFK and Jackie), and an ideal place to spend the night while exploring Virginia wine country. The quiet, 1-mi (1.6-km) Middleburg Historic District has several historic inns, antiques and fine art, and equestrian shops to help you play the part of mon-eyed socialite spending a casual weekend in the country. It also holds The Christmas Sleigh (5A E. Washington St., 540/687-3665, www.thechristmassleigh.com; 11am-5pm daily, holiday hours vary), the German-style Christmas shop owned by the late Linda Tripp (yes, that Linda Tripp) and her husband. The National Sporting Library & Museum (102 The Plains Rd., 540/687-6542, www.nationalsporting.org; 10am-5pm Wed.-Sun.; $10 adults, $8 seniors/youth ages 13-18, free for children 12 and under) showcases fine art related to equestrian sports and country activities from the 17th century to present day.

Virginia Horse Racing

While Middleburg gets significantly more crowded, the best time to visit is during one of the famed steeplechase races. Since 1911, the Middleburg Spring Races (540/687-6545, www.middleburg-springraces.com) have drawn, as one local newspaper wrote in 1936, "turf folk representing high society of New York, Philadelphia, Baltimore, Washington, and Virginia." The event traditionally takes place annually on the third Saturday in April. Similarly, the Virginia Fall Races (540/687-9797, www.vafall-races.com) on the second Saturday in October have attracted top equestrians and fox hunters from across the country since 1955. Both happen at the 112-acre Glenwood Park (Rte. 626/Foxcroft Rd.,), the oldest continually operating racecourse in Virginia, where you can reserve a tent for a crowd or tailgate with your family.

RESTAURANTS AND WHERE TO STAY

Rooms in Middleburg book up months in advance for the horse races, so plan ahead. It may be cheaper to rent a car or get car service from DC to Middleburg for these events and make it a day trip.

Established in 1728, The Red Fox Inn & Tavern (2 E. Washington St., 540/687-6301, www.redfox.com; $285-355) is the top place to dine and dream in Middleburg. First Lady Jackie Kennedy was a frequent guest, as was, some believe, young George Washington. The inn has 17 historical but luxe rooms—think four-poster beds and luxury toiletries—plus one two-story, two-bedroom house with a full kitchen. And the cozy tavern (8am-10am and 5pm-9pm Mon.-Fri., 11am-2pm

Red Fox Inn & Tavern

and 5pm-9pm Sat., 11am-2pm and 5pm-8pm Sun.; $28-46) showcases local ingredients and wine.

In the heart of wine and hunt country, the five-star Goodstone Inn & Restaurant (36205 Snake Hill Rd., 540/687-3333, www.goodstone.com; $395-545) is an idyllic haven perfect for a romantic getaway, with 18 rooms and suites with their own personalities set on 265 acres. In addition to an outdoor pool, hiking trails, and spa, the estate has a working farm and gardens, which supply the stately restaurant.

Salamander Resort & Spa (500 N. Pendleton St., 844/303-2723, www.salamanderresort.com; $385-515) is a getaway itself, as you'll never want to (or need to) leave the 350-acre estate, with 168 contemporary rooms and suites and dozens of amenities and resort activities. Spend the day lounging at the 23,000-square-foot spa and outdoor pool, play tennis or lawn games, or even go horseback riding at the on-site stable. The hotel has several restaurants and bars, as well as kids' activities.

For a quick meal in the village between shopping or wine-tasting, Market Salamander (200 W. Washington St., 540/687-8011, www.marketsalamander.com; 8am-2pm Wed.-Thurs., 8am-4pm Fri.-Sun.; $5-10) has excellent made-to-order sandwiches and picnic-ready food, with several outdoor tables. Or, grab a coffee, tea, or breakfast or lunch sandwich at Middleburg Common Grounds (114 W. Washington St., 540/687-7065, www.facebook.com/middleburgcommongrounds; 6am-6pm Mon.-Fri., 7am-6pm Sat.-Sun.;

$5-10), with a cozy space to sit and plan your next adventure.

INFORMATION AND SERVICES

The Middleburg Visitor Center (12 N. Madison St., 540/687-8888, www.visitmiddleburgva.com; 11am-3pm daily) is in the village, or you can visit the website to plan your trip and obtain more information on wineries, shopping, and special events.

TRANSPORTATION

Middleburg is approximately one hour (45 mi/72 km) west of Washington DC. Take I-66 W to U.S. 50 W (exit 57B toward Fair Oaks/Winchester) and continue on U.S. 50 W about 25 mi (40 km) directly to the historic center. Glenwood Park is just under 2 mi (3.2 km) north of the historic district via Foxcroft Road, and the wineries and inns are spread around Middleburg. If you don't have a car, or want to explore the wineries worry-free, car service is recommended; Reston Limousine (703/478-0500, www.restonlimo.com) is popular for point-to-point service to and from the District as well as wine tours. The center of Middleburg is easily walkable, though you'll need transportation to the countryside sights.

Middleburg is approximately 45 minutes (30 mi/48 km) from the closest Skyline Drive entrance at Front Royal. Or, head about one hour (36 mi/58 km) west to Little Washington, where you can reach Skyline Drive and Luray Caverns via the Thornton Gap entrance.

BACKGROUND

The Landscape

GEOGRAPHY

Washington DC gets a bad reputation for being a swamp, both literally and figuratively. This may be an exaggeration, though it's easy to see why the nickname sticks if you visit during July and August, when the humidity can be overbearing. Built on the banks of the Potomac River, an important waterway for trade and transportation during most of the city's history, the nation's capital is on sturdy land, and while you don't need to worry about sinking into the marsh while exploring the monuments, DC is nonetheless a water town, selected for the prime location nestled between the Potomac and Anacostia Rivers, which connect to the Chesapeake Bay. While part of the National Mall is, indeed, built on marshland, George

dome of the U.S. Capitol

Washington certainly did not choose swampland for his great experiment.

But he did choose the site for the strategic location in the middle of the 13 original colonies, easily accessible from the most important ports and the earlier capitals New York and Philadelphia. Today, it comprises 68 square miles (109 km) between Maryland, Virginia, and the Potomac River. By design, Washington, District of Columbia, is not a state but a territory under federal jurisdiction, created in 1790 from land from the surrounding states specifically to serve as the independent capital of the young nation.

CLIMATE

DC has four distinct seasons—though the temperate and glorious spring and fall are far too short, giving way rather quickly to high heat and humidity for most of the summer and cold, dark winters. The occasional snow or ice storm debilitates the city, which is mocked by northern states for being unable to handle a winter storm and thus shutting down. (But, cut us some slack, because we're the southernmost northern city—or, the northernmost southern city, depending how you want to look at it.) In recent years, the climate has gotten extremely unpredictable, so unless you're traveling in the dead of winter or summer, pack layers and be prepared for sunshine or rain.

ENVIRONMENTAL ISSUES

The unpredictable climate has led to environmental issues, which have an impact on one of DC's top industries after governing: tourism and hospitality. Specifically, the erratic temperatures make predicting the peak bloom of the cherry blossom trees, which draw 1.5 million visitors to DC annually, nearly impossible. In 2017, for example, the blossoms started to bloom early after an exceptionally warm winter, but they were quickly damaged by a cold spell just before reaching their peak. DC had a beautiful display nonetheless, but not to the extent of past years. Not to mention, environmentalists warn that the sheer magnitude of visitors traipsing around the trees at the Tidal Basin each year could lead to the trees' demise.

Another environmental concern is the notorious pollution of the city's rivers. Why can't the home of the Environmental Protection Agency keep its own waterways sewage-free and thriving? Thanks to extensive cleanup efforts, the Potomac River has improved in recent years, but the Anacostia River, DC's "forgotten river," still has a long way to go to address the sediment, chemicals, and sewage as well as, sadly, the garbage floating in the rivers and Tidal Basin. While the rapid growth and development around the District has led to runoff, it's also led to residents waking up to the need to clean up and preserve the natural habitat. If you're interested in learning more about the history of the Anacostia River and present-day environmental challenges, Anacostia Riverkeeper (www.anacostiariverkeeper.org) runs free boat tours. These tours, and more importantly, the cleanup efforts, are funded by 5-cent fee charged for every disposable paper or plastic bag at any business that sells food or alcohol (with a few exceptions for things like restaurant leftovers in a paper bag).

Given the focus on the famous Maryland blue crabs and crab cakes served at many local restaurants, it's important to know that, while the species was overfished about a decade ago, the population has since rebounded; in 2019, the female adult crab population was the largest it had been in seven years. You should feel free to enjoy the regional specialty, knowing you're contributing to an important aspect of the economy, and knowing the Bay region is actively addressing this environmental issue.

ANIMALS

You may notice a somewhat unusual animal while walking around the city, particularly the Northwest quadrant: the black squirrel, which will have no qualms sprinting across your path even in heavily trafficked areas. These melanistic squirrels first arrived in DC from Rondeau Provincial Park in Ontario, Canada, which sent eight of them to the National Zoo in 1902, then eight more a few years later, in exchange for some of America's gray squirrels. Rather than put them in a cage, the zoo simply released them into the park. The squirrels thrived in their new habitat, and today, they make up about 25 percent of the District's squirrel population.

History

BIRTH OF THE CAPITAL

Needless to say, George Washington and his contemporaries were not the first people to inhabit the land around the Potomac River. When European settlers first arrived, several Algonquin-speaking tribes lived in the Chesapeake Bay region, including the Piscataway. While colonization forced these tribes to new settlements, or tragic demise, they left their mark in the names of major geographic features; "Potomac" (or "Patowmack," as it was spelled on early maps) is their name for the river that played such an important role in the choice of this region as the capital city, while "Anacostia" is the evolution of "Nacotchtank," as the area tribe was named by Captain John Smith in 1612.

George Washington, however, knew the area perhaps better than anyone in colonial America, having worked as a land surveyor in the region from the age of 17 and having inherited Mount Vernon (on the banks of the Potomac) in his 20s. Washington, Virginia, near Shenandoah National Park, was the first town of many to bear his name. So it's no surprise that, when he led the team to select the site of the new capital city, he chose this area.

After the American Revolution, the United States Constitution called for the creation of "a District (not exceeding ten miles square) as may, by cession of particular states, and the acceptance of Congress, become the seat of the government of the United States." For the Founding Fathers, it was important that the capital remain independent, under federal control and not a state, though this has caused contention in more recent years. Pulling land from Georgetown, which was part of Maryland and remains part of DC today, as well as Alexandria, Virginia (given back in 1846), the location was a compromise between Alexander Hamilton and northern states, who wanted the new federal government to pay the debts of the war, and James Madison and the southern states, who agreed to the plan in exchange for placing the capital in the south.

To build his vision, Washington hired Major Pierre Charles L'Enfant, the French engineer who served with Americans in the war, to design the new capital. He was inspired by the baroque architecture and grand landscapes of Paris and Versailles, with their wide, tree-lined boulevards and major buildings in prominent positions in the city (such as the Capitol and presidential mansion). While his plan was never fully realized, any visitor to both DC and Paris will recognize the similarities.

In August 1814, during the War of 1812, British troops invaded the young capital and burned many of the buildings, including the Capitol, Library of Congress (with 3,000 books), Treasury, and White House, which First Lady Dolley Madison fled in the nick of time. Less than a day after the invasion, thunderstorms put out the fires, and the resourceful government quickly began reconstruction, with the new White House ready for President James Monroe's inauguration in 1817.

THE CIVIL WAR TO THE NEW DEAL

The government and capital continued to thrive—though as northern states began to abolish slavery one by one, tensions heightened between the north and south. Alexandria, a major hub of the slave trade, petitioned the federal government to return the land to Virginia in 1846; just a few years later, the federal government ended slave trading (though, notably, not slavery) in the capital, while newly returned Alexandria continued to sell slaves through the busy port to the more southern plantation states. For a detailed look at the slave trade in Washington DC, visit the corner of 7th Street NW and Independence Avenue NW, near the Federal Aviation Administration. Signs describe the horror of the Williams Slave Pen, where Solomon Northup, whose story was told in *12 Years A Slave,* was held after being kidnapped. Nearly one-third of the slaves brought to the United States were brought through the ports of DC, Maryland, and Virginia, and many built the new capital city, including structures like the Capitol and White House.

Shortly after Abraham Lincoln was elected the 16th president (in 1860) on an antislavery platform, tensions broke. The Confederates seceded, hoping to make Washington DC their capital. Lincoln, who freed the slaves of the District of Columbia eight months prior to the Emancipation Proclamation, built the Union military, bringing troops from all over the country to defend the capital, including many freed blacks.

The Civil War had a huge impact on everyday life in Washington DC—namely, creating massive growth of the federal government, to manage the war effort and then the reconstruction of the nation, and the population, which continued well after the war. Thousands who had moved to the capital to serve in the military or provide service to the war stuck around, and slowly but surely, this swampy backwater with limited infrastructure would grow to become a cosmopolitan city on par with New York and Philadelphia. As the federal government grew in size and scope, so, too, did the District of Columbia, with monuments, museums, and government buildings sprouting up amid the District's creeping borders. This growth and development continued into the 20th century.

CIVIL RIGHTS ERA TO PRESENT DAY

The civil rights era brought turmoil to this racially diverse, growing city, once on the rise but destroyed by the racial divisions continuing to divide America, 100 years after the end of the Civil War and Lincoln's assassination in Ford's Theatre. Nearly 250,000 people gathered on the National Mall to watch Martin Luther King Jr. deliver his "I Have A Dream" speech from the steps of the Lincoln Memorial on August 28, 1963. And less than five years later, when he was assassinated, the District of Columbia was torn to shreds by five days of violent riots, which burned many of the vibrant African American neighborhoods, once centers of jazz and culture, to the ground. As in so many cities in America, the white and middle-class populations fled to the nearby suburbs, leaving burned-out, and increasingly crime-ridden, DC to deal with the remains. Through the 1980s and early 1990s, Mayor Marion Barry, one of the most

iconic and controversial figures of late 20th-century DC, brought more attention to DC, first in his work as a civil rights leader and popular city official who brought social programs and growth projects to the city. His waning years as mayor were notorious because of scandal, when he claimed "bitch set me up" during a crack cocaine sting at a downtown hotel.

The 1990s brought reinvestment in the city, and interest once again in moving to the federal metropolis, and slowly but surely, the city rebuilt after the turmoil of the 1970s and 1980s. With Presidents Clinton and Bush II, the federal government, and the city it calls home, began growing once again. As tanks rolled into the streets on September 11, 2001, the future of the city was briefly uncertain, but again, more federal growth in the aftermath of the terrorist attack and the wars in Afghanistan and Iraq led to more growth, period.

When President Barack Obama was inaugurated on January 20, 2009, in the largest inauguration to date with some 1.8 million people crowding the National Mall and the city's hotels and businesses, Washington DC finally seemed to have overcome the turbulence of the 20th century, embarking on a renaissance of growth and innovation that continues today.

Government and Economy

TAXATION WITHOUT REPRESENTATION

"Taxation without representation" is the way of life for Washingtonians, because, as the Founding Fathers intended, Washington DC remains a territory of the federal government rather than a state. Until 1961, Washington residents had no voice in the government, but the 23rd Amendment gave them three electoral votes in the presidential election—the same as the least populous state—and these votes have gone to the Democratic Party candidate ever since. Since 1970, the District has, theoretically, had representation in the House of Representatives, as well, but while the at-large delegate has an office on Capitol Hill, she cannot vote. Of course, like the residents of the 13 original colonies, who were required to pay taxes to the King of England without having representation in the British Parliament, residents of Washington DC are still required to pay federal taxes, despite the fact that their legally elected Representative cannot voice their concerns on federal tax policy, or any other policy, for that matter.

The District of Columbia Home Rule Act of 1973 allowed DC a mayor and 13-member city council to make laws and manage services, schools, and social and cultural programs for the increasingly growing population. But Congress still has the final say—like when DC voted to legalize medical marijuana in 1998, for example, and Congress prohibited the city from using funds to start the program. In 2014, voters legalized possession by nearly 65 percent, but Congress continues to try to limit DC's ability to regulate the sale of the substance even today.

A COMPANY TOWN

If you aren't comfortable talking about, or hearing about, politics and policy differences—well, you'd better get comfortable, because Washington DC is a company town, and policy is the product. Nearly one in three jobs in the District is a federal government job, with many DC residents working in these roles; the rest are filled by residents of neighboring suburbs in Maryland and Virginia, who, while they may not have a DC zip code, spend their workdays, and many evening and weekend hours, contributing to the economy.

As for the rest of jobs in the District? It's hard to get a totally accurate count, but it's safe to say that most of them are related to the government in some way: lobbyists and lawyers and communications experts employed by the famous firms on K Street, or representing companies, trade associations, and constituencies large and small; a massive media presence, who report on the minutiae of politics and life in DC, and hold elected officials accountable; private consultants who are hired at large salaries to manage government projects when federal employees can't, or won't; nonprofits and charities, who either try to influence or fight the government at any given time; think tanks that, well, think about the issues (and sometimes provide recommendations); international bodies, like the World Bank, and international embassies, because this is the most important city in the world, if you ask a Washingtonian; even hospitality employees, who have undoubtedly heard many state secrets as those government employees meet with reporters or friends across the aisle for clandestine cocktails in restaurants and hotel bars across the city. And everyone, from the head of the public relations firm to the bartender to the reporter, has an opinion, even if the report claims they're neutral.

In other words, you can't escape politics in DC—but really, why would you want to? And the key, whatever your politics, is that there's someone here who's working for your candidate or your cause—even if they voted the other way.

Washington DC does have other important industries. Related to hospitality and tourism, DC has a booming dining and nightlife scene, and more and more critically acclaimed chefs are setting up shop in this city where there's always disposable income. Increasingly, there are niche industries, too—food manufacturers and distilleries, boutiques and designers, and small businesses of all shapes and sizes—though, of course, they'll all be glad for the gossip column blurb when the VIP patronizes their business.

Local Culture

DIVERSITY

Washington DC is a racially and culturally diverse city where all races, ethnicities, sexual orientations, and backgrounds are welcome and represented. And we mean diverse: Of the nearly 700,000 residents, 47.7 percent are black or African American, 36.4 percent are white, 10.9 percent are Hispanic or Latino, and 4.1 percent are Asian. The demographics have shifted rather rapidly; until 2011, the population was 50.7 percent black or African American, the first city in the nation to have a black majority, but this is no longer the case. As DC grows and neighborhoods once in turmoil in parts of Northeast and Southeast are now experiencing growth—and getting very expensive—white people, especially young white people, are moving to the city in droves, while black and immigrant families who have historically occupied these neighborhoods since the mid-20th century are moving to the more affordable suburbs in Maryland and Virginia.

LITTLE ETHIOPIA

Washington DC has a large Ethiopian population, and the Washington metro region has the largest Ethiopian population in the country. While Ethiopian immigrants are increasingly priced out of the District and now live and open businesses in suburbs like Silver Spring, Maryland, and Alexandria, Virginia, parts of the U Street Corridor and Shaw around 9th Street NW are still known as "Little Ethiopia," as evidenced by the many Ethiopian restaurants. It's more likely these days, however, that you'll encounter a young Ethiopian immigrant driving your Uber or Lyft, rather than opening a restaurant.

LGBTQ LIFE AND CULTURE

In 2017, Gallup found 8.6 percent of DC residents self-identify as gay, lesbian, bisexual, or transgender; Vermont came in second, with 5.3 percent. According to the U.S. Census, 4 percent of DC households are same-sex couples, compared to the national average of about 1 percent—and DC legalized same-sex marriage in 2009, well before many states. Dupont Circle has historically been the center of LGBTQ life and culture in DC since the 1970s, and while 17th Street has several of the most popular gay bars and annual events like Capital Pride and the High-Heel Drag Race, the neighborhood isn't really seen as the gay community hub anymore, as gay bars are everywhere throughout the city—and the LGBTQ community is wholly embraced.

MUSIC AND THE ARTS

Believe it or not, Washington DC is an artsy town, home to world-class theaters and performing arts venues, outside-the-box troupes, and concert halls and music clubs even the professionals love. If you're lucky, you'll see street musicians performing around Metro stations or busy, downtown intersections, some of them large bands, or you can always go to Meridian Hill Park to see the famous drum circle on Sunday afternoons.

Historically, DC was one of the nation's hubs for African American performing arts (even before Harlem), especially jazz. Duke Ellington was born in Washington DC and spent much of his life here, starting his career playing in the city's jazz clubs around "Black Broadway," along with stars like Ella Fitzgerald, Marvin Gaye, and The Supremes, until the riots of 1968 decimated the area, which didn't bounce back until the 1990s. Today, you can walk by the ghosts of some of these clubs, including Bohemian Caverns on U Street, or listen at Blues Alley in Georgetown and even The John F. Kennedy Center for the Performing Arts, which has a robust jazz program.

In the 1960s and 1970s, DC gave birth to an important musical tradition: go-go, made famous by Chuck Brown, "Godfather of Go-Go," who lived in DC most of his life, though there were dozens of go-go groups in the Washington area. At go-go shows, the music continues seemingly nonstop for hours. Today, you can see some of the remaining top go-go bands, like Rare Essence and Experience Unlimited (EU), at The Howard Theatre and The Lincoln Theatre.

In the 1980s and 1990s, DC had an influential hardcore punk movement, as well, with bands like Minor Threat and Bad Brains creating socially conscious music.

ESSENTIALS

Transportation

GETTING THERE

AIR

The Washington metropolitan region is served by three airports.

Ronald Reagan Washington National Airport (DCA, 2401 S. Smith Blvd, Arlington, Virginia, www.flyreagan.com) is just over the DC line in Arlington, Virginia. It's 10-20 minutes from the city center by car via the George Washington Memorial Parkway, and 20 minutes from Metro Center via the Metro Blue and Yellow Lines (National Airport station). This small, easy-to-navigate airport provides service on 10 domestic carriers, and while it's the most convenient, flights can be a little more expensive.

Ronald Reagan Washington National Airport

Washington Dulles International Airport (IAD, 1 Saarinen Cir., Dulles, Virginia, www.flydulles.com) is in Dulles, Virginia, about 45-60 minutes (26 mi/42 km) by car via I-66 West or the George Washington Memorial Parkway/VA 267 West and the Dulles Access Road; follow signs for airport traffic to avoid the toll. This is the largest airport in the region, serving national and international destinations via many major carriers. Leave yourself plenty of time to get to the airport, especially during weekday rush hour (3pm-7pm). Taxis cost $70-100 with tip each way, though ride-hailing app services cost as little as $35-40. From the airport, you can get an airport-approved Washington

Flyer taxi to your destination or have your Uber or Lyft driver pick you up at the arrivals level.

Dulles is accessible by public transportation, too. Take the Metro Silver Line to Wiehle-Reston East station, about 40 minutes from Metro Center. From there, catch the Silver Line Express Bus to the terminal, which costs $5 for the 15-minute trip. This route may feel inefficient, but it can be faster than driving during rush hour. Eventually, the Metro Silver Line will go directly to the airport; construction is expected to be completed in 2021.

Baltimore/Washington International Thurgood Marshall Airport (BWI, 7035 Elm Rd., Baltimore, Maryland, www.bwiairport.com) is another option for domestic budget carriers and a few international carriers, including Air Canada and British Airways. It's about an hour from DC via the Baltimore-Washington Parkway, but only 30 minutes from Union Station via Amtrak or 50 minutes via MARC (Maryland Area Regional Commuter) train; take your train to BWI Marshall Airport and catch a free shuttle every six minutes. (If you time it correctly, it's possible to get from Union Station to your gate in one hour.)

CAR

"Inside the Beltway" is the phrase used to describe the political baseball in DC, played by career politicians and lobbyists and media and Washington insiders, and often has a negative connotation to anyone who doesn't live here. Where does it come from? These Beltway insiders live and work within the Capital Beltway, or I-495, the 64-mi (103-km) highway that encircles Washington DC and a few close suburbs of Maryland and Virginia (like Chevy Chase and McLean, where many lobbyists live), and a road you'll probably have to travel if you're arriving by car. The Beltway connects to I-95, the longest north-south interstate in America, and it's notorious for heavy traffic, especially during rush hours (6am-9:30am weekday mornings and roughly 3pm-7pm on weekday evenings). Other major routes through DC include U.S. 50, which crosses the National Mall, and I-66, which ends at the road's easternmost point in DC.

If you're driving to DC, your best bet is to ditch your car at your hotel and utilize public transportation, taxis and ride-sharing apps, and walking. In addition to heavy traffic in and around the immediate vicinity of DC and unexpected road closures due to motorcades and security concerns, parking can be difficult; parking garages are typically expensive, and street parking is challenging to find and maneuver, especially with so many one-way streets in the city.

TRAIN

Amtrak (800/872-7245, www.amtrak.com) serves **Union Station** (50 Massachusetts Ave. NE, 202/289-1908, www.unionstationdc.com) on Capitol Hill. Amtrak Acela Express service runs hourly to major East Coast cities including Baltimore, Philadelphia, New York, and Boston, getting to New York's Penn Station in less than three hours, though tickets for the higher-speed service are often more expensive unless you plan far in advance. (Don't be surprised if you see DC celebrities, or even real celebrities, traveling this route.) The Northeast Regional is the other major East Coast route, serving dozens of stations between Boston and Newport News, Virginia. Other services passing through DC include Silver Service/Palmetto from New York to Miami, Florida; the Capitol Limited and Cardinal, which head west to Chicago; and the Vermonter, which starts in Washington DC and travels to cities in Connecticut and Vermont.

Union Station is easy to navigate and generally efficient, with quick-service dining and shops on the same level as the tracks, as well as table-service restaurants and a food court. Amtrak announces the track early, sometimes more than one hour in advance, so travelers line up at the tracks, but you can arrive 10-15 minutes before the train and have plenty of time to spare if you're not checking luggage; there's plenty of space to bring normal-sized luggage on board. If you're traveling first class or have ClubAcela or United Club membership, you can enter the lounge and board the train through the lounge about 10 minutes earlier than other passengers, allowing you time to choose your seat and get comfortable before the rush.

From Union Station, you can catch the MARC train (866/743-3682, http://mta.maryland.gov/marc-train), Maryland's commuter rail service, a cheap and relatively efficient route to Baltimore and Baltimore Washington International Airport, as well as the Virginia Railway Express (703/684-1001, www.vre.org), Virginia's commuter rail service to suburbs of Northern Virginia. Union Station connects to the Metro Red Line and Metrobus service, as well as DC Circulator and tour buses.

BUS

Greyhound (202/789-4318, www.greyhound.com) arrives at and departs from Union Station (50 Massachusetts Ave. NE, 202/289-1908, www.unionstationdc.com) on Capitol Hill; the bus terminal is connected to the main station terminal, so just follow the signs for buses. The bus terminal does not have any amenities, so grab food or coffee from the shops in the train terminal before heading to your bus.

There are several relatively inexpensive bus services between DC and New York City, which are especially popular among 20-something travelers. From Union Station, BoltBus (877/265-8287, www.boltbus.com) and the double-decker Megabus (online reservations only at www.megabus.com) have daily, nonstop departures to New York as low as $15-20 each way, if you're willing to book a few weeks in advance; both offer service to a few other cities, as well. Washington Deluxe (866/287-6932, www.washny.com) has departures from Union Station and Dupont Circle Metro station to several stops in New York, with prices ranging $20-30 each way in advance.

GETTING AROUND
NAVIGATING THE CITY

Washington DC is a walkable city, with broad, well-maintained streets and sidewalks. And it's relatively easy to navigate, especially around the central tourist areas like the National Mall and Capitol Hill, once you understand the layout. True to L'Enfant's original plan, DC has four "quadrants" around the U.S. Capitol: Northeast, Southeast, Northwest, and Southwest. When traveling to a new address, check for the quadrant signifier (NE, SE, NW, SW), because some streets will cross two quadrants. Most, but not all, of the streets are arranged in a grid around the U.S. Capitol. The numbered streets run north to south, the lettered streets run east to west, and the diagonal streets are named after states (Pennsylvania Avenue and Massachusetts Avenue are two you'll likely encounter). There's no J Street, so don't be alarmed when you walk from H Street to I Street, which is sometimes written out as "Eye Street." And "B Street" is now Constitution Avenue and Independence Avenue. The letters stop at W Street, which is near the boundary of the original capital city; now, as you pass W Street and head north into Columbia Heights and Upper Northwest, east-west street names will continue in alphabetical order (Belmont, Clifton, Euclid, Fairmont, etc.) and start over again until you reach Maryland, always skipping X, Y, and Z.

PUBLIC TRANSPORTATION

Washington Metropolitan Area Transit Authority (202/637-7000, www.wmata.com) operates Metrorail (more commonly referred to simply as "Metro"), DC's network of underground and above-ground subway service, and Metrobus. Together, the services reach every neighborhood in DC as well as nearby Maryland and Virginia suburbs. While locals love to joke about the inefficiency of Metro and frequent delays during rush hour, the rail system is simple to navigate, cheap, and efficient, most of the time, especially if you're traveling across quadrants to destinations close to a station. While Georgetown and some farther-flung destinations, like Union Market and the U.S. National Arboretum, don't have stations nearby, most everywhere else you'll visit does, especially downtown and around the National Mall and Capitol Hill. Metrorail operates 5am-11:30pm Monday through Thursday, 5am-1am Friday, 7am-1am Saturday, and 8am-11pm Sunday; trains run anywhere from every four minutes during rush hour to every 10-20 minutes in the evening, but you'll want to check the trip planner for the last train from your particular station.

Metrobus, on the other hand, is a little more difficult to navigate, with 325 routes hitting more than 11,000 stops; don't hop on a bus unless you know where you're going. DC Circulator (www.dccirculator) is more straightforward, with six routes in prime tourism areas; this is a good option to get to Georgetown or to travel around the National Mall. For both bus options, schedules vary by route.

Metrorail, Metrobus, and DC Circulator accept the reloadable

SmarTrip card, which you can purchase at blue fare vending machines in every Metro station. Each person must have their own card to travel on these services, though up to two children under age 5 may travel for free with each paying adult. Metrorail fares vary depending on how far you're traveling and the time of day, with peak fares ($2.25-6 per ride) from opening to 9:30am and 3pm-7pm weekdays; Metrorail accepts only SmarTrip cards. Metrobus fares are $2 for regular routes, $4.25 for express routes ($1 for regular routes and $2.10 for express routes for seniors or those with disabilities) but can be paid with SmarTrip or cash with exact change on the bus. If you're planning to use public transportation a lot, a SmarTrip card provides free bus-to-bus transfers and discounted rail-bus transfers.

The **DC Streetcar** (www.dc-streetcar.com, 6am-midnight Mon.-Thurs., 6am-2am Fri., 8am-2am Sat., 8am-10pm Sun. and holidays) operates every 10-15 minutes between Union Station and the Atlas District/H Street Corridor. The streetcar is currently free, though it's not especially efficient; it's a little easier to take a taxi or ride-sharing service to your destination on H Street NE, or even walk from Union Station if you're a fast walker. From Union Station, follow the signs for the streetcar through the bus station and look for yellow DC Streetcar signs to lead you to the stop outside the station.

As in any major city, be aware of your surroundings at transportation stations, and you'll want to use common sense with regards to your valuables and traveling late at night,

but generally, you can feel safe using all of these services.

TAXIS AND RIDE-HAILING APPS

You can hail taxis throughout the city, though there's no one, main taxi company, so service and car quality can vary greatly. Taxis are required to accept credit cards, and most have touch-screen payment machines in the backseat, but it's honestly not uncommon to encounter a taxi driver whose machine doesn't work. Rates are $3.50 for the first one-eighth mile and $2.16 for each additional mile. The DC Department of For-Hire Vehicles has an authorized **mobile app**, www.dctaxi.com, to allow you to hail and pay for a vetted taxi. Virginia-based taxi companies, including **Washington Flyer** (888/927-4359, www.flydulles.com/iad/washington-flyer) and **Red Top Cab of Arlington** (703/522-3333, www.redtopcab.com) can pick you up to take you to the Virginia airports, and both accept reservations.

Ride-hailing apps are just one of the reasons why there has been such a boom in more far-flung parts of Northeast and Southeast Washington, and these apps, including **Uber** (www.uber.com), **Lyft** (www.lyft.com), and **Via** (http://ridewithvia.com), are strongly recommended for travel around the District and to/from nearby suburbs in Maryland and Virginia. You can save a substantial amount of money—as much as 50 percent—using lower-cost services like UberX to get to and from the airports versus a taxi. Uber and Lyft can pick you up at all three airports; check in the app for your meeting point.

DRIVING

Unless you like the adventure of confusing traffic circles, surprising one-way streets, road blockades and motorcades, and of course, crazy traffic, it's best to leave driving to the pros, and utilize public transportation, taxis/ride-sharing apps, and walking to get around the city. If you decide you want a car—say, to explore the U.S. National Arboretum, or drive to Mount Vernon—there are major car rental agencies convenient to downtown, and car-sharing services like **Car2go** (877/488-4224, www.car2go.com) and **ZipCar** (866/494-7227, www.zipcar.com) have pickup points around the city and rentals by the minute, hour, or day.

BICYCLE

DC is a great city for cycling, with a growing number of on-street bike lanes and marked routes as well as parks and trails to explore. If you want to explore DC by two wheels, you'll be in good company—about 4 percent of Washingtonians city-wide bike to work, with as many as 20 percent from neighborhoods in Upper Northwest. For traveling from point to point around the city, **Capital Bikeshare** (www.capitalbikeshare.com) has 440 stations and nearly 4,000 bikes available 24/7 daily in DC, Maryland, and Virginia. You can rent a bike for $2 per ride, up to 30 minutes, or purchase a day pass for $8 or three-day pass for $17. When you're finished, just drop the bike at any station with space. If you want to rent a bike for a longer journey, such as to ride the Mount Vernon Trail to Virginia, you can rent bikes, helmets, and locks from **Bike and Roll** (202/842-2453, www.bikeandrolldc.com), which has locations at the National Mall, Union Station, and Old Town Alexandria. Increasingly, many hotels offer bikes for guest use, as well.

Health and Safety

HOSPITALS AND EMERGENCY SERVICES

DC has several major emergency rooms. The hospital that's most likely the closest to your hotel is **George Washington University Hospital** (900 23rd St. NW, 202/715-4000, www.gwhospital.com) in Foggy Bottom, which treated President Ronald Reagan when he was shot in 1981. If you're having an emergency, don't try to figure out which emergency room is closest to you—just dial 911.

For urgent but not emergency situations, **MedStar PromptCare** (www.medstarhealth.org) offers walk-in services in **Capitol Hill** (228 7th St. SE, 855/546-1970; 8am-8pm daily) and **Adams Morgan** (1805 Columbia Rd., 855/546-1973; 8am-8pm daily). In addition, several **CVS Pharmacy** (www.cvspharmacy.com/minuteclinic) stores operate walk-in clinics; hours and locations vary.

PHARMACIES

CVS Pharmacy (www.cvspharmacy.com) has dozens of stores in the Washington metropolitan area, with prescription pharmacy services as well as over-the-counter medicines and personal care products; several locations are open 24 hours daily, including the store and pharmacy one block from the Metro on Dupont Circle (6 Dupont Cir., 202/785-1466, www.cvspharmacy.com). Walgreens, Rite Aid, and local pharmacies are available, as well.

CRIME

In the latter half of the 20th century, DC got a bad reputation for violent, often drug-related crime, which peaked in the 1980s and early 1990s as the nation's capital earned its "murder capital" nickname and got caught up in the crack epidemic. This has changed, and tourists should not fear visiting any major sight, or any neighborhood in this guide, for that matter, especially during daylight hours.

As in any major city, however, tourists are advised to use common sense, in any neighborhood: Take care with your valuables, don't talk on the phone while pulling out your money to buy a Metro fare card, use public transportation and stick to well-lit and busy streets at night, and avoid walking alone on deserted streets or empty parks in the middle of the night, especially if you're not familiar with the neighborhood. And be wary of locals' advice. We never fear our city and will venture to the most desolate corner for interesting food or off-the-beaten-path sightseeing or art, but it doesn't mean visitors should necessarily walk there.

Thanks especially to the ease of ride-sharing apps, many neighborhoods once considered dangerous are experiencing a boom of growth and development. While neighborhoods like the Atlas District/H Street Corridor, Anacostia, and Union Market/Ivy City, best accessed by taxis/ride-sharing apps, have important tourist sights, growing dining and nightlife scenes, and friendly residents, keep your wits about you at night, when parts of these neighborhoods can become more deserted. However, it's important to note that no neighborhood, including Shaw or Dupont Circle or Georgetown, for example, is immune to crime, and you're advised to take care anywhere you go, especially after dark. When in doubt, use public transportation or taxis/ride-sharing apps.

HOMELESS POPULATION

More than 7,000 people in Washington DC are homeless, and while walking in almost any part of town, especially downtown and near popular tourist sights, parks, and major Metro stations, you're likely to encounter friendly (but persistent) panhandlers. It's kind to give them your change if you desire, but you will not encounter any problems if you choose to keep walking. If you'd like to help the homeless while you're exploring the city, look for people selling copies of Street Sense (www.streetsense.org), a biweekly newspaper written and sold primarily by the DC homeless population.

REGULATED SUBSTANCES

The drinking age in the United States is 21 years old, and this is strictly enforced in Washington DC; don't be surprised if you're asked for identification at restaurants and bars, even if you're in your 20s or 30s, and expect to show identification to enter live music venues and dance clubs. While some venues, including the 9:30 Club and Black Cat, have some "all-ages" or "18 and over" shows, most nightlife venues are 21-plus. Bars in DC may serve alcohol until 2am on weekdays, 3am Friday and Saturday, though a lot of bars will shut down around 1:30am or 2am on weekends and much earlier on weekdays—DC is generally an early town.

Smoking is prohibited in all enclosed public spaces in DC, including restaurants, bars, and clubs, though there are a few cigar bars.

In 2015, possession of small amounts of marijuana for personal use became legal in Washington DC (though Congress wasn't happy about it). Adults 21 and older may possess two ounces or less of marijuana and transfer one ounce or less to another adult, as long as no money is exchanged. A growing number of local businesses legally sell marijuana paraphernalia or other items like T-shirts and provide a "free gift" of marijuana with purchase. You may use marijuana on private property, but it's prohibited on public property, and this law is enforced especially on federal property—so don't try to smoke around the monuments, because you can be arrested. (It's not uncommon to catch a whiff around populous nightlife areas like the U Street Corridor on a weekend night, but we can't recommend you take the risk in public, because arrest is a possibility.) If you do acquire marijuana in DC, don't cross the border: It's illegal for recreational use in Maryland and Virginia, though possession of 10 grams or less in Maryland has been decriminalized and both states are expanding medical marijuana programs.

Travel Tips

ACCESS FOR TRAVELERS WITH DISABILITIES

DC is relatively flat and easy to get around, including in the main tourist areas, and even sights like the Lincoln Memorial and Thomas Jefferson Memorial have elevators. Most attractions, museums, and performance venues offer accessible tours, seating, and other accommodations, and many offer frequent ASL-interpreted tours and performances. One exception may be Georgetown, which has hilly, uneven sidewalks. All Metro stations, rail cars, and buses are accessible, and there's an elevator at every station; if the elevator is not working, Washington Metropolitan

Area Transit Authority will provide free transportation to the next station. Visit the Metro Transit Accessibility Center (600 5th St. NW) for the Metro Disability ID card, which provides fare discounts for up to one month.

TRAVELING WITH CHILDREN

Washington DC is an excellent city for a family vacation, with a wealth of free, fun, and educational sights, museums, and activities. No matter how long you're visiting, you can spend your entire trip taking advantage of free activities, though attractions with admission fees typically offer discounts for children and free tickets for very young children with paying adults. Most of DC's hotels and popular, bustling restaurants welcome families with children, with the exception of a few of the finest restaurants specializing in tasting menus—your kid is unlikely to enjoy Komi or The Inn at Little Washington, and nor will anyone else around you. For quick meals when kids are restless, diners, fast-casual restaurants, and food trucks are plentiful.

SENIOR TRAVELERS

While most of the major sights and museums are free for everyone, those with an entrance fee typically offer discounts for seniors, though age requirements may vary. The Senior SmarTrip card allows adults age 65 and older to get reduced fares on Metrorail and Metrobus, which can be purchased at the Metro sales office (600 5th St. NW) by showing government identification.

LGBTQ TRAVELERS

Headquarters of the Human Rights Campaign and home to annual pride events, Washington DC is extremely friendly to LGBTQ travelers. The city celebrated the Supreme Court's 2015 gay marriage ruling near the White House, which was illuminated in rainbow colors, and DC's status as one of the most gay-friendly cities in America did not change when the new administration took office in 2017. (If anything, it's become even more gay friendly as locals resist the administration's rhetoric about social issues.) Two local LGBTQ publications, Washington Blade (www.washingtonblade.com), which has been around since 1969, and Metro Weekly (www.metroweekly.com), provide news and information on DC's LGBTQ community and events.

INTERNATIONAL TRAVELERS

All international visitors are required to have a valid passport to enter the United States. Canadian citizens traveling by air need a passport or NEXUS card, but those arriving by land may show an enhanced driver's license/identification card instead. Depending on your country of origin, a visa may be required, or you may be eligible for the Visa Waiver Program (VWP), allowing travel to the United States for business or leisure for 90 days or less without a visa. All visitors and their baggage may be subject to an interview or inspection by U.S. Customs and Border Protection; be prepared to provide details about the purpose of your visit, where you are staying, and when you plan to leave. For more information on entry requirements and restrictions, including prohibited items, visit www.cbp.gov.

MONEY
DC ON A BUDGET

Washington DC is one of the most expensive cities in the United States, after San Francisco and New York City, and high prices extend to tourism. Luckily, the best sights are free, and it's possible to spend your entire trip exploring the national parks and monuments and Smithsonian Institution museums, which offer free guided tours and other special programs. In addition, the Kennedy Center has a free performance at 6pm, every day of the year, including Christmas Day and New Year's Day, while other theaters and performance venues will offer last-minute or under-30 discounts on tickets for many shows.

Generally, hotels are expensive year-round, and rates are exorbitant during major events like the National Cherry Blossom Festival and presidential inaugurations, though conferences can cause rates to spike regularly, too. Book in advance, or look at some of the new, lower-cost pod-style hotels; conference hotels that gear to business travelers (like the Washington Hilton) often have good deals on weekends. Many Washingtonians put their homes on Airbnb, and you can find private apartments in prime neighborhoods like Dupont Circle and the U Street Corridor for much cheaper than hotels.

Restaurants and bars have gotten more expensive; extravagant tasting menus are the trend, and it's not uncommon to spend $15 (or more) on a cocktail. At the same time, foodies on a budget will find good diners, delicious fast-casual dining, food trucks, and markets with inexpensive vendors serving the city's innovative cuisine without the restaurant markup. If you're willing to dine 3pm-7pm, even some of the finest restaurants have happy hour drink and appetizer specials, which you can make into a meal. The Riggsby has one of the best, but almost every nice restaurant with a bar has happy hour. And many restaurants offer late-night happy hours, like Hank's Oyster Bar's late-night oyster deals, or half-price bottles of wine on slower weekdays. If you're a big eater, weekend brunch is extremely popular—almost every restaurant serves it—and can provide bigger bang for your buck with an abundance of food and bottomless beverages.

Save money getting around by buying a SmarTrip card and taking advantage of public transportation.

SALES TAX AND TIPPING

The DC sales tax is 5.75 percent (groceries and prescription and nonprescription drugs are exempt). Tourists need to account for the much higher tax on dining and accommodations; DC charges 10 percent on restaurant meals, alcohol (both in restaurants/bars and liquor stores), and rental cars, and 14.5 percent on hotel accommodations.

Standard tipping guidelines in the United States apply in DC, although 20 percent is the minimum for good service in restaurants, bars, and lounges. In many quick-service restaurants and independent coffee shops, you'll have the option to add tip via the touchscreen payment terminal; if you're grabbing a bottle of water, for example, a tip is not necessary, but if you're ordering made-to-order food or beverages, add $1-5, depending on the cost of your order. The same rules apply for tip jars; it's much appreciated if you drop the change in the jar at a food truck. In bars, $1 per drink is acceptable, but tip more generously if you're ordering complicated cocktails, getting advice from the bartender on wines or beers, or sitting at the bar for a long time.

TOURIST INFORMATION
VISITOR CENTERS AND INFORMATION

Destination DC (901 7th St. NW, 202/789-7000, www.washington.org) is the official tourism office for Washington DC. Explore their comprehensive website before your trip, and download their free, interactive guide, or place an order for a paper copy, in advance.

Around the National Mall (www.nps.gov/nama), you'll find National Park Service kiosks providing information, maps, and souvenirs; the National Park Service website is the best resource for up-to-date information on closures and special events.

Located in the Smithsonian Castle, the Smithsonian Visitor Center (1000 Jefferson Dr., 202/633-1000, www.si.edu/visit;

8:30am-5:30pm daily) has information about every museum and volunteers who can help you decide which museum to tackle first. The Smithsonian website has downloadable maps and brochures, as well as a mobile app to help you access information while you're on the go.

The White House Visitor Center (1450 Pennsylvania Ave. NW, 202/208-1631, www.nps.gov/whho; 7:30am-4pm daily) and U.S. Capitol Visitor Center (1st St. & E. Capitol St. SE, 202/226-8000, www.visitthecapitol.gov; 8:30am-4:30pm Mon.-Sat.) have exhibits, information on tours, and gift shops.

COMMUNICATIONS AND MEDIA
TELEPHONE

In the United States, dial 1 followed by the area code (202 in DC) and the seven-digit phone number. There are several area codes in Virginia and Maryland. Calls to area codes 800, 866, 887, and 888 are toll-free from any U.S. phone.

In case of an emergency, dial 911 from any U.S. phone to reach emergency services.

POSTAL SERVICES

The United States Postal Service (www.usps.com) has several branches throughout the city; check the USPS website for locations and hours. There is no central post office in DC, as the historic post offices have since been turned into the Trump International Hotel Washington DC and the Smithsonian's National Postal Museum.

WEIGHTS AND MEASURES

Washington DC is in the eastern time zone and observes daylight saving time between the second Sunday of March and the first Sunday of November. International travelers may need an adapter and a converter for appliances to fit the outlets; in the United States, electricity is set at 110 volts. Most hotels will provide hair dryers, and inexpensive personal appliances and device chargers are available at most pharmacies.

RESOURCES

Suggested Reading

HISTORY

Asch, Chris and Musgrove, Derek. *Chocolate City: A History of Race and Democracy in the Nation's Capital.* Chapel Hill: The University of North Carolina Press, 2019. The definitive history of two centuries of race relations in Washington DC.

Lewis, Tom. *Washington: A History of Our National City.* New York: Basic Books, 2015. This is a comprehensive but readable introduction to the history of the nation's capital, describing in captivating detail everything from how George Washington chose the site to the impact of the 20th century's wars and riots on the city and its residents.

Savage, Kirk. *Monument Wars: Washington, D.C., the National Mall, and the Transformation of the Memorial Landscape.* Berkeley: University of California Press, 2009. Discover American history and key players through the dramatic story of the development of the National Mall and the capital's iconic monuments and memorials.

POLITICS AND MEDIA

Bernstein, Carl, and Woodward, Bob. *All the President's Men.* New York: Simon & Schuster, 1974. Before you visit The Watergate Hotel, read the *Washington Post* investigative reporters' telling of how they uncovered the political scandal of the 20th century.

Brower, Kate Anderson. *The Residence: Inside the Private World of the White House.* New York: HarperCollins, 2015. Fans of *Downton Abbey* will devour this White House correspondent's look at life inside the presidential mansion, based on her interviews with the household staff for first families from the Kennedys to the Obamas.

Caro, Robert A. *Master of the Senate.* New York: Vintage Books/Random House, 2002. At over 1,000 pages, this biography of Lyndon Johnson's 12 years in the U.S. Senate provides in-depth insight into power in Washington, and how Congress really works.

Leibovich, Mark. *This Town: Two Parties and a Funeral— Plus Plenty of Valet Parking!—in America's Gilded Capital.* New York: Penguin Group, 2013. In his juicy tell-all, a *New York Times* correspondent introduces you to the city's power players and wannabes, and how things get done in "this town," as the locals call Washington DC.

Wolff, Michael. *Fire and Fury: Inside the Trump White House.* New York:

Henry Holt and Company, 2018. Washington gleefully ate up this exposé of the new political landscape, a tome that blurs the line between fact and fiction.

ARTS, CULTURE, AND SOCIETY

Davis, Margaret Leslie. *Mona Lisa in Camelot: How Jacqueline Kennedy and Da Vinci's Masterpiece Charmed and Captivated a Nation.* New York: Da Capo Press/Perseus Books Group, 2008. Art lovers will enjoy this delightful read about first lady Jackie Kennedy's mission to bring the Mona Lisa to the National Gallery.

Hopkinson, Natalie. *Go-Go Live: The Musical Life and Death of a Chocolate City.* Durham: Duke University Press, 2012. A former *Washington Post* reporter explores black life and culture and racial divisions in DC through the lens of the city's homegrown music genre.

Onwuachi, Kwame. *Notes from a Young Black Chef: A Memoir.* New York: Alfred A. Knopf, 2019. Before you visit his District Wharf restaurant Kith/Kin, learn about this young chef's journey from Brooklyn to Nigeria to *Top Chef.*

FICTION

Buckley, Christopher. *Thank You for Smoking.* New York: Random House, 1994. There's a lot of truth in this satire about lobbying, in which cigarette company spokesman Nick Naylor promotes the benefits of smoking.

Cutler, Jessica. *The Washingtonienne.* New York: Hachette Book Group, 2005. Long before the days when adult film stars and the Steele Dossier were part of the Washington news cycle, a Hill-staffer-turned-sex-blogger lit up the local gossip columns with her salacious novel inspired by her real-life exploits with DC power players.

Kafka-Gibbons, Paul. *Dupont Circle.* New York: Houghton-Mifflin, 2001. In this charming romantic comedy, meet the diverse residents of Dupont Circle as the DC Court of Appeals prepares to hear a groundbreaking case about same-sex marriage.

Mengestu, Dinaw. *The Beautiful Things That Heaven Bears.* New York: Penguin Group, 2007. Both joyful and heartbreaking, this novel tells the story of an Ethiopian immigrant who owns a bodega near Logan Circle, and his budding romance with a white woman who moves into the neighborhood during a time of racial divisions in the city.

TELEVISION

Homeland. Showtime, 2011-2020. The writers consult with Washington experts, including former undercover CIA agents—but it's still a little eerie how they're able to predict what's next in foreign policy. They get the personalities right, too.

Veep. HBO, 2012-2019. Yes, this is exactly how people speak and interact in Washington politics.

Internet Resources

GENERAL INFORMATION

DC.gov
www.dc.gov
The official website of the Washington DC city government has information about parking and transportation, recreation facilities, and citywide events.

Destination DC
www.washington.org
The official website of DC's tourism authority, Destination DC is the most thorough guide to the city's neighborhoods and happenings.

POLITICS AND MEDIA

Congress.gov
www.congress.gov
Find your Senator or Representative, see the congressional calendar, and learn about the history of the legislative branch on the official website of the U.S. Congress.

POLITICO
www.politico.com
This print and digital publication dives into the nitty gritty of national politics and policymaking, and publishes the early morning newsletter Playbook, the morning must-read for those inside the beltway.

The Hill
www.thehill.com
In addition to comprehensive coverage of Capitol Hill, this rag is known for the annual 50 Most Beautiful list of hot and high-profile Washingtonians.

The Washington Post
www.washingtonpost.com
In addition to publishing some of the best national, international, and local reporting, DC's major newspaper has excellent dining, arts and culture, and nightlife content; food critic Tom Sietsema can make or break a restaurant with one review.

Washington City Paper
www.washingtoncitypaper.com
For everything other than national politics, from coverage of the city council and public transportation to concert reviews, locals turn to this print and digital publication; the annual crowd-sourced Best of DC list will help you find everything from the best cupcake or dive bar, to the best drycleaner, bike shop, or dance company.

Washingtonian
www.washingtonian.com
This magazine combines original reporting about life in the Washington metropolitan area with some of the best coverage of dining, shopping, real estate, and day trips; foodies will want to check out the annual 100 Very Best Restaurants and Cheap Eats lists.

ARTS, CULTURE, AND SOCIETY

Brightest Young Things
www.brightestyoungthings.com
This colorful lifestyle website has the most complete list of concerts, happy hours, and comedy events geared toward young partiers.

Cultural Tourism DC
www.culturaltourismdc.org
In addition to organizing free walking tours and embassy open houses and maintaining a comprehensive list of cultural events, Cultural Tourism DC manages more than a dozen Neighborhood Heritage Trails throughout the city; find the trails, and download interactive mobile apps, here.

DC Theatre Scene
www.dctheatrescene.com
What's on stage? This website covers everything from Kennedy Center productions and national tours to local troupes and fringe festivals in detail.

Metro Weekly
www.metroweekly.com
This publication is one of the most comprehensive guides to LGBTQ events and nightlife, with excellent arts and entertainment coverage.

Smithsonian Institution
www.si.edu
The Smithsonian's website is a one-stop shop for planning your museum hopping, with information on opening hours, exhibits, and special events at every Smithsonian museum and cultural center.

Washington Blade
www.washingtonblade.com
This publication has been covering LGBTQ news, life, and culture since 1969.

Washington Life
www.washingtonlife.com
This local glossy covers the city's power players and the events they frequent; check out the "My Washington" feature for locals' dining and nightlife picks.

PARKS AND RECREATION

National Park Service
www.nps.gov
Whether you're planning a tour of the National Mall's monuments and memorials, or an excursion to Rock Creek Park or Shenandoah, the National Park Service's website details operating hours, tours, travel tips, and more.

Index

T

U

VWXYZ

INDEX

Restaurants Index

Nightlife Index

Shops Index

Hotels Index

Photo Credits

Photos by Samantha Sault, except:

Title page photo: Jon Bilous, Dreamstime.com; page 2 © Joe Sohm, Dreamstime.com; Vlad Ghiea, Dreamstime.com; Richard Gunion, Dreamstime.com; page 4 © (top left) Jon Bilous, Dreamstime.com; (right middle)Wangkun Jia, Dreamstime.com; (bottom) Adam Parent, Dreamstime.com; page 6 © Kmiragaya, Dreamstime.com; page 9 © (top) Mrcmos, Dreamstime.com; (bottom) Vichaya Kiatyingangsulee, Dreamstime.com; page 11 © (top) Leslie Banks, Dreamstime.com; (bottom) Vitalyedush, Dreamstime.com; page 12 © (bottom) Smithsonian; page 13 © (top) Meinzahn, Dreamstime.com; (bottom) Nicole Glass Photography, Shutterstock.com; page 18 © (bottom) Ioan Cnejevici, Dreamstime.com; page 19 © Anna Krivitskaia, Dreamstime.com; page 20 © (top) Mira Agron, Dreamstime.com; page 27 © Eq Roy, Dreamstime.com; page 28 © (bottom) W Washington D.C.; page 29 © Michael Kleinberg; page 30 © James Blinn, Dreamstime.com; Louise Rivard, Dreamstime.com; page 31 © Michael Wood, Dreamstime.com; page 32 © (bottom) NPS Photo; page 34 © (bottom) Luiz Gustavo Freitas Rossi, Dreamstime. com; page 37 © (top) Sandra Foyt, Dreamstime.com; page 38 © (bottom) Peng Ge, Dreamstime.com; page 41 © Marcos Souza, Dreamstime.com; Zhi Qi, Dreamstime. com; Claudia Uripos, eStock Photo; page 45 © (top) Richard Gunion, Dreamstime.com; page 46 © (bottom) Scott Jones, Dreamstime.com; page 49 © (top) Marcos Souza, Dreamstime.com; page 50 © Smithsonian; page 53 © (bottom) Vitalyedush, Dreamstime. com; page 54 © Smithsonian; page 55 © Jon Bilous, Dreamstime.com; page 56 © Erik Lattwein, Dreamstime.com; page 57 © (bottom) Edwin Verin, Dreamstime.com; page 59 © (bottom) Itsadream Dreamstime.com; page 60 © (top) Cvandyke, Dreamstime.com; page 64 © (bottom) Erik Lattwein, Dreamstime.com; page 65 © (top) Kmiragaya | Dreamstime.com; page 66 © (bottom) Ritu Jethani, Dreamstime.com; page 67 © (top) Vitalyedush, Dreamstime.com; page 69 © (bottom) Peng Ge, Dreamstime.com; page 71 © (top) Sherryvsmith, Dreamstime.com; page 73 © W Washington D.C.; Lmel900, Dreamstime.com; Jon Bilous, Dreamstime.com; page 76 © (bottom) Alberto Dubini, Dreamstime.com; page 79 © Zrfphoto, Dreamstime.com; page 82 © (top) Think Food Group; page 84 © Greg Powers; page 85 © (top) Think Food Group; page 88 © (top) W Washington D.C.; page 89 © RP3 Agency; page 92 © (bottom) Vitalyedush, Dreamstime. com; page 98 © Jon Bilous, Dreamstime.com; page 103 © Ioan Cnejevici, Dreamstime. com; Jakub Zajic, Dreamstime.com; page 106 © (bottom) William Perry, Dreamstime. com; page 109 © (top) Warren Rosenberg, Dreamstime.com; page 110 © Konstantin Lobastov, Dreamstime.com; page 113 © (top) Ardent Vibe; page 115 © Askoldsb, Dreamstime.com; page 125 © Littleny, Dreamstime.com; Robert Lautman, Courtesy of The Phillips Collection; page 130 © (bottom) Lei Xu, Dreamstime.com; page 132 © (bottom) Kimpton Hotels & Restaurants; page 136 © (top) The Jefferson, Washington, DC; page 138 © (bottom) Robert Lautman, Courtesy of The Phillips Collection; page 140 © (bottom) Richard Gunion, Dreamstime.com; page 145 © Jon Bilous, Dreamstime. com; page 150 © (top) Shootalot, Dreamstime.com; page 153 © B Christopher, Alamy Stock Photo; page 154 © David Harmantas, Dreamstime; page 159 © Abby Jiu; page 171 © Zrfphoto, Dreamstime.com; A Rake's Progress; page 175 © A Rake's Progress; page 177 © (top) Sticky Fingers; page 180 © Ivan Mateev, Dreamstime.com; page 182 © (top) Richard Gunion, Dreamstime.com; page 183 © (bottom) Joaquin Castillo, Dreamstime. com; page 187 © Erik Lattwein, Dreamstime.com; Reema Desai; page 190 © (bottom) Jon Bilous, Dreamstime.com; page 192 © Lunamarina, Dreamstime.com; page 193 © (bottom) Think Food Group; page 194 © Park Hyatt Washington; page 195 © Richard Gunion, Dreamstime.com; page 196 © (bottom) Robert Miller; page 197 © Richard Gunion, Dreamstime.com; page 198 © Bourbon Steak at Four Seasons Hotel; page 200 © (top) Avmedved, Dreamstime.com; page 202 © (bottom) Cvandyke, Dreamstime.

Acknowledgments

Thank you to the savvy team at Avalon Travel for your guidance and support over the years, especially Kim Ehart, Scott Kimball, Kat Bennett, Leah Gordon, Nikki Ioakimedes, Bill Newlin, and the entire publicity team. It's always a joy to work with you and I'm so proud of what we've done with the DC guidebook. Here's to hoping we'll be able to celebrate another edition in person soon.

I'm lucky to have many great writers, mentors, and friends in my life who have supported and encouraged me throughout this process, offering brilliant ideas, invaluable advice, and treasured company when I need to try new spots in DC. These include Kevin Chaffee, Chuck Conconi, Janet Donovan, Kevin Fisher, Linda Mercado Greene, Pat Harrison, Danielle Mohlman, Shannon Schaper, Becky Schindler, Jean Schindler, and Karin Tanabe. Thanks also to Franco Nuschese and his team at Café Milano for hosting one of the best book parties I've ever been to in DC—and I've been to a lot!

Thanks to my parents, for your unconditional love and instilling an early love of books in me, to Casey, for your smart perspective and support, and to Chuck and Maribeth for cheering me on.

Thank you, Matt, for believing in me, for challenging me, for your brilliant eye, and for putting up with me on deadlines. I can never thank you enough. I love you and I'm so lucky to call you my partner and my friend.

And finally, thank you to DC. You'll get through it.

MOON ROAD TRIP GUIDES

Drive & Hike
APPALACHIAN TRAIL

THE BEST TRAIL TOWNS, DAY HIKES,
AND ROAD TRIPS IN BETWEEN

TIMOTHY MALCOLM

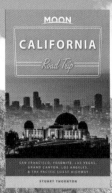

BLUE RIDGE PARKWAY
Road Trip

INCLUDING SHENANDOAH & GREAT SMOKY
MOUNTAINS NATIONAL PARKS

JASON FRYE

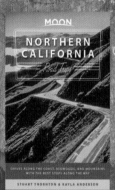

CALIFORNIA
Road Trip

SAN FRANCISCO, YOSEMITE, LAS VEGAS,
GRAND CANYON, LOS ANGELES,
& THE PACIFIC COAST HIGHWAY

STUART THORNTON

NASHVILLE TO NEW ORLEANS
Road Trip

NATCHEZ TRACE PARKWAY • MEMPHIS •
TUPELO • MISSISSIPPI BLUES TRAIL

MARGARET LITTMAN

NEW ENGLAND
Road Trip

BOSTON, ACADIA NATIONAL PARK, WHITE
MOUNTAINS, BERKSHIRES, NEWPORT, AND CAPE COD

JEN ROSE SMITH

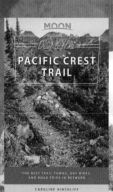

NORTHERN CALIFORNIA
Road Trip

DRIVES ALONG THE COAST, REDWOODS, AND MOUNTAINS
WITH THE BEST STOPS ALONG THE WAY

STUART THORNTON & KAYLA ANDERSON

OREGON TRAIL
Road Trip

HISTORIC SITES, SMALL TOWNS, AND
SCENIC LANDSCAPES ALONG THE LEGENDARY
WESTWARD ROUTE

KATRINA EMERY

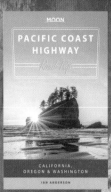

PACIFIC COAST HIGHWAY
Road Trip

CALIFORNIA,
OREGON & WASHINGTON

IAN ANDERSON

Drive & Hike
PACIFIC CREST TRAIL

THE BEST TRAIL TOWNS, DAY HIKES,
AND ROAD TRIPS IN BETWEEN

CAROLINE HINCHLIFF

Advice on where to sleep, eat, and explore

Detailed driving directions including mileage and drive times

Itineraries for a range of timelines

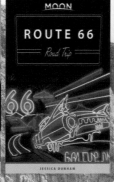

MOON

PACIFIC NORTHWEST
Road Trip

SEATTLE, VANCOUVER, VICTORIA,
THE OLYMPIC PENINSULA, PORTLAND,
THE OREGON COAST & MOUNT RAINIER

ALLISON WILLIAMS

MOON

ROUTE 66
Road Trip

JESSICA DUNHAM

MOON

SOUTH FLORIDA & THE KEYS
Road Trip

WITH MIAMI, WALT DISNEY WORLD, TAMPA &
THE EVERGLADES

JASON FERGUSON

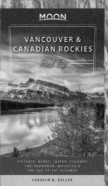

MOON

SOUTHWEST
Road Trip

LAS VEGAS, ZION & BRYCE, MONUMENT VALLEY,
SANTA FE & TAOS, AND THE GRAND CANYON

TIM HULL

MOON

VANCOUVER & CANADIAN ROCKIES
Road Trip

VICTORIA, BANFF, JASPER, CALGARY,
THE OKANAGAN, WHISTLER &
THE SEA-TO-SKY HIGHWAY

CAROLYN B. HELLER

MOON

YELLOWSTONE TO GLACIER NATIONAL PARK
Road Trip

JACKSON HOLE, CODY, THE GRAND TETONS
& THE ROCKY MOUNTAIN FRONT

CARTER G. WALKER

MAP SYMBOLS

═══ Major Hwy	▓ Pedestrian Friendly	------- Trail	········· Ferry
─── Road/Hwy	▒ Tunnel	▪▪▪▪▪ Stairs	⊶⊶ Railroad

■ Sights	⊛ City/Town	▲ Mountain	
■ Restaurants	◉ State Capital	✦ Unique Feature	
■ Nightlife	○ National Capital	⧖ Waterfall	
■ Arts and Culture	✪ Highlight	⚲ Park	
■ Recreation	★ Point of Interest	≜ Archaeological Site	
■ Shops	• Accommodation		
■ Hotels	▼ Restaurant/Bar	TH Trailhead	
	■ Other Location	P Parking Area	

CONVERSION TABLES

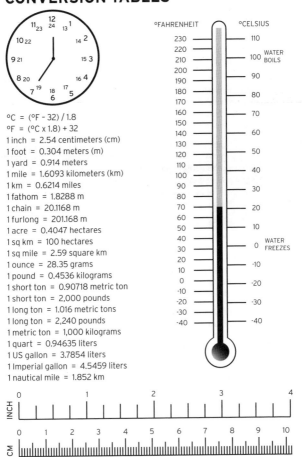

°C = (°F - 32) / 1.8
°F = (°C x 1.8) + 32
1 inch = 2.54 centimeters (cm)
1 foot = 0.304 meters (m)
1 yard = 0.914 meters
1 mile = 1.6093 kilometers (km)
1 km = 0.6214 miles
1 fathom = 1.8288 m
1 chain = 20.1168 m
1 furlong = 201.168 m
1 acre = 0.4047 hectares
1 sq km = 100 hectares
1 sq mile = 2.59 square km
1 ounce = 28.35 grams
1 pound = 0.4536 kilograms
1 short ton = 0.90718 metric ton
1 short ton = 2,000 pounds
1 long ton = 1.016 metric tons
1 long ton = 2,240 pounds
1 metric ton = 1,000 kilograms
1 quart = 0.94635 liters
1 US gallon = 3.7854 liters
1 Imperial gallon = 4.5459 liters
1 nautical mile = 1.852 km

MOON WASHINGTON DC
Avalon Travel
Hachette Book Group
1700 Fourth Street
Berkeley, CA 94710, USA
www.moon.com

Editor: Kimberly Ehart
Acquiring Editor: Nikki Ioakimedes
Series Manager: Leah Gordon
Copy Editor: Kerry Smith
Graphics Coordinator and Production Coordinator: Scott Kimball
Cover Design: Faceout Studios, Charles Brock
Interior Design: Megan Jones Design
Moon Logo: Tim McGrath
Map Editor: Kat Bennett
Cartographers: Mark Stroud, Brian Shotwell, Kat Bennett
Indexer: Greg Jewett

ISBN-13: 978-1-64049-922-5

Printing History
1st Edition — 2018
2nd Edition — November 2020
5 4 3 2 1

Front cover photo: William Perry, Dreamstime.com
Back cover photo: Blackghost600, Dreamstime.com

Printed in Malaysia for Imago